DIGITAL LIBIDO

SEX, POWER AND VIOLENCE IN THE NETWORK SOCIETY

Alexander Bard
Jan Söderqvist

Translated by John Wright

DIGITAL LIBIDO

SEX, POWER AND VIOLENCE IN THE NETWORK SOCIETY

ALEXANDER BARD JAN SÖDERQVIST

CONTENTS

1
Civilization, uncivilization, and their discontents 9

2
The human constant, the technological variable, and the metahistorical tsunami 33

3
From the plastic nomadic tribe to The Global Empire 55

4
Socioanalysis as the critical theory of The Internet Age 77

5
Instinct, drive, desire and transcendence 107

6
The dialectics of libido and mortido 133

7
The night of the world as the core of the temporal subject 157

8
In search of the lost phallus in the digital plurarchy 179

9
The fetish and the abject – the symbols that drive the social theater 209

10
Plato's, Kant's and Einstein's mistake – the autistic ape's dream of the perfect machine 235

11
Our network-dynamical Universe – chronocentrism, emergentism and relationalism 257

12
Individualism as the opium of the people – hypernarcissism, pornoflation and interpassivity 283

13
The dialectics of ressentiment – identitarianism as the curse of the consumtariat 311

14
The digital class struggle – the netocratic swarm versus the consumtarian mob 341

15
Sensocracy, tribal mapping and the digital priesthood 361

16
The informationalist apocalypse and the three heads of the netocratic hydra 385

Glossary 413

1
Civilization, uncivilization, and their discontents

To look or not to look? Naked female breasts can cause a problem for the man who for one reason or other happens to come across them. The correct stance is determined by environment and context. There are clubs where more or less naked bodies are displayed at a price, and there one could reasonably stare to one's heart's content (since one has paid). That anyone would object to the staring as such is hard to imagine. However it is not hard to imagine that many would object to this whole business of naked breasts at a price, which confirms the problematical aspect of nudity in general and naked breasts in particular. It is possible to – in certain cases with good reason – claim that the staring in itself only is a pretext and a sort of foreplay, that the stared-upon breasts are meant as advertisement for sexual intercourse which is to follow upon the potential client's ocular inspection of the naked breasts, this too at a price in which case, something which is strictly forbidden according to many law books, including current Swedish one. There is, in any event, a set of cultural taboo regulations that governs all kinds of dealings with naked female breasts, which explains why payment even exists. But what if the naked breasts are on display for free? Then what?

The protagonist in Italo Calvino's novel *Mr. Palomar* from 1983 strolls along a desolate beach with only a few sunbathers in sight.

Suddenly he spots a young woman sprawled on the sand. Her torso is not covered by anything, she is bathing her naked breasts in the sun. And Mr. Palomar immediately and instinctively averts his eyes. It is a way for him to respect the remains of the taboo of nudity that in spite of everything still lingers. His action also entails, at least in his own eyes, a measure of chivalry towards the half-naked woman. Her breasts are her own, even though they are at the moment naked and at the mercy of everyone's eyes. They have nothing to do with him, all staring could be perceived as intrusive because breasts are precisely breasts.

But when Palomar has taken a few more steps and the naked breasts have disappeared from view, he has second thoughts. A refusal to look at the breasts does, of course, mean that he himself adheres to – and moreover contributes in reinforcing – an obsolete custom based on the conception that the sight of naked breasts is something shameful that should be avoided; it means, Palomar now thinks, that he furnishes the naked breasts with "a kind of spiritual bra," which is both discourteous and reactionary. For the woman with the breasts has actually herself chosen to shed her bra, if indeed she even owns one. And the breasts in question seemed, judged by the little glimpse he succeeded in catching before his glance quickly drifted towards the sea and the waves, to be eminently "fresh and easy on the eye." Therefore Palomar opts for another strategy when he on his way back walks by the same woman. He both looks and does not look, that is: in fair democratic spirit he allows his eyes to sweep across the entire vista – sea-foam, boats, the bath towel, the breasts and the coastal outline – without giving any special scrutiny to anything in particular. Palomar thus acts as though the naked breasts are nothing special at all. Which fills him with self-satisfaction: the breasts thus become a natural part of the landscape, neither more nor less.

However, this contentment unfortunately does not last; soon enough Palomar catches himself having committed a reprehensible act: he has observed an individual fellow human as though she were an object. He has reduced her to the level of a thing and overlooked what is specific both to her and to the female sex. This is, or might at least be understood to be, an upholding of patriarchal oppression. Therefore he must do it again and do it right, so Palomar turns around anew and walks back to the woman, and this time grants the naked breasts a considerable measure of factual interest. This time his eyes do not wander, but he soberly registers the uncovered torso's lines and curves, only to later return to the sand and the sea as though nothing in particular had occurred.

Now there is nothing that might be misconstrued, Palomar muses, only to once again be afflicted with doubt. This cursory matter-of-factness – might it not be perceived as hauteur and a refusal to acknowledge what a woman's breasts by time-honored tradition represent in our culture? What he would most of all like to express with his look is of course encouragement and appreciation for the change within and the modernization of society's customs that is entailed in the acceptance of breasts being naked, without this constituting a sexual overture. This new openness in society appeals to him, and therefore Palomar once again turns back and approaches the woman and the naked breasts with firm steps, to finally and emphatically express benevolence and agreement with his eyes. But no agreement is forthcoming, it will soon be made clear. The woman with the naked breasts snatches her towel, covers herself with it, and scurries off with an irritated shrug.

So what really happened? Was it a misunderstanding? In that case, who misunderstood whom and who is it that decides what a pair of naked breasts, or for that matter something completely different, actually means in the one context or the other? This, as with most things, is ultimately a question of power. And moreover a question of geography: A pair of naked breasts means one thing on the Italian Mediterranean coast (where we might imagine that Calvino's Mr. Palomar finds himself) and something else in Egypt or Jordan (where there are no naked female breasts on any beaches, precisely because they would mean something totally different, namely a completely unthinkable depravity that would cross the border to madness). The prerogative of interpretation belongs to he or they who have wrested power over, or at least for the moment dominate, the cultural production of meaning. Not seldom, this power position is disputed and in practice divided between the combatants, a division that over a great span of time remains unclear and mutable, which entails that wholly or partly irreconcilable meanings and definitions over a long period coexist in parallel, and that a more or less irreconcilable tug-of-war continues until one of the parties is forced to give up and leave the stage.

Another way to speak of the same process is to say that the *Zeitgeist* changes. It might for example mean that certain words can no longer be used, at least not in the fancy salons. And certain behaviors are forced to go underground. Which of course does not mean that these behaviors disappear; they have merely received a new meaning. Take for example antiquity's same-sex love between adult men and tender youths, which is mentioned by Plato and others. In other contexts this affection, as we know, has been handled differently. These processes are constantly ongoing, the battles rage back and forth. Meanings thus change continuously over time, which occasions enthusiastic adherents of social and political progress to imagine that the outcome of power struggles of this kind is preordained, that it only is a matter of time before the "reasonable" and "civilized" alternative triumphs and forever consigns the "primitive" and "outmoded" challenger to the garbage dump of cultural history. If so, this would mean, if we return to Mr. Palomar and the naked female breasts, that all controversies around topless beach fashion ought to be completely obsolete – now that we actually find ourselves well into the third millennium – either because we (men) now are ideologically drilled to clothe all (female) breasts in a "spiritual bra" precisely of the kind that Palomar imagines, or because we (men) quite simply have stopped regarding female breasts as something which possesses a sexual and thus revolutionizing charge.

A quick glance at the development in what we call real life does, however, clearly tell us that this is merely pious wishful thinking; that the battle for power over the production of meaning still rages with undiminished force. The breasts may be regarded as the female body's commanding heights: strategically interesting hills that many lay claim to with varying rationales. Many women claim that their breasts, and how these should be defined, is an issue that only belongs to women, but even if they were to gain support for this viewpoint, it of course does not mean that the issue of the breasts' sexual charge thereby is decided, since different women answer this question in different ways. Even women who call themselves feminists assume different positions regarding their breasts. Some, for example members of the feminist network Femen, bare their breasts for ideological reasons and in the name of gender equality on beaches and in public baths: they claim that they own their own bodies and refuse to accept a sexualization of their own breasts. Which probably must be regarded as naive and overly optimistic when the society around them persists in doing precisely that andcarries on sexualizing women's breasts. Which is why this standpoint has been accused of being both naive and foolish by both men and women.

In our native Sweden, public swimming pools have become a venue for this constant battle for power over the production of meaning in terms of women's bodies: in many places one has succumbed to pressure and taken the drastic step of introducing separate bathing hours for men and women respectively, generally with reference to women's need of a safe space and an opportunity to swim and bathe without the eyes of men constantly upon them. We are not speaking of naked breasts or any form of nudity whatsoever, but only of women and men together within the same space, which in Sweden in the 21st century is considered a problem that must be handled. The historian of ideas Karin Johannisson has in this context written about a sense of uneasiness that arises "at a certain sort of look." "We put on clothes when we bathe in public," she continues, "because we do not want to expose ourselves to the wrong kind of look." And what is meant by "the wrong kind of look" is quite simply an unwillingness or inability (in men) to provide the woman's naked breasts with precisely the spiritual bra that Mr. Palomar is musing about. The surrounding world's intense interest therefore causes the breasts to need a bra of one sort or another. Individual people may have their diverse convictions, but the collective nevertheless insists on certain rules in order to be able to function; some are formalized as laws while others exist as partly tacit agreements that at least are assumed to be recognized by a majority. These customs thus require a bra in some form applied on the outside of the woman's breasts. But the straps of the bra chafe on all those who are of a differing opinion and who regard the bra requirement as a violation. And if it is not a bra requirement that is at issue, it is something else.

There is always a lingering conflict between what Sigmund Freud, the father of psychoanalysis from Vienna of the previous turn of the century, calls *the pleasure principle* and what he calls *the reality principle*, or if you will, between the child's quest for maximal pleasure and the adult, socialized citizen's quest for acceptance within the community. That the child has grown up and been enfolded into the collective does of course not mean that desire for (often forbidden) pleasures in any way has disappeared, which in turn means that adulthood is characterized by a long series of enforced compromises, something that engenders a sense of constant and growing aversion that results in – and this is also the title of one of Freud's most influential works – *Civilization and Its Discontents* (*Das Unbehagen in der Kultur*) from 1930. This conflict between drive impulses and decreed discipline is unavoidable, argues Freud. Order and progress require diligence and hard work, stable families and regulated forms of reproduction. This means that society at any cost must suppress various excesses and richly reward a highly developed impulse control. "The program that the pleasure principle foists upon us, namely to be happy, is impossible to fulfill," Freud remarks dryly.

According to Freud, both a functioning process of civilization and robust growth assume that all efforts towards happiness in general and sexual pleasure in particular be subordinated to an austere regime based on abstention, monogamy and hard work. Repression is therefore unavoidable in a society that satisfies citizens' material needs and that offers at least a minimum of security. The alternative would not be preferable; put a bra on for the good of the collective, in other words. This line of argument is consequently not so much a criticism directed at society and civilization, as a call for factuality. Raging against the bra requirement would be childish and pointless, becoming an adult entails accepting sacrifices and restrictions, particularly as these deprivations are anything but wasted. "Drive sublimation is", writes Freud, "a particularly prominent element in cultural development, it enables the significant role that higher mental activities – scientific, artistic, ideological – play in our cultural life." Civilization in broad terms – that is: the entire societal development that has enabled various spectacular gains in all sorts of areas – hinges on being able to drain energy away from sexuality: "Since Man does not possess unlimited amounts of mental energy, one must master one's tasks through a purposeful distribution of libidos."

What cultural development ultimately does and has as its goal is, according to Freud, to illustrate the constant struggle between *libido* and *mortido*, "the will to life and the death drive," a struggle that constitutes what is central in Man's life in the first place. Freud is caustically sarcastic towards all those who anxiously try to mitigate the furious force in this grandiose defining drama by wrapping the conflict in sentimentality and mendacity: "And this clash of the giants our pediatric nurses want to silence with lullabies about Heaven." Suffering is part and parcel of being an (adult) person; the tension between libido and mortido is permanent, while the reality principle is unimpeachable. A considerable measure of libidinal satisfaction must unconditionally be sacrificed on the altar of social community; the alternative is disintegration and chaos. We are forever doomed to be discontent in civilization, and whining about chafing bra straps and the like is, according to Freud, just infantile nonsense.

He who whines the most and most vocally about culture's and society's repression of Man throughout history is probably the Swiss-French philosopher Jean-Jacques Rousseau, who also claims that the civilization process inhibits and deforms that which is "natural" and original in Man, and thus one may of course assume that Rousseau and Freud carry out a similar analysis. But in all other respects they differ radically. Rousseau claims in his dissertation *Discourse on the Origin and Basis of Inequality Among Men* (*Discours sur l'origine et les fondements de l'inégalité parmi les hommes*) from 1755 that what is the very foundation in society, the gradually growing web of mutual dependencies, is what corrupts Man and creates a hierarchic system that promotes and cements inequality, oppression and slavery. Rousseau imagines the "natural state" that prevails before the genesis of society, when audacious, independent "savages" – filled with a healthy self-love that does not reflect itself in the appreciation of the world around them (*amour de soi même)* and a warm empathy for their sisters and brothers – roam freely through expansive forests where there is enough food to easily feed all mouths. And it would, Rousseau maintains, be impossible here for a person to coerce obedience from someone else, since the necessary surveillance is not possible to organize. No one dominates anyone else, simply put, no one is master and no one is slave. Rousseau's savage neither possesses nor requests language, reason or collective community; he lives in accordance with a powerfully sentimentalized variant of the pleasure principle, the only things that interest him are "food, a female and sleep."

That is: all this is played out in Rousseau's own, sentimental fantasy. His savage – presocial Man – has of course never existed. Mutual dependencies and organized collaboration are our species' only significant competitive advantages vis-à-vis other species and the main reasons for us having survived in the first place and moreover having multiplied on a large scale. And Man arises simultaneously with, and cannot possibly be separated from, spoken language. If his colleague Friedrich Nietzsche now and then philosophizes with a hammer, Rousseau thus during long periods philosophizes in his hat. Which in no way has prevented his thinking from setting an example or him attracting large numbers of devoted adherents – rather the reverse (which time and again forces us in our work to return to Rousseau, who constantly creates problems). His conceptions of love in the natural state – or more correctly: his line of argument around the insouciant absence of what we corrupt societal creatures call love, an absence that made sexuality uncomplicated and pleasantly free from jealousy, lies and feelings of guilt – appeal to generation after generation of thinkers who are discontent in civilization and who in their naive ignorance handle this through longing for a gospel of satisfied drives.

In Rousseau, males and females couple willy-nilly, when they happen to bump into each other in the forest, and since they do not have a language to speak of they cannot declare any feelings for each other. People mate and say goodbye to each other without any fuss. Just as he or she has no concept of death or their own mortality – for this one does not have in one's natural state, according to Rousseau – they never think in terms of ownership rights or a common future as a couple. Particularly since they never think about anything at all ever, since they do not master the art of thinking, and nor do they have any language suitable for formulating abstract concepts such as love, for instance. Love therefore does not exist, and no one misses it. Sexuality cannot harm or shake the society that does not even exist and that no one asks for either; sexual energies need not be fettered but can flow freely. The access to females is good and they are available for sexual relations year-round. Consequently the issue of bra or not, spiritual or of any other kind, never comes up. The sex drive is sound and pure – and above all natural.

So then the question that many pose is whether Freud still may be overly pessimistic when he claims that our discontentment in civilization is incurable, since the conflict between the pleasure principle and the reality principle by definition is permanent. Is it not still possible to cure, or at least alleviate, our discontentment in civilization somewhat through some sort of socio-political plan of action? Must we sacrifice our personal happiness for the good of society? Is the gateway to the lost paradise of uncomplicated drive fulfillment really closed for all eternity? So with the purpose of so to speak, "softening up Freud" in this respect, the German-Jewish social philosopher Karl Marx is recruited during the 20th century to a rather dysfunctional, Freudo-Marxist marriage of convenience, an alliance that both Freudians and Marxists of a more orthodox bent often angrily reject. Among the more renowned of these matchmakers there is the psychoanalyst and sexologist Wilhelm Reich and the philosopher and sociologist Herbert Marcuse. According to them, the antagonism between sexuality and society is something that one can use by consciously intensifying it to liberate sexual energy, thus loosening up the repressive system with the aid of sexuality.

The time for sacrifices and restrictions is therefore regarded as past and the naked body is transformed into a weapon in a struggle for liberation. The mandated bra is tossed into the trash can. Or else one burns it in front of the flashes of the press photographers' camera. For Reich – who in time succeeds in antagonizing both communist parties across Europe and the psychoanalytic movement by virtue of his theories about the orgasm as a cure for neurosis and about the blessings of pubertal sexuality – the connection between Marx and Freud is self-evident. While Marxism is the sociological expression of how Man becomes conscious of how the financial laws work and how a minority exploits the masses, psychoanalysis constitutes an expression of how Man becomes conscious of precisely the social repression of sexuality that Freud speaks of in *Civilization and Its Discontents*. But Freud has, as mentioned, no intention of blowing civilization to bits with the aid of orgasms, but accepts repression and discontentment as the price one has to pay for the many gains of the civilization process in a large number of areas. And the organized communists of Europe generally prove more focused on societal economics and class analysis than on well-to-do neurotics. All this resistance leads to Reich constantly roaming from the one country to the other, even being forced to publish his later works through his own publishing company.

Marcuse opts for another approach, above all in the book *Eros and Civilization* (with the subtitle *A Philosophical Inquiry into Freud)* from 1955. He argues that all the sacrifices and restrictions that Freud speaks of – and thus also patiently accepts – possibly can be defended with reference to scarce resources under certain special historical circumstances that necessitate hard work, but in the industrialized Western world from the 1950s onwards the situation is completely different. Unparalleled productivity increases lead to an abundance of consumption goods that causes the demands on hard work and abstinence from pleasure to no longer remain, at least not fully. The civilization process finally reaches the point where reality insists that the reality principle must be modified, which offers increased space for the pleasure principle.

Thus there is reason for optimism, an optimism that actually, argues Marcuse, also is built into Freud's own reasoning, but is concealed, even to the progenitor himself. Liberated from the harsh conditions of scarcity Man can in Marcuse enjoy shorter working hours and allow his strained and haggard body to be resexualized. Eros should no longer have to submit to the harsh restrictions of monogamy and reproduction. The liberated body is instead meant to become "a thing to be enjoyed – an instrument of pleasure." This libidinal paradise is the Freudo-Marxists' equivalent to the classless society where all social – and now also sexual – tensions are dissolved; capitalism has thus vanquished itself to death and has lost both the access to and need for all its coercive measures. The female breasts may by all means be naked. Men are welcome to look at them. No bra – not even of a spiritual kind – is necessary any longer, since there is no reason to regulate pleasure. Progress and an increase in growth has become a player piano thanks to production-increasing technology.

It is easy to imagine that Marcuse, and possibly even Reich, would greet the coming development within digitalization and robotization that liberates – or lays off – the human work force, with particular joy. If the machines carry out the work, we humans can concentrate on our pleasure and explore it without social stress. According to Marcuse, Freud's direct connection between civilization and repression thus is a misunderstanding: when the one coincides with the other it is because of special, time-bound factors and the exercise of power. But with other political prerequisites everything might be different. That demands for a postponed and/or inhibited satisfaction of needs are portrayed as necessary is merely an expression of the capitalist ideology having to legitimize injustices that actually are products of a class interest and that can be remedied with a little good will. The libidinal paradise that both Rousseau and in part also Freud – even if he is notoriously vague on this issue – place in a precivilizatory past, and to which the gateway, according to the two of them, is locked, since it is not possible to dismantle civilization, then actually awaits us in an enlightened future, this according to Marcuse and the psychoanalytically inspired Marxism.

But against this sunny utopianism, a few objections can be raised. To start with, we have the lamentable but nevertheless indisputable fact that the profits that are now made thanks to the productivity increases and cost cutting that follow from technological innovations are distributed highly unevenly, which leads to differences in income and wealth increasing rapidly both within and between rich and poor countries. That large and growing groups of unemployed people will have more leisure time to spend – more than they have ever feared or might have imagined – will not entail a renaissance for sophisticated, sexual pleasures, but rather an alarming increase in various sorts of addiction. As well as an increase in depression and suicides. One should therefore be careful what one wishes for, since there is a risk that one's wish might come true.

Which brings us to the next objection, namely that the price for the coveted wish fulfillment would – if it was possible to carry out at all – be much too high and the positive effects of it would constantly be overestimated by the propagandists of wish fulfillment, simply because they close their eyes to the inherent conflicts of objectives, while they engage in wishful thinking and fantasize about the effects of an abolition of the regulatory system around the satisfaction of needs. There is, to start with, no consensus on how a deregulation of the drive economy could be carried out and above all no agreement on what it may entail. What about polygamy? Should we lift all restrictions around promiscuity? Pedophilia, bestiality, incest – is it really time to revoke or ameliorate all prohibitions and restrictions that culture commands? If so, what about legalization of organized forms of football hooliganism where supporters of different teams agree on a time and place to fight each other, even with potentially lethal weapons? It would probably never be a question of any particularly radical form of deregulation, at most just a softening up of written and unwritten rules in certain limited respects. There is always a boundary for most things – if we are to maintain a society at all – and this is a boundary that either is written into law and is patrolled by guards, or else is merely symbolically marked in the collective subconscious. But *the boundary* most definitely does exist.

The greatest problem with the libidinal paradise is however that it never has existed nor can it ever exist, since it is basically just a Rousseauan fantasy that partly, but just partly, rubs off on Freud as he writes *Civilization and Its Discontents*, where he establishes that the discontentment really is incurable and fundamental, with an origin in Man's mental constitution. Which means that Freud's theory of culture does not harmonize in all respects with his topological model of human consciousness, something that Marxists with an inclination towards the utopian and psychoanalytical eagerly take to heart. But even if there were some truth in the paradisiacal myth, and if it were possible to imagine a human before or outside civilization, free to devote himself to boundless pleasure without reprisals, this "natural state" would at any rate not constitute some peaceful idyll, quite the contrary. Cultural restrictions are actually a blessing in cunning disguise, since they facilitate continued fantasizing about the unrestricted pleasure – something that is relatively innocuous and that in itself provides certain pleasure – while they also liberate the fantasizing subject from the burden of having to make the painful discovery that the drives, in the words of the American psychoanalyst Adrian Johnston, are "constitutively dysfunctional."

The drive machinery is not meant to produce our happiness, it is not compatible with something like family weekend bonding with snacks in the sofa. The sought-after and awaited delight never materializes, or else it proves completely illusory and is quickly scattered, to be replaced by discomfort and anxiety. In a way, Johnston writes in the book *Time Driven: Metapsychology and the Splitting of the Drive* from 2005, the drives are their own worst enemies. The actual satisfaction simply does not entail any real satisfaction. Which is why repression definitely has its advantages. Just as Freud himself does, Johnston uses the ancient tragedy's king Oedipus as a representative of the libidinal subject that within itself harbors desires that civilization kits out with a strait jacket, and that through the game of chance acquires and avails itself of a unique possibility to commit and experience these extreme boundary transgressions without requiring any interventions from the surrounding society.

Neither Oedipus himself nor anyone else suspects what he is actually doing when he slays his father Laius and marries his mother Jocasta; according to Freud he is following impulses that stem from repressed wishes hiding in the subconscious of every human subject, wishes that it takes a whole battery of mental mechanisms to keep in check – here we are speaking of the superego, castration anxiety et cetera.

But does this make Oedipus happy? No, not exactly. Once it dawns on him what he has done, he gouges out his eyes and goes into exile. So where does the tragic part of the tragedy really lie? The conventional answer is that Sophocles' famous drama shows us how helpless Man is in the face of the colossal forces of destiny. Oedipus is informed in advance by the Oracle of Delphi on how his life will be shaped and what actions he will carry out, which naturally appalls him and makes him take what he imagines to be efficient countermeasures – just as Laius believed he had cheated destiny by letting a servant kill his newborn son after he too had been warned in advance – but it is of course unfortunately precisely these countermeasures, Man's vain squirming in the net of destiny that inexorably envelops him, that result in the oracle's predictions coming true. Against the powerful machinery of destiny Man stands powerless and defenseless. Freud however argues that Oedipus' drama moves the reader and the spectator for other reasons: that the actions he actually carries out involve a staging of every human's secret, aching, repressed wishes. Therefore everyone can identify with the events on the stage: Oedipus lives out these forbidden wishes – and pays a high price.

Against this view, one might claim that Freud reads into the story psychoanalytical theories that actually are not present in the text, but one might of course also, argues Johnston, take the position that Freud does not relate psychoanalytically enough to Sophocles and that therefore the reading of the drama ought to be taken several degrees deeper. The result is that Oedipus himself becomes *an Oedipalized subject*, a person who is subordinated to the complex that nowadays bears his own name. And in this perspective he succeeds in doing what he most deeply longs for – even though it happens purely instinctively and without intention – when he makes visible that which has been made invisible. Oedipus quite simply succeeds in doing that which Rousseau fervently dreams of; he lives out the secret wishes that society censors. He has committed the perfect crime, he has been allowed to taste – to feast on – the most forbidden of all forbidden fruit. And then the question is: should he not in so doing have liberated himself from all his neuroses? If it is only cultural prohibitions that hold us back, and when no one else in the city of Thebes makes the least effort to punish him, should not Oedipus be the happiest, most peaceful and most complex-free person in the whole world? If so, then why does he gouge out his eyes?

Well, Oedipus punishes himself solely on his own initiative. He is totally devastated by the insight of what he has done. Instead of absolving himself, since it all happened unconsciously and inadvertently, he takes full responsibility for his crimes and imposes the harsh punishment himself. Which ought to make us at least somewhat suspicious: does not Oedipus thereby also admit to a considerable measure of participation when it comes to motive and driving force? Has he not stared deeply into his dark soul and glimpsed the repressed desires that make him a criminal, since he actually carried through on them? And if so, is someone ever innocent of anything? In the same way that Freud in Marcuse is a closet optimist, he becomes an even darker pessimist in Johnston than he is aware of himself, and Johnston argues considerably more convincingly. There is a fundamental and paradoxical opposition between drive and satisfaction that is impossible to reason away or come to grips with, and thus reason to contemplate all the dimensions of pessimism. But we must also note that Oedipus' tragic insight presents itself only after the transgression is a fact. That is: at the optimal time – guilt is something disagreeable and there are repression mechanisms that handily take care of this as well.

Nothing comes more naturally than finding excuses for one's own guilt and happily passing it on to someone else. Meanwhile the discontentment with civilization and the stubborn pounding from repressed drives and wishes causes *transgression* in various forms to constantly appear irresistibly alluring, particularly in a collective form, in groups where the restrictions of the surrounding society are more or less temporarily rescinded. Just as it is easy to project one's own guilt upon others, it is similarly easy to find good reason to hate others. They look strange, they speak strange languages, they have usurped unjust advantages in some sense, they believe in the wrong god, they support the wrong team. And actually, it is not even important to find an excuse – they are quite simply not we. That is reason enough. Few things are as intoxicating as shedding one's personal responsibility and all the restrictions of civilization to be part of a community that runs amok and eliminates all anxious and tidy regulatory systems. It is herein that modern terror's great attraction lies.

Our project *Digital Libido* has gone through several metamorphoses during the writing process, but the work has its origin precisely in contemporary Islamist terror and in a conversation between the authors that happened to arise in a hotel room in Moscow while we were watching a news report on television about the Islamic State, who just had committed another act of atrocity, had cut the throat of some kidnapping victims or had executed the population of an entire town somewhere in the Middle East. What primarily interested us about the Islamic State at the time were two aspects that oddly enough seldom or never come up in the discussion about the phenomenon: in part to what extent the Islamic State is an Internet-based phenomenon, in part how extraordinarily little this entire terror activity has to do with religion, but how strong is the connection to cultural discontentment.

The combination of terrorism and book reading was during this period – around 2014 – a subject to which a number of newspaper articles were devoted. It is a quite interesting, albeit a possibly discouraging chapter, for those who want to understand why youths in Europe of Muslim background in large numbers have been enticed into joining the terror network the Islamic State to fight in the Middle East. Two of these youths were particularly noted: Mohammed Nazon Ahmed and Yusuf Zubair Sarvar, two 22-year-olds who left their families and friends in their home town of Birmingham in the United Kingdom to join the Islamic State in Syria. Sarvar wrote a farewell letter to his mother in which he told her that he and his friend would go off to "do jihad." It is interesting to note here what travel literature the two of them ordered from the Internet bookshop Amazon to prepare for the holy war. Was it perhaps advanced dissertations in Islamic theology? Or anti-colonial treatises where all the crimes of the Western world in the Orient are analyzed and condemned? No, actually not. Instead it was the most light-hearted beginners' introduction to their own religion that one might possibly imagine: *Islam for Dummies*. And to be on the safe side, also *The Koran for Dummies*.

Which means that Ahmed and Zarbar just learned – if indeed they even did – a few elementary phrases about their religion before they travel off to fight for the caliphate and slaughter Muslim brothers who believe in the wrong things and various religious minorities in the area who are even more wrong in their beliefs. And nothing indicates that the already established terrorists, by whom they allowed themselves to be recruited, were one iota more versed in either the religion or its history either. This confirms what emerges in a report on what is called radicalization from the British MI5, which was leaked to *The Guardian*: Most of those who are recruited to terrorism neither practice Islam nor any other religion in an organized form, but should on the contrary be regarded as true novices. In truth, a distinct religious identity functions as protection against this violent radicalization. This fact is confirmed constantly: the murderers from the terror attacks in Paris or Copenhagen shortly thereafter did not either belong to the most exclusive elite amid learned scholars. They were not recruited from a Quran school, but from the correctional services. They were petty gangsters who looked forward with excitement to ramping up their activity level, and we can for good reason assume that they had motives other than religious ones. Thus it is not, as the French political scientist Gilles Kepel claims, a case of a radicalization of Islam, but instead, as Kepel's colleague and antagonist Olivier Roy maintains, a case of an Islamization of an unarticulated radicalism.

The unpleasant truth is that the Islamic State – and similar organisations and cults – constantly find new recruits in the tens of thousands by enticing them with the prospect of exercising delirious group violence with no consequences whatsoever. All these video clips of cut throats and mass executions are by no means primarily meant to frighten adversaries: they must rather be regarded as recruitment commercials for a medially exceptionally driven cult with bloody terror on the agenda. This – along with the Dionysian rush of group cohesion – is precisely the organization's main *selling point*. One offers participation in a collective who by virtue of being so heavily armed holds itself above all societies' aggregate laws and rules and gives aggression free rein. One skillfully exploits the fact that people evidently enjoy exercising violence together in groups as well as the liberation from responsibility that becoming part of a collective ensures. This in turn means that "doing jihad" has become little more than an upgraded charter travel option for restless youths of European football hooliganism.

Allah is therefore innocent of this. So who is guilty? Well, completely ordinary, despicable people in groups are guilty. When the appetite for torturing and massacring afflicts us, we just use the pretext that happens to be closest at hand. For many, it happens to be religious belonging in a time colored by comprehensive and enforced migration, for others it is something else. And thanks to the Internet we quickly and easily find innumerable like-minded people. Cannibals and body snatchers, pedophiles and assorted bullies – they all find their kindred spirits on the net; they form their communities, build their alliances and promote their interests. Many become scared of the image they form of the development, while the increasing segregation pulls society apart and thins it out. Law and order is constantly at the top of the political agenda, the security business sector expands, and frightened people with a lot of money pull away from society and hole up in *gated communities*. These are cordoned-off, walled residential areas to which not every Tom, Dick and Harry has access. And this is of course the market's answer to what is perceived as the state's failure to protect property rights and personal security. Here one need not see poor people, here one need not experience social tensions. But does one thereby escape human nature and its repressed desires?

Few novelists take as enduring and intense an interest in the very problem associated with *gated communities* as the Englishman J. G. Ballard, who constantly revisits the complications that seemingly inevitably arise in the enclosed idyll in novels such as *High Rise*, *Cocaine Nights* and *Super-Cannes*. In Ballard the well-structured idyll explodes in unrestrained orgies of violence and kinky sex. His literary universe is a space where the thoroughly regulated agreements and the well-trimmed garden hedges go out the window when the discontentment in civilization becomes so desperate that the liturgical consumption no longer can dampen people's anxiety or ameliorate their tedium. It is hardly surprising that Ballard to a large extent draws his animating creative impulses from psychoanalysis and from surrealist painting. What we learn from Ballard is that we should indeed be careful what we wish for, since it actually can become reality in a nightmare scenario. Well-being is never permanent; the death drive is a reality. This is quite similar to what we see in the Francis Fukuyama who philosophizes about the end of History; it is in a similar state of satisfaction of material needs and existential insouciance that several of Ballard's memorable novels unfold. In every well-disciplined paradise there is always a snake concealed. Balance is but a chimera, a transient anomaly. At the same moment that history, according to the beautiful theory, ought to be ended, it starts moving anew. Not seldom through violent convulsions.

It is just an impossible situation. When everyone should have every reason to be happy, there is always someone who finds a new reason for discontentment and worry. The realized utopia fills us with a dangerous restlessness that sooner or later will claim its victims. The enclosed reserve proves a powder keg. Ballard's short novel *Running Wild* from 1988 describes a crime investigation that is conducted precisely in an orderly and well-guarded *gated community*, Pangbourne Village *o*utside London, a luxurious idyll surrounded by and built with sophisticated technology, an ideal place for children to grow up in. Then one day it is suddenly completely empty. All the adults are brutally murdered, all the children have vanished without a trace. The investigation treads water for several months, until the psychiatric adviser Richard Greville is put on the case. And when all other theories have been tested, there remains but one, the most terrifying of them all. The reason that there has not been a demand for ransom for the children is that they never were kidnapped, it was the children who carried out the murders of the parents. Why? How could these pampered, seemingly well-bred and probably spoiled youths be transformed into the welfare idyll's own Baader-Meinhof Group? The answer is, they were restless and bored. They were discontent in civilization. "They were rebelling against a despotism of kindness. They killed to liberate themselves from the tyranny of love and care."

Digital Libido is a book that with its starting point in psychoanalysis explores Ballard's well-manicured quasi-paradise and that attempts to describe the somber energies and the repressed wishes that threaten to blow up the entire splendiferousness at any moment. For the History that just ended has set itself in motion again. We argue that there are indications of in what direction it will move and what this in turn will mean for the informationalist network society that is taking shape beneath our feet. It is possible to discern tendencies and patterns. And we further argue that an updated reading of Sigmund Freud and a carefully chosen selection of his many successors gives us well-functioning tools for this work. We advocate more psychoanalysis to the people. During the course of the journey we will touch upon subjects such as class and class conflicts, dominance and subordination, the patriarchy and the matriarchy, libido and mortido, gendered power structures and feminism, adultification and infantilization, globalism and identity politics, cosmopolitan mobility and national romanticist anchoring in the local, et cetera. We are obviously aware that all these things are extremely charged in a situation where many hope to win decisive debate points by pretending to misunderstand someone else's argument in order to thereby be able to become publicly enraged and victimized. So for this reason, in order to as well as possible avoid both genuine and phony misunderstandings, we want to declare here and now what *Digital Libido* is not.

Digital Libido is not a book that promotes any views about the development that is depicted in it. It is not for or against digitalization or globalization. It is not a book that wants to advocate for one opinion or the other in regard to the ongoing development. It does not attack the new underclass, on the contrary it warns of the risks of a new upper class that completely cuts its ties with the rest of society. Nor does it have a hostile inclination towards *feminism*, on the contrary it wants to deepen the discussion around gender roles and distribution of power in a way that leads to increased gender equality on all fronts, towards an *egalitarianism* that includes both sexes and that makes feminism as unnecessary as an otherwise necessary *masculinism*. And so on. Nevertheless we will allow ourselves the occasional sharp turn of phrase for the sole reason that we persist in believing that just as being clear-sighted always is better than wishful thinking, frank language is always better than euphemisms. So welcome to a world filled with sex, power and violence in a digital version, a brave new world underpinned by a high tech platform of intense networking. Welcome to *the digital libido*, the only thing that keeps us alive in the emerging global network society.

2
The human constant, the technological variable, and the metahistorical tsunami

Meaning – here we have a truly thrilling dilemma. We cannot live without it, quite simply because without meaning existence lacks all . . . yes, precisely, meaning. This is an unbearable state of affairs and something which we must at any cost remediate one way or another. Therefore, we are searching for meaning, at all times and all over the place, a search made considerably harder by the lamentable fact that meaning does not exist and cannot exist, at least not in the tangible sense we so dearly would like it to exist, that is: in the sense that the stove and the saucepan exist in the kitchen over there. Which is why the search for an already existing meaning, ready to welcome and be occupied by new tenants, always is and always must be doomed to fail. So why this constant search for meaning? According to an explanatory model from evolutionary biology the need for it is related to our brain never having had the task of to uncovering truth about existence, but instead, within the boundaries of what is possible, enables a functional orientation and navigation in and through a largely unknown surrounding world full of potential threats. And that task becomes so much easier to carry out with an established meaning to navigate by, completely irrespective of whether it actually exists.

There is a cracking sound coming from the bushes over there, not far away, and the listener wonders whether it was just the wind blowing or perhaps a perfectly harmless badger that happened to step on a dry twig. Yes, it might have been. But there is also the risk that it might have been a dangerous predator or malevolent enemy who at this moment is watching and contemplating an attack. In this context, caution is a virtue, natural selection favors he who immediately gets a sense that danger lurks in the near future and who acts accordingly. What was true or not is therefore of secondary importance; there is no harm in being cautious one time too many, while incautiousness sooner or later will be penalized. So we interpret nature and the world surrounding us to the best of our abilities, ascribe causes and intentions to things, find contexts and patterns – or else we create them ourselves in our own head when there are none to be found. A systematic trying-out of created causal contexts and explanatory models is called "science," a high status occupation. When a certain hypothesis does not hold up on closer scrutiny, it must be rejected; what we believed to be true was actually erroneous, but now we believe that something else is true, that is: we believe this up to the point when what now is new proves old and erroneous, after which we believe in something else that is now new. And so on. And we carry on like this. However, what we do not believe in is chance or a purely material causality without intention we can relate to. These kinds of things make us nervous. Which means that if we can choose between necessity and contingency, we cling to necessity as long as humanly possible.

There are different ways of managing the insight that the search for meaning is meaningless. We can stare this insight in the eye and accept it, which could lead to either despair and powerlessness, or alternatively to the impulse to actually create or participate in creating a meaning that ties the collective together and bestows form and maneuverability on existence, in complete awareness that the cherished meaning consists of fiction. But what is simplest and also closest at hand is of course good old-fashioned repression. We compartmentalize the bothersome insight and do not admit it. We find and assume a meaning that serves our purposes, and we refrain from questioning it so strenuously that it risks collapsing. We do not hesitate to carry out the intellectual acrobatics that the defense of this meaning requires. An important element in this never-ending project of manufacturing and continuously maintaining a functional meaning is, of course, the *historiography* that creates a legitimate context for the power relations that happen to currently prevail in the society. Writing history, historicizing existence and connecting different events with different values along the timeline, is obviously never equivalent to establishing a more or less exhaustive record of these events, or even of the most important events, of the past, but it is intended precisely to manufacture functional meaning in the form of a cohesive story about how the now appears. It is a question of selection and arrangement of suitable facts, as well as creativity in terms of useful fictions.

Every paradigm in world history must comprise its own historiography, that is: a society's view of history constitutes the foundation of its self-image and its worldview. Historicization is the lens through which society views itself. It lays down the conditions for the relevant perspective, which in turn governs the selection of relevant facts. Or conversely: The very fact that there is a reprioritization in a society of what is regarded as relevant or irrelevant in the past, in itself reveals that powerful forces are in motion and that a paradigm shift has begun. Moreover, historians seldom work for free; one might assume that they for instance strive for remuneration in the form of land or money, and above all reasonable recognition for their endeavors from the world around them. Consequently one has strong incentives within the profession to produce a history that meticulously leads up to and glorifies the prevailing – or maybe rather the new, emerging – power structure.

Therefore the produced history must become completely understandable in the context in which it is created, and thus cannot depart to any considerable extent from what the forces of power and the commissioning body expected, without running the risk of being perceived as divergent, in the sense of being odd, irrelevant and hard to comprehend. Thus an important dimension of written history is always ideological in the sense of what it selects and what it discards, this regardless of the author's stated or tacit intentions. Naturally this also applies to the authors of this book to the extent that we devote ourselves to historiography: the fact that one is conscious of the problem does not mean that one is let off the hook. The only reasonable approach to this dilemma is openness and transparency. We are of course part of the power relations of our age just like everyone else, our view of history is governed by the present we share with the surrounding world. But we do hope that awareness will sharpen our gaze and provide a multi-faceted image of the present time, which is going through revolutionary changes. If the overarching power structure that ultimately rests on a dominant media technology (see *The Netocrats* for a more extensive elaboration) is dramatically changed, or rather is replaced by a completely new one, since a new metamedium's arrival means talents and skills are judged in accordance with a brand new system of rewards and punishment, the poor historian is compelled to seek new employers. And to whistle a different tune.

The need for a new historiography with a different focus follows naturally from a new power elite commissioning a glorification of themselves. The smoothest way of carrying out this maneuver is to recast historiography as an interpretation of the past, a succession of simplified protovariants of precisely the social configuration that is in the process of taking shape in one's own present. That is; the coronation of a new power elite is portrayed as the objective for the entire historical process quite simply because this is how the rulers-to-be and their historians wish this process to be perceived. A new history bestows a new and much-needed meaning on a new age. The events once again appear to be a logical targeted development. If the objective and meaning of history was, for instance, to one day produce the industrialist's factories, history is transformed into a voyage leading to this very factory building through a series of domestications, or acts of taming, of sundry raw materials lying around in nature waiting for civilization to reach the level where Man could make use of these exact substances. Concepts such as "Stone Age," "Bronze Age" and "Iron Age" are applied to the events afterwards precisely because that perspective is in line with the conception of the factory and the industrial economy as the final stop of the historical process and the preceding era's metaphysical completion. People who lived during the Stone Age were of course blissfully unaware that they were Stone Age people. Thus the word "Stone Age" does not occur in a single history book until the emergence of industrialism.

The reason for this metahistorical necessity is that every person and every collective first and foremost seeks *social identity*: a person who has been stripped of or has never satisfactorily been able to create his social identity ends up in a *psychosis,* and psychotic people are, as we know, generally dysfunctional in everyday life to the extent that we, both for their own sake and for that of their surroundings, habitually lock them up. This identity as a *dividual* (see *The Body Machines* for more extensive reasoning on this concept) in a social context arises through a constant authoring and editing of dividual and collective biographies, or life stories, interpretations and rewrites of what afterwards is apprehended as that which gives meaning to an imagined timeline that stretches from a more or less vague introductory phase, where the configuration of the present slowly starts to take shape, up until its full-scale manifestation in the present.

History in itself is actually *contingent* – full of surprises that cannot possibly be predicted and which only can appear self-evident or necessary afterwards. This is a result partly of the infinite complexity of existence in the form of incalculable interaction between an immeasurable amount of variables, partly of existence being fundamentally *indeterministic* – open to the future and full of randomness at every moment along the timeline. It is possible to describe and reason around this contingency in theory, but in practice it is impossible for Man to handle, just as it is impossible for the perception apparatus to fashion a true picture of *the mobilist chaos* that surrounds us at every moment (see primarily *The Global Empire* for elaboration), leading us to a constant freezing of this chaos of impulses and giving us on the one hand arbitrary but on the other quite functional *eternalizations* – seemingly sustainable fictions that the brain can handle and that produce an soothing illusion of meaning.

Emphasizing this fundamental contingency serves neither the old nor the new, emerging power structure's interests. Power does not want to hear – and above all will not allow the spread of – the fact that the state of affairs, so advantageous to the elite, is unconnected to any meritorious achievements. We tend to forget that evolutionary processes in all contexts, biological as well as cultural, essentially are lotteries. The winners become winners thanks to the good fortune that happens to favor their own predisposition above that of others, and thus really do not have much to boast about. Social Darwinism is vulgar and stupid. But power is of course more interested in legitimacy than in truth, which is why it quite simply commands from its historians – more or less openly – a morality that elevates the virtues that have been rewarded by the prevailing conditions into universal ideals for all ages. At the same time, these conditions entail that only a certain type of historiography becomes comprehensible, which merely further reinforces the glorifying tendency. The result is that the power structure appears to be the result of a logical, ordered process that cannot be questioned, but that instead must be defended and glorified within the prevailing paradigm's incessant identity production.

Therefore *metahistory* is built on the principle that all historical events that are prioritized out of the prevailing value base must be ascribed *necessity* afterwards. What has happened has happened by necessity, which insinuates that the current power structure also must be necessary, which makes it virtually impossible to question it. Historiography thus manages to kill two birds with one stone: the new power structure at once becomes both glorified and impossible to criticize, at least as long as the underlying current information-technological paradigm is resilient to fundamental changes. G W F Hegel, the German forefather of process philosophy, observes in the early 19th century that there is absolutely no necessity *per se* in history, rather, necessity is always established afterwards when Man feebly projects his wishful thinking about his own power position and his own historical significance, pompous to a fault, onto the completely pointless contingency of existence in itself. This is what we keep doing, whether we gaze around the world or look back through history: through our historicizing we implement measures that create meaning.

It is therefore in complete agreement with the rules of the game that historiography confers on the sitting or incoming power an aura of significance and dignity. Nevertheless it is ultimately a case of power's wishful thinking about itself and its own historical role, something that merely can be maintained by force of the prevailing paradigmatic communication advantage, which is reinforced by the established feedback loop that arises when the projected proficiency is rewarded with an intense *libidinal* attraction from the other parts of society, something which in turn confirms and reinforces dignity, and so on. The master and the slave – concepts handed down from Hegel and his antithetical successor Friedrich Nietzsche – have their carefully scripted roles to play in this context. The slave's mortidinal needs to subordinate himself to and curry favor with the master are both powerful and constant, since this simultaneously confirms and reinforces the system's social identities. Actually, idolatry is the engine of the entire social theater, and there is a tremendous, almost intoxicating allure both in assuming the role of the idol and in being part of the worshipping collective in front of the stage. The social sadists always constitute the minority, while the social masochists make up the majority, as Nietzsche in resignation observes. The slaves are always by necessity many times more numerous than the masters in every society.

This in turn means that the idols are easy to substitute and often inherit each other's roles (a priest is replaced by another priest, a king is replaced by another king, an aristocrat is replaced by another aristocrat); the only thing that is really required is that the substitute is relatively familiar with his role and his script. A trenchant rewrite of this script occurs only rarely, namely in connection with an information-technological paradigm shift when a brand new class, favored by the new rules of the game that result from the new technology, enter the stage with new lines of dialogue and replace the old guard who have now made their final performance and are hopefully courteously but nevertheless firmly ushered off to instead play the role of loser in the new elite's historiography, produced in accordance with given directives. While new masters enter into new agreements with new slaves about mutual recognition in accordance with established patterns. It is only then that, for instance, a new ruling bourgeois class steps forward and ensures that the priest is replaced by an academic, the king is replaced by a politician and the aristocrat is replaced by an industrialist, and so on. The metahistorical constant is Man's eternal need for mortidinal submission, while the object of this submission can and must vary with the circumstances. Harsh winds may blow atop the power pyramid, but both the pyramid and its peak stand firm as long as the paradigm in itself is not threatened. The earthquake only occurs when the paradigm's fundamental communication flows are rerouted and its information storage is reorganized. But then the change occurs all the more quickly and intensely.

This state of affairs entails that all biographies that are written within a specific paradigm, both the dividual and the tribal or some other form of collective, must revolve around what the prevailing power structure perceives as relevant for one's own identity production. The constantly ongoing selection process – whether carried out via authorized monasteries, universities or websites – continuously culls amidst all that tells of, or is being told about, the past. Historiography is thus governed by *relevance* and not by some magnanimous endeavor for an exemplary *factuality*. The justification of one's own power and the conditions under which it is exercized occurs through constructing and maintaining a pattern in what is said to be a development, a pattern that is said to be the historical necessity. That is: the prevailing power structure tends to prioritize the events and changes that have or at least appear to have been relevant for its own genesis. In a metahistorical perspective it is the prevailing power structure that decides what is relevant for the entire story about the emergence of the present, since it is the structure that in various ways rewards the historian to write a biography of the same that portrays its emergence in an appropriately flattering light.

History is of course always written in hindsight, the meaning put in place when the image of the recorded past corresponds to the image of a development, which thereby appears necessary. Eternalization always works best as a certainly illusory but nevertheless necessary and hopefully functional node in a contingent, mobilist chaos (see *The Global Empire* for an extensive treatment of this process). Our continuously updated biographies – the stories about who we are and how we fit into the given context, constantly extended and rebuilt in real-time – are placed into the surrounding world and immediate environment, in what the German philosopher Markus Gabriel calls our *field of sense*, and it is there that they give the appearance of offering value and meaning. The meaning-filled field-of-sense clusters that this gives rise to are what we call *models*. It is these models that Man takes as his point of departure, both individually and as a collective, when he constructs his *worldview* – that is: the meta-model within which other models are posited to be able to generate relational values for each other. It is then from this worldview that Man lets himself be programmed to make the prioritizations that he thinks will give him that eagerly coveted social identity without which all production of meaning is impossible.

This veritable *quest for status* naturally becomes all the more intense the closer to the prevailing power structure the dividual approaches, since it is there that identity is the most libidinal. *Libido*, the will to live, is maximized when it is associated with freedom. And freedom first and foremost requires power over one's own destiny, the status to say yes to what one wants and no to what one does not want. This explains why Nietzsche refers to libido as *the will to power*. Thus libido is at its most intense – providing that all other factors are equal – closest to or perhaps even within the halls of power. Little wonder that many of the men who have approached power over the ages have paid for this approach through castration, administered by the men who had got there ahead of them. Political history is replete with eunuchs as well as more or less binding vows of chastity. The important thing is that this means that the identity production's circle is closed, and will continue to be closed as long as the societal structure's underlying paradigm retains its legitimacy and the social punishment and reward system remains intact. Afterwards, when the old paradigm is phased out, a painful and often violent process is launched, directly connected to information-technological development. Technology is the only thing in Man's surrounding world and immediate environment that in a genuine sense actually changes over time – everything else is a consequence of this fundamental change. Metahistory is therefore invariably, at its deepest level, a history of technology. Or as we ourselves call the first chapter of our first book: *Technology is the motor of history*.

Understanding and remembering that Man has enormous difficulties in accepting new models is of great importance. Man is after all an organism, and all organisms are primarily conservative. The instinctive reaction to external stimuli in every organism is to spontaneously distance itself. This preprogrammed cautiousness is, as already stated, what the evolutionary process rewards; every change constitutes a possible threat, which does not preclude that even painful and unwanted changes occasionally may be necessary and even vital in sustaining life. So when Man finally accepts new biographies, models and identities, even when this occurs under duress, he often becomes very fond of them and later finds it even harder to question these accepted models, since that would require a questioning of himself and the social categories that he now believes himself to have conquered, rather than merely passively have taken over. After all, they represent a massive investment from which Man bitterly seeks dividends before he considers himself able to proceed.

Social identity in turn rests completely on the models that Man uses to navigate through existence: "Tell me your model and I will tell you your identity." At a certain age, which varies from one person to another but takes place sooner or later, most people give up their attempts to question and change models in life, and would rather cling to the model that they most recently, with great effort, learned, and would be happy to do so until death if need be. It is this moment that for the father of psychoanalysis, Sigmund Freud, constitutes, the shift from *libido* (the will to life) to *mortido* (the death drive) as the dominant mode in the dividual's life. People quite simply stop absorbing new information of the sort that would compel any form of revision of the models that are the bedrock of their self-image or worldview. Past a certain age people change for instance cars, phones, computers, life companions or professions much more rarely and reluctantly than do younger people, and instead these older people put great effort into explaining to themselves and their immediate environment why their own media habits already are sufficiently sophisticated and why further changes would be detrimental.

This is also part and parcel of the issue: not only are changes in themselves bothersome inasmuch as they require a measure of adaptation work and rethinking; it is moreover the case that the person who has been accorded a fairly high status under the prevailing circumstances would not be particularly keen on changing the conditions that are the foundation for their own present status. An established power elite will for good reason interpret all forms of novelty as bad news. Since we are living at the very start of *informationalism* or *the Internet Age*, and since we who are writing and reading this book are part of the new, rapidly emerging netocratic power structure, it is also we who get the enjoyment of rewriting history as our own collective biography in accordance with the new legitimization needs that have arisen, and thus can create a both credible and attractive social identity for ourselves. Divisions that define previous eras serve old purposes, which is why we need new ones; what is natural (a treacherous word that one always should be suspicious of) in the current context is a division of human history into four information-technological paradigms: one for *spoken language*, one for *written language*, one for *printed language* or the mass media, and one for *interactive language* or digital media.

Every preceding era should therefore be understood as a necessary starting point and prerequisite, an undeveloped protovariant, of the new paradigm which now, as we speak, emerges before our eyes – that is: the *informationalist* paradigm. Every fundamental, social change also has a material, external and technological foundation. Thus we can logically deduce the necessary steps in the *paradigmatic dialectics* between technology and Man in the following way: First there is the fundamental technological disruption causing the metahistorical tsunami. One example is the launch of Johannes Gutenberg's printing press in Germany in the mid-15th century. The development of a new metaphysical fundamental idea follows, a new ideological center for historiography that directly or indirectly lauds the new emerging power elite and its, by necessity, self-aggrandizing worldview. For instance, René Descartes laying the ground for *individualism* and rejecting God as the center of existence (in favor of this newly-created individual), as summed up in the quote "I think, therefore I am" from 1637. An idea that spreads through cheap, printed books in large and ever-increasing editions.

In a third step, the force of the new technology explodes while the instigators behind it don't yet really understand what is happening. We call this dramatic phase *the great chaos*. A striking example is the French Revolution in 1789 (which therefore is no authentic revolution, but merely a symptom of the real revolution that occurred as early as 1450). Paris was, even at that point in time, teeming with citizens who could read and write, devouring pamphlets and broadsheets as well as encyclopedias and books replete with enlightened agitation. Only after this stage, in the fourth step of the paradigmatic dialectics, comes the taming of the force of new technology and the realization of the metaphysical idea via the shifting and intensified information flows of the current society. Only then is the paradigm shift complete and it finds its ideal organizational form. For instance, in Napoleon's army's victory parade around Europe, with Napoleon himself as the most perfect individual of all in 1806. Napoleon's army, eagerly cheered on by the thinkers of the day – with Hegel as the standard-bearer – over the next 200 years becomes the model for all institutions created under the banner of the nation-state for the state, markets and academies. This is the golden age of mass media and thus also of proficiency in reading, writing and mathematics. As a result of these communication flows we get both capitalism and industrialism, as well as bourgeois democracy – with all that brings in the form of educational systems, et cetera. All this is developed with great energy up until the next metahistorical tsunami, which is launched with the stealthy arrival of the Internet in the 1980s. At this time much of the old disappears, while other things are embedded in a brand new context and thus acquire new meanings.

In this way we can observe how spoken language leads to what we call *primitivism*; how written language leads to *feudalism*; how the printing press leads to *capitalism*; and how the Internet throws us into *informationalism*. As the pattern shows, every paradigmatic leap entails that the amount of information available to Man explodes. And the explosion undoubtedly occurs in a very different place than inside the halls of the old power. The streets of Paris in the 18th century is a completely different environment from that of the logbooks for grain collection in ancient Egypt. Just as technology clusters such as Silicon Valley in our 21st century is a completely different kind of environment than the cotton mills of Manchester in the early 19th century. This in turn means that information and knowledge is disseminated to new, power-hungry actors that previously have been tangibly marginalized. In this way, they receive a forceful, sought-after injection of libidinal empowerment, while new conditions disfavor old rulers. This process is depicted in great detail in *The Netocrats*.

The social breakthrough of new metatechnologies occurs ever more rapidly. The printing press needed more than 350 years to produce the changes that resulted in early capitalism; The Internet has in just a few decades already changed the prerequisites for politics, culture, economics and the production of social identity beyond recognition. However, we humans also change – our physiology – with the slowness of biology, a process that has been constant throughout history up until now when cyborg technology opens up transformative and, for many people, disagreeable perspectives. This assuredly plastic but in fundamental aspects immutable human nature – where cyborg technology still is nowhere close to success in comprehending or being able to modify the human brain to any real extent – entails that our genes not only are created under, but to a large degree also live on in the original paradigm, characterized by the unrestricted power of spoken language, namely the primitivist nomadic society. A tribe in constant motion, with a membership of between 50 and 150 adults, plus a number of children and a few still fairly lithe seniors who contribute to the survival of the collective with their experiences and their wisdom: despite the entire civilization process and all the changes that has brought, this tribe is the social environment where most people, because of their genetic programming, feel most at home.

This explains why constant fantasies about the original nomadic tribe characterize people's yearning and search for functional ways of life, expressing itself in the social psychological myth that we call *the tribal nostalgia*. Ever since Jean-Jacques Rousseau, philosophers have briskly churned out poetry about the innocent and happy life in the nomadic tribe, a myth built on nothing but the nostalgic wishful thinking of the many Rousseauians, which always finds like-minded listeners in great numbers. Thus the human psyche's basic stance is not freedom and radicality, as Nietzsche desires in the 19th century, but quite the contrary, submission and conservatism. Or to express the matter in Nietzschean fashion: most people prefer to live their lives as mortidinal *slaves* rather than libidinal *masters,* as that supreme heckler of hypocrisy, Marquis de Sade, remarkes with brutal honesty in writings such as *Philosophy in the Bedroom*, where he attacks the sentimental reverie about human nature of Rousseau and others. Slavery is Man's normal state, not freedom.

Further, human history displays a constantly ongoing tug-of-war between the tribal on the one hand and the universal on the other. The tribal gives a robust and clearly defined identity, but in return requires a marked distancing from that which deviates or in any way lies outside the narrow, locally anchored framework. This dichotomy in turn sooner or later leads to an unavoidable conflict of interest between those within the tribe who are fascinated by that which is alien and those who build their status on and get their security from the familiar. Pitted against the tribal there is the universal: the story of empathy and even of identification with the stranger. There is a focus on that which unites us humans across arbitrarily drawn boundaries – national identities are always fictitious, but nevertheless often very functional – rather than that which separates us. The universal narrative can entice us with a long list of attractive attributes in the form of possible non-zero-sum games of a social, political and cultural character, but it can never produce the social identity that satisfies humanity's most basic needs. The universal quite simply never bestows on anyone the delightful satisfaction of being in the focus of what we call *the phallic gaze*, which is the key to many of the political conflicts that have taken so many commentators by surprise. Globalization has its socio-economic logic and dynamics, but it is inevitable that it scares the daylights out of many people, primarily poorly educated rural people who have no ability to compete in a post-industrial labor market, people who quite rightly observe that this process brings further marginalization on their part. For these people the tribal identity becomes a promise of a salvation, albeit a temporary one, and its negative definition in relation to the hostile and frightening world around them receives a clarity that forcefully generates security. The surrounding world in this scenario is accorded the role of a menacing background against which one's own social identity shows up with sharp contours.

The primitivist tribe did not only find itself in constant movement, but was above all *plastic*. People's dividual differences (see *The Body Machines* for a more extensive discussion) are connected to the fact that what survived (or not) in the Darwinian evolutionary process was not a few individual people but entire tribes – precisely in the capacity of entire tribes. Either they survived and procreated, or they perished. Thus it was the tribes with the most favorable collection and combination of properties at the time that survived, and the tribes that had the least suitable collective features that perished. This was true to such a great degree, moreover, because of the constant life-and-death conflicts between tribes that encountered each other from time to time, tribes that competed with each other for the extremely limited resources offered by nature. The groups that were least prepared for these brutal conflicts were annihilated on the battlefield with no man spared. This means that the myth of the noble savage always has been precisely that, a myth, and that life in this period hardly was the cozy pacifist love fest that history naivists in Rousseau's wake still dream of to this day.

The tribe was every individual member's entire world, and also their life insurance policy – as long as one had both useful and practical skills to offer the collective that in return provided protection and fellowship. Should members of one tribe happen upon members of another on the savannah, one group either beat the other to death or ran for their lives, depending on who was more powerful. The concept of *a human* was never projected in any way whatsoever on anyone outside of one's own tribe. The stranger bore marks on his forehead different from those chosen within one's own tribe and in addition spoke an unintelligible and therefore menacing language. There was no option but to draw one's weapon upon an unexpected meeting in the outskirts of the tribal arena. Cooperation was confined to one's own tribe, as the researcher and author Jared Diamond shows, precisely because everyone else was a sworn enemy in the eternal fight for survival between the various nomadic tribes. These other tribes were not us, did not share our stories, did not carry out our rituals, did not speak our language, did not share our frames of reference or our understanding of the meaning of everything, and therefore they by definition did not deserve our trust and instead could – and should – be annihilated without further ado. They were quite simply not even humans.

This basic approach is and remains the psychological foundation of all warfare: the extensive *demonization* of the stranger who is thereby transformed into the adversary and who is no longer regarded as fully human. It is only then that killing can be justified. And the primitivist nomadic tribe to a large extent lives on today in the form of more or less aggressive clan communities that still strive to redraw the world map. That these structures live on in spite of civilizing pressures is connected to the fact that the same brain that triggers a sense of strong well-being – indeed, almost a mild rush – when we are together with our loved ones, in a flash switches over to sudden aggression and a brutal distancing from strangers and outsiders, above all in situations where one's own tribe/clan/family is experienced as facing an immediate threat from the outside. This libidinal and fundamentally genetically conditioned mode of action – forceful aggression aimed at a threatening environment – is what we throughout history have regarded as *heroism*. In other words, militant aggression is the very fabric of the primitivist nomadic tribe's (orally conveyed) historiography. This timeless storytelling also speaks to the children of today as they sit there playing more or less violent games on their computers, as well as the adults that watch TV series rife with threats and aggression hour after hour; the connection to our neural pathways is biological.

The history naivists within, for instance, the utopian Left and the eco-moralist environmental movement are thus fundamentally wrong about life in the primitivist nomadic tribe, and so have absolutely nothing of value to contribute to a meaningful discussion on the informationalist modern human. Everything that is akin to this thoroughly false and rose-colored romanticization concerning Man's social origins and deep-seated drives must actually be discarded if we are to achieve a reasonably credible, critical analysis of what is going on within ourselves and in our environment in the turbulence of the informationalist society. But unfortunately, our self-image and worldview are still clouded by these long-winded history naivists who follow in Rousseau's footsteps and convince themselves (and us) that it is society and civilization that have corrupted a pristine, angelic and unspoiled natural state characterized by peace and concord, and who portray Man as an intrinsically harmonious and good-natured bon vivant rather than as a restless neurotic with a pathological death wish, despite this being demonstrably much closer to the truth. The truth we can infer from existing research has constantly and without any notable misgivings been sacrificed over and over again on the altar of moralism, unfortunately still to this day. But no kind of pacifist, peaceful paradise populated by noble savages has, to judge from all available facts, regrettably ever existed. And this hardy, ideologically colored propaganda lie is not merely untrue, which in itself is bad enough, but is in fact exceptionally destructive. Building a society based on great amounts of wishful thinking is a surefire recipe for widespread problems, which we have witnessed and which we still can see in our lives. Tribal nostalgia leads us straight into the most destructive of blind alleys.

At the dividual level the evolutionary process primarily favored those genes underpinning the success of the collective, but that were not too close to the internal competition within the tribe, since a similarity of this kind meant that one viewed as a dividual was more or less replaceable, and thus also tangibly vulnerable. A functional dissimilarity, on the other hand – that is: a dissimilarity of the right kind, one that was rewarded by the prevailing circumstances – entailed a rare winning ticket in the gene lottery. This explains a fact that on the surface may appear puzzling, bordering on the inexplicable, namely that homosexuality within a population stays at a fairly constant rate worldwide and in the most disparate societal structures. It turns out that between five and ten percent of the population is primarily sexually attracted to their own gender, always and everywhere, rather than the reverse, which in theory is procreatively objectionable. Tribes with a greater number of homosexuals than this level have indeed managed poorly in the intense competition, but this occurs also to tribes with a lower number. The optimal percentage of homosexuals for a tribal population's long-term survival has been proven to lie precisely in the range between five and ten per cent.

This state of affairs leads to the question of what role various forms of what often is called "sexual deviations" – homosexualities, bisexualities, transsexualities and also asexualities – have had in the evolutionary process and in what way they have been beneficial to the collective in question: in particular with respect to the plastic nomadic tribe. We can then logically assume that the explanation does not lie in the various sexual practices, which have varied considerably more over time than sexual orientations: the distribution of majorities and minorities has remained constant throughout history. And this in turn means that the fight for rights and equality of sexual minorities – significant for the informationalist society – must be regarded as a highly serious effort to protect the entire plastic tribe's survival, and not as some trendy decadent phenomenon where loud-mouthed special interests put forward various destructive lifestyles as false ideals, which is what politically and religiously motivated adversaries constantly try to claim. The truth is of course that sexual orientation in itself is a superficial phenomenon. But beneath this visible surface lurks something precipitous and decisive for the dividual identity, namely *the tribal map*. The singular person may wish this and that from life, but the following fact remains: his specific placement within the tribe in question is largely decided by others – above all by *the elders*, the leaders of the tribe – with regard to his biologically conditioned talents and nothing else.

The Swiss psychoanalyst Carl Gustav Jung calls these tribal roles *archetypes*. This means that all conceivable archetypes are present within the tribe's aggregate gene pool in order to optimize the tribe's chance of survival. All men and women bear the genetic potential for both homo- and heterosexual offspring. The most necessary or at least the most immediate archetypes – we call them alfa- beta-

and gamma characters – constantly recur. But the predispositions that underpin rare but nevertheless necessary roles are handed down in plastic gene clusters that yield different outcomes depending on varying circumstances. The transborder archetypes are quite simply hyperplastic precisely because they are both more unusual and more complex than the primary archetypes. This means that they seldom have the daily, central role that we find in the alfa- beta- or gamma characters. But where the transborder archetypes really are needed – the shaman and the trickster are the two most common – their roles prove to be directly decisive for the survival of the tribe. It is little wonder that we find significant elements of for instance androgyny and other transborder and hyperplastic properties within what we call *the shamanistic caste*. And the shamanistic caste's role is never more important than during the metahistorical earthquakes that we call paradigm shifts, something that we are living through now, at the time of writing.

3
From the plastic nomadic tribe to The Global Empire

Day-to-day life during primitivism was permeated by a deep religiosity in that the search for food occurred in parallel with the constant search for meaning, a search that could never cease since in essence everything in the surrounding world was confusing and inexplicable, except for religion itself. Creating meaning was (and is) synonymous with creating oneself, both at a dividual and collective level. Another way of expressing the same thing is to say that there was no religion at all during primitivism since there was nothing other than religion. Everything was religion. And if everything is religion, then nothing is more religious than anything else. At the same time, existence was permeated by playful experimentation. As long as the tribe was not at war with competing rivals it was possible to make hunting and gathering more effective so that these chores only took a few hours a day – considerably fewer than a regulated work day in our own age, where our social identity up until now has been connected to just that, work – which freed up time for other activities. So the daily schedule was full of gaps, primarily because there was no point in accumulating a surplus of food, since it was not possible to store it to any significant extent. A not insignificant part of the day could be devoted to various types of games, originally lacking in any practical purpose, and which were important because of their own inherent qualities.

When these intratribal games grew in scope and were carried out by ever larger groups, they went through a gradual regulation and ritualization that cemented social identity and constituted the basis of the collective culture. This is an important observation made by several researchers and authors, for example the Dutch cultural historian Johan Huizinga and the German social theorist Herbert Marcuse, who was active within the neo-Marxist Frankfurt School. Being part of the ritual game meant that one confirmed and manifested one's membership in the primitivist nomadic tribe. That the game was, or could be, stimulating and amusing does not mean that it should be understood as a childish pastime. The game was always serious in a fundamental sense, where the ritual game frequently was brutal rather than mild and loving. The outcome of the game could often be deadly. And yet the game was generally tolerated, which should not be interpreted as implying the tribe in question was torn asunder by internal conflicts or sectarian strife that had to be channeled and managed under controlled circumstances. Quite the contrary.

The key to understanding the playful collectivization process lies in the principle called *intracollaborativity*: a network of institutionalized cooperation at various levels within the tribe. For this network to be productive, a large measure of adaptation to a constantly changing and unpredictable social environment was required. This can be interpreted solely in religious terms, which in turn required that the dividuals of the tribe developed a large measure of *plasticity*. This intransigent demand for dividual plasticity was what gave rise to the brutality of the ritual game. We can see how this pattern recurs among informationalist contemporary humans. We are not referring to illegal violence in the form of for instance football hooliganism and the like which society fights with all means at its disposal, without ever succeeding in eliminating these expressions of cultural dissatisfaction. What we want to focus on is instead how this brutal violence is channeled and made uniform as an exercise of authority, an officially sanctioned domestication of the plastic dividuality that is found in everything from the violence monopoly of the police and mandatory schooling to involuntary psychiatric care. This large-scale domestication is in practice invisible since the prevailing power structure portrays it as both natural and necessary; these social processes are created and maintained solely for what is in the best interests of the dividual, and lack any other purpose according to the official ideology. However the result, as if by coincidence, is the coveted plasticity in the form of more or less docile citizens.

The natural approach within the primitivist nomadic tribe was therefore *cooperation*, not *competition*. An *intracombativity*, a competition for positions and resources within one's own tribe, generally only arose in extremely desperate situations. That kind of competition has never been a primary purpose in itself, which the influential standard-bearers of individualism for ideological reasons tend to claim for the purpose of portraying selfishness and ruthlessness as exemplary and from a broader perspective beneficial to society at large. Man's closest relative among the great apes in Africa is not the fierce gorilla from north of the Congo River, a species whose alpha males do not hesitate to kill members of the group not closely related to them, and which therefore has been enthusiastically used to construct and underpin all sorts of vulgar Darwinian quasi-ideology about Man. No, Man's closest relative, considerably closer than the gorilla, is the consensus-seeking bonobo (the pygmy chimpanzee) found south of the Congo River, which among other attributes distinguishes itself by using sex to resolve conflicts and by tolerating vulnerable members who can count on protection thanks to a sophisticated system of branched alliances. The primitivist tribe operated in the same way, where alliances and generally advanced social structures on many levels were constructed through language.

It is, as we mentioned, primarily in connection with confrontations with competing tribes that Man demonstrates a gorilla-like aggressiveness. In day-to-day life within the nomadized tribe, Man acts for the most part as a peaceful, powerfully libidinal bonobo who creates meaning with others in a collective through cooperation on various social projects, and who tends to have, or perhaps fantasizes about, sex on a large scale. There is competition between the tribes – literally a matter of life and death – but within the tribe competition is outcompeted by cooperation. But this cooperation is not – as Rousseauan history naivists are wont to claim – an expression of the protodemocratic spirit of noble savages, but should instead be understood as members acting under duress in the form of threats of violence and clear demands for plastic adaptation in accordance with the tribe's material needs. The tribe's everyday existence is no picnic, and institutionalized violence lives on in a refined and more effectivized form in today's informationalist society. We are so fond of, or at least accustomed to, almost bound by, this libidinal structure that we are fundamentally unable to seriously imagine alternative platforms for human co-existence. The point is that violence is institutionalized and so made invisible, which makes it possible for us to worship it devotedly while we preen our disingenuously pacifist self-image. And its name is *Phallus*.

Ever since the heyday of the primitivist nomadic tribe, dividual Man has a strong yearning to be part of the masses and be one with the ritually playing swarm, a yearning that is combined with and complemented by an equally intense terror of being placed outside the collective fellowship that gives us our social identity and constantly reproduces our vital meaning. There arises a complex and contradictory relationship with the collective, which expresses itself both in libidinal ecstasy and in mortidinal submission, two sides of the same coin that both constantly recur in the ritual game. The more than 12,000-year-old temple Göbekli Tepe in Turkey tells us that advanced religious rituals were a significant part of daily life in the primitivist nomadic tribe long before written language, agriculture and permanent settlements started to dominate history. Furthermore, life in the tribe – for lack of future communication technologies such as written language and electronic mass media – was full of constantly recurring *purification rituals* that were meant to establish control, or at least an acceptable illusion of control, of outer as well as inner turbulence. It says a lot that purification rituals generally have been connected with truth production, and up until modern times to clergy or *the shamanic gene* in the population, in other words, the most phallic of all institutions.

The purifying behavior largely lives on in informationalist contemporary Man in the form of ritual consumption of the performance that is presented at *the medial theater*, which responds to a recurring, internalized demand for expressing and constantly reformulating social identity through more or less superstitious incantations. A typical medial production, such as authoring a text, should consequently – as the Bulgarian-French philosopher Julia Kristeva expresses the matter – rather be regarded as the optimal purification ritual. For what is a blog written by (and about) a dividual purporting to be working on his or her own personal development filled with if not these constant purifications, followed by a steady stream of purported transformations? Thanks to social media we can now continuously ritually purify ourselves, almost in real time. We carry out this ritual in front of what we tend to imagine to be everyone's gaze. In reality, other people are generally not so interested, mainly because they too are also fully occupied with showing themselves off to the same imaginary mass audience. Here we have an unsolvable dilemma, one that arises when everyone arms themselves with a keyboard and a smartphone with a camera and a microphone: the irresistible urge to cleanse oneself in the digital public sphere and an escalating lack of attention. For lack of a patient god who has the tenacity to witness everything that all self-obsessed people spew into media channels left, right and center, culture explodes in what we call *the hypernarcissistic condition*, where the formerly rare exhibitionists quantitatively take over, while their longed-for voyeurs are conspicuous in their absence. The purification ritual runs amok in the Internet Age.

So what does primitivist metaphysics look like? It is primarily centered around the figures that constantly recur in the stories of feats told around the camp fire, which serves to spread light, warmth and create security in the menacing nocturnal darkness, the equivalent in this age to late capitalism's soothing, community-building and anesthetizing television. These stories had many functions: providing momentary diversion and escapism, conveying knowledge, building up and continuously maintaining a societal moral code that promoted the public good and handling the need for mysticism. The stories were subject to evolutionary pressure that was both genetic and memetic: they were performed by the most popular storytellers, selected by virtue of their genetically predispositioned talent, and the stories competed with each other for popularity in a constantly ongoing memetic knock-out competition where the reward was survival in the collective memory and a passing-down of the stories, usually in modified form. So what does the social environment upon which these stories reflect and comment look like? And which of the various features of the nomadized tribe might the moral part of these stories be reinforcing and dampening, respectively?

Initially, it is important to clearly state that there never existed what we today refer to as *civilization* during primitivism. By definition, a civilization is an extensive accumulation of knowledge: every new generation can build on the achievements of their predecessors, and above all one can at least to some extent avoid constantly repeating the same old mistakes of previous generations. But this is not possible to any considerable extent in a society that is not underpinned by media technology more sophisticated than spoken language. In this society, which essentially is based on spoken language in terms of knowledge transmission, the human brain is the only receptacle where information can be stored. This means that when a knowledgeable and most likely elder member of the tribe finally died, the information that had been stored in this particularly valuable brain also vanished for good from the tribe's radar. The grief was enormous, understandably, and the crisis was tangible. Until all the knowledge that had been lost could be learned anew by a new generation, the tribe was vulnerable and prone to be at a disadvantage in the constant conflicts with competing tribes in the area, since these rivals were favored by a temporary knowledge advantage.

This dramatic information advantage explains why representatives of an elder generation demanded and received homage from the younger members of the tribe. The older and thus richer the dividual was in terms of experiences, the more important the person in question became from a strategic perspective, and the stronger the position of the dividual in question within the tribe. Elder tribe members could quite literally be carried around purely for their value as the tribe's memory banks. This is also the evolutionary biological reason why Man has developed the ability for both sexes to survive for several decades after his own procreative ability has disappeared. The elder, no longer fertile women did not merely participate in but *de facto* governed collective child care while the elder men constituted an important asset by virtue of their experiences and knowledge, of critical importance in terms of managing crises, not least the crises that were connected with competition and conflicts with other tribes in the immediate environment. Once again we see how a sophisticated collaboration within one's own group constituted the primary competitive means in the fight for resources. We call the heroized primordial figures of the flock *the primordial patriarch* and *the primordial matriarch*: primordial figures who are the presumed predecessors of the current *patriarch* who heads the hunting party with a near-religious authority, and the current *ma-*

triarch who firmly controls the reproductive cycle and child rearing within the tribe with an iron fist. We express this by saying that the patriarch controls *the outer circuit* while the matriarch controls *the inner circuit* within the tribe.

However, by no means does this signify that we see within the primitivist nomadic tribe something even remotely akin to a forerunner of the modern conjugal family, something that moralizing historians, too colored by their present-day values, for ideological reasons tended to do during the emergence of industrialism in the 19th century. Quite the contrary. The conjugal family was invented, rather, as a temporary solution to many of the problems that arose as a result of the transition from an agrarian to an industrial society, a solution that meant that one did not have to compromise concerning the prevailing individualist ideology. However, the conjugal family, with its blinding focus on the, biologically speaking, minimal family size, lacked a substantive function earlier in history. The primordial patriarch should rather be understood as a symbolic, historical depiction of the actual patriarch of a certain tribe, and similarly the primordial matriarch was a symbolic, historical depiction of the tribe's matriarch. Thus the roles of patriarch and matriarch should be viewed as symbolic. It really does not matter who at the moment assumes the role of the patriarch or the matriarch; these parts might well be played by several actors, or else merely be used as projections. What is really important is that these figures are ever present in and are at the disposal of the tribe's collective fantasy, as its supremely elevated authorities.

The story of the primordial patriarch actually has but one primary task, and that is to confirm and reinforce the position and the power connected with the patriarch who is active at the present time in any given society, in order to more efficiently tame and school the boys of the tribe into socially useful men and maximize the benefit to the collective. The same obviously applies to the primordial matriarch: these stories and the concepts they reward are an important part of the socialization process that shapes the collective into a functional, coordinated structure. In Freud's psychoanalytical spirit we call this process *social castration*; ultimately this is the same meta-historical logic that causes the kings, priests and aristocrats awaiting their forthcoming ascension to support the historiography that emphasizes their own specific roles and places them in the absolute center of power. It is not a question of pure power ambitions for one's own part to any great extent – we are, as mentioned, speaking of a system built on a large measure of intracollaborativity, rather than intracombativity – but rather about an endeavor that optimizes the functionality of power itself. Without the legitimate matriarch *the imaginary order* with its cyclical reproduction myth is razed, which would lead to young women no longer being prepared to allow themselves to be subjected to the life-threatening role of producing the next generation of the tribe in their own bodies. The risk these women took was not negligible; before the 18th century revolution within health care, at least one in ten women died in childbirth. And without the patriarch *the symbolic order* is razed, which would lead to young men no longer being prepared to submit to the social castration that shapes them into obedient and efficient team players in the group's collective hunting and fighting, as well as in the strictly ritualized and controlled orgiastic tribal rituals.

In this primitivist historiography the primordial matriarch does of course play the necessary role of the matriarch's mythical foremother, while the primordial patriarch in a corresponding way plays the necessary role of the patriarch's mythical forefather. By tabooing all questions about the primordial parents' own origins – this, too, is necessary, they are after all and must be the only humans in history that themselves lack parents – the matriarch's and the patriarch's respective statuses become absolute. Their positions in relation to their environment end up in the mysterious zone of social axioms where nothing can or should be questioned any longer – even discussing their positions is *taboo*; unthinkable. Which in turn means that as long as the matriarch and the patriarch act in accordance with the prevailing norm, they claim the honor for all attained and purported progress, while they can blame the mythical primordial parents' capriciousness if things do not go according to plan. They are quite simply fully metaphysically covered, just like all other purposive and self-confirming clergy who follow in their wake through the course of history.

The primordial matriarch and the primordial patriarch are by necessity both admired and feared. Otherwise the taboo status of their illogical and undecipherable origin would not work particularly well. There must be acceptance from the common people of the implied miracle. Considering that so many aspects of one's existence appear unfathomable and miraculous, there are no obstacles in talking about it. Thus it becomes impossible for the tribe members to identify themselves with these idealized mythical figures. To achieve the desired identification there is instead a need for *heroes*. And the first heroes are of course the primordial parents' own children, *the primordial son* and *the primordial daughter*, whose relations to their primordial parents are characterized by passionate ambivalence. As a direct consequence of the ambivalent relationship between primarily the primordial patriarch and the hero, there arise the first myths of *patricide*, the murder of the patriarch, which entails the violent onset of the tribe's history, a history that for lack of civilizational linearity must be radically circular. Patricide is then the germ of *the eternal recurrence of the same*, as Friedrich Nietzsche strikingly terms this central event in primitivist historiography. It is the case of a historical cycle whose severe tribulations only can be parried through the tribe's recurring sacrifice to the primordial parents' spirits. With this, the primitivist religion has established its own foundation.

As soon as the primordial parents are connected to the capricious forces of nature, the first gods arise. This storytelling and identity-building later explodes when the tribes build sacrificial sites, to which they regularly return. The first god is the rain god. The sun god arrives only later. The clearest example of this is the dominant god in the Middle East at the dawn of feudalism, Baal, who started his career as a local rain and fertility god, but who later also would serve as a global sun god. It is the sun god that one holds onto and that becomes the only god in connection with the transition from polytheism to monotheism. Polytheism and monotheism then live on side-by-side over a long period. Polytheism was primarily a decentralized folk religion, driven by the need for spiritual proximity, which triggers what we call *metaphysical distancing.* Monotheism was an overarching intellectual explanatory model that could bridge boundaries between tribes and cultures, and was driven by *metaphysical intimacy.* The local icon was worshipped and adored privately because of its tangibility and proximity in relation to the individual practitioner, while the global god instead was bestowed upon an audience, general worship across tribal boundaries on the imperialistic arena. The overarching purpose of religion was twofold: on the one hand to satisfy a never-ending need for meaning, and on the other hand to provide the social glue that held the collective together in a tribe united by the same faith and the same rituals. Other people who believed in other gods, were of course not to be trusted. And the most obvious sign that they were unreliable strangers was their strange rituals.

Polytheism is thus local and folksy, while monotheism is global – at least in theory – and elitist. The foundation for this division can be traced to theism's two fundamental relational issues. First of all the fundamental issue of what the gods really want, and then the necessary follow-up question about how Man should relate to whether and when the gods refuse to answer the first question. The local gods of polytheism can always answer the first question, in which case the second question need never be asked. If nothing else, polytheism's local gods are regarded as so intellectually uncomplicated that they cannot even answer the question of what they want, and therefore they settle for whatever Man comes up with to satisfy them, which in turn explains the disparate *kitsch* – a checkered mishmash of icons and other cult objects – that dominates the interior decoration in polytheist temples as well as teenagers' bedrooms. On the other hand, monotheism's global god might well choose to ignore Man and his petty troubles completely – the state that is called *hester panim* in Hebrew, *the divine absence* – and only the believer who can handle *the transparental absence* is ready to accept monotheism as the only religion. Within Christianity the division between the local gods and the global god happens through the distancing between the concrete saints and the abstract, three-headed god. Within Hinduism the same dislocation occurs between the local gods with which one communicates via offerings at the altar in one's home on the one hand, and the in-every-respect absent creator god *Brahman*, the expanding breath of the Cosmos, Hinduism's and above all the yogis' monotheist god, who is concealed behind the polytheist diversity of minor gods presumed to occupy themselves with the many trivialities of daily life.

How difficult – or rather how impossible – it is to break the power of polytheism over the masses is clearly illustrated by the radical, top-down endeavors to intellectualize religion that have been carried out ever since the Axial Age (800-200 BC). As early as 3,700 years ago Zoroaster attempts to fashion such an enlightened religion without superstitions in Central Asia. Akhenaten repeats the attempt, inspired by Zoroaster, in Egypt 400 years later. Gautama Buddha carries out the same maneuver in India in the 6th century BC, when he separates his doctrine from chaotic-but-tolerant Hinduism, and in a manner similar to Zoroaster and Akhenaten, preaches universal consciousness as the new and only god. A similar elimination of the distance to the divine is conducted by Jan Hus, Martin Luther and Jean Calvin, the Protestant rebels in Renaissance Europe, when they – among other things – reject Catholic saint worship as a response to the gradually emerging proto-Enlightenment's requirement for the individual's central role in existence. By getting rid of the saints and thus reducing Christianity to a direct, unmediated and intellectually demanding relationship between the believer and the believed, without intermediaries which of course increased the risk of the message being corrupted – primarily through translating the Bible to the vernacular, printing and disseminating it via the potent printing press with this purpose – the protestant reformers attempt to salvage Christianity's reputation in a Europe where the darkness of superstition is increasingly dispelled. In the countries and regions where the Protestant Reformation made gains, Catholicism held sway longer and more intensely where superstition was the most deeply rooted.

In the short run the result was formidable, though came at the price of several extremely bloody religious wars; in the long run it was a lost cause trying to save Christianity from internal and self-made disintegration. For despite the recurring enthusiasm for all these fundamentally monotheist reformations and their charismatic prophets, every attempt throughout history to intellectualize metaphysics – a movement away from populist polytheism, onward towards elitist monotheism – has eventually collapsed. As soon as the neatly arranged mental garden has been cleared of sundry weeds, polytheist folk religion and its ravings about the local and supernatural has nevertheless clawed its way back into day-to-day life. The actual practices of Zoroastrianism and Buddhism are merely vulgar and often highly intolerant absurdities in relation to the advanced theories that the founders once proclaimed. Akhenaten was even aggressively erased from Egypt's history by the polytheist counter-reformation that ensued after his and his family's death. And to this day it is enough to take but a few steps away from the most advanced natural scientific conferences and we will be met by hoards of New Age adherents with crystal necklaces, chattering away unabashedly about purifying contacts with spirits, ghosts, energies, chakras and all kinds of conceivable and inconceivable reincarnations. In other words, there is nothing new under the sun.

Please observe that there is no distinction between the polytheist folk religion of the Indian man who sacrifices food to a blue elephant god and of the Catholic woman who lights a candle before the Virgin Mary, or the American teenager who cries and feels she is communicating important matters with some rock idol or another in connection with the latest album release. The small, local gods keep their grip on the small, local people. And therefore the grandiose ideologies constantly crumble into small, local sects. This applies to religious bodies and political parties, as well as the persistent online following of the music, film and web stars of our age. And it could hardly be otherwise as long as we humans do not change from within. Which we, as we mentioned, do not do – what we actually do is inadequately scrape away to try to adapt to new circumstances. Thus our polytheist sects and cults replace the long-lived primitivist nomadic tribe, which we so earnestly miss while we are earnestly unhappy in our culture, which unfortunately is necessary in order to handle a growing, collective subject that follows from the development of technology. Pitted against Freud's pleasure principle there is the relentless reality principle. Which means that *tribal nostalgia* constantly returns and afflicts us anew with full force.

Deep down, Man is a fundamentally conservative creature. Just like all other organisms his initial reaction vis-à-vis all forms of change is to regard it as an annoyance, something that one instinctively rejects the moment it is no longer possible to deny. This is true regardless of whether we are talking about *distal stimuli,* which is the external germ of perception, or *proximal stimuli,* which is the energy which in itself constitutes the perception process in the sensory organs. In spite of all talk in connection with revolutionary breakthroughs that embracing *change* in itself is a good thing, every human more or less still hits the brakes when they drive into the future. Being radical, progressive or change-prone is in fact nothing other than being slightly less conservative than other social actors in the same or in a comparable situation. The distinction lies in certain people braking a little softer and less desperately, and others who do so considerably harder and more decisively. But we all hit the brakes. And those that brake the softest tend to be both younger than those who brake in wild desperation for one thing, and that they have good reasons to feel they have less to lose from the change in question.

The distinction between radicalism and conservatism is particularly clear during a genuine paradigm shift, when those considered down and out by the old power structure – for instance by being regarded as a lower race, a less talented sex, being sexually attracted to the wrong things or living in the wrong place – suddenly perceive that there arises a longed-for possibility for *empowerment*, an opportunity for social recognition and an existential realization previously thought impossible for them to attain. If these potential class travelers and status maximizers actually possess the new paradigm's most coveted talents, they may even count on being promoted to the emerging power structure's new upper class. For the underclass, material changes that propel the emergence of new regulations for conferring and calculating social status by definition is something to be considered good news. But the human organism's propensity for change or *radicality* at these historically unique paradigm shifts is no stronger than this. Above all, there is no mysterious, built-in radicality in the one group or the other, whether we are talking about farmers, workers, women, homosexuals or various kinds of ethnic minorities, as some erroneously imagine for purely political and/or ideological reasons, confusing lucid analysis with romanticizing wishful thinking. Seeing the world through rigid categories is unfortunately not unusual. Unless a person is served up a concrete and obviously libido-reinforcing identity change in a simple and easily understandable way, he will not on his life freely embrace any crucial change of any kind. It is just not in him, or us.

The social changes that still do occur are compelled by our environment and directly connected to a preceding technological revolution. From this insight it is not possible, as we have already pointed out, to claim that there was any real revolution in the streets of Paris in 1789. Nor that there was an "industrial revolution" in North-West England in the early 19th century. What happened there and then was rather a series of symptoms of an actual revolution that had occurred far earlier, namely the literally epochal arrival of the printing press in France's north-eastern neighbor Germany in the mid-15th century. Paris had merely become the major city where literacy had enjoyed its greatest dissemination in the late 18th century, the place where the printing press had for the first time provided in the form of books, tabloids, encyclopedias and banknotes an emerging and libidinally famished literate bourgeoisie with real prerequisites for an explosive sense of sudden empowerment. It was quite simply there that a political pamphlet could cause the greatest possible uproar, where there was a receptive audience, which stimulated the writing of more pamphlets, and so on. In England there were conditions that enabled a rapid, industrial development, which would have been quite unthinkable without the multi-branched consequences of the printing press. Compare this to Europe's greatest empire during the Renaissance, the Ottoman Empire, that in a contrary way tried to prevent the use of the printing press the longest and most stubbornly of all, and *de facto* reduced the Balkan Peninsula to Europe's poorest back alley a few hundred years later.

What we later, in the state-administered educational institutions called elementary schools, were taught to regard as a revolution in Paris in 1789, was thus merely an eye-popping materialization of the information-technological revolution that had taken place more than 300 years earlier. Technology trumps politics, as the Swedish business entrepreneur and media mogul Jan Stenbeck once remarked; additionally, it is also the case that technology conditions and shapes politics. Please also note that the most famous tweet in world history "I think, therefore I am" is formulated by a certain René Descartes in 1637, more or less right in the middle of the period between the advent of the printing press in 1450 and the materialization of "the French Revolution" in 1789. Thus the gradually emerging paradigm's forceful truth production, colored by Cartesian rationalism, is introduced: the Enlightenment. There's no doubt whatsoever in Paris in 1789 which metaphysical idea is driving the new development: it is the nouveau riche burgher with his Cartesian *cogito* as a firm platform for an ingratiating self-image and worldview who without further ado sends the already anesthetized Abrahamic god off into the wings. It is this metaphysical shift, from *monotheism* to *individualism*, this metahistorical event, which enables and produces what we today call the French Revolution and the new paradigm's continued progress. Descartes has already prophetically produced the literate burgher – presumably he regards himself as the first and most archetypal paragon – as the new, deified *individual* around which existence itself revolves.

The attribute that defines Man, according to Descartes, is the ever-questioning and constantly doubting process of thinking; the cornerstone of his rationalism. He was not formally a republican or an atheist himself, it was a little early for that, but it is, as the historian Claude Nicolet claims, impossible to later become a republican (and an atheist) without taking the route via Descartes. That the new individual would experience and start to manifest his empowerment in terms of being a political subject after having read Descarte's ground-breaking thoughts in a book from a printed mass edition, is a logical truism. The mass editions created a mass audience, which in turn created even larger mass editions, and so on. So from having been a luxury for the rich, literacy relatively quickly became a social must for anyone with the least bit of ambition. The Cartesian revolution and the ensuing Enlightenment arose as a direct result of the Catholic Church's efforts to silence the new, heretical ideas and their attempt to introduce the death penalty for using a printing press in France in 1517. It is completely logical that a revolutionary technology of this kind encounters embittered resistance from those who quite rightly regard it as a threat, but in the long run it is always technology that holds all the cards. This is why banning the printing press naturally was doomed to fail, since all-too powerful forces had already been set in motion, in the same way that the war the nation states of the modern world has waged on drugs over the past few decades always has been doomed to fail, or the entertainment industry's awkward campaigns against digital file-sharing in the early 21st century. The last-mentioned issue could only find a satisfactory solution through technology – that is: streaming – and not through legislation, no matter how aggressive.

One can always put a spoke in any wheel that happens to be within reach, but one cannot obliterate or prohibit the wheel as such. In emergency situations one can delay the social and cultural development in line with a highly potent, dominant metatechnology, but only temporarily and at tremendous cost. And in the long run one cannot stop this development in any meaningful sense. Since the Catholic priests resisted the idea of individualism – they did of course have the most to lose from its successful dissemination, since it destroyed their monopoly on truth production – they also became the first of the revolution's many victims that were led to the guillotine. There was no defender left who was able to mobilize efficient protection for the monarchy or the aristocracy, for that matter. The defensive line was penetrated. Therefore the guillotines could methodically chew up the entire old, feudalist power structure in and around Paris during the age of revolutionary terror in the late 18th century. After this revolutionary maneuver, they gave the university, which the upwardly mobile bourgeois class loved, the role of the church of the new age – science supplanted theology; without René Descartes there would be no Isaac Newton – and their primary task was of course to rewrite humanity's history from scratch. This time with the necessary, incremental emergence of the individual as the leading story.

The Freudian superego now briskly moves aside in order to survive. Metaphysics no longer revolves around tempering God's wrath and attaining salvation for us flawed sinners in the afterlife, but instead is concerned with giving individuals the scientific knowledge that is increasingly necessary, through an increasingly intensive moralizing, imposed self-realization *before* death. Please observe the striking resemblance between the university and the monastery as institutions. Actually, the university only really distinguishes itself from the monastery by making more and cheaper books available to more readers, books whose message therefore enjoys a greater dissemination, so that their authors can spend more time adopting a more detailed and specialized style of writing. *Progress* supplants *eternity* as the engine and horizon of metaphysics, a shift that in itself is portrayed and perceived as progress and that was practiced even when Napoleon, undisturbed, built his military career as the first bourgeois general ever – since his aristocratic rivals were of course all executed. This is how he was at hand in 1804 to assume the role of France's phallic dictator and lift the country out of the revolutionary chaos that long since had served out its purpose – a new type of commander of a new type of army where the soldiers were literate. Behind all these dramatic changes we constantly sense the discrete clatter of the printing press.

Please note how Napoleon does all this in the capacity of an individualist superhero, as *the Cartesian Individual par excellence*, that is: exactly the figure that G W F Hegel later holds aloft and acclaims in his book *The Phenomenology of the Spirit* from 1807 as the *Zeitgeist*, the personification of the new age. And what then is Hegel's own extolling description of the taming of the new age's technologies, forces and ideas if not the very completion of *paradigmatic dialectics* in itself, that is: *the authentic revolution* in its dazzling entirety? It is really not so odd that Hegel, intoxicated with both Napoleon and himself – with Napoleon as his pharaoh and with himself as Napoleon's own spokesperson and press secretary – even reckons that he has seen the completion of history and ecstatically describes how the *absolute* steps forward in the distance at dialectical history's final stop. For now the metamodel was ready for the organization of the individualist society, with Napoleon's army as an emblem and metaphor for the new, victorious paradigm, the organizational form that Hegel terms and hails as *the absolute state*.

Hardly surprising, the academization of human knowledge, the cataloging afterwards of all the necessities of history, in the service of the absolute state, quickly picked up pace. But the quarrels about which academic statements are true and which are false are presumably always as intense among those that regard themselves as summoned to take on the role of truth producers. It is merely the underlying information technology that is supplanted, affecting the quantity of the discourse but hardly its quality. New phenomena occur, others end up in a new context and acquire new meanings, but the patterns are recognizable. This has, during many other paradigm shifts as well, occurred when the old power, in this case the church, ironically created and released the monster, in this case the university, that later annihilated it. The parallel to how the social monster of our age, the Internet, first was created by the military and universities of the nation state for the purpose of reinforcing their power and influence but then was turned against them, is striking.

We always imagine that we can harness a technology and that its creators can steer its use in the desired direction. But history proves over and over again that technology, as the American media theorist Neil Postman says, always plays its hand, regardless of what more or less change-prone people fear or wish. Nor do you control your private smartphone or your private laptop, it is the machines that create, shape and then control you too. While both the social and technological engineers have a fascinating tendency to repeatedly, throughout history, dig their own graves without ever understanding that this is exactly what they are doing with such great energy. So never ask an engineer what the future holds. That question can instead preferably be posed to a young and curious shaman, a historically cultivated observer who has had the good sense to establish a solid observation spot alongside the culture that during major convulsions sheds its skin and assumes another shape; a shaman who observes these convulsions and sees how Hegel's time-bound dream of the perfect citizen in the absolute state is vaporized and disappears like slender streaks of smoke in the wind. It is about time that we all realize it is not only God that is dead; so, too, is Napoleon.

4
Socioanalysis as the critical theory of The Internet Age

First of all there is of course eating, or if you will, gobbling (*das Fressen*), as Bertolt Brecht observes in *The Threepenny Opera* from 1928. But there's no moral to this, regardless of the impression the budding Marxist Brecht was under at the time, but something much more basic, namely the dividual identity. We are of course primarily animals who in the capacity of animals have primary, physiological needs in the form of food, liquid, warmth and shelter from weather, et cetera – needs that are impossible to prioritize away without the organism in question, the dividual, expiring. Once these needs are suitably met and the organism's earthly existence is secured, at least for the foreseeable future, the hunger for meaning and context becomes urgent. And the tool we then use is the dividual identity that we manage to produce with the knowledge and perspectives that are at our disposal in the current situation.

Identity assumes two complementary and mutually conditioning and conditioned expressions: partly in a dividual self-image, partly in a worldview. These images belong together and arise within the friction that is generated by the collective, which means that identity primarily is a relational phenomenon. Self-image and worldview are simply two sides of the same coin. Without the self, no world.

And vice versa. Or to put it slightly differently: without the internal subject, there is no external object (and vice versa), for the self is of course also part of the world – what else could it be? In this way, the world is also the self; it springs into existence in the confirming eyes of the self. This intimate interdependence naturally applies to all collective constellations and not just to dividual people. Every family, clan, nation or subculture both offers and demands its own relational identity that clarifies that the we that is seeking a definition is this or that, and around this identity there is a boundary that clarifies that the same we definitely is not this or that, and that this we acts in a world that is inclined this or that way, but not this or that way. Thus identity production is both a psychological and sociological phenomenon – but above all it is a dialectical phenomenon. It is in the constant interaction between self and world in the form of social *input* and *output* that identity takes shape, both for the dividual and for the group, in a process that in principle follows that same pattern irrespective of the level. We can therefore sum up the entire human identity production and orientation within one's surrounding world with the concept *social relationalism* (see *Syntheism – Creating God in The Internet Age*).

Psychoanalysis is the philosophical study of psychological identity production, from which follows that the philosophical study of sociological identity production is called socioanalysis. In the turbulence that now prevails, as we are heading into the relationalist network society at great speed, socioanalysis is the most important tool we have at our disposal to actually understand ourselves as social creatures, and our collective present and future. Our identity is of course constructed from the models we have created, both for how the external world around us is expected to function and for how the internal consciousness of the dividual and/or the identity-creating collective is expected to develop and interact with the surrounding world at different levels. These models in turn hinge on the production of dividual biographies and/or the collective's historiography.

We are, quite simply, the people and the societies that our biographies and our histories depict; we can only get a sense of our past through the perspectives and the information at hand; as for our future, we can only speculate about it with more or less acuity and precision with our history and the processes that are playing out in our present time as the main parameters.

However one might just as well turn the tables. If we are indeed studying *metahistory*, that is: the history of historiography, what appears before our critical gaze is how every historiography at every point in time faithfully reflects and thus also confirms the prevailing power structure. This is of course exactly what made it relevant, useful and – ultimately – even comprehensible. This is what historiography *de facto* is: a mirror for princes, a flattering portrait in tribute to the prevailing power structure. And it is, as we have already observed, the prevailing power that commissions and funds this tribute to itself. This story, whose purpose and function is to portray the current state of affairs as fated and natural, constitutes the metaphysical axiom from which all the paradigm's psychological and sociological identities are constructed. The metaphysical axiom is *the truth par excellence* about Man and the world, and the story of their complicated interrelationship. It is little wonder that metahistory shows that there is constant editing work that entails this historiography undergoing incessant changes, more or less subtle. Some old stories are phased out to be replaced by new and continuously added biographies, while all existing biographies are subject to constant revision.

In exceptional and extremely rare cases there is a revolution that upends the entire old history and that entails a short period full of chaos and uncertainty, followed by a new build-up phase where new axioms are created in accordance with new prerequisites that are in line with the new metamedium's agenda. This revolutionizing process is of course extremely painful for old rulers who took maximum advantage of the conditions that prevailed under the old paradigm. For obvious reasons, since it does not serve their purposes. Every alteration of the fundamental conditions must be disagreeable and unwelcome for those who are favored by the conditions that happen to prevail at the present time. Which in turn means that there is room for a new historiography in that a new power structure is starting to develop in parallel with the old power structure losing ground, strength and relevance. By insisting on a completely new history, built on new models and which propels completely new forms of identity production, the new elite seals its power grab. Right now, for instance, we find ourselves in the transitional stage between capitalism and informationalism, a paradigm shift that basically is triggered by a new media technology having secured a prerogative of interpretation and which thus puts its stamp on all societal activity, which in turn entails new conditions and rules in all areas, which in turn means that the old power elite no longer meets the presently prevailing specification of requirements and thus inexorably is shoved aside thanks to the incessant Darwinian selection mechanisms.

New conditions in this case entail a new system of reward and punishment that values various talents and skills by yardsticks different from previous ones, so there is a requirement for talents and skills completely different from those that only recently were viable in conquering and retaining power on the new playing field. It is ultimately the dominant information technology and its medial structures that decide what thoughts a society can think, how truth is defined, what prioritizations are perceived as most urgent, and so on. The old elite became an elite and retained its power by force of talents and skills that were rewarded by the old system. In conjunction with a paradigm shift the value of these talents and skills is drastically reduced, and this now demoted group, along with its historiographers and other courtiers and ladies-in-waiting, is compelled to bid adieu to power and glory. The mythology they once cherished, propagated and used as support for their claims on power, is now rapidly converted into the new superstition of the underclass. It is, for instance, not the bourgeoisie that nurture and polish the myths around the old kings, the noblemen or the clergy with their outdated faith in God when industrialism displaces the feudalist structures. No, royalism, fascination with the aristocracy and the traditional faith in God now live on – inasmuch as these antique phenomena can even be said to have any life left in them – as bedtime stories and daydreams for the new underclass, which then is manipulated into or voluntarily has chosen to soak up sundry vulgar variants of the phased-out paradigm's dated rulership ideology.

The underclass is – as Nietzsche claims, in contrast to Marx during the second half of the 19th century – fundamentally reactionary rather than progressive or proactive. Which hardly ought to be particularly controversial, it is of course among other things exactly this that makes it just that, the underclass. And Marx's analysis of capitalism may be ever so brilliant, but the communist ideology can never be anything but an aged Christianity that has been adapted to fill the void left from the poor workers' lost faith in the eternal life after death. The communist utopia and the classless society thus replaces the heaven that Christianity promises and holds the same lure for those who yearn for an existence where nothing changes anymore, which – naturally – is the same as an existence that actually is no existence and that never can become a reality in a world that has any similarities to ours. This occurs in parallel with the bourgeoisie's emerging, individualist rulership ideology fueling Marxism's political adversaries – a *de facto* right in the form of conservatism and a *de facto* left in the form of liberalism – who constitute the capitalist paradigm's ruling elite. It is with the starting point in this gradually phased-out elite's powerful individualism and economism that the new Internet Age starts to take shape; not from Marxism's capsized quasi-Christianity, which has had the time to implode even before the Internet establishes itself as the metamedium that dictates the terms for a new historical paradigm.

Fundamentally, the revolution is first and foremost technological; it is entirely a matter for the new ruling class that is orchestrating it, while it is the revolution that carries forth and holds aloft the incoming elite. Through this entire course of events the underclass is sitting in the auditorium, regardless of what the political rhetoric says. The peasants never rose up against the aristocracy to any significant extent, any more than the workers ever removed the bourgeoisie from power. Nor does anything suggest that the consumtariat will oust the netocracy, rather the reverse: the netocrats are extremely adept at recruiting every talent from the underclass to their own networks – this is precisely among the qualities that characterize the netocracy – something that moreover is very much in the elite's own interest. Thus one kills two birds with one stone; in part one provides one's own class with the best possible talent, and in part one robs the underclass of the very talent that might constitute its rebellious-minded leaders. The talents are continuously promoted, the permeability in the social stratification is optimal, and what remains at the lowest tier of society will therefore be an underclass without eloquent leaders and consequently also without the ability to express its dissatisfaction in an effective way, controlled and deadened through entertainment, consumption and fast carbohydrates.

Genuine radicality is nothing other than the curious and innovative use of the latest technologies. Netocratic radicals can at best only acquire indirect attentional power through building platforms based on *open source*, rather than the direct attentional power that follows from the netocratic libertarians' construction of insular talent-concentrated networks based on *imploitation*. Informationalism's political ideology production cannot possibly be either more left or more right than this. Thus the idea of a revolutionary underclass has never been more unfounded and mendacious than now – a sentimental bedtime story with which an increasingly irrelevant capitalist left rocks itself to sleep, one of history's near-scandalously deceitful myths, created and maintained by the many banal moralists of the ruling class. The simple reason for the underclass' purported, revolutionary potential in practice being non-existent, is that this class, if we for a moment use a phrase borrowed from Nietzsche, is driven by a slave mentality.

If we instead view the matter from a socioanalytical perspective, we observe how the underclass constantly seeks *the matrichal mortido* rather than *the phallic libido*: its instinctive, collective reaction to that which one might regard as social injustices is more or less powerless indignation and various political compensation claims as a result of someone else having enriched themselves at the expense of this group. This in contrast to acting resolutely with the starting point in what one considers oneself able to create by one's own devices through one's own entrepreneurship (in the broadest sense of the word). What makes the underclass the underclass is precisely this lack of visions and ideas, its every bit as vague as embittered demands for leveling, its eternal sucking of the comforting *mamilla*, a readiness to passively consume itself to sleep and to sleep tight in the shadow of the many projects that the phallic power conducts. Not infrequently this passivity gives way to scattered outbursts of aggression with no direction or objective. It is hard to illustrate Freud's theory of the death drive any clearer than this.

By definition a paradigm shift requires a new worldview, since the old one by necessity must be discarded when new truths replace the old ones. A new worldview in turn requires new models. And new models in turn require a new historiography. This new historiography must take its point of departure in the new power structure and its industrious search for and creation of its own specific identity. This process is often dramatic and painful. Moreover, every paradigm shift occurs in four different, partially overlapping phases. The introductory phase is made up of a technological revolution that upends the material fundamental prerequisites for the old paradigm. In this context, Man is *the historical constant*. We change with evolutionary slowness, that is: in principle not at all over periods of tens of thousands of years, periods when the world around us and the technology that conditions our prerequisites for life can undergo the most revolutionizing changes. As for our biological equipment, we are for this reason essentially identical with the people who were part of what we call the genesis of civilization a little more than 5,000 years ago. Technology is the historical variable in this context, which means that all these essential changes in Man's existence fundamentally should be regarded as technological. The very concept of technology is derived from the Greek word *techne*, which means elongation. Thus technology is the process – and the study of this process – with which Man extends his body and by extension also expands his world. Technology is what ultimately causes epochal social changes and drives what later turns out to be historical development: this entire process is fundamentally technological. Technology constantly creates new conditions for the interaction between itself and Man; Man adapts to the best of his abilities. And that ability is immensely comprehensive.

The second phase in the paradigm shift is a fundamental idea that drives a completely new metaphysics, which in turn forms the foundation for the new paradigm's historiography and thus also forms its worldview. We call this *the ideological revolution*. The new metaphysics paves the way for and, in advance, tells the story of the new ruling class in the new paradigm – which at a later stage enables this very power shift – partly as an expression of the new ruling class' internal (self-confidence) and external (propaganda) marketing. This second phase does not primarily claim to be underpinned by any form of objective truth, instead it now revolves around what ideology the new, emerging social conditions actually support. Metaphysics is built on a set of borrowed fantasies, for instance primordial parents in a distant past, a God in a heaven somewhere far away and beyond reach, or the Individual that hides inside an enigmatic gland in the brain. The point here is how these fictions even by definition resist every form of empirical control and investigation. In this way they also become immune to all criticism that emanates from antagonistic premises, and thus the reasoning is ushered into perfect circles.

Metaphysics is of course no exact science; rather it constitutes the prevailing power's self-congratulatory metastory. It always pays to build metaphysics on something that *cannot* be controlled, but that is attractive and intriguing enough to function as an axiomatic vantage point. The originally Hegelian idea of a network-dynamical universe where everything is dependent on everything else, and where something (an *actant*) or someone (an *actor*) is accorded a role and a value connected to its own function in this constantly ongoing interaction, does not claim to be supported by objective reality either. This idea just happens to be an apprehension about reality that becomes functional and relevant in a society dictated by the dynamics generated by the Internet. It simply reflects the prevailing technological prerequisites, which does not mean that it says anything of value about any kind of eternally valid truth beyond this very society and these very prerequisites. That metaphysics itself says differently, is a completely different matter; all cracks in one's own presentation are harbored in the very comprehensive blind spot. This grandiose self-deception is part and parcel of the nature of the matter; it is not up to the emperor to point out that he is naked. Nor does he even see it himself, with the possible exception of the odd moment of cold sweat and nightmarish lucidity that he does his best to quickly shake off.

At its deepest level, metaphysics, as Nietzsche emphasizes, is about what and how a ruler prioritizes to safeguard survival and status at the very moment of his own hold on power, nothing else. What is central is that the transition to this paradigm's second phase is experienced as credible and relevant for the emerging power elite. And one prerequisite for relevance and credibility is that the story which supports this second phase concurrently pulls the rug out from under the old paradigm's metaphysical center. Paradigm shifts are quite simply enormously violent. Power shifts brutally because the prerequisite for power has already shifted. Moreover, paradigm shifts invariably leave a lingering discrepancy between Man's sociobiological prerequisites and the current technological environment, with all its at least initially arcane innovations. This discrepancy has only increased with every paradigm shift, through Man having been removed further and further from the original primitivist nomadic tribe, away from the biologically programmed, locally anchored intratribal security to the challenging, globally comprehensive *intertribalism* with its constantly increasing and for most people demanding interdependence between the originally scattered communities. That war and peace has shifted in violent waves during this entire development is a direct result of the most basic paradigmatic conflicts.

When the nomadized tribes become settled, it is necessary to say goodbye to the *primordial patriarch* and the *primordial matriarch* that evidently are not able to unite several groups into dynamic and stable societies, a task that one therefore must hand over to *God*, the universal metaprimordial patriarch, who for practical reasons was accorded completely different, upgraded powers. A monotheism that with credibility lays claim to at least a measure of universality is required to do the job – since all tribes live under the same life-bestowing sun, it is the *Sun God* that through and through is entrusted with playing this part – and that unites constellations previously kept separate and that may even have been each other's enemies; and with this monotheism there follows an intertribal clergy that disseminate the true doctrine and administers the counseling. With this, one phases out the cadre of intratribal shamans that previously frightened people by demonizing strangers. But over time even monotheist religion with its autocratic God loses its authority and is degraded to fill a purely decorative, ceremonial function.

The urban bourgeoisie that steps onto the platform of the printing press, that conducts trade and colonization all over the known world, that eagerly explores the parts that are yet unknown and that replaces the landed aristocracy as the new society's power elite, has scant need for a fictitious chief custodian, but instead creates a fictitious, deified version of themselves: the *Napoleonic Individual.* This becomes a credible and highly functional ideal for a ruling class dominated by global industrialists and entrepreneurs, politicians who extol progress and academics steeped in the humanities. As soon as the Individual has been complemented by the atom and the nation, *humanism* is complete as a religion. That its own self-image says that it is no religion at all, but merely common sense, is revealing. It is only when metaphysics has lost its relevance as a producer of truth that it starts to regard itself as precisely a religion amid other religions. But also this glorified Individual, apparently eternal and universally relevant, is wholly dependent on the social and cultural ecosystem that is connected to a specific paradigm. In the Global Empire of the Internet Age the same Individual is brutally degraded to a dysfunctional therapy patient that completely lacks the talents and skills that now are in demand and being rewarded – of what use would a self-aggrandizing individual in an increasingly refined network culture be? – which is why an idealized image of the *Net* comparatively quickly emerges as society's propelling metaphysical idea.

All we have to do is to let the Internet envelop the entire planet Earth and the Net as an idea will jump off the map (see *The Global Empire*). The main reason for this castling is that during the Internet Age the overarching purpose in every form of creative activity is to implement network-dynamical principles as quickly and as efficiently as possible. The result for the dividual person will then, in broad terms, be that the primary individual is transformed into the secondary dividual. The idealized *event*, the network-dynamical peak experience followed by the transformative memory of the same, supplants mythical *progress* as the prevailing paradigm's metaphysical engine, in the same way that this progress once supplanted the just as highly mythical *eternity*. The Net then takes over the position as the metaphysical center of the Internet Age, and dethrones both the Individual and God. The dividual is therefore subservient to the Net, in contrast to the outdated Individual who himself was the objective, meaning and measure of everything. Network dynamics kills individualism. Or rather: individualism succumbs because of increasingly unfavorable conditions and is replaced by network dynamics, which responds to the new rules that are dictated by new prerequisites.

The new metaphysics must, as mentioned, posit the new power elite at the center of existence. And it primarily does so through forcefully evicting the previous paradigm's metaphysical axiom. The primordial father and primordial mother of primitivism must disappear to give way to feudalism's God at the center of the feudalist paradigm. Feudalism's God must then in turn disappear for capitalism's Individual to be offered necessary leeway at the center of the new paradigm. It is precisely this maneuver that René Descartes carries out as he kick-starts the European *Enlightenment* in 1637 with the epochal statement: "I think, therefore I am." What Descartes thereby does, is to discretely and courteously, but nevertheless efficiently, put God to sleep, while he launches the very Individual that assumes God's place at historiography's metaphysical center. This naturally has transformative consequences: the church is robbed of its monopoly on truth, to start with. And gradually all the prerequisites for the monarchy as well as the aristocracy erode. All these country estates where mangy aristocrats in vain tried to uphold the splendor of yore: suddenly these were something that the bourgeois nouveaux riche bought and sold on a market to use them as symbols of a newly-acquired status. All this unsentimental peddling, all this conspicuous consumption, was something completely unthinkable during an earlier paradigm: country estates were something one inherited, cherished and handed over to the next generation of hereditary nobility with age-old lineage, and for these to ever be bought and sold for money was utterly unimaginable. For this new way of thinking and this new practice to gain a foothold, a completely different metaphysical system was required.

The monopoly on truth then falls to the scientist, who obviously cultivates and affiliates himself with an ideal that is in line with the individualism that follows from Descartes, namely *atomism*. Together these two superideologies pave the way for the parliamentary politician's (again a completely new person in the public arena, unthinkable during previous conditions) assumption of power with the aid of *nationalism*, as well as for the manufacturer's and merchant's assumption of power with the aid of *capitalism*. The scientist, the politician and the business entrepreneur quite simply take over the functions that the priest, the monarch and the aristocrat had during the previous paradigm, and around this *triad* there forms a power structure that is sustainable over the long-term through its devastatingly efficient internal *balance of terror*. For as soon as any one of the three attempts to expand his territory at the expense of the others, the other two will join forces to put the challenger in his place. The distribution of power is delicately balanced, and the structure is just as it was when the priest, the monarch and the aristocrat constantly watched, challenged and roughed each other up during feudalism. This power structure in the form of a *terror triad* then lingers on with remarkable efficiency as long as no new form of dominant information technology requires a new set of talents on a new level of immanence and thus opens the door to a new historical paradigm. Once this ending actually comes to pass, the entire foundation for the old terror triad erodes; all three participants are concurrently afflicted with a gradually more urgent crisis of legitimacy. The structure's entire foundation, and thus its metaphysical story, collapses under the pressure from the new mode of information processing.

When Isaac Newton – who is seven years old when René Descartes freezes to death in Stockholm in 1650 – lays the ground for what is called classical mechanics with his book *Philosophiæ Naturalis Principia Mathematica*, it means that he in practice translates the Cartesian conception of God's absence to an updated worldview in physics terms. In doing so he sets a pattern for all economics and social sciences that in the future will supply the truth that the capitalist paradigm needs: immense amounts of intellectual energy is then spent on building thoroughly fictitious models to illustrate dreamed-up equilibria that never, with a few exceptions, were possible to observe in any social reality, that instead were dramatically alterable and that precisely for that reason generated an intense yearning for security, order and stability. Newton provided nourishment to the hope of a world and a society that is regulated by eternal, immutable laws of nature, this in contrast with an existence where a more or less capricious creator god incessantly intervenes and changes the prerequisites. For the vigorous, status-conscious and power-hungry Individual it entails a significant competitive advantage to acquire trenchant knowledge of these laws of nature. Nature is lying there, waiting for the entrepreneurs to come and exploit its seemingly inexhaustible resources for their own, well-earned gain; it is merely ignorance and a lack of innovation that throws up roadblocks. For the well-informed there is in principle no limit at all to what can be accomplished.

Facilitating for these enterprising Individuals became the primary task of science, in particular enterprising Individuals that head colonial empires and commercial corporations. Science is enrolled in the service of the bourgeoisie, and the Cartesian Individual, the fiction that capitalism has elevated to a transcendental ideal, hovers over the entire project. This development runs like clockwork after the transformative revolutions in America and France in the late 18th century, storied events that still resonate across the world. But actually it is not at all an issue here of any authentic revolutions, but merely of completely logical, expected power shifts that confirm and derive from the technological and ideological revolutions that had taken place several centuries earlier. It is the twin synchronized innovations of the printing press (1450) and the Individual (1637) that constitute the only truly revolutionary phenomena in the context. Everything else – literacy as a mass phenomenon, education, scientific progress, the new political public sphere with cafes, salons and later on political parties, industrialism, parliamentary democracy, the bourgeoisie's dethroning of the aristocracy, imperialist Europe's conquest of the so-called Third World, and so on – is quite simply effects related to the printing press and its ideological consequences, and they are all completely unthinkable without these.

The third phase is the unbridledly violent gearing of the power of the new technology. This suddenly arisen state is essentially anarchic; we call it *the great chaos*. Since we humans tend to overestimate the importance of ourselves and our ideas in driving social change, while we usually underestimate the impact of technology, we not infrequently confuse this gearing – that is; the ramifications of the revolution – with the revolution as such. To begin with, the new masters in the great chaos will continue to operate according to the old paradigm's metaphysics and models, a mode of action that we subsume under the heading *the great naiveté*. But sooner or later it becomes evident for these gentlemen that the great naiveté fills no purpose, but on the contrary has counterproductive consequences, which is why one is forced to channel the energies in the great chaos in accordance with the new prerequisites that appear in conjunction with the agenda of the new metatechnology becoming clear.

It is quite simply the case that the new terms that arise with increasing clarity and emphasis generate mechanisms that start to weed out the elements that brought success under the old system, and instead reward quite different behaviors and talents, upon which the process continues into the fourth and final phase of the paradigm shift. This transition can occur at the moment when the new, upwardly mobile class are at the greatest possible distance from the old paradigm's power elite as well as the combatants of the great chaos, and when this group wises up to exploiting the fact that one now actually has the best conceivable overview of the ongoing tumult and concurrently realizes that what determines how the events unfold is the domestication of the force inherent in the new paradigm. This is exactly what the main actors of the fourth phase do – they tame the social dynamics that arise as a result of the technological revolution and shape these forces after their own purposes, personify the new metaphysics through essentially creating it themselves, thus claiming power. The similarity between, for instance, the pharaohs of ancient Egypt and the industrialists of modern Europe is not insignificant nor random. When this threshold once has been crossed, the paradigm shift can propagate itself throughout the societal body and gradually make its mark on absolutely everything by virtue of the new metaphysics as well as the new worldview and the new models that the new main actor of the playing field either constructs himself or adapts to the unique prerequisites of the new technology – an interaction between Man and technology where Man is the historical constant.

What ultimately determines the final power struggle is control of the talent and the skills that the new paradigm requests. It cannot but end with the actors who are favored by the new conditions grabbing power. The new, highly valued and intensely requested talent – or rather the control and curating of new talent – is the resource that allows itself to be turned into a hold on power. Once the dust has settled over the battlefield, the paradigm shift is completed. It is necessary then to redecorate the entire store: a new metaphysics glorifies the new ruling class, while the old metaphysics tumbles with the fall of the losers and is made to serve as insufficient solace for the new underclass when the new power carries out necessary, painful changes. For what makes the underclass precisely an underclass is that it merely is able to react to all the change that causes everything solid to become transient; it completely lacks the ability to act, as Nietzsche observes. When the primitivist nomadic tribe becomes settled and agrarian, it is consequently the impoverished peasants toiling in the cropland who cling to and place a sentimental value on outdated polytheism and the worship of ancestors that the new elite already has phased out. And similarly it is the worn-out workers toiling in filthy factories who stubbornly cling to feudalism's monotheist religion. This religion could of course assume various expressions and preach either the eternal paradise after death or the classless paradise after the revolution – on the whole it didn't matter which one, they are both examples of the same form of linear superstition complex.

This in turn explains why Christian peasants so freely allowed themselves to be converted into communist workers merely through a minimum of literacy. One immediately recognized the narrative, it was quite simply the same fantastic story on repeat, this time touched up with a veneer of urban factory soot instead of rural loam. It is remarkable how independent churches with their hybrid theology – individualist Protestantism – sprung forth in parallel, literally side by side with the nascent trade unions and the temperance movement of the 19th century. The various membership registers not infrequently overlapped to a great extent. And when these seemingly disparate ideologies now meet their end, they do so together, hand in hand, as feeble, barely discernible ghosts of old identities that today lack contours as well as substance, wiped out by the prevailing conditions in the network society. Neither the independent churches nor the trade unions nor the drunk tanks are nourished in a society where nationalism – with its demands for dividual responsibility vis-à-vis a real or internalized authority figure – is made irrelevant by the Global Empire and its virtual network dynamics. They resemble dinosaurs after the fateful meteorite impact. Digitalization and globalization together constitute the two-headed death squad that without mercy executes all three of them.

When the new consumtariat in the network society is the group that most eagerly of all clings to the old paradigm's metaphysical ideals and fictions, history thus repeats itself with near-terrifying clarity.

It is just as self-evident as it is counterproductive and pointless for the consumtarian underclass to fantasize about individualism's, atomism's, nationalism's and industrialism's magical but hardly probable resurrection. Whenever we hear someone bear witness of their convinced faith in themselves as an Individual, or when we observe how someone desperately claims a national identity for lack of a sense of belonging in any vital, subcultural community, we can be certain that we are dealing with a bonafide consumtarian. We call this popular but not particularly well thought-out digging of one's own grave *the tragic nostalgia*. It is hard to see the tragic nostalgia as anything other than the most dangerous ideology of all those that sprout during and after a paradigm shift. A few examples of tragically nostalgic infatuations in the history of ideas are the nomadic Mongol invasion in Central Asia in the 13th century, German Nazism of the 1930s and Islamism in the Middle East in the early 21st century. Thus it is not the emerging power elite one needs to fear, at least not at first: the groups responsible for the most brutal and at the same time the most confused eruptions of violence and atrocities throughout history are the tragic nostalgics, who set their gaze firmly backwards on a set of fictions that lack tangible relevance in a present that the tragic nostalgic dreams of tearing to shreds at any cost.

This is the banality of evil in its real sense: not an evil that is cunning and calculating, as it often can be in the literary stories of antiheroes, but on the contrary an infantile and unreflected evil that primarily is driven by the suction that arises in the pathological vacuum that we call *the absent phallus syndrome*. What is most terrible is thus not that there is some demon hiding behind evil, but that true evil by force of its banality becomes so powerful and spreads so terrifyingly rapidly and easily precisely because it conceals no demon whatsoever. It is quite simply captivating, the collective exercise of aggression is intoxicating. Behind all the myths that speak of irrational and therefore violent gods, there is always an insight that violence lacks a god which means there is no one who takes responsibility for it. Instead of demons, it is self-pitying humans who are responsible for what we call evil. If one sees oneself as a victim, one has already justified all the means considered necessary to achieve the restitution deemed owed by the world. He who feels really sorry for himself is the one who commits the worst atrocities and who lacks the ability for empathy with others. The demon of evil is invariably a spoiled brat who yields to every whim that happens to surface, a child fettered to the *mamilla*, the boundlessly generous matrichal breast, terrified at the thought of the authentic phallus' demanding representation of the harsh and onerous world outside the infantile and mendacious fairytale world. It is better to hide in the army of the false phallus, where the innocent *abject* is blamed for absolutely everything that has gone wrong, in order to avoid a confrontation with the phallic truth at any cost.

If Gutenberg's printing press was the technological innovation that from 1450 onwards paved the way for the following 500 years of the mass media age, the arrival of individualism with *the Enlightenment* in the 17th century is the second step in the previous paradigm shift. And this golden age of individualism is, as mentioned, introduced with the most popular tweet in world history: "I think, therefore I am", formulated by René Descartes in *Discourse on the Method* from 1637. It is with this phrase, approximately in the middle of the period spanning the arrival of the printing press in Germany (the technological revolution) and the outbreak of the French "Revolution" in Paris in 1789 (the great chaos) that Descartes lays the ground for the ensuing *Enlightenment philosophy* – which thus has the printing press as a material/technological prerequisite and the French Revolution as its most apparent consequence – but also its truth-producing relative *science*, its ruling class *the bourgeoisie*, and thus also the individualism, atomism, industrialism and nationalism that would come to dominate the historical configuration that we sum up in the concept *the capitalist paradigm*.

God is not yet dead, but Descartes retires God from the role of metaphysics' necessary foundation by escorting him from the world where all the hectic activity is occurring and where we struggle to make ourselves the masters of creation. The most prominent actor in the Cartesian revolution is instead the free-thinking and self-critical *Individual*, the human byproduct of the printing press and the daily newspaper, who captures considerable power for his own sake in the rapidly expanding city by using the new printing press for producing banknotes – rather than the old monarchy's appointments and alms – and through exerting control of the increasingly efficient and profitable factories – rather than conquering the country estates' production of foodstuffs and attempting to use this as a power base. Individualism constitutes the foundation for the modern society and its supporting supraideology, *modernism*, with the historical *progress* as its metaphysical engine; conservatism, liberalism as well as socialism are therefore expressions of the same fundamental modernist supraideology where the development ultimately is projected onto the Individual himself. Within this religion there is always something for everyone to constantly strive to improve – without receiving either mercy or forgiveness – for the purpose of attaining the essential subject experience, which in spite of all efforts never arrives. Thus capitalism builds the perfect, libidinal rat wheel, *self-realization*, spurred on by the strictest of all Freudian superegos, namely the internalized police officer that the French philosopher and historian Michel Foucault devotes the lion's share of his career to identifying and charting. Late capitalist Man is thus best described as a mechanical *desire machine* that is constantly chugging along at idle speed, a kind of manic, masochistic loop waiting for a home stretch that never appears and a finish that never comes to pass.

Descartes' courage lies in formulating for the first time in Western history a metaphysics that ignores the creator god as the origin of everything when he instead turns the Individual himself – in the capacity of philosopher and scientist, and above all in the capacity of the bourgeois reader of texts that speak of the philosopher's and the scientist's gains – into the center of existence. When Nietzsche proclaims that "God is dead, and we have killed him" in his work *Thus Spoke Zarathustra* from 1883, he is thus merely summing up a development that begins with Descarte's imposed retirement and marginalization of God as a metaphysical axiom more than 200 years earlier. Nietzsche completes the Cartesian revolution by emphasizing Napoleon as the ultimate *Individual,* in his capacity as the one who with supreme self-discipline realizes and completes individualism's inherent promise. Napoleon's literate army – the first of its kind in history – does according to both Hegel and Nietzsche point upwards towards Napoleon himself as *the realized Individual par excellence.*

Just as with God before him, the Individual soon becomes the object of zealous studies and endless discussions amid the theologians of the new age: the humanist academics. The Individual can of course be described as a physiological phenomenon, in the approach of *psychiatry*. He can also be described as a social scientific phenomenon, in the approach of *psychology*. But the Individual can also be described from his inner fantasy worlds and how these constantly collide with the problematic surrounding world: as an ideological phenomenon, which is what occurs in *psychoanalysis* by way of case studies where the entire history of philosophy is projected onto the dividual person. Since psychoanalysis is carried out through speculative considerations and not through empirical production of evidence, it must, just as its relative, philosophy is, be regarded as an art form rather than as a regular science. Within psychotherapy the Individual is regarded as a sick *patient* who is to be cured through medical and social scientific research, attaining happiness and productivity in order to thus realize his inherent potential. Within psychoanalysis the dividual person is however treated as a confused *analysand* that hopefully can achieve philosophical enlightenment on the illusory aspect of his own subject experience in the midst of a society that is itself built on pathologically conditioned mythologies.

We might express this by saying that psychiatry seeks the cure that will pave the way to happiness in the medicine cabinet, without questioning the surrounding society. Similarly psychology seeks the cure that is to lead to happiness within social scientific empiricism, without questioning the surrounding culture's ideological credos. But within psychoanalysis there is no other cure than the insight that ultimately there is no cure for Man's existential predicament in a fundamentally pathological world. The pleasure principle will always be at loggerheads with the reality principle. Even our conscious conviction that we at any cost want to survive in all situations, our *libido*, is actually a denial mechanism, a repression of our even more deep-seated but elaborately hidden death drive, our innermost wish to cease to exist, the *mortido* that drives our subconsciousness. But to this deeper level Man has no access by way of any empirical research; science might possibly wrestle with Man's search for happiness, but it has nothing to say about any form of existential truth. Here there are consequently no other tools than *speculative logic,* based on the dividual person's historical prerequisites in each specific case.

It should come as no surprise that psychiatry and psychology, which are oriented at explaining and controlling the dividual person, sooner or later would turn their scientific ambitions towards the social collective to explain and control this as well. Thus in the 19th century *sociology* arrives – represented by notables such as Auguste Comte, Karl Marx, Herbert Spencer and Emile Durkheim – with the ambition to explore and position the Individual in the society that emerges after the French Revolution. Of course, even Plato in ancient Greece, Confucius in ancient China, Zoroaster in ancient Iran and Ibn Khaldun in medieval North Africa write comprehensive texts about the social arena and pit various ideals against each other. But sociology in the 19th century still breaks radically with all previous social theories, since it starts from individualism as the axiom. It is the reading, writing and counting – and thus also autonomous Man (which is extremely central: if Man is the center of existence he is now placed in the social sphere, instead of the other way around). It is no longer about how hopefully kind-hearted monarchs and priests shall lead a host of underlings to happiness, but about how the Individual shall realize himself as the center of existence in the midst of a society populated by innumerable other, competing Individuals. The sociologists therefore roam free in the borderlands between empirical research and political idealism, where they assume the role of the self-appointed ideology producers of capitalist society.

However, if psychiatry and psychology cannot access Man's basic existential predicament, but are forced to surrender the critical phase of this exercise to psychoanalysis, the same must apply to the human collective at least in equal degree in its application in the dividual person. Sociology can never do anything other than dance atop a series of more or less arbitrarily composed assumptions about Man and society and their interaction with each other, assumptions that are taken for granted merely because they appeal to the prevailing power structure, though this does not make them eternally valid or even close to empirically verifiable. It is here that the need for *socioanalysis* becomes obvious. In order to understand what is happening with and within us humans in conjunction with the arrival of the Internet Age – with its explosive development of *digitalization*, *globalization* and *nodalization* – it is not nearly enough to start from the same old outdated models and sit around tinkering with the same old empiricism over and over again. The problem is not that the measurements are erroneous, but that we are quite simply measuring the wrong things, and are doing so from irrelevant fundamental assumptions. The models themselves, the very view of humanity and the world, must be fundamentally questioned, and for this there is a requirement for a philosophical rather than an empirical revision of the activity. Socioanalysis is precisely this deeper, speculative logic, in contrast to sociology's empirical research oriented towards superficial phenomena. If philosophy is the metaperspective around the scientific and empirical disciplines – there is for obvious reasons a philosophy of science but no science of philosophy – it means that psychoanalysis is best understood as *metapsychology* and socioanalysis correspondingly must be regarded as *metasociology*.

Socioanalysis and the need for it does of course not arise all of a sudden out of a vacuum. As early as the 1920s the "neo-Marxist" sociologists and social psychologists at the so-called Frankfurt School (Institut for Sozialforschung) – with representatives such as Theodor Adorno, Max Horkheimer, Erich Fromm and Herbert Marcuse – start to carry out an *ideology critique* through blending Karl Marx's political sociology with Sigmund Freud's increasingly influential psychoanalysis. At the same time, old Freud himself shifts his focus from the treatment of the dividual analysand to society's collective delusions and the mechanisms behind these in books such as *Totem and Taboo* (1913), *The Future of an Illusion* (1927), *Civilization and its Discontents* (1930) and *Moses and Monotheism* (1937). Freud and the Frankfurt School are followed later in the 20th century by a long line of thinkers in the borderlands between philosophy and socioanalysis, for instance George Herbert Mead, Jacques Lacan, Michel Foucault, Jürgen Habermas, Gilles Deleuze, Julia Kristeva and Slavoj Žižek. A socioanalysis for the Internet Age worth its salt naturally has to build on these social theoreticians' achievements. But it is not afraid of questioning the individualist myths that these thinkers inherit as axioms from Descartes and his many influential interpreters, such as Jean-Jacques Rousseau and Immanuel Kant. A serious socioanalysis for the Internet Age therefore must tear up and deconstruct the entire individualist worldview and its view of history. Individualism is dead. It no longer works in an increasingly refined network society. So what supplants it? And how?

Let us begin by stating that informationalism is dominated by three gigantic movements: *digitalization*, *globalization* and *nodaliza-*

tion. The Internet Age receives its name from the *Internetization* of Man and society. Billions of people and objects are interconnected into complicated, interactive networks with each other, and these networks and their nodes and data flows constitute the new digital society, rather than the increasingly secondary urban and rural societies in so-called real life. The virtual world is the new primary world from which everything else departs; the previously wholly dominant physical world has become secondary. The digital society is flat in structure and increasingly transparent compared to the modernist society we are leaving behind. But this definitely does not mean that we are *en route* to the classless society (see *The Netocrats*). New power structures arise, not between dividual people but between the various networks that people create with those around them. All nodes are not equally powerful. Certain nodes influence millions of human actors and technological actants every second, other nodes barely influence anything in their environment. An original chaos that by and by acquires nodes as centers is called a *plurarchy* within socioanalysis (see *The Netocrats*). The network society is thus at an early phase first and foremost a plurarchic society, which means that it ought to pay off for us to study earlier plurarchies in history, rather than for instance democracies, in order to understand in depth what is happening in our present.

For instance, having millions of followers or simply having a few dozen followers on social media creates an enormous discrepancy in influence. But we would go astray if we speak of these discrepancies in power and influence as connected to dividual people. It is rather the case of discrepancies in power and influence between different networks, depending on where in the prevailing network pyramid the networks in question are located (see *The Netocrats*). Power has been converted into a network-dynamical rather than an individualist phenomenon. Therefore a correct and functional power analysis of the network society must use network-dynamical rather than individualist models, otherwise it searches for the new power structure in all the wrong places and completely misunderstands the entire complex of problems. Individualism has become as outdated an explanatory model for network society as when theology collapsed as an explanatory model for the natural sciences after the breakthrough of the Enlightenment in the 17th century. If individualism is punished rather than encouraged in the new power-generating networks, it is of course irrelevant both as an ethical ideal and as a socioanalytical explanatory model. Theology, in the same way, became an encumbrance in the natural scientific laboratories and nowadays lives out its final embittered days as a remnant from the past in the mainly American and Arabic madness that is called *creationism*.

In our book *Syntheism – Creating God in The Internet Age* we give a detailed account of the incremental transition from Kant's completed Cartesian individualism in the 18th century – the correlationist metaphysics between the subject and the object – via Nietzsche's revolutionizing relativism in the 19th century (all objects are in constant motion in relation to each other and the subject is but one object among others) – up until the relationalist revolution that Alfred North Whitehead conducts within philosophy and Niels Bohr within quantum physics in the 1920s. Whitehead thereby completes the Nietzschean revolution, "more Nietzschean than Nietzsche himself", through smashing the fundamental object and building metaphysics on merely dividual events that have passed as soon as they arise, where *relations* are what is fundamental, that create their *relata* instead of the other way around. From a philosophical perspective Bohr then simply transfers the Whiteheadian revolution to quantum physics by making the field instead of the particle the primary aspect of physics. Instead of quantum mechanics we should therefore talk of *quantum organics*.

When the Internet arrives in the 1980s, there is really nothing else required but classic speculative logic in order to understand that Whitehead's relationalism suddenly becomes highly useful as a metaphor for the new, emerging digital arena. The new social relationalism consequently teaches that there are actually no dividuals at all to begin with, but merely what we call *pure relations* without any material substance in the classical sense. And it is out of these pure relations that dividuals rather than individuals arise as illusory phenomena after every encounter between human bodies and brains, both physically and virtually. The experience of *dividuality* arises only as a consequence of the dividual leaving the room or the conversation with the other actors in which the relations are occurring. There is no dividual that conducts relations, there is only a dividual that is the byproduct of the relations that are constantly ongoing and that spur the dividual towards constant change, which makes the dividual a constantly altered event and nothing else. Or to use the ancient Greek philosopher Heraclitus' classic one-liner: "You cannot step into the same river twice." It is not just a case of the foot not being the same twice, as one of Heraclitus' disciples quickly points out. It is not even the same owner of the foot in question. Everything has changed, everything is differently disposed; time is another word for change. *Panta rei*, everything flows, as Heraclitus also expresses the matter. The problem is not, as Marx maintains, that capitalism entails that all that is solid melts into air, but the entire notion that something even could be solid is a pure and ideologically conditioned illusion. Stability was the fiction that Newton supplied on demand. But only events exist, as Whitehead maintains, there are ontically speaking, no objects whatsoever.

The sense of community between the dividual events, the sense that one and the same immutable or at least only slowly alterable dividual constantly populates a certain body is thus a delusion. The network society has not just revealed this sense to be a hallucination, but has also been forced to send it out into the cold since it constitutes a serious encumbrance. Individualism has already moved down into the digital underclass. It is the new consumtariat at the lower tier of society that devotes itself to narcissistic compensatory behaviors in the Internet Age. The ruling netocracy, on the other hand, entertains itself by networking for its own sake. According to its new ideals it is the *swarm*, the suddenly arising event of collective creativity, that is the objective and meaning of being a successful citizen in the network society. The name of this event is *Syntheos*, the god that the netocrats create themselves rather than anyone or anything one might consider oneself created by. Netocratic syntheism in this way replaces individualist progress as the metaphysics of the Internet Age. For what is this Syntheos if not the definitive *phallus*, not given beforehand from above by nature or history, but first created and then worshipped by the netocratic swarm.

Authentic psychoanalysis is the only forum where we are not allowed to without disturbance devote ourselves to enjoyment in an otherwise pleasure-obsessed contemporary society. Above all, psychoanalysis succeeds in questioning and attacking three areas where enjoyment has become the undisputed axiom of our time: sexual, professional and spiritual life. Within all three areas the Internet Age's enjoyment is mandatory. But beyond the infantile enjoyment there is the lure of the yearning for *the phallic intrusion* and the promise of one day personifying the adult autonomy. So do you choose the red or the blue pill? Do you choose happiness or truth? If you choose matrichal happiness, take your pill and slip into your sweet Sleeping Beauty slumber. Remain an innocent child forever. But if you choose the phallic truth, socioanalysis will awaken you back to life, admittedly into a harsh and brutal world, but into a world that is worth loving and being fascinated by. As an adult. As an autonomous person. For this is the task of phallus, to seduce us with adulthood's existential freedom and responsibility, which makes us move away from the mamilla's mendacious security in an undemanding make-believe world. To make us finally tire of the phony, infantile cuddling with and among pleasant illusions. To instead make us want to grow, despite the toil and the risks it entails. Charting the course that leads there is the mission of socioanalysis: to offer the Internet Age's sole opportunity of critical awakening. The Enlightenment project of the Internet Age starts, in other words, here and now.

5
Instinct, drive, desire and transcendence

Organisms are fundamentally conservative. Changes are always foisted upon them in some way. This is in the nature of the organism since change costs energy and energy is hard currency in the daily fight for survival in one's existence. The *status quo* is always preferable as long as there is no impending threat that gives rise to urgent countermeasures. To proactively begin a process of change with the purpose of gaining presumed long-term advantages is usually something too abstract and uncertain to even be considered. Therefore the organism treats the world around it with a good measure of caution even from the outset and tries to avoid every form of change as long as possible. When an organism acts, despite this, the reaction should be understood as one conditioned by external and by definition unwelcome stimuli. It would prefer to strive towards the catatonic state rather than the hyperactive. This is the default setting: a pull towards the equalization of energy levels.

The father of psychoanalysis, Sigmund Freud, calls this fundamental stance regarding the surrounding world "the longing of the organism back to the inorganic." He terms this primary wish of the organism *the death drive*, or *mortido* in Latin, and the fundamental assumption is thus that the living being invariably is in a state of motion towards the inorganic, towards extinction and – ultimately – death. Since this gradual dissolution goes hand in hand with reduced tension – both within the organism and between it and the world – the death drive is paradoxically connected with what Freud calls *the pleasure principle*, that is: the dividual's impulsive pursuit of enjoyment and gratification, and implies where an explanation for masochistic pain's fusion with pleasure might be sought. In this light, self-destructive behavior becomes wholly logical as part of an instinctive exertion towards the inorganic, enabling a deeper view of what instinct actually is: a series of innate defense mechanisms that organize the organism's behavioral patterns. Thus we can also state that *instinct*, which is the basis of Man's complex drive machinery, is a reactionary and mortidinal phenomenon rather than something active and libidinal.

So what does this really mean? Does the living organism not want to live? The answer is not a simple one. Well, yes, the organism can be said to want to live, but not primarily, only secondarily. Just look at the newborn infant, which after the shock and pain of being delivered is thrust into a world that is in sharp contrast to the pleasant and above all, safe, womb – *matrix* in Latin – from which it now is eternally banished. The child wants to go back in, but this of course is impossible. The delivery is an experience so terrifying that the child never can remember it afterwards, which is why it must be repressed. Therefore the French psychoanalyst Jacques Lacan calls birth *the great trauma* – with a pinch of ingenuity we might even call it *the mother of all traumas*. The point is that even in connection with birth, Man's repressive mechanisms vis-à-vis all forms of discomfort go into overdrive. When the child, usually shrieking, by necessity fails in its endeavor to return to the womb, there instead emerges an instinct to crawl to its mother's breast, where the child then in vain does everything it can to realize the next impossible fantasy. This project is designed so that if the child can just manage to suck the maternal breast intensely enough – in psychoanalysis the Latin concept *mamilla* is used – the reward is that a reunion is granted with the mother's body. The suddenly arisen existence as an autonomous creature, never sought by the child itself, would thereby receive an every bit rapid as longed-for ending.

As soon as the newborn child spots the maternal breast, there awakens a will to regard the mamilla as its private property with no restrictions whatsoever. This voyeuristic viewing combined with the incestuous touching of the mamilla kick-starts what will later develop into one of Man's most afflicting curses: *the desire to appropriate the object*. From the child's naive and undeveloped perspective, food and maternal love does of course flow from the mamilla without any sign of a demand for reciprocity. All the child need do is suck and swallow. So why not expect everything to be just as simple also later in life? In the child's fantasy world the mamilla is thus nothing other than the matrix 2.0: *in part the optimal protection against a hostile surrounding world, in part the undemanding and bottomless enjoyment par excellence*. Therefore, during the rest of its existence, the child will fight bitterly, primarily to be able to maintain and safeguard this paradise that it would rather not see as lost, secondarily, to be able to dream of a restitution of this *matrichal state*.

All these human fantasies and pipe dreams of idyllic rest, balance in the economy, a harmonious worldview, snug security, the creation of comfort through nesting – that is: everything that we in our contemporary society subsume under concepts such as *nesting* and *cocooning* – an undemanding bosom, warm hugs, peaceful heavens, serene paradises, lush Edens, soothing oases, beds with fluffy duvets, puffy sofas, steamy bathtubs, spas and everything else in that genre that promises cozy forms of well-being – these are endless variants of the same basic dream of *the return to the matrix*. Since this matrix is always located in the past, which by definition is impossible to return to, while all these fantasies are merely pale copies of and highly unsatisfying substitutes for the original, this yearning for the matrichal state in itself will always be conservative and nostalgic. This in turn means that the more unsettled Man feels in terms of his relationship with the chaotic world around him, the more tempting a conservative and nostalgic approach will be. The child's first instinct, *nota bene*, thus springs from the will to die, not from a will to live. And if life really must be lived, in spite of everything, the first and most important prioritization will be to minimize this living of life as much as possible, that is: transforming oneself to a living dead person.

What this drive in its purest form strives for is nothing other than a state of perfect rest and uneventfulness. And when – or rather, if – the organism makes other prioritizations and decides to make the effort to live, motivated by an experience that the will to life – *libido* in Latin – manifests itself, this libido is nothing other than the repression of mortido, the deeper and primary will to leave life for death. Libido should instead be regarded as the very *repression par excellence*, and its appearance above all indicates that the more deep-seated mortido already has been phased out. But as everyone understands, it does not mean that the death drive disappears, merely that it is repressed, beneath the horizon of consciousness where it covertly continues to work (and ache). Its new arena is Freud's big discovery, the most treacherous and impenetrable of all hiding places: *the subconscious.* Thus the child from this moment of fragmentation onwards has made itself unaware of its nature and original instinct, instead elevating the culturally acceptable libido as an ideal and guiding star. *Culture* and its imaginary universe is therefore based on the elevated libido as an ideal, while *nature* and its real universe constantly remind us of the repressed mortido, our disposition and our origin, which remains alive and highly active, constantly influencing our behavior and our conceptual world without us understanding what is happening or the forces of which we are at the mercy.

The logical separation in the child's fantasy world causes culture to be represented by *phallus,* while nature is represented by *matrix.* Man's system of drives is essentially determined by the tension and ambivalence that constantly prevails between phallus and matrix, which also, among many other things, is the prime prerequisite of religion. It probably goes without saying, but just to be on the safe side: we are not speaking here of genitalia in any tangible sense whatsoever, nor of anything connected with anyone's biological sex or indirectly connected with actual genitalia. These Latin concepts quite simply signify two philosophical concepts that in part constitute each other's diametrical opposites, in part the two poles in Man's complex drive machinery, where *matrix* represents the holistic, cohesive and infinite, while *phallus* represents the separating and differentiating, the limited and finite. Matrix represents *the imaginary order*, while phallus represents *the symbolic order* in Man's fantasy world; matrix represents instinct, phallus represents desire. Drive then arises in the charged conflict zone between matrix and phallus, that is: between instinct and desire. The fundamental idea behind psychoanalysis is to raise awareness of and emphasize these processes that are under the surface, to spread light and clarity where dusk and obscurity prevail. How we then handle our newly-acquired insight is another matter, since there are no guarantees that satisfaction will be stable.

If we employ a metaphoricity from military and society life, we might express what we just mentioned as though instinct takes the shortest route to its target – like a heat-guided missile charting its course via the exhaust of the target's jet engine – while desire for its part rather would dance and excitedly continue its dance around what we call *the cathexal object* (from the Greek word *kathexis*, which is best translated as "emotional investment"). The entire job description of desire of course focuses on one thing alone: proclaiming the grass to invariably be greener on the other side, regardless of which side is involved and on which side desire and the desirer happen to be located. It is a matter of principle. Drive is dancing, but only initially, around its object, and as soon as the possibility presents itself it will head straight for its target, to immediately incorporate this object into its own identity. He who uses Freud to orient himself in the human psyche will at great advantage connect instinct with the "id," drive with the "ego," while desire is located in various incessant disputes with the "super-ego." A concrete way of distinguishing between the three different phenomena is to observe their distinct reactions after the conquest is a fact: Instinct is immediately satisfied; while drive, on the other hand, feels as though it has depleted all its energy while at the same time has expanded its contents; while desire is heavy with disappointment the moment the objective has been fulfilled since this does not match its expectations, which it cannot possibly do, because desire has already started to direct its attention towards the next seductively green lawn on the other side of some sort of fence.

The symbolism we are speaking of here is however not completely unconnected from gender, and above all not from the different roles that the sexes play in the life of the small child. In her book *Powers of Horror: An Essay on Abjection*, the Bulgarian-French philosopher and psychoanalyst Julia Kristeva traces the ambivalence between matrix and phallus directly to the small child's experience of the mother's and father's disparate roles in the child's fantasy world. Or to be consistent with the central role of symbolism in our argument: since Man is a symbolic-tribal creature, and the child has many parents of both sexes within the tribe, let us then speak of *the matriarch* and *the patriarch* rather than the mother and the father as the two dominant adult representatives of the sexes in the child's imagination, entirely without relation to any actual biological kinship. The matriarch then plays the present and concrete adult role, while the patriarch constitutes the distancing and abstract adult role. According to Kristeva it is not merely the small child who fights to maintain the sense of belonging to the matriarch. Kristeva's major insight is rather that the matriarch does not either want to loosen her grip on the child. The matriarch and the child are living in a sort of mutual semiotic-symbiotic container, in what Kristeva terms *the semiotic soup*, an apparently cohesive, prelinguistic fantasy world.

The patriarch steps into this fantasy world with his phallus – the symbol of language, law and the ambivalent reality outside – and thus drives a wedge into the intimate togetherness that prevails between the matriarch and the child, a lever that the child must have access to in order to later be able to liberate itself successfully from the matriarch through a process that Kristeva calls *abjection*. Kristevian abjection occurs when the child is around one year old. A number of different research projects confirm that the child is the most similar to its father and its other male biological relatives at this very age, which indicates that the patriarchal role evidently is the most important one for the child at this particular time. However, abjection is not a clearly defined one-off event, but rather divided into three different steps. We express this by saying that the first abjection is *post-matrichal*, the second abjection is *post-mamillic*, and the third abjection is *post-phallic*.

The first abjection is nature's own, namely delivery itself, but it is only the surrounding tribe, not the child itself, that understands that birth actually entails the child's separation from the matriarch. The second abjection is the Kristevian, which occurs at the age of one and which primarily revolves around the child's fundamental distancing from the matriarch, where the body of the matriarch and above all the *mamilla* becomes the first detested abject, while the phallus as the first fetish has a lure more or less off in the distance with a tough and conditioned, real love rather than the devalued, unconditional and therefore increasingly worthless phantasmic love from the mamilla. Actually it is precisely the matriarch's admiring gaze towards the phallus – and everything it represents – that unleashes that which in psychoanalysis is called the boy's *Oedipal complex* and the girl's *Electra complex*. What is this mysterious force that the phallus holds and represents, and that the child does not have itself? What happens, as *the phallic intrusion* occurs the way it should, is that the boy starts to *imitate* and the girl starts to *erotisize* the phallus. But if the phallic intrusion goes missing, the child sinks its teeth into the mamilla and is permanently infantilized. An infantilization that unfortunately also can befall entire cultures and societies, according to socioanalysis, if the phallic intrusion does not occur and society straps itself to the mamilla of undemanding support.

The task of the phallus is not to separate the child from the matriarch with the purpose of depriving the child of its enjoyment, but rather *to seduce* the child with the many enticements of adulthood: If you covet and therefore fight for and take responsibility for your autonomy, your reward will be the power and freedom of the phallus. Real life on the outside is much more exciting than the fabricated fairytale life within the mamilla. It is quite simply libidinal, not mortidinal. This gives rise to the child's first yearning for the phallus, for adulthood, for the challenge from the rough but stimulating and rewarding life outside the safe but unexciting bubble that has been established around matrix and mamilla. As proof of this second abjection phase there is the terrible twos that entails a constant and conflict-ridden testing of the phallic limits. The process is later concluded with the third phase: the *teenage rebellion*. We call this event *the uprising against the phallus*, since the attack is directed at the phallus rather than at the matriarch, even though the primary objective is to establish and test one's own identity vis-à-vis the old forms of authority. Hence, the dialectical voyage from the dependence and irresponsibility of childhood to the autonomy and sense of responsibility of adulthood is completed.

It is only after the Kristevian abjection that the child succeeds in disentangling itself from the matriarch and converting a previously experienced "we" in a symbiotic relation with her, into an "I" on the one hand, and a "you" on the other hand. In this abjection process, the phallus becomes the symbol of what the child feels it has lost – I cannot have everything I want, thus a *desire* arises directed towards what I cannot have quite simply because I cannot have it (the inaccessible grass must be greener) – a lack that also is the mysterious force that the phallus appears to exercise over the child and the surrounding world, but that the matriarch apparently lacks. The phallus is of course accessible to the matriarch but inaccessible to the child via what Freud terms *the incest taboo.* Thus desire in itself starts and ends with the worship of the distanced phallus through which all other desired objects receive their value. If mamilla is the metasubject, phallus is the metaobject.

Culturally this is manifested through the dance around the tribe's uniting phallus, its *totem*, whose higher and long-term purpose is to cultivate cooperation rather than competition between the members of the tribe. Around this totem the most phallic project of all is established and maintained: *the law.* And nothing is punished more severely by the law than crimes against the symbolic order itself. The murder of the patriarch, *patricide*, is therefore the ultimate transgression of the law and also the only way in which the law can be vanquished – which can pave the way for a new *paradigm*, a new power structure with a new historiography and a new social identity. Patricide is either carried out by a frustrated younger generation who want to usurp power over the law; or more likely, by the patriarch himself by voluntarily stepping aside when a new paradigm is due. But up until this happens, it is obedience to the law that is required, it even castrates the successfully autonomous adults in the tribe and puts the tribe before the dividual member. We call this *the social castration.*

Since the matrix and the imaginary order are psychotic in nature, while phallus and the symbolic order are neurotic – that is: since these two ways of relating to the world are structured in completely opposing ways – the child can only manage on its own by maintaining and identifying itself with an at least fairly stable balance between these two opposites. To be human is to be both an imaginary and a symbolic creature, to constantly carry out a precarious balancing act between mortido and libido, matrix and phallus, yin and yang, psychosis and neurosis. But the abjection process, the movement towards this life-sustaining independence, runs from matrix to phallus, from the imaginary to the symbolic, without allowing itself to be totally devoured by the lure of the phallus, for that matter. For it is only in a balanced relation between matrix and phallus that the child becomes a functional human, and it is the ambivalence between matrix and phallus that keeps up and stimulates Man's imagination.

The ambivalence between the imaginary and the symbolic is actually the germ of *the sublime*, the engine of human creativity and the arena for humanity's greatest and most bittersweet stories. What prevents the imaginary and the symbolic from meshing is namely history's indomitable forward movement and the constant change of the surrounding world. Or as the psychoanalyst Lacan expresses the matter: *The real* constantly steps in and tears up the stubborn attempt of the imaginary and the symbolic to merge into a cohesive universe. The real, according to Lacan, is not some form of hyper-reality detached from Man's conceptual world, but quite simply that which constantly rushes in and upsets Man's dream of the existence of a cohesive, well-ordered and fixed world. The fantasies and the symbols never find each other, since existence is in constant flux. The real is quite simply the recurring annoyance and reminder of history's contingency where time as the constant of the Universe – that which the Iranians of antiquity call *Zurvan* and the Greeks later christen *Kronos* – is the only absolute constant, beyond both matrix and phallus. Only the metalaw of contingent change endures over time.

All the while, time, in the capacity of the ultimate phallus, is constantly outside of human reach. Man can only live in the past. So of course the world is cohesive purely ontically – for physicists as well as for metaphysicians this is completely unproblematic – but it can never be ontologically cohesive for Man himself, since his symbolic and imaginary universes respectively remain in several respects separate and mutually contradictory. The world itself thus offers Man no cohesive ontology, what it has to offer him is merely the ambivalence between these worlds, the ontic meets Man only in, for instance, quantum organics' counterintuitive but nevertheless indisputable uniformity. Thus the ontological project never succeeds in leaving the philosophical metalevel. No externalization, not even a fictitious freeze of the Universe in itself, holds fast when time is set in motion and contingency becomes the only necessity.

If we view the human drive machinery from yet another perspective, we discover the following: *instinct* belongs to the wild animal in Man, while *drive* belongs to natural Man, *desire* belongs to the cultural creature in Man and *transcendence* belongs to enlightened Man. The organism's reaction to stimuli from the surrounding world is determined by instinct, while instinct is the aggression that dwells in the real. Drive is the metainstinct, as well as the repetition that belongs in the imaginary. And desire is the metadrive: the transgression that belongs in the symbolic. Transcendence, finally, is the metadesire and transcends (as the name implies): it exceeds both aggression, repetition and transgression in one and the same movement without creating any universe other than *the infinite now* as an extremely temporary ecstasy, where the memory of the experience along the timeline constitutes the engine that keeps the machinery running and at the same time reflects on the activity. Or to express the entire drive system metahistorically, with the aid of the four information technological paradigms: Instinct is propelled towards the tribal *life cycle*, drive is attracted by monotheist *eternity*, desire entices with individualist *progress* and transcendence is attracted by the network-dynamical *event*. Without a drive to match, Man cannot step into and identify himself with the new paradigm's metaphysics.

All existential choices can in principle be reduced to the choice between the two ideals *enjoyment* or *truth*: the conflict that drives, for instance, the story in the film *The Matrix* from 1999. The conflict between enjoyment and truth also cuts right through the four categories in Man's drive system. Drive and desire are connected to enjoyment as an ideal, while their shadows – instinct and transcendence – are connected with truth as an ideal. While consciousness apprehends these expressions as different categories and degrees of wills, subconsciousness is merely concerned with pressure and repressions. The French philosopher Paul Ricoeur compiles this into four steps: First there must be a *source*, then a *pressure*, thereafter a *direction* and finally an *object*. Syntheologically we personify Ricoeur's four steps as *Atheos* (the source), *Pantheos* (the pressure), *Entheos* (the direction) and *Syntheos* (the object) (see further *Syntheism – Creating God in The Internet Age*). Source and pressure are connected with mortido, while direction and object are connected with libido.

It follows that the displacement from mortido to libido, from matrix to phallus, from passivity to activity, occurs between pressure and direction. Phallus is the organ that determines the direction of the matrichal pressure, that tames the natural force (mortido) to the cultural will (libido). Matrix creates the raw materials in abundance, phallus delimits and shapes the raw materials to the object, and thus the object receives its longed-for fetishistic value. The consequence is that the abject always precedes the fetish, but that the abject controls culture only if and when the fetish is missing. We sacrifice to the gods before we worship them. And we continue to sacrifice to them even when they are clearly absent, which they have a tendency to be. But if the gods make their presence felt, we stop sacrificing to them and start to worship them instead. For mortido operates according to *the iteration principle* – it displays a compulsory repetition in accordance with the philosophical ambition to come ever closer to the coveted externalization. Libido, on the other hand, operates in accordance with *the alteration principle* – it acts with the poetic ambition of keeping everything in a constant state of flux and expanding the entirety that arises between the phenomena. This explains why instinct and drive are defined as iterational, while desire and transcendence are regarded as alterational.

Within Man there is the struggle between *instinct* and *desire*. We can then add *drive* as instinct's shadow and *transcendence* as desire's shadow. Instinct's nature is contingent, ambivalent and confused. Syntheologically it is connected to the source, *Atheos*. Drive, on the other hand, is intimately connected with the direct satisfaction of concrete needs. Syntheologically it is connected with pressure, *Pantheos*. Desire is an exclusively human phenomenon, since it is a byproduct of language. Syntheologically it is connected with direction, *Entheos*. Transcendence represents our endeavor to reach beyond nature, society, culture and death – its phantasmic playing field is *the infinite now*. Being within transcendence is seeing oneself as one process among an infinity of other processes, within an infinite number of processes, *ad infinitum*, where the subject emerges when the metaprocess is manifested as the active agent, as the phallic curator within the matrichal information chaos of existence, to itself. Syntheologically transcendence is connected with the concept of *Syntheos*.

It is only he who first has experienced transcendence and who later also allows himself to be led by transcendence as a metaphysical ideal that can take part in the netocratic building of Syntheos. This in turn means that if we are to build *the event* that drives the netocracy during informationalism – a project that many contemporary theoreticians investigate and advocate, for example Jacques Derrida and Alain Badiou, after the collapse of modernist progress as a metaphysical ideal – then we must experience transcendence beyond instinct, drive and desire and only then, from this experience, can we build Syntheos. We then attain the insight that *the construction of God is the netocratic event par excellence*. But it is not a case of a permanently higher level where libido dies from lack of oxygen: what we are talking about is merely a highly temporary, transient and ecstatic experience. The event has as rapid an end as it has a sudden beginning. It is a very separate event and not an eternity in a heaven or in another utopia with the ambition of being enduring. Or else the event would be unbearable, like a constantly ongoing orgasm without an end in sight, ever. Which causes the syntheist sacral to take shape in the productive and inspiring *memory of the divine experience* and nothing else. Syntheos thus bestows a rich and inspiring meaning on what has transpired, but does absolutely does not give saturation. Syntheos does not threaten, but reinforces libido, which continues to be driven by the quest for one's own historical completion (which will never occur). Wanting to live is wanting to experience, to become rich from experiences and affirm one's own inevitable incompleteness, while it is only within the confines of this incompleteness that libido can be developed and produce new shoots.

Another way of summing up the drive system syntheologically is to describe instinct as *animalistic*, drive as *mechanical*, desire as *human* and transcendence as *sacral*. We humans share instinct with other animals. It is actually the animalistic aspect within Man. Desire is exclusive to Man. It is, as mentioned, a byproduct of the language that Man alone possesses. Drive is the playing field that stretches out in between instinct and desire – the conflict between the animalistic and the human within Man. It is therefore distinguished by a kind of grinding monotony. Thus instinct belongs with mortido and desire with libido, while drive gets its energy from the dialectics between libido and mortido. If we venture into Lacan's psychoanalytical universe, we can posit instinct in *the real*, drive in Man's *imaginary universe* and desire in Man's *symbolic universe*. For the progenitor Sigmund Freud, instinct, as previously mentioned, would come from *the id*, drive belong with *the ego* and desire would get its energy from *the superego*. Please note how transcendence literally transcends all these three categories. It is quite simply nothing other than the consequence of the insight of how the other drives operate.

Transcendence is thus the final destination of Lacanian psychoanalysis. But it can never be anything but temporary and makeshift, there is no possibility of permanently existing in the transcendental drive. This insight is nothing new in itself. The Tibetan philosopher Chögyam Trungpa argues that the celestial state that we call *ecstasy* – another name for the network-dynamical event – cannot possess any continuance, partly because it makes the agent dysfunctional (there is a completely logical and legitimate reason for psychotics to be locked up in psychiatric hospitals), partly because the ecstatic enjoyment sooner or later would be transformed into hellish torment if it continued eternally. A paradise and an eternity are thus by definition two irreconcilable quantities. What is divine must be brief. Instead, transcendence and its experience, syntheism's *the infinite now*, must be temporary and generate its power from this very happenstance and fleetingness that makes it so much more desirable and thus meaningful.

An educated transcendence is therefore an ecstasy connected with memory. It is the *memory of the ecstasy* that lifts and carries the agent after the experience, that enriches life, and which therefore in the post-cultural transcendence must be taught in order to be attained and experienced. It is, for instance, *the infinite now* that should be sought in *the psychedelic experience* and other shamanistic practices and not – regardless of what enthusiastic psychonauts often claim – some kind of secret knowledge that has been preserved in and for various insular societies for the purpose of preserving their imploitative exclusivity. The experience, the memory of the experience and how this memory influences how, from the moment on, the world is valued outside this experience – this is what is central about the infinite now, not some suddenly discovered shortcut in individualism's struggle for an academic power position and/or media attention. This also explains why we categorize transcendence as sacral rather than human.

Curiously, we rarely see psychoanalysts confront themselves with what is expected to happen in the drive system beyond psychoanalysis in itself. The objective here is actually identical with *enlightenment* or *realization,* what one strives for in most of the Eastern philosophical schools, a kind of metalevel above the drive system, an observation spot that is both internal and external vis-à-vis the drive system in its entirety. This fourth category – which is strangely missing in the teachings of the main protagonists of psychoanalysis, Freud, Lacan, Kristeva and Žižek – is exactly that we call transcendence. The point is not a naive hope that someone will be able to live permanently within transcendence in some sort of eternal bliss, just as it is impossible for someone to be permanently enlightened. But the very fact that transcendence even can be attained, albeit temporarily, provides a motivation for ascribing it a significant role as the fourth category in the human drive machinery. The thinker who cannot see this does not merely gamble away his spiritual riches, but also harbors a completely erroneous understanding of the structure of the human psyche and the full potential of the drive system.

From a historical perspective, underestimation in psychoanalysis of its own potential ability to alter the analysand's drive system is the blind spot of the entire discipline. It is not then a question of curing the analysand as though he were an unruly patient, but concerns achieving a sublime change of the drive system itself, and thereby enables the transcendental event in an analysand who accepts not only his own mortality but also mortido as the deep-seated engine of libido. However, there is a reasonable explanation for philosophers and psychoanalysts rarely reaching all the way to the mystery of transcendence. The explanation is quite simply that the experience of transcendence in its entirety never has occurred, and if transcendence is not experienced, then it cannot be expected to be conceived of and/or suggested. The reason is of course that the preceding *desire* is a gigantic, not to say inexhaustible subject in itself. Desire of course starts with libido suddenly not getting what it wants and therefore fetishizing what it cannot have and converting the desired into the cathexal object. Thereafter, desire thinks it is certain of what it wants and has a clear goal in sight.

Desire's constant search for desire itself is desire's innermost nature. And since Man is a gregarious animal, desire – having conquered a certain fetish or having annihilated a certain abject – might very well be imitated and rapidly disseminated among people. Lacan terms this memetic as well as mimetic pattern *the desire for the desire of the other.* There is actually nothing to prevent the desire for the desire of the other from triggering a synchronous chain of *prohibition* of its own, followed by an intense desire that transcends the desire for the desire of the other. The subject initially wants to want the same thing that its partner (in the broadest conceivable sense) wants. When the subject feels it has attained the desire for the desire of the other, there arises a prohibition against going further than its partner. This prohibition produces a new and even stronger desire beyond the desire of the other. Obstacles are torn down and desire turns into an emotionally aggregated hyperstate beyond the phallic confines upon which the subject has relied from the start. There are now only two possible exits from this impasse: either the desirer is locked into an isolating and destructive psychosis – the contact with its partner being broken down completely – or the desirer moves on from desire to transcendence, where intimate relations can be built from a starting point in the shared memory of the joint ecstasy.

When the syntheist agent sees through the metatruth about desire as a desire for itself, she also has the possibility to, at least temporarily, detach herself from desire's constantly grinding mechanisms to the extent that the fourth category is motivated as a definition of the syntheist agent's ambitions. Desire sort of wears out the subject, but without libido being the least bit weakened. Transcendence is thus metadesire's dialectical outcome, a pure enjoyment within the drive to distance oneself from desire, which in a Hegelian sense has turned against and seen through itself. Precisely this conscious return from desire to drive is transcendence in itself. Instead, it is possible to cultivate a consciously blind, unreflected enjoyment within transcendence, not unlike instinct's worship of phallus and matrix, all the while in enlightened consciousness rather than as some kind of subconscious mysticism. We express this by saying that transcendence confronts the subject with its own *asubject* – the asubject is that within the subject that it otherwise is unconscious of, that is: the greater part of the subject that resides in subconsciousness rather than in consciousness – and with this expanding self-realization the subject will also act differently in the future, in comparison to drive or desire being the final stops of psychoanalysis. This tangibly new mode of acting is *de facto* the empirical proof of the existence of transcendence. Or as the Swiss psychoanalyst Carl Gustav Jung expresses the matter: He who has no contact with his own *shadow* is not a complete human being.

Thus it appears as though psychoanalysis from a historical perspective is uncomfortable with discussing its own enlightenment project – for naturally there is such a project, why else would one bother to go into psychoanalysis? – even though this kind of enlightenment in a sort of Lacanian sense would be a meta-enlightenment that teaches us that there is no enlightenment in the classical sense. It is only after a successfully completed psychoanalysis that the asubject receives a place in the subject's worldview and prioritizations. Drive's surprises are allowed to disturb desire's calculating, both as a plasticity vis-à-vis the ravages of the real and as drive's veto against desire's most neurotic ambitions. It is thus quite simply after transcendence that a person can experience *freedom* as a cultural rather than as a natural creature. We are then speaking of a freedom to, not a freedom from the ravages of the real in fantasy, life as a kind of enduringly enthusiastic wait for the next network-dynamical event, connected with an expectation of this event's *novelty* rather than a superiority connected with a fictitious ranking of events: a novelty liberated from every kind of burdening hierarchization. Socioanalytically we express this by saying that a person who is in contact with his own shadow, who senses and has included his asubject within his subjective identity, is a person who identifies himself with the factual truth, and who therefore is ideologically coherent in his worldview and thus also reliable in social relations.

Or as Friedrich Nietzsche would put it: We are speaking of a person who has learnt to live beyond morality's banal extremes *good* and *evil*. So what could be a more flagrant example of Nietzsche's ethical ideal *amor fati*, love of fate, than the subject's affirmation of its own capricious asubject, its mobilist rather than eternalist nature? Enlightenment is in this context after all no literal enlightenment of all the murky nooks and crannies of the subconscious, but an understanding and acceptance of the sublime's creative effect on subjectivity itself. The Zoroastrian word for enlightenment is *asha*, which in ancient Persian means "this is how it works" and nothing else: in other words, transcendence is the psychoanalytical understanding and acceptance of the subconscious mortido as the necessary engine of the conscious libido without which there will be no supply of energy. The subject is, so to speak, completed and shifts its point of departure from desire to transcendence when it realizes that without its asubject it would be nothing. Knowledge of ourselves actually makes us more free, not the other way around. If one wants to call this enlightenment, we will not argue against it. The subconscious does not, of course, steer us via some form of matrichal chaos, it definitely has its own phallic order, namely *the phallic order of the drive*. When we, so to speak, "surprise ourselves," what is striking about the surprise, is not its chaos but rather its tangible order.

"He who loves does not know why he loves what he loves," writes the Slovenian philosopher and psychoanalyst Slavoj Žižek of love in desire's symbolic universe. But Žižek overlooks something central when he gets stuck in desire's endless corridors, and this is that he who loves within transcendence knows perfectly well what he loves and why. And he who loves can precisely therefore appreciate current phenomena, relations or situations ecstatically, fully aware that ecstasy only can be experienced temporarily lest it becomes unbearable, and that it thereafter must be nurtured tenderly as an extraordinarily valuable, libidinally productive memory. Thus within transcendence *the infinite now* can be experienced and then re-experienced as a memory. Enlightenment cannot eliminate desire – nor is this the point – but desire is tangibly altered by enlightenment and *this* and nothing else is the Hegelian shift in perspectives that is sought. Desire can thereafter pass through transcendence – even if not always, still often – and then attach itself to another dividual identity than the cyclically mortidinal or the dialectically libidinal. Thus it is a voluntary *eternal recurrence of the same* that wishes to be exactly that, an eternal recurrence of the same, amused by its voluntary monotony, as a *de facto* mortidinal libido, without making a distinction between mortido and libido. And without this distinction, without being followed either by the urge for prohibition, the shifting of the focus of desire, or the consumption of the object, libido becomes genuinely uninhibited.

We call this *transcendental freedom*. But transcendence cannot be attained and understood without a thorough amount of work and a conscious sacrifice of all ambition if it is to last. That is: if fate, beyond the work itself, proves fairly generous toward the analysand. Transcendence is after all the reward of successful psychoanalysis. Just as it is impossible to determine a particle's position and movement simultaneously in the world of physics, neither can one maintain longevity and commitment simultaneously within the drive system. Actually, this is the very shift from desire to transcendence: In exchange for sacrificing the longed-for permanence – and so to speak settling for a brief ecstasy with a concomitant memory – you actually are allowed to and also able to maintain the attraction to exactly that which desire really seeks, namely phallus itself. The reason is quite simply that desire is limited after the arrival of transcendence. Or to employ the terminology from the *dialectics of eternalism and mobilism* (see *The Global Empire*): The syntheist agent ceases to seek her own eternalization and instead accepts and welcomes her mobilization. Or to reconnect with Nietzsche: What is transcendence if not the very driving force behind the Nietzschean *Übermensch* after God's (welcome) death?

When desire awakens anew within the confines of a reawakened libido, it finds its way back to the event whereit previously found fulfillment to seek an eternal recurrence of the same, rather than moving on to yet another new objective of the non-durable goods type, an objective that tries to conceal that desire deep down only wants to preserve itself and allow the machinery to constantly run on overdrive. Desire only wants itself, it wants to never cease desiring, and brings this about by constantly postponing its own satisfaction in constantly discovering the emptiness of the desired object and therefore, constantly hurrying on towards new objectives and new predetermined disappointments. Every time a desired object is conquered, there is a sense that it was not actually this particular object that was really the desired one, that there always is an essential dimension in the experience that after all is missing, as long as the object finds itself within desire's symbolic universe. When, on the other hand, desire ends up in the mysterious universe of transcendence, it instead attains what it first thought it wanted and *de facto* really wanted, namely the ultimate and definitive limit setter and value creator, phallus itself.

Desire does of course require that the subject attempts to conquer and eternalize the object, but within transcendence the subject stops at cultivating a relationship with the subject, which means that the temporary, high-intensity relationship and not the permanent, low-intensity ownership is what becomes central. This in turn, ironically, means that transcendence forces desire back into drive and makes it function as it once thought it could function there. The dialectics of libido and mortido is completed and we attain *the libidinal absolute*, a "here, but absolutely no further" in the syntheist agent. This Hegelian absolute of psychoanalysis, this existential contentment with the situation, this *union with the divine*, as Sufi mystics would express the matter – rather than some kind of life-denying and self-castrating asceticism – is Eastern enlightenment in its full splendor.

In this context, it is important to understand what makes desire so unique. Prohibition and transgression are, for instance, fundamental sub-drives behind desire. As soon as Man through language is posited in the symbolic universe, the words start to be accompanied by hidden subtexts, virtual agglomerations of ice beneath the dark water, invisible but with great meaning and much power, subtexts that the fascinated subject tries to guess. This becomes apparent to the child when it first understands the ambivalence of language and the symbolic abjection from both the matriarch and the patriarch becomes necessary. Simply put, the child suddenly understands that the matriarch and the patriarch do not mean the same thing when they use the same words. Their intentions with the same choice of words evidently differ, since they build different contexts, use different tones of voice, et cetera, when they utter wordings that at a cursory glance, or in writing, appear identical.

Fundamentally there are two different approaches. The matriarch tests the sustainability of the environment and its reliability through a mobilist use of language. The patriarch, however, puts trust in the words' literal meaning through an eternalist use of language – actively ignoring the obvious but short-term consequences of the word choices – and thereby demonstrates his power through seemingly being able to afford to ignore the consequences of his use of language, the phallic marker *par excellence*. The child perceives the ambivalence between these two language uses and has to navigate between these two positions and form an impression of its own. The subject is awakened and shaped by the path the child chooses between the matriarchal and patriarchal complications. The symbolic gender is shaped when the child in the end is not allowed to play with any compromises, but is forced to imitate either the matriarch or the patriarch in public. And it is only there and then that such secondary phenomena as, for instance, sexual orientation start to attain a structure – phenomena that are subservient to the symbolic gender and its infernally grinding identity production.

The major mistake of the postmodernist project is to not understand that the symbolic sex is at least as strong and adamant as the imaginary or physiological sex can ever be. This does not necessarily mean they are unequal. There is no ethical nor any evolutionary advantage in using language in a mobilist or eternalist way *per se*. Both these language uses exist, both these language uses work. Rather, the diversity of language arises partly in the distance between what language is presumed to represent and what it actually represents, partly in the distance between matrichal ambiguity and phallic unequivocality. It is actually thanks to matrichal ambiguity at the camp fire that language can offer poetry as an instrument, while phallic unequivocality within the hunting party is necessary both for the sake of logic and an exact conveyance of instructions.

Enter here the specific aspect that gave the patriarchy its temporary upper hand over the matriarchy, from the permanent settlements onwards: the new power instrument with which one could erect the platform that constituted the foundation for societally necessary bookkeeping and legislation. In this context phallic unequivocality trumps every form of poetic ambiguity and wealth of meanings. Efficiency could come to good use and prove its utility. The hunting parties and warrior collectives that had acted in the outskirts of the nomadized tribal culture suddenly ended up at the center of society in the capacity of the state's registrars and the custodians of the law. The phallic energy gained a five-thousand-year, temporary advantage over the matrichal approach. *The patriarchal hegemony* was born and has ever since, bit by bit, grown in strength and power at the expense of the matriarchy, since other changes in society have favored it. Thus men's dominance over women has a great deal to do with the character of information flows, and is tied to specific technological, rather than ideological paradigms, a dominance that might well be flipped to its opposite depending on what sort of information flows generate the valuable order in chaos, but hardly otherwise. Whoever best tames the information flows in any given society will also master this society. This applies equally to gender and all other social categories. As it was during informationalism. And thereafter.

6
The dialectics of libido and mortido

When René Descartes formulates his famous proposition "Cogito ergo sum," it spells the beginning of the end of God the Almighty as the guarantor both of Man's security in his existence and of the truth of the knowledge revealed to him, even if Descartes himself makes a Herculean effort to deny the scope and gravity of the coup he stages through what *de facto* entails a divinization of the individual self. Dethroning God is of course a challenging act of rebellion and nothing one does casually; it leads to a great deal of anxiety since it opens the door to devastation in the form of revenge from a God who in the opening stages of the coup still possesses considerable power. Therefore Descartes was compelled to carry out his precarious operation beneath dense layers of camouflage. In this context, the German psychoanalyst Horst Richter speaks of "an ostensible motivation that one with the aid of psychoanalysis can designate as a classical rationalization." That the self now steps forward with these monumental claims must, argues Descartes, be completely in line with God's will; the individual self-consciousness of Man that now and hereafter is the linchpin of all knowledge production in this world must have its origins in God quite simply because ... well, here we end up in yet another of these cognitive blind alleys called "evidence of God," but that are actually circular reasoning with scant evidentiary value in any respect whatsoever, constructed under duress.

In his book *Der Gotteskomplex*, Richter focuses on the transition from the Middle Ages to the new age that eventually results in the modernity with which we have lived up until now. Medieval Man's leap from a pious faith in authority to rationalist self-reliance has generally been lauded as an expression of grandiose liberation and a victory for reason. Actually, argues Richter, it was "fundamentally a neurotic flight from narcissistic powerlessness to a narcissistic illusion of omnipotence." Deposing God made us feel infinitely small, insecure and defenseless – feelings that were both unbearable and impossible to admit. The solution would be repression and what Richter terms "an infantile megalomania." When the child no longer can bear being left in the custody of parents who are perceived as unreliable, it responds by transforming itself in its own imagination into an almighty parent figure. And similarly, says Richter, our civilization suffers from self-inflicted, partly paralyzing excessive demands. We self-medicate with the aid of illusions of total control of the many processes in nature we find threatening. We are no longer safe in our faith in God, but are left to seek solace and edification in human reason that promises divine independence. This boundless self-overestimation neutralizes the panic anxiety over powerlessness. The risks that follow in the wake of rationalist megalomania appear negligible juxtaposed to the fear of having to admit to oneself an infantile dependence on a degraded authority.

Each of us becomes his own God! It is an ingenious maneuver, but the price in the form of isolation and loss of reality – what Karl Marx later calls *alienation* – is steep. The sociologist Norbert Elias speaks of the conception of a *Selbst in Gehäuse* – the encapsulated self – as a bedrock concept in European thinking ever since the Renaissance. The prime example is Immanuel Kant's transcendental subject that even beforehand, by definition, is doomed never to attain the so-called "thing in itself." Which leads to the conclusion, or at least a strong supposition, that Man makes himself unable to participate in a genuine community, that our species instead has developed into what Richter calls "a swarm of egocentrics with concealed megalomania." The objective was to achieve mastery of the world by acquiring useful knowledge of the world. For he who still was loath to completely let go of the venerated authority, Kant staged a deification of reason, to which nature has to adhere. God became reason, reason became God.

He who no longer is sure of having God, must himself become God – that is: must become omniscient and constantly carry out new feats with the purpose of convincing primarily himself that he is not in a position of dependence. This meant that febrile activity increasingly was extolled, while passivity was viewed with increasing and ever more intense disdain, which in turn entailed that the relationship with one's own body with all its regrettable needs became problematic. The downside of the uninhibited cult of reason was – of course – that emotional life was disparaged. And which figure was connected with everything that this society, on its way towards enlightenment and modernity, associated with helplessness and dependence, namely passivity, corporeality (in contrast to intellectualism) and unbridled passions? Who was it that represented all that Man felt compelled to leave behind at any cost? The answer is of course the woman. The man, however, took the opportunity to don all the desirable qualities that indicated a magnificent future where Man could dictate his own destiny. He could of course maintain that he elevates the woman, puts her on a pedestal and accords her the purest, most courtly worship, which naturally does not entail anything other than that he places the institutionalized oppression in an elegant little doll's house and admires himself and his own splendor. Worshipped or not – the woman was routinely likened to an immature child. She was shallow, fickle, foolish – she could not be entrusted with anything of real gravity. That the human self that was knighted by Descartes, possessing god-like reason and a desirable strength of will, assumed markedly male contours, was quite simply right and proper. Gender differences were refined and reinforced.

However, with the entrance of the patriarchal law in society and history – the phallic energy as a recorded and thus eternalized and independent setter of limits and preserver of the divine order *par excellence* – there follows a connection between *prohibition* and *transgression*. As soon as there is a clear prohibition, the desire to be able to violate this prohibition also arises. Drive ignores the prohibition without comprehending the consequences of this act. Desire, on the other hand, is fully conscious of the prohibition, and immediately starts experimenting with the imaginable consequences of violating the prohibition. As a matter of fact, the desire for transgression is so strong that it basically fuels historiography in the emerging feudalist society. The creation myth no longer becomes a story of how God created the world and merrily posited Man in it, but instead a story of how God created a perfect world in accordance with the word and the law, and how Man then violated this order and therefore was thrust into a rebellion against God, how this rebellion failed, and how Man ever since has been waiting for a savior who will restore him, returning him to the original perfect state that prevails within divine law.

This is of course one long imaginary game with *phallus*, where Man is abandoned in desire's eternal trap: I want the phallus, I do not want the phallus, I can have the phallus, I cannot have the phallus. Whereupon libido gets completely jammed up in transgression's cast-iron grip. From now on it becomes necessary to break the law and hope for salvation in order to be able to establish contact with and experience libido in the first place. Everything from feudalism's eroticized salvation doctrine to the postmodern therapy industry is built on this *logic of transgression*, in which Man constantly is reduced from a responsible adult to an infantile child. This state is from a psychoanalytical point of view desire in its purest form, without any form of transcendence. Desire that only can desire itself in a single eternal dance around the exceeding of its own limits. The longing for the eternal return to the safe *mamilla*.

It is important to point out here that it should not be seen as a sign of some kind of adult taking of responsibility to follow the letter of the law in accordance with the neurotic ideal of the browbeaten petty bourgeoisie. There is no reason whatsoever to believe that the law has factual substance, any kind of metaphysical point over and above the concrete phallic exercise of power. No, seeing through the logic of transgression must instead take place from the opposite direction. Transgression can only lose its power when prohibition is revealed in all its miserable banality. For it is prohibition that propels transgression in a near-animalistic way. What is presumed to be behind the closed door will precisely, because of this, have much greater value than what is at hand in front of the door. It is therefore only when prohibition has been revealed as a piece of social theater that the law also, in the capacity of the social superego, loses its attraction. And with this there is also the disappointment over transgression losing its libido. The last holdouts in the crumbling temple of transgression will then be the postmodern sadomasochistic cults with their incessant nagging about leather, lace, rubber, whips and pseudoreligious symbolism – symbols that for the rest of humanity have long lost their transgressive explositivity.

The historical shift from feudalism's moralism via individualism's ambivalence and fantasies about omnipotence to the relationalist ethics of interactivity, means that humanity disposes of the form of pleasure it previously preferred and allowed itself to be dominated by, but that now appears increasingly banal: transgression directed towards prohibition. When nothing is forbidden anymore, when nothing can shock us any longer, then the libido of transgression also dies. And it is precisely here that we humans end up when we are drowned by the uncensored and uninhibited flow of attention-demanding social pornography that is called *the Internet*. The law as the social superego dies, and with it both prohibition and transgression, which now lose all attraction and meaning. *Pornoflation* kills libido and erotic depression reaches pandemic proportions. All that remains is the vacuous hunt for attention for attention's own sake, a kind of grinding quest for affirmation on autopilot.

The nature of the real is compulsive repetition. When it pierces through to Man's fantasy, the real does so with both frenzy and stubbornness. Without bearing any meaning of its own over and above the fact that the real disturbs the prevailing equilibrium. The imaginary universe is built on the *dialectics of eternalism and mobilism* (see *The Global Empire*). It is characterized by a metonymic fluid state. Mobilist chaos must be interpreted as projected eternalizations connected to other equally projected externalizations. Ontic fields of intensity are transformed into ontological phenomena. But at every moment the externalizations are set in motion, both within and between themselves, and must therefore be eternalized anew to become tangible, functional. This means that nothing ever is what it purports to be – strictly speaking there is no being, merely a becoming – which entails that seemingly adjacent phenomena will represent what is being referred to at every moment.

The symbolic universe consists of a language meant to describe the imaginary universe, and the distance that slowly but surely is built up between the imaginary ontology and the enchanted world of language causes the symbolic to soon consist of a long series of metaphorical misplacements. It is already given that nothing is what it purports to be – it becomes clear even in the imaginary universe – but how something is described no longer has anything metonymic about it, but instead constantly misses the mark and therefore must be redefined in all eternity without even being close to hitting the mark. Therefore Man is forced to search for a sustainable meaning on the symbolic metalevel – he builds or embraces ambitious explanatory models that we call *ideologies* – without ever being able to create an enduring meaning within his symbolic universe.

On the other hand, he who is unable to reach the symbolic metalevel at all gets caught up in a chaos that engenders either a psychosis or a desperate search for salvation through complete submission to an arbitrarily chosen phallic idol. The phallic idol becomes the very idol that happens to be available at this moment, regardless of how foolish or destructive this idol is perceived to be by the environment that already exists at the symbolic metalevel. It is actually precisely the dramatic encounter between the submissive's idolatry and the ideology at the metalevel that brings about the fundamentalist reaction in the former – the submissive idol worshipper literally becomes *literal*, the symbolic universe is ascribed ontic qualities, the truth is suddenly available in the form of the words, or if you will, the riddles, that escape the lips of the phallic idol. These words are *the law*, and the law is immune to the hauteur of those who have attained the symbolic metalevel. But if only the law can be upheld, the lost harmony in existence will be realized. These mechanisms are exploited, even as we write this, with devastating efficiency within politics around the world.

This brings us to *rejection*, which is the attempt to externalize internal disturbance. Libido is of course rejection *par excellence*. Mortido requires freedom from frustration and irritation, a state that Man can only experience in total resignation, that is: not until he is faced with his own death. Libido, which thus dominates the drive system up until then, is driven precisely by the tensions that frustration and annoyance over the repressed mortido generate. Libido is nothing but the very externalization of this tension. What happens is that tension becomes an obsession which must have an outlet, and this outlet requires an object onto which it can be projected. This could equally be a *fetish* to worship or an *abject* to hate, the main thing is that the mind succeeds in projecting *the rejective passion* onto the object in question and libidinalizing it. So worship and hatred are not each other's opposites, but rather two corresponding sides of the same coin. The topological opposite of these passions is instead *the erotic depression*, the false mortido, which believes it is missing a libido which in turn is built on the repression of the authentic mortido.

If instinct must be understood as always occurring at the right point in time, drive is instead characterized by something we call *the paradox of the constantly erroneous moment in time*. It should be regarded as an inherent quality of *ecstasy* or libidinal intensity that it constantly turns up when least expected. This in itself is proof that libido is operating there. While instinct governs a creature that is completely unaware of its own mortality – thus the direct connection between cause and effect in the instinctive reaction – drive governs a creature that has understood but has still not succeeded in incorporating its own mortality and whose time is always out of synch. Libido can therefore be described as the reaction to mortido's inability to find its place. The American philosopher and psychoanalyst Adrian Johnston calls this *phenomenal ontogenesis*. It is precisely because the subject not even in its wildest imagination can envisage its own death that its mortality is its fundamental repression. The subject hangs in the air, convinced of its own immortality, while its dark underside, what we term the *asubject* (a concept first used by Czech phenomenologist Jan Patocka), is completely preoccupied with wrestling with the body's aging, fragility and tangible mortality. The subconscious is therefore best described as vampiric. Admittedly, it does not believe in its own death, but still longs for it tirelessly. This reveals that subconsciousness is governed by mortido and not by libido, which instead is directed off to consciousness and its fantasy worlds in the form of the imaginary drive and the symbolic desire.

In ancient Greece, love was divided into three categories: *eros* (sexual attraction), *philia* (brotherhood in its deepest form), and *agape* (divine love). A fourth category is added by the Dutch philosopher

Baruch Spinoza in the 17th century: *amor intellectualis*, intellectual love. The parallels to the four drives are striking: Eros is connected with instinct, philia is connected with drive, agape is connected with desire and amor intellectualis is connected with transcendence. Transcendence of course is the realized dialectics of libido and mortido as complete insight, the ultimate form of enlightenment in a syntheological sense. Hegel's beloved absolute meets Freud's feared libido in a sublime union.

To be human is to be torn between violently contradictory forces. On the one hand we have consciousness, which is dominated by *the will to live* – our almost furious ambition to survive at any cost and in various ways, to make an impression on the world around us as distinct and independent creatures, to appear in clear relief both to ourselves and to our fellow humans. The Latin term for this will to live is *libido*, and when it is at its maximum we experience a sensation we call *ecstasy*. On the other hand we have the subconscious, the domicile of the constantly grinding *death drive* that pulls us towards submission, irresponsibility and extinction – an end to existence's compulsive and demanding change and renewal. The Latin term for the death drive is *mortido*, and taken to its extreme it expresses itself in *depression*: a paralyzing ennui in the face of an existence that inundates us with its boundless diversity. This fundamental conflict does not preclude libido and mortido from being two sides of the same coin, namely human drive in its most elementary form. Further, these two energies are intertwined in an infinitely complex, dialectical system that is developed and continually changed over time. It is never possible to refine them or imagine them as disconnected from one another, but they are part of a dynamical structure of mutual dependence and mutual influence.

It may even happen under certain circumstances that the one is transformed into the other with a measure of regularity. Consequently we have everything to gain – and absolutely nothing to lose – from meticulously studying how the complicated *dialectics of libido and morbido* actually works. Then we discover that mortido is mobilist and primary, while libido is eternalist and secondary. The Taoist philosophers from East Asia express this *dialectical monism* by saying that *yin* – which is the mortidinal, matrichal, negative and passive force – precedes *yang* – which is the libidinal, phallic, positive and active force – before they together form the universal unit called *tao*. Libido is quite simply the both necessary and fundamentally unsatisfactory channel through which mortido expresses itself. Therefore it is only libido that is accessible in consciousness, and when mortido finally penetrates into consciousness and in this way makes its presence felt, it forms what one within psychoanalysis calls a *trauma*. For the sake of pure self-preservation consciousness must encapsulate this trauma and, so to speak, rise above it, and does so in the form of *repression*. The trauma must not exist, and therefore may not exist, so it does not exist. At least not above the horizon of consciousness.

So where and when does this comprehensive but productive denial process begin? Well, the beginning of our trauma, *the mother of all traumas*, actually is our birth. The delivery is painful and therefore harrowing; and entails an unmanageable separation from the *matrix*, which is why the experience quite literally is traumatizing and must be repressed. Therefore birth, according to the French psychoanalyst Jacques Lacan, constitutes *the great trauma*. All the traumatic experiences following birth can consequently in some sense be regarded as a more or less covert threat of a repetition of this great trauma, which even in itself triggers strong emotional reactions. This means that this original repression is activated anew in situations that metonymically or metaphorically bring about a subconscious reminder of the great trauma, which often expresses itself in the form of *compulsive repetitious behaviors*.

In Greek mythology libido is represented by the love god *Eros* and mortido by the death god *Thanatos* (their predecessors within Iranian mythology are called *Ohrmazd* and *Ahriman*, the twin sons of the primordial god *Zurvan*, the Old Persian name of *time* as the origin of everything). Sigmund Freud argues that the struggle between Eros and Thanatos characterizes not only the individual's inner drama – for instance in Freud's own analysands – but also the drama that constitutes the entire human history of different civilizations and their rises and falls. The dialectics of libido and mortido thus drives civilization and thereby ultimately all of history. This means that it is not sufficient to bury oneself in all that pertains to the newest technology if one has the ambition to understand the present in any depth. A complementary and indispensable dimension is added when we understand how the dialectics of libido and mortido has controlled our senses and shaped our cultures throughout history. With this understanding it is then possible to draw conclusions about what expressions these dialectics will assume in the future and – not least – how these dialectics will relate to the technological development.

What we are talking about here is thus dialectics in two steps: In the first phase we have the eternal, incessant fight between libido and mortido within the dividual person, and in the second phase we have the dialectical relation of the bisectional and conflict-ridden person's to the increasingly complicated surrounding world that technological development produces. If we use the syntheological conceptual toolkit to describe the dialectics of libido and mortido, libido corresponds to *Entheos*, mortido to *Atheos*, while dialectics in itself uses *Pantheos* as its arena. Entheos – which represents "the divine within us" – is the metaphysical umbrella term for the timeline, diversity and consciousness. Atheos – "the divine as the non-existing" – is then nothing other than a virtual potentiality, the ontic nothingness out of which both the Universe in itself and all its emergences, including human consciousness, arise. Pantheos is existence as it *de facto* ontically exists in its entirety. Syntheologically the dialectics of libido and mortido is therefore described as though a potentiality in Atheos suddenly is transformed into an actuality in Pantheos, which immediately wants to return to its non-ontic potentiality in Atheos, but when faced with the impossibility of this desire reinterprets yearning for extinction as a will to existence.

This dialectically compelled will to existence is manifested as Entheos, the completed libido, before existence finally returns to its original non-state as the completed mortido. In front of us we thus have a chain of events where Atheos (step 1) transitions to an incomplete Entheos (step 2), after which Entheos is completed (step 3) only to then return to Atheos (step 4), and where Pantheos acts the playing field for this entire dialectical drama in four acts. Or to express the matter psychoanalytically: If subconsciousness had possessed a self-consciousness of its own, this self-consciousness would be desperately suicidal. Without the distancing of consciousness from the environment – fundamentally viewed as synonymous with the distance between subject and object – mortido cannot be transformed into, let alone be interpreted as libido. Thus subconsciousness has a structure that psychoanalysis tries to trace and understand. But by definition it lacks self-consciousness; it is an *asubject*, not a subject. Repression is and must be, from the great trauma onwards, the engine of the will to life. With this, we have prepared the ground for an overarching chronology concerning the dialectics of libido and mortido, a foundation we can use to trace, chart and define the various expressions of the driving force, both in the dividual person (through *psychoanalysis*) and for civilization in its entirety (through *socioanalysis*).

Just as consciousness' will to live masks the subconscious' yearning for death, faith in the irreplaceability of one's fellow human masks the fact that Man's greatest and deepest longing revolves around the *intrasubjectivity* that has been made invisible. The intrasubjective relation is *the sublime*, the encounter between the human subject and its own divine shadow in regard to itself at the moment of death, that is: the syntheological completion of the project Entheos, the personification of the divinity that dwells within the subject itself. This is because the subject's encounter with Entheos entails its *completion*, how it attains a state where nothing else is needed anymore, including otherwise cherished relations to other people and how we interact with them. Actually, it is this experience that enables *the acceptance* at the moment of death, the sensation that the dialectics of libido and mortido has been completed – that *yin* and *yang* at last have meshed as an assuredly empty but still manifested *tao* – and can fade out. The dividual's separation from the tribe is at this moment neither menacing nor anxiety-ridden, but instead liberating. The reason is that the reunion with the Cosmos entails that every kind of distance disappears. This in turn means that mortido eventually is victorious in the battle against libido, whose task ultimately is impossible to carry out. It is actually quite possible to purely logically attain the insight that mortido is the subject's innermost propelling force much earlier than this. But this state can *de facto* not be experienced fully until the acceptance of mortality right before the moment of death. Up until then, the Freudian *repressive mechanism* which causes libido to overshadow mortido, which thus disappears from sight, will dominate the subjective experience of existence.

A consciousness without contact with a subconsciousness is the very definition of a *neurosis*. And the converse relationship – a subconsciousness without contact with a consciousness – is the very definition of a *psychosis*. From this, it follows that the subject primarily perceives itself as being basically neurotic, while it views the external object as basically psychotic, that is: as a chaos that it desperately tries to eternalize. The parallel to Werner Heisenberg's uncertainty principle within quantum physics is striking: the more precisely the subject tries to define itself, the more chaotic and unfathomable the object appears. This indefatigable endeavor to constantly eternalize phenomena induces consciousness to appear to govern the subconscious. This is *the eternalist subject* (see *The Global Empire*), a fundamentally phallic subject that acquires its substance merely from its visible ability to eternalize the mobilist chaos that surrounds the subject. The neurotic state thus considers itself in command of the psychotic state. The subject in itself acts as a stamp of approval to show that the externalization has succeeded. This first phallic impulse arises even in the infant's experience of owning the *mamilla* in conjunction with breast-feeding. Therefore it does not matter if for instance a Buddhist monk sits meditating and contemplates for thousands of hours to attain *nirvana*, such a mortidinally accepting state beyond both enjoyment and suffering still cannot be attained until right before the moment of death. Or to express the matter in a Taoist way: During the course of life *tao* dwells within *yang* and does so in constant movement. But at the moment of death *tao* instead moves over to *yin*, where it is fixated for eternity, as though it, viewed afterwards, had actually always belonged there.

The eternalist subject as such becomes a roadblock to all genuine identification with someone else or something else. It imbues how we view everything, both present and absent. It is quite simply impossible to remember anything from the past – and to an even greater extent to relate to or fantasize about this past – without the memory passing through the filter of the experienced subject, which requires an objectification of memory itself. The subject is the optics through which we perceive and structure the world. All this in turn means that libido tends to be reinforced rather than weakened by the influence of subconsciousness on consciousness, irrespective of how powerful or disagreeable it may appear. Consequently we set libido's prophet, Zoroaster, against mortido's proclaimer, Buddha, within the ranks of the great Eastern progenitors in this area when we claim that repression *de facto* is the whole point. Libido shall exercise its erotically tinged control of the experienced subject up until the moment of death. There are no sustainable arguments for anything else. This means that all attempts to attain the mortidinal state in advance – and to later brag about this as though it were some sort of "enlightenment" – tell us more about the need of boastful ascetics and monks to conquer status within various hierarchies – and to use this status as a platform from which to moralize about their fellow humans – than about something that is pertinent to genuine spirituality.

Zoroaster quite simply claims that it is only the actor who completely accepts repression who also credibly and successfully can seek and attain the truth about existence. Repression is thus the conditions of enlightenment itself and thus also the engine of truth. The Old Persian language *Avestan* even has the same words for repression, enlightenment and truth, namely *asha*. He who in vain seeks some kind of enlightenment beyond repression will on the other hand merely become mired in myth creation, without any ability whatsoever to see the truth about existence beyond the myths. This explains why the phallus constantly returns as the symbol of factual truth while matrix returns as the symbol of the circumscribing mythology. Phallus tells the truth and does so directly and brutally. The most phallic figure in history is therefore the soothsaying prophet – or *Spitama* which is Zoroaster's and Buddha's titles in *Avestan* and *Sanskrit* respectively; that is: the highest rank within the tribe falls to the priest who provokes thinking to go forward – while the matrix is content to reiterate the protecting and security-creating myths for the children who are not yet ready for the phallic truth.

This is what in turn explains why Zoroastrianism, in contrast to Buddhism, was constructed without any authoritarian monk and nun system. For there is nothing higher within Zoroastrianism than following one's own libido. Libido is entirely fundamental for Zoroastrian ethics, which interestingly is totally void of moralist commandments and rewards beyond death. Thus everyone and no one within the Zoroastrian doctrine is also their own priest, shaman, monk or nun. This libidinalized subject experiences a constant frustration connected to a surplus of impulses. For the subject *de facto* ultimately arises through a series of events that results in an unmanageable chaos, where the subject plays the part of the illusory coordinating agency that ties up all the loose ends fluttering freely in the gale that prevails in the turbulent surrounding world. When existence no longer holds together, when incoming impulses appear contradictory and hard to interpret, there suddenly arises the autosuggesting sensation that there still is a subject that unites everything. Self-consciousness is nothing other than a necessary oasis – albeit in the form of a mirage – of order in the chaos of the subconscious. The need for a cohesive worldview compels the emergence of a subject at the center of this worldview, as the dialectical response to the intrusive chaos. The fundamental lack of cohesion is in itself the experience of the subject. Libido must quite simply repress mortido into the subconscious for *the phallic impulse* to create a conscious subject to occur.

As a network-dynamical alternative to *the Cartesian subject* or *the individual*, which Descartes launches in 1637, we call this phenomenon *the anti-Cartesian subject* – or *the dividual*. In contrast to the Cartesian subject, which only can assume the main part in Descartes' individualist and fundamentally megalomanic and highly compensatory metaphysics in the capacity of being the agency that precedes everything else, the anti-Cartesian subject is quite simply a purely illusory cohering waste product of the chaotic process that consists of conflict between different forces and impulses. Or to express the matter with a starting point in the dialectics of eternalism and mobilism: *The dividual subject is* actually the human psyche's *externalization par excellence*. And since libido corresponds to eternalism, while mortido corresponds to mobilism within the dialectics of libido and mortido, it means that the dividual subject also is *the libidinal subject*. The identification with the externalization process generates the libidinal conviction that the subject exists and wants to live and manifest itself. The need for an admittedly fictitious but still functional order in chaos drives the repression of mortido, which then in turn paves the way for libido's explosive growth. The subject process is quite simply the phallic response to the matrichal chaos that surrounds the child and that instills in the child a sense of frightening diminutiveness and exposedness.

Please note that even if the human drive machinery can be divided into the four categories *instinct*, *drive*, *desire* and *transcendence*, libido is still understand by the libidinal subject itself to be one single, coherent force. Feel free to compare with how the four syntheological concepts *Atheos*, *Pantheos*, *Entheos* and *Syntheos* are encompassed within a single relationalist metaphysics (see *Syntheism – Creating God in The Internet Age*), this since the syntheist story is the chain that runs between the four concepts, and not the separate entities in themselves. This means that a libido that for some reason is mentally or physiologically weakened, or possibly even depleted of energy, also is weakened when viewed in its entirety. Culture is therefore full of practices that give advice on how libido should be preserved, accumulated and above all maximized ahead of both circular as well as dialectical events such as hunts, ceremonies, parties and rituals, where a strong libido is associated with pride and status, while a weak libido is associated with shame and guilt. The sex organ between the legs and the sex organ in the head are quite simply driven by one and the same force. The point is of course that the tribe on the whole should maximize its own collective libido. Social theater with its various metaphysical practices therefore becomes a priestly statement on how libido should and must be generated, nurtured and handled, that is: all that is subsumed within the concept *tantra* in Eastern philosophy.

The basis of tribal ethics is thus the story of how libido either serves the collective, and in that case, of which collective it serves, or else is squandered by the dividual, who thus puts aside the interests of the tribe. It is consequently the patriarch's and the matriarch's primary task to jointly tame and supply the tribe's common libido. The moralizing stories therefore revolve around the inner or outer evil that afflicts he who does not adhere to the patriarchal law or the matriarchal custom that regulate the tribe's existence. The gadabout, the thief, the rapist and the whore are all variants of figures who commit this fundamental, libidinal betrayal against the demands that the collective regard as justified and necessary. Mortido is circular while libido is linear, which means that mortido constantly finds its way back to one and the same spot, which it apprehends as the original, while libido never repeats itself but constantly seeks manifestation in the form of new actualities in a future that it never quite catches up with. While mortido implodes, libido expands, and this in turn creates alternately stimulating and frustrating surpluses of libidinal energies.

Libido thus has a dialectical temporality, while mortido has a cyclical temporality. This means that a metaphysical structure built on a dialectical linearity is fundamentally life-affirming, while a metaphysical structure built on cyclical repetition fundamentally constitutes death worship. This state of affairs has ethical consequences: If we are to devote ourselves to a credible enlightenment project in our present digital age, there must be a process-philosophical criticism of Nietzschean caliber of the cyclical society that conducts a conscious or unconscious death cult by placing all its enjoyment in the safe darkness of mortido. In the conflict that prevails between existential freedom and existential compulsion, libido's dialectical repression of mortido is a prerequisite for the freedom of expansion and innovation that the dividual person can acquire. But most people either do not know how to attain this existential state, or else they are – which is only too common – more or less paralyzed by fear at the thought of their own possible freedom, which causes them to insist on living out their days in voluntary house arrest inside the cyclical mortido, bound tightly to the *mamilla*, doomed to constantly repeat the same monotonous pattern of trivialities in order not to miss out on the fervently desired sense of security.

Letting oneself be embraced by the intoxicating freedom means affirming libido's repression of mortido and devoting oneself to direct *pleasure* (comparable to *plaisir* in French) rather than indirect *enjoyment* (comparable to *jouissance* in French) in the mental force field made available. For the sophisticated netocrats around whom this revolves it is consequently not a longed-for extinction that gives life a framework and a (lack of) meaning, but the primary focus is instead *the ecstatic event*, what syntheists call *the infinite now* – first as *experience* and then, above all, as a constantly inspiring *memory*, with a syntheist subject tied to this memory. The event as an idea is quite simply netocracy's metaphysical engine and motivation in the same way that *eternity* as an idea propelled feudalism and its monotheism, and *progress* as an idea propelled capitalism and its individualism. For no matter how much contemporary Man thinks he is yearning for a life after death as well as a better future for his children, these credos have lost their credibility. This shift can clearly be seen in the constant and escalating search for *the transformative event* as the defining experience of the entire Internet Age.

It is worth noting that the female population on the whole is more suited to handle mortido worship than the male population. Women can always turn to reproduction to obtain an easily discovered albeit risky and demanding *raison d'etre*. And since child bearing from a tribal and biological perspective is a collective project – the child does not belong to the mother nor to any male partner of the mother, all such fabrications are merely modern footnotes to history, the child is both the tribe's property and its responsibility from the very outset – the maternal role for the woman gives her an adequate place in a universe that is apprehended as entirely cyclical. If she so wishes, that is. For the man there is unfortunately no such possibility. Without the dialectical libido and its ambitions the man is viewed as completely unnecessary, and this insight is extremely threatening and associated with discomfort.

Right after the phallic separation of the boy from the mamilla – in the midst of a burning, compelled *abjection* – the boy stands helpless, screaming in desperation for any kind of *meaning* to his existence. The boy has of course no central place within reproduction, particularly not now in the age of in vitro fertilization, and his discovery of and fascination with the phallus is at the deepest level the discovery of the dialectical temporality, where phallus is the symbol of the original male existential pointlessness *par excellence*. But this status as superfluous also entails freedom from obligation. Freedom is the great opportunity for creativity, within the very limitations that creativity in turn requires. Here we are of course not speaking of a matrichal psychotic freedom; such a boundless freedom does of course make every form of esthetic hierarchization impossible. It is rather the case of the artistic freedom that arises in the shadow of the phallus, like a playful, fundamental pointlessness within the clear limitations of phallus. And it is, as the American cultural historian Camille Paglia points out, the phallic freedom that *de facto* creates and drives the entire human civilization, which also explains why it largely is exclusively men who have not only are responsible for war and destruction throughout history, but who also have drawn up and built all the numerous, magnificent constructions – bridges, palaces and cathedrals – that surround us today, and are the cultural products we are most proud of.

This transformative discovery of phallus after the lacerating abjection is thus human creativity's fundamental origin. All that is harbored within the confines of a repetition is namely not literal repetition – if that were the case the various species would not be able to develop and natural selection would not have any variations to work with. Within repetition there are also novelties, which both Friedrich Nietzsche and Gilles Deleuze demonstrate and make an important point for in their respective philosophical systems around the productive concept *the eternal recurrence of the same*. The child goes from copying, to repetition as pure repetition, to *imitation*, that is: repetition with elements of novelty, and creativity immediately picks up the pace as there is now play with various, more or less conspicuous, varieties. If we then identify the child with civilization, phallus can be the symbol of pointlessness, freedom, playfulness and creativity. Thus this phallus also is a representative of a dialectical and libidinal worldview – which first and foremost the boy as a future man can identify with – rather than with a cyclical and mortidinal one. It is precisely this experience, which Paglia also notes, that spurs men to build society's skyscrapers as well as its criminal networks. Men excel both in the constructive as well as the destructive.

The phallic man constructs and builds assiduously, but constructing and building in itself is beyond good and evil, as Nietzsche would put it. This activity does not stand above the cyclical and mortidinal, rather its function lies in creating a complement, something that is necessary for the tribe's survival and expansion. This explains why men end up in what best can be described as an existential on/off-position – something that is mental rather than biological. Under the libidinal influence men are connected and develop enormous, creative energies. Under the mortidinal influence these men shrink into little boys who desperately call for the mamilla, pitifully paralyzed in their pining for what in practice is the death dance of breast milk, and they dream steamy dreams of the union with the Cosmos that is mortidinal extinction. It is little wonder that the most prominent goddesses, those who are at the top of the hierarchy, are not connected to reproduction; instead they are feared representatives of chaos and destruction, war and dissonance. Examples of such terrifying goddesses are Kali in India, Mazu in China and in Taiwan, Chalchiuhtlicue amid the Aztecs in Central America, antiquity's Eris (cause of the Trojan War) amid the Greeks, and Discordia amid the Romans.

We might also include in this list the most markedly matrichal metaphor of them all, namely the inscrutable, all-engulfing sea with its oceanic emotions – the phenomenon that Freud with good reason considers the origin of religion, the emotional longing back to the dissolution into the Cosmos: The matrix that ultimately devours the phallus and lays waste to both creativity and reproduction. In this, we find an explanation for why "overgrown kids" are so much more predominantly boys than girls in the network society. And yet we are talking about the boys who really are exposed to the phallic intrusion that leads to the abjection of the mamilla, precisely in the way that the patriarch in the nomadic tribe physically makes sure that this actually happens. For the modern men who have not experienced the phallic intrusion, and who thus never have completed any form of mamillic abjection, there is no real hope that they ever will take on the responsibility of the adult man themselves, and even less that they will succeed in learning how to enjoy the libidinal freedom and the possibilities for acting creatively. This core troupe of the consumtariat instead gets caught up in the life-long, counterproductive cycle that is constituted by hypernarcissism, pornoflation and interpassivity. Women instinctively smell a rat and stay away for good reason. For what is it worth, a phallus without libido – for women, for men, for any human or for society at large? Absolutely nothing.

Observe that neither libido nor mortido in themselves can be described as any form of energy. Libido should rather be described as the agency that is located between the body and the subjective experience that "devotes itself to enjoyment." Mortido is the agency beyond the libidinal enjoyment that does not do much of anything, except create frustration and annoyance for the libido every now and then. This is also why we talk of subconsciousness and not of unconsciousness. There is thus a tangible consciousness of the subconscious' presence in consciousness, but there is no possibility to peer into the subconscious in the same way as consciousness constantly observes and fixates itself. Where the gaze of consciousness inwardly generates the dividual identity, subconsciousness' absence of mind has precisely the opposite effect. Mortido is simply the agency within the subject that makes it impossible for the dividual identity to attain permanence and stability, that which constantly frustrates and annoys, that which invades fantasy as *the real* without for that matter allowing any harmonizing or creation of accord in the whole whatsoever after its invasions. In his book *Disparities*, Slovenian psychoanalyst Slavoj Žižek convincingly demonstrates how the subject constitutes this bleeding aperture, this tangible and bothersome shortcoming in terms of worldview, this desperate attempt to first detach and then associate separate moments and to there and then "make the world hang together." Which of course it does not. And never will.

7
The night of the world as the core of the temporal subject

The European enlightenment philosophers develop humanism, atomism and nationalism in parallel as three different, complementing aspects of the same individualist core ideology. The kinship is confirmed by the etymology: both *atom* in Greek and *individual* in Latin mean indivisible. Up until Immanuel Kant, in the late 18th century, the Enlightenment philosophers constantly return to the human subject as *the enlightened and enlightening brightness* in the darkness of existence, which they all regard as axiomatic. This conviction thus constitutes the innermost backbone of the new religion *individualism*. The indivisible and enlightened human is quite simply the world's savior and the starting point of all thinking as well as every form of action. The Kantian transcendental subject must instead be regarded as a well-executed philosophical completion of the Cartesian subject that is launched 150 years earlier.

However, with G W F Hegel's arrival in the early 19th century, the conception of the subject as the light of existence undergoes a 180 degree reversal. According to Hegel, the subject is instead what he terms *the night of the world*: literally the very opposite of the light that illuminates existence. The explanation is that Hegel is the first Western philosopher who actually understands that mortido lies in wait beneath libido and constitutes its actual driving force. The only thing we apprehend within ourselves is a constant frustration, caused by a vague and ambivalent surplus. But it is this very surplus that *de facto* is our libido. The Swiss psychoanalyst Carl Gustav Jung terms this the surplus of frustration, this night of the world, Man's *shadow*, a terrifying monster that hides behind the subject, where an encounter entails a trial that only the hardiest psychoanalysands can hope to endure. Or to use even more accurate philosophical parlance we call this subconscious night of the world *the asubject* – the part of the subject's very core that it constantly tries to repress – which lurks under the conscious subject, as its main and driving component. So we are talking about *the mortido as the libido's underlying engine*. We would be wise to become better acquainted with this night of the world. Indeed, *knowledge of one's own shadow* is actually a condition for us to be able to trust another person. And it is only after the Hegelian subject's arrival that we can begin to psychologize the subject – the psychological discipline is later developed by Nietzsche and Freud in Europe, and by the pragmatist philosopher William James in the United States, all three influenced by Hegel's process philosophy – which one then begins to do with devastating frenzy, though varying success. The psychologization of ourselves and of society becomes somewhat of a popular movement – the mass activity that more than any other characterizes the emerging modernity. But there was also a need for process philosophers of this caliber – Hegel, Nietzsche, Freud, Jung, James – to succeed with the comprehensive work that is required for the fundamental dismantling of the individualist Enlightenment project.

What we call *the dialectics of eternalism and mobilism* in our work (see *The Global Empire*) is actually the contemporary, phenomenological development of the Hegelian subject's dialectical development via intellectual reflections. The pioneer Hegel opens his dialectics with *the positioning reflection*, which corresponds to fundamental *eternalization*. It is then followed by *the externalizing reflection*, which corresponds to the secondary *mobilization of the eternalization*. Finally Hegelian dialectics is rounded out by *the completed reflection,* which corresponds to *meta-eternalization*, that is: the completed eternalization of all other, preceding eternalizations, set in motion in relation to each other and thereafter perceived, written down and cataloged as a cohesive worldview in the form of *a hierarchy between different levels of fixated movements*. The Hegelian subject then arises as a reaction to this process, as a *negation* of the same. Fetishes and abjects might well function as points of departure for subject production, but the subject in itself is, according to Hegel, a purified negation and nothing else. So without an asubject, no subject at all.

In his books *Less Than Nothing* and *Disparities* Slovenian philosopher and psychoanalyst Slavoj Žižek amuses himself by developing the details behind the Hegelian subject as the night of the world. The fundamental eternalization is a purely formal description of the observed object in question. The ensuing, secondary mobilization of the eternalization corresponds in Žižek to the externalizing reflection that arises when the object is posited in a chaotic and complex surrounding world and thus becomes subject to a host of different interpretations from a great variety of perspectives. Hegel then conducts a philosophical stroke of genius in describing how this reflection "bends inwards towards itself," after which it morphs into a completing, all-encompassing reflection, *the Hegelian absolute*, where the variation in interpretations and expressions is allowed to modify and deepen the object afterwards. That is: exactly what we within the dialectics of eternalism and mobilism call *meta-eternalization*, where admittedly the world ontically speaking always is *a matrichal and mortidinal chaos*, while this of course must be subjected to reflection, after which it in the end ontologically will be understood as *a phallic and libidinal order* (rather than as a particular fetish or an abject), and will be furnished with clear boundaries, thus becoming practically manageable. We thus arrive at a particularly functional platform for an ontology, a phenomenology and an epistemology for dialectical process philosophy. As a bonus we also succeed in positing the libidinal subject where it belongs: at the end, not at the beginning of the dialectics of eternalism and mobilism, as *the Hegelian negation* which constantly escapes eternalization, as a last confused sign of life that points forwards in an otherwise ossified subject process, as *the eternalization par excellence.*

The ego appears as the illusory but functional and seemingly fixed starting point that the mind creates when nothing else is available with which to orient oneself within a world that actually is completely chaotic. And since consciousness merely constitutes the visible but, in terms of scope, insignificant apex of the iceberg that is the human psyche and that otherwise is constituted by the subconscious, it is by definition impossible for every dividual to ever be completely honest with itself or others in terms of drives and desires. Should one then regard this dividual in its social context, the complexity increases exponentially. If one were to put this unavoidable loss of reality into play and multiply it with all the relations that are part of the collective weave, the blind spot would assume colossal proportions. In practice there is no perceptive reflection on the drive machinery, whether we are talking about instinct, drive or desire. What *de facto* does exist is a hodgepodge of partially separate monologues that together constitute an incomprehensive collective drama where all the players constantly are at cross purposes precisely because they lack both self-awareness and perspicuity. Therefore, in this particular respect we speak of the common intercourse within the tribe as *the social theater.* And both farce and tragedy are on the playbill.

For lack of knowledge we fantasize. This is how our brain works; it fills in the many gaps in our perception with assumptions that appear to agree with the patterns that so far have been proven fit for the purpose. The brain is actually completely disinterested in what is actually true or not, it is constructed to most efficiently produce predictions that favor survival. We can then divide these fantasies about ourselves and our surrounding world into two distinct categories. On the one hand we have *the imaginary order* – our more or less functional fantasies about the social theater and the roles we ourselves play within its confines – which is connected to instinct and drive. On the other hand we have *the symbolic order* – the forms through which the social theater reveals itself to us via linguistic statements, artistic expressions and religious experiences – which instead is connected to desire and transcendence.

The lack of authentic contact with both the dividual subconscious and the actual motives of the world around us causes the reality that is played out outside our imaginary and symbolic orders to remain pure chimeras. It is only exceptionally, when the imaginary and symbolic orders are upended by various sorts of annoying surprises, when *the real* penetrates into the fictitious conception of how the world is constituted and underlines the distinctions between terrain and map, that we are reminded that these orders are not, nor can possibly be, anything but fabricated orchestrations, built on fantasies. Moreover, the real is not actually a piece of objective and reliable reality that reveals itself through magic of some sort and thereby exposes the truth about the world for us. Fundamentally it is only the case of a signal saying it is time to adjust structure and substance in the fantasies about the world that we are currently entertaining. This very disturbance as such may be just as phantasmic in nature as the imaginary and symbolic orders that it upsets. Or not. We are not equipped to decide this.

The cosmological correspondences to the human mind's libido and mortido are called *centropy* and *entropy*. We are living in the backwash of *the Big Bang*, which occurred almost 14 billion years ago, and scientific research long had its focus on the evident entropy within existence. But the Universe would not be able to exist had entropy not been balanced by an every bit as forceful centropy, which is the Universe's built-in ability to not only maintain its existence, but also to expand and organize itself by way of ever more complex systems. The similarities are many and the four concepts are highly useful as metaphors for each other. But while centropy and entropy are involved in a direct power struggle with each other – the Universe can in principle expand forever as long as matter and gravity cancel each other out in a cosmic zero sum game of sorts – libido and mortido are pitted against each other in a complex dialectics, where it is the very *ambivalence* between them that keeps the human drive machinery up-and-running.

It is hardly surprising that this state of affairs readily can be expressed in syntheological terms: Atheos and Entheos with all due respect, but it is within Pantheos that the really fascinating things happen, connected to the fact that the venue for the cosmic struggle, rather than the combatants as such, is what piques our interest. Or to express the matter from a libidinal perspective: It is precisely because we cannot actually decide whether we deep down want to live or die that we are so resolutely convinced that we want to survive at any cost. Beyond all these existential passions there hides a simple temporal logic: We can still die if we survive for the present, but we can never live again once we have died unless we take the absurd doctrine of reincarnation seriously. And it is precisely this fundamental imbalance between libido and mortido that gives libido the symbolic advantage in the struggle between these two agencies that appear to control consciousness. Which in turn explains why premeditated *suicide* – that is: the materialization of a mortido that has shifted from its given place in subconsciousness to play a tragic main part in consciousness – is and must be one of culture's strongest moral taboos.

In the colorful and passionate history of psychoanalysis, Jung eventually ends up in numerous and extended conflicts with his master Sigmund Freud. But one issue where Jung goes further than Freud, and where Freud later has to give in and admit that Jung is correct, is the principle of *monolibidinalism*. Jung argues that the mind tends to compress libido into one solid force for maximal effect, not unlike how light in our age can be compressed into one single compact and powerful laser beam, rather than it being fragmented into a number of distinct expressions. This explains why libido is so powerful and convincing where it manifests itself, and also why every form of depletion of libido influences the entire libidinal status dramatically. It is one and the same. When Freud writes *Beyond the Pleasure Principle* in 1920, he is still convinced that libido must be understood as a host of disparate expressions without any direct connection between each other. But in *The Ego and the Id* a few years later Freud takes Jungian monolibidinalism so far that he even describes libido and mortido as one and the same, rather than as dialectical counterparts.

Freud maintains that all drives merely are variants of one and the same drive, and that the only underlying force is the death drive. He thus takes the position that everything fundamentally is mortido. The only thing the organism wishes is that the constantly irritating surrounding world would leave it alone so that it may cease to exist. Libido can thus only be understood as a repression of a stronger and constantly underlying mortido. And in the guise of one big single repression, Libido is one single force irrespective of whether we reduce it to a chemical-hormonal complex or regard it as a logical way of organizing a momentarily limited resource. According to the German existentialist Martin Heidegger, death is not merely the dividual's death from the world, but also *the world's death as world for the dividual.* But the great terror that haunts us humans neither has its origins in the insight of our mortality, nor – which if possible would be even worse – in a conviction that we actually are or might be immortal, with all that this would entail in the form of an eternal future as restlessly itinerant vampires.

It is not a question of horror of the phase shift from libido to mortido within the mind on the deathbed, from the presumed will to survive to an acceptance of and a sense of liberation connected to impending death. No, the real horror instead concerns the past rather than what is to come. It concerns the understanding of how incredibly unlikely *actuality* is, which leads to an icy finger of insight of how incredibly unlikely and therefore cumbersome and exposed the experienced subject actually is. Heidegger's famous state of being, his pure consciousness without direct subjectivity – *Dasein* – has always hung and always will hang on an especially delicate thread. This is *the sublime* along the timeline. In the borderlands between consciousness and subconsciousness, libido hangs by a slender thread in a tempestuous, gigantic ocean of mortido as far as the eye can see. If the eye could see anything that lies beneath the horizon of consciousness. Which of course it cannot.

The shift in question is logical if we view it as an inversion of the dialectical shift within philosophy from German philosopher Gottfried Wilhelm von Leibniz's question "Why is there something rather than nothing?" to Frenchman Henri Bergson's question "Why is there so much of everything?" as philosophy's most fundamental question. Leibniz's question of course takes its starting point in an understanding of libido and mortido as some form of self-evident axioms: Libido is for Leibniz that which is something and mortido is that which is nothing, and thereby Leibniz reduces, which is fully understandable, philosophy's foundation to yet another issue of the philosopher's own subjectivity – the Enlightenment's Cartesian *cogito* elevated to an existentialist axiom. Leibniz thus turns himself into the Enlightenment philosopher *par excellence*, the most prominent of all individualists, where his radical atomism with its bizarre monads follows with a high degree of predictability, along with all the other philosophers who are steadfast in the Leibnizian paradigm.

Bergson's shift of metaphilosophy's focus from existence in itself to *diversity within existence* as philosophy's fundamental inquiry is primarily based upon the insight that the state *nothing* really does not exist anywhere – it is neither possible to think nothing as nothing, nor to think outside time – which means that Leibniz's question is fatally erroneously put. For it is of course built on a non-existing contradiction, which *de facto* makes it completely uninteresting and useless as a basis for further philosophizing. For if the state of nothing has some form of ontic and thus ontological-significance, it definitely does exist, and then it is by definition no longer "nothing"; thus there is no "nothing" at all, either in an ontic or an ontological sense, outside our own highly human fantasy about ourselves as "non-existing existences" before our birth and/or after our death.

Rather, Bergson observes a world of self-sufficient, independent *emergences*, and it is in the middle of the most evident of these emergences for Man, namely Man himself and his immediate environment, that Bergson initially observes a world where there always is dizzyingly much of everything, both lots of realized *actualities* and beyond these an enormous amount of virtual *potentialities*. It is this that Bergson, just like his contemporary Heidegger in Germany, grasps as the really great riddle that philosophy is forced to wrestle with: a philosophy at the center of the world, created by and for Man as an actor rather than as an observer, a philosophy that problematizes all of Man's desperate attempts to orient himself within existence, in the midst of the drastic *momentum*, along the immutable axis of time. In terms of the diversity of existence there is, as Bergson observes, no doubt whatsoever. Diversity itself is hard to top as the starting point of the philosophical discourse. And from Bergson's reasoning it also follows that time is the great mystery of existence and moreover fundamentally absolute, since it is precisely along the stubbornly ongoing, incessant and constantly unidirectional timeline that all this diversity reveals itself and becomes a universe.

Observe that Bergson presents two different dimensions of time in his philosophy: first *local time* which is relativist, just as his contemporary, the physicist Albert Einstein demonstrates. But Bergson also maintains – not least in a classic debate with Einstein himself in Paris in April 1922 – that we must also factor in what Bergson calls *duration* or *global time*, which is absolute – that is: a fixed time for the

Universe as a whole. It is along the endless grinding duration rather than in relative time that diversity upon diversity arises in the ingenious phenomenological system that we develop into *the dialectics of eternalism and mobilism*. On closer consideration it is of course considerably easier to imagine two temporal dimensions than one. First of all, it is reasonable to assume that the Universe operates in a completely different way along its surface than in its core. Along the surface, the expansion of the Universe does not encounter any direct resistance whatsoever, while everything within the Universe is intertwined with everything else, which, according to Einstein himself, influences the speed of relative time (including for instance the movement of particularly local clocks). This is the fundamental distinction between *global time* (or *hypertime,* if you will), with which we measure for instance the age of the Universe itself, and *local time* (or *relative time*), which Einstein from his more limited worldview presumes to be the only dimension of time.

It is striking how global time, with its inexorable forward movement, is so reminiscent of the Lacanian drive, while local time with its relativity vis-à-vis its environment bears strong resemblance to the Lacanian desire. The physicist Lee Smolin and the philosopher Roberto Mangabeira Unger jointly explore both the physical and philosophical implications of these two temporal dimensions in the book *The Singular Universe and the Reality of Time* (2014). For it is precisely this lack of resistance that makes global time so dramatically different compared to local time. It is precisely along the surface of the Universe that the decisive *lack of resistance* arises, such boundless flexibility exists nowhere else inside the Universe, where there instead always are fields and forces that influence absolutely everything and therefore relativize all forms of existence inside the Universe, a necessary *relativization* that thus shifts to an equally necessary *absolutization* along the surface of the Universe.

So what then is this physical absolute if not the only phenomenon in a complex system that both ontically and ontologically is truly one? The British-American physicist and mathematician David Bohm's concept *holomovement* – the Universe as a single cohesive unit within that which, with reference to the process-philosophical pioneer Alfred North Whitehead, is called *the Whiteheadian momentum* – is therefore not just the sum of everything else that is ontic, but also the only thing in the Universe that fundamentally is one single, cohesive and clearly delimited phenomenon. Everything else exists inside this universal *holomovement* and is therefore, as Nietzsche observes, always at least two, multiplicities piled upon multiplicities, which later through Nietzschean perception is arbitrarily eternalized into coherent ontological *phenomena* or *objects*. Metaphysically this has the consequence that diversity does not simply spring from *univocality*, but univocality is the constantly ongoing continuation of *the Big Bang*, which therefore is not only the origin of the Universe but also its still intact and coherent surface, which expands at a speed that might well be tremendously much faster than that of light – and the speed of light is, as we know, simply local time's top speed, that is: the speed at which local time stops – since global time at the surface of the Universe is unaffected by external factors and thus will not let itself be slowed down by anything.

It might be tempting to portray global time as some kind of revenge for Isaac Newton's *absolute time*, but we would probably do well to put off such a celebration for the moment. First of all, according to Newton, absolute time must be regarded as the only form of time. And secondly, absolute time, with its divine design, also has a curiously even pulse, which global time actually need not have at all. Constants should instead be kept to an absolute minimum in a network-dynamical cosmology. This means that it is quite reasonable to imagine *chrono-emergences* during the development of global time. Cosmic history demonstrates several signs of these speed shifts, wholly in accordance with *cosmological emergentism*. The total expansion of the Universe can both slow down and then pick up pace anew. Rather, it is enough to state that we are correct in defining global time as something other, and above all something more stable, than local time, so that we then can establish *univocality* as the fundamental principle of the Universe in its entirety in relation to *multiplicity* as the fundamental principle of the chaotic core of the Universe.

However, this does not mean that the unity of the Universe enables any eternalization of the world as a whole other than that which perception *by default* invents. Admittedly, univocality has the greatest ontic status in the relationalist worldview. But it is a presentist univocality that ontically merely lasts momentum by momentum. The enduring ontological world is nothing other than a phenomenological invention by Man himself. This because the Universe as a whole also is in a constant state of flux, in exactly the constant pace of change that we refer to as *hypertime* or *global time*. However, note that nowhere in this philosophy of time need there be any *infinities*, it is quite sufficient with an arsenal of microscopic and cosmological *enormities* respectively to describe our monist universe with its two main attributes, the univocal surface and the multiple inside. Thus for once the metaphor *celestial body* really is motivated.

What Bergson focuses on is however Man's *experience of time*, a complex phenomenon that mechanical clocks cannot pinpoint, no matter how precise they may be. To him, a strict natural scientific approach to time was viewed as the prison of emotion. For Einstein, on the other hand, it was essential to disregard the subjective experience of time if we are even to have a possibility of capturing what is common in this experience, which is why all the concepts that are used must be particularly well-defined. Synchronizing clocks located in different places mainly becomes a practical problem that induces Einstein to make detailed calculations. Physics and philosophy here speak two different languages about two different things; the lines of reasoning run in parallel and will never meet, not even in a provisional agreement. In any case, temporality is fundamental for the existential experience since it is fundamental even for the underlying dialectics of eternalism and mobilism. Or as Heidegger expresses the matter: "We are time."

Modern time philosophy starts for real with the publication of J M E Taggart's *The Unreality of Time* in 1907. As an antecedent to the debate between Bergson and Einstein 15 years later Taggart posits two alternatives which he terms the B-theory and the A-theory of time. The B-theory is the bedrock of Einstein's beloved *eternalism* – past, present and future are all real, and what we experience as time, and even measure with our clocks, is actually an illusion. That is: it is the case of exactly the same eternalism that we find within the dialectics of eternalism and mobilism, but according to Einstein it is eternalism, not mobilism, that is primary. It is no longer the human being Einstein that freezes a chaotic world with his perception, but it is existence in itself, which according to Plato's obedient disciple Einstein is frozen beyond the illusion of time and all movement and change that is illusory. Precisely when this mysterious freeze is supposed to have occurred is however something that Einstein and the other eternalists never want to answer, for they also maintain that there is no time outside relative time despite its mysterious tendency to only move forward in one direction (one might of course opine that time that merely is an illusion might well be allowed to go wherever it wants to, it would undoubtedly be mathematically tidier, but this is evidently not just any illusion).

Einsteinian spacetime is thus one big *block universe*, a kind of Platonic cosmological fantasy beyond our experience of relative time's immutable movement forward. All dividual objects in an eternalist world consequently must be understood as the sum of what they have been, what they are and what they will be. We sum this up as *the perdurantist worldview*. So do not believe even for a moment – pardon if you will our childish sense of humor – that you merely are whom you feel that you are right now. According to Einstein, subjectivity is *de facto* forced to include everything it has ever experienced itself to be and above all everything it ever will experience itself as being – at this very moment and as long as the subject exists. All change, even in its own subjective identity, is of course according to Einstein a complete illusion. Taggart's A-theory, however, is the foundation of modern *presentism*. Only the current moment is real, what has already happened has at the same time lost all ontic value, and the future is actually both open and indeterministic, precisely because it has not, even in our wildest imagination, happened yet. There are no fixed objects over time in the presentist world, but that which has ontological significance is merely the constantly mutable *fields of intensities* or *phenomena* within what is called *the endurantist worldview.*

Thus according to presentism it is not time, but the Einsteinian block universe that is the real illusion. Time is very real, actually the most real thing that exists, the bedrock on which both space and matter rest. The moment is the center of existence; moreover the entire Universe is synchronized to one single moment on the global axis of time, a worldview that Whitehead and Bohm investigate in detail in the 20th century. Bohm's idea of existence as the *holomovement* should be understood as the logical and total opposite of Einstein's *block universe*. It is hardly a secret that relationalist metaphysics, which we present in this text, is built on presentism and rejects Einsteinian eternalism as a metaphysical axiom. With this, we return to the point where Bergson is correct in his conflict with Einstein in 1922. When we are wrestling with time we are not only forced to accept its ties to the *hyperontic momenta* of presentism. It is also necessary to distinguish between global time, the modern heir to Isaac Newton's absolute time, and local time, which is the relative time on which Einstein's models are built.

However, what Bergson does not seem to understand is that with his revolt against the Leibnizian paradigm he also upends Man's obsession with his own *mortality*. For only a die-hard Leibnizian can maintain that Man's struggle between his own something and his own presumed nothing is the conscious or subconscious propelling force behind the existential project as a whole. A Bergsonian, on the other hand, must in all honesty view himself and his immediate environment as one long series of diversities posited along a mysteriously pulsating absolute duration, where every moment is a struggle to find what Lacan calls *the master signifier*, a single *fetish* or a single *abject* in the perceptive maelstrom onto which the illusion of a cohesive worldview can be latched. It is a case of producing a fundamental *primordial eternalization* on which the entire ensuing dialectics of eternalism and mobilism can be built. This primordial eternalization is thus not primarily a something pitted against a nothing, as Leibnizians from Leibniz himself to Heidegger imagine, but rather an overwhelming diversity frozen in a single phantasmic (fictitious) moment – the event that is called *the infinite now* within syntheology (see *Syntheism – Creating God in The Internet Age*) – to the illusion of one single cohesive object, that is: *the master signifier par excellence.*

All the while it is the enormities in all directions within this ontic, mobilist chaos and not his mortality that frightens and fascinates Man in equal degree. *The sublime* lies lurking – not merely in the form of what Freud calls *discontentment* (*die Unbehagen* in German) but also as what we in Bohm's spirit can call *overpowerment* – in the enormous diversity of existence rather than in its stated existence. An expression of this relation is the post-Bergsonian dividual's fundamental question to itself: How would the much more likely chance of a world without my participation have appeared vis-à-vis the world where the inquisitive subject still seems to find itself and where it unavoidably also participates? The answer to this question is the existential unruliness that the Danish existentialist Søren Kierkagaard in the middle of the 19th century calls *angst.* And how then does Man handle this fundamental, existential anxiety, this infinite fragmentation of himself in the equally diverse directions of existence? He represses it into subconsciousness where his vertiginous *angst* is pushed aside and is compressed into a more or less productive *trauma.*

It is on top of this trauma that Man builds the illusion of an eternally frozen primordial eternalization, that is: the master signifier. During this fictitious eternalization the trauma naturally continues to pulsate menacingly, like a smoldering volcano with constantly recurring eruptions, what Lacan calls *the real*, and this pulsating movement beneath the surface gives rise to perceptions in equal measure of menace and fascination within the confines of Man's fantasies about himself, his immediate environment and, not least, his subconscious. It is this menacing and fascinating underworld cloaked in darkness that is *the sublime*. Hegel's "night of the world," Jung's "shadow," our own "asubject," returns as the innermost core of the subject. Individualism's attempt to depict Man as the cohesive representation of the Universe collapses. We are not just time, as Heidegger puts it, we are enormous and chaotic diversity along the unidirectional timeline. The Bergsonian revolution directed against Leibnizian metaphysics is completed only when we also understand that it is *the sublimeness of Man's existence*, and not his mortality, that maintains the human subconsciousness and that thus also supplies the fuel that powers Man's fantasy worlds.

The sublime is best described as the cataclysmic and ambivalent collision between libido and mortido, the place where ecstasy and terror, beauty and evil meet. The ultimate experience, beyond ecstatic happiness, where happiness is dissolved by linear time's inexorable forward movement – that which within syntheology is called *the infinite now* – is a state of endless sorrow and endless beauty at once. This is the conscious, syntheist moment of death, the experience of looking death in the eye right before the imaginarily autonomous existence's final and inexorable cessation, a cessation that entails mortido's ultimate victory over libido once it happens at a certain point along the timeline. Since this experience imbues everything else in the existential experience – since it masters subconsciousness and colors fantasies long before it actually occurs – we refer to it as *the sublime*. Therefore the metaphysical contemplation must start from the sublime as an axiomatic foundation. Everything else in a person's life receives its specific value depending on its position vis-à-vis the sublime.

The Heideggerian question is quite simply: "What does this mean for me on my deathbed?" Not because anything really means anything at all on the deathbed, but because this is the only horizon against which it is possible to posit a value *before* the moment of death. And not because we are mortal humans, but because we are creatures that are conscious of the explosive force of the sublime, that which boils under the lid of the pot that we call the subconscious. Man is compelled to finally handle all his other conflicts in relation to *existence*, *civilization* and *death* from the sublime's role as a cohesive fetish and/or abject in his fantasy world. Therefore we refer to the sublime as the engine of drive. And drive is fundamentally repellent. It reacts with violent force towards the repellent and terrifying in the sublime. But it is just as forcefully but *subconsciously* thrown back to the sublime as its own engine.

This fundamental element already exists in instinct as a craving for the immediate remedy of an experienced acute shortage. Since drive is equal parts instinct and desire, it also comprises a consciousness, or even a subconsciousness, both about the subject's mortality and its sublimeness. Consequently drive's reaction to *discontentment* or *overpowerment* is not merely instinctive, but also comprises an experienced threat towards one's own identity and its concomitant fantasy worlds. Life is experienced as beleaguered from all sides and the fantasies risk being drowned in the brutal darkness of the sublime. This precarious situation generates an enormous ambivalence. While we are searching for *the phallic gaze*, we are also longing for *patricide*, the murder of the patriarch. Even while we want to stay within the mamilla's mendacious but comfortably undemanding security we are disgusted by it and want to be thrown out into the coldness of freedom's unknown outside mamilla – in the same way that Adam and Eve were thrown out of the Garden of Eden – where we can only hope that phallus awaits in the tempests of the sublime.

This means, first of all, that freedom in all respects is a particularly double-edged sword. In his famous work *Escape From Freedom* (1941) the German-Jewish psychoanalyst Erich Fromm, who originally was affiliated with the Frankfurt School (The Institute for Social Research), argues the thesis that the liberation from God and external authorities, as from inherited traditions and conventions, that follows from individualism and the Enlightenment, can result in an urgent anxiety and a feeling of helplessness akin to the infant's paralyzing insecurity when it separates from the womb. Freedom is far from unambiguously pleasurable, it can have catastrophic consequences when the terrified collective are exposed to political manipulation and, as the German petty bourgeois did during the chaotic 1930s, in social masochist frenzy willingly submit to extreme totalitarian oppression simply so they could at any cost avoid carrying the terrible burden of freedom. The ravages of Nazism are – this will be the contemporary Frankfurt School's official position – a sadomasochistic psychodrama that is played out in the theater of the societal collective. This massive submission is connected with enormous pleasure. It expresses itself in that the estheticization of politics reaches unsuspected heights. "Humanity's increasing alienation vis-à-vis itself has reached a degree where it is able to experience its own annihilation as an esthetic pleasure of the first order," writes the culture critic Walter Benjamin, loosely affiliated with the Frankfurt circle, in *The Work of Art in the Age of Mechanical Reproduction* (1936).

Secondly, this fundamental ambivalence, regarding freedom, means that it is drive that is speaking. Unfortunately, it gives us no indication of what direction we ought to follow. Drive merely rages within us, spurred on by the mind's ambivalence vis-à-vis its own existence. And its unpredictable violent behavior makes us long for patriarchal banishment, the phallus as the limit setter *par excellence*, a banishment that however only increases ambivalence – prohibition increases rather than decreases attraction – and thereby also increases drive in itself. This is the dialectics of libido and mortido at full volume, not as a struggle between life and death, but rather as an endless, ambivalent dance above the sublime in subconsciousness. The sublime is quite simply the smoldering stones on which libido dedicates itself to the bizarre dance that keeps us alive. A dance where one single misstep is enough – slipping on a single stone – to be devoured by the bone-chilling mortido that lurks below.

If socioanalysis is built on *the dialectics of libido and mortido*, phenomenology is built on *the dialectics of eternalism and mobilism*. And unsurprisingly there is a plenitude of parallels. Libido and eternalism display a kinship with each other inasmuch as they first and foremost are chimeras, if extremely productive and necessary ones. They are ontological but not ontic, to put it in a Heideggerian manner. That is; they only exist as necessary pawns in our consciousness and in our perception respectively. Beneath the thin libidinal veneer, in the subconscious, mortido rules. And beneath the thin eternalist veneer, in the material reality that envelops and permeates us, mobilism rages unrestricted despite Einstein's Platonic fantasies. Mortido and mobilism are not just ontological, but also fundamentally ontic. Thus they are always guaranteed to win in the end – just as mortido and mobilism ruled the world with an iron fist before we were born – and our subjectivity is nothing other than the sublime, ambivalent and thus libidinal protest against their unavoidable, coming victory.

The fact is that a world without our consciousness and without our perception would not contain any of these dialectical relations, it would be a world with a single furious mortido in a single mobilist chaos. Dialectics in all its variants arises only in our relation to the surrounding world. We perceive mortido as a libido because we are being lured into trying to multiply and survive as libidinal subjects. And we perceive mobilism as an eternalism because this surviving creature that succeeds in procreating also must be able to orient itself phenomenologically and communicate with its surrounding world only to succeed in surviving and procreating. But neither libido nor eternalism in themselves bear any higher values whatsoever over and above these fundamental, logically deduced functions. And nor do they even exist outside our necessary but illusory fantasy worlds. So Plato, like his disciple Einstein, is fundamentally wrong. Everything that actually exists, lives and has meaning for us is to be found inside the cave itself; outside the cave there is merely frozen death.

8
In search of the lost phallus in the digital plurarchy

Libido is a massive and often violent force. The opposite of the libidinal society is of course the mortidinal society, which by definition is *decadent* inasmuch as it is built on *the subconscious attraction to one's own downfall,* about which the German philosopher Walter Benjamin speaks in his essay *The Work of Art in the Age of Mechanical Reproduction* (1936), an attraction that increases as humanity's alienation vis-à-vis itself grows. The conflict between these two forces – the libidinal and the mortidinal – creates enormous tensions. An example every bit as illuminating as it is absurd of the contradictoriness that arises as a result of this eternal tug-of-war, is when a secularized society calls upon the practitioners of a violent and violence-glorifying religion to act peacefully and tolerantly toward society's many deviant groups, despite the religion in question proclaiming its inherent libido which is anything but tolerant towards deviations. Which is in the nature of the matter, because the libido that allows itself to be grayed out through compromises and vagueness in part loses ground to other groups in the incessant Darwinian fight for survival between different memes, in part also suffers defeat in the incessant tug-of-war with the mortido that is driving this compromise and leveling out.

The secularized society thus requires, wholly in accordance with its equally authoritarian and decadent discourse, that the religion, which by its' own nature is religious, should act as though its adherents actually are not convinced and not believers at all, but actually are secularized and dressed up in masquerade attire, that is: a notch more decadent than the decadent themselves. This requirement might appear reasonable and appealing, at least in accordance with the secularized discourse, but it is built on a profound ignorance of what religious faith is and how religious communities function. It is also impossible to carry out, of course, regardless of what material advantages one might offer to tempt with and regardless of the threats one uses as deterrents. Mortido meets libido terrified at its phallic ascension, but libido can never apprehend mortido with anything but disdain for its literal sexlessness. Which entails that mortido's recurring demands for self-inflicted castration of both ideology and activism lead to recurring conflicts between, on the one hand a decadent, multicultural and thus also decorationist society, and on the other hand its monocultural rivals that by virtue of being considerably more libidinal also are considerably sexier and thus find it easier to enthuse their adherents and generate a potent social identity. Or to express the matter as simply and as crudely as possible: *The virile rod of the wilderness will always emit more powerful enticements than the guarded tittle-tattle of the stylish salons.*

This relation between *libidinal potency* and *mortidinal decadence* explains why the Internet Age's strictly delimited, militant subcultures offer the perfect hotbed for recurring virtual as well as physical conflicts with the surrounding world, where it is the most libidinal and not seldom minoritarian alternatives, not the watered-down, lifeless, mortidinal and majoritarian organizations that triumph in the most intense conflicts. Thus it is the case of an extensive and escalating culture of violence – often in the form of perverted guerrilla cults, intoxicated by their own romanticizing rhetoric – and not of some kind of anarchist realization of a global, pacifist dream, which both the libertarian right and the post-Marxist left preach in their naive blindness. The Internet Age is *plurarchic* rather than democratic (see *The Netocrats*). It is governed by a *plurarchy* of various nodes in a gigantic, flattened chaos, which lack the ability, incentive and will to understand each other and/or cooperate for the common good, since it is precisely in the isolating distancing from competing power nodes that the coveted libido escalates. Indifferent *capital* is displaced by passionate *attention*, for the simple reason that in the plurarchic chaos that the dynamics of the Internet brings forth, it is, naturally, libido, not the politically correct ideology, that exercises the most powerful force of attraction.

Moreover, there is the fact that plurarchy in itself efficiently precludes all attempts to maintain a cohesive global arena. The corrupt nation-state, torn asunder by bureaucracy, collapses – no nation-state has ever, irrespective of the ruling regime's ideological color, scrapped more laws than it has produced – when all the central players in the global power game turn their back on it (*The Global Empire* contains a more thorough analysis of this phenomenon). Moreover, it is also a development that is accelerated by the emergence of the digital cryptocurrencies and of the gradual erosion of state taxation. The social theater is therefore fragmented into innumerable separate subcultures, which in practice lack closer connections between them, and which at best merely keep sporadic checks on each other via data-anthropology and sensocratic surveillance systems. When the old, democratic society because of a string of collaborative factors can no longer be maintained and is forced to admit its obsolescence in one area after another, we are instead forced into *the plurarchic society*. The question we should rather put to ourselves is whether the democratic society even existed, and in particular whether it existed in a way that even remotely comported with its own marketing campaign, or if the only reasonable view is to regard it as a stale myth. Anyway, the new (dis)order is primarily occasioned by the Internet's flat and incomprehensive comprehensive structure. Plurarchy offers no short-cuts. The strongest power position in the nodalized society is the apex of the network pyramid. But no actor has over and above this local virtual power any kind of quasi-divine overview of the entire plurarchy. Never previously has the Nietzschean god's death been more obvious.

The pattern that emerges when we start to analyze *big data* in a meaningful way is that everybody lies (which also is the title of a popular book on the subject: *Everybody Lies* by the economist and philosopher Seth Stephens-Davidowitz). Everyone lies to their friends, bosses, children and parents, siblings and cousins, boy- and girlfriends – indeed, everyone lies to everyone. Above all, everyone lies when they are interviewed in various surveys on habits and attitudes. And everyone lies, not least, to themselves. People lie about how much they eat and drink, they lie about how often they have sex, they lie about everything in a more or less subconscious ambition to fit into their own fantasies about whatever the collective considers normal and/or desirable. And all this lying of course means that our conceptions of what actually is normal and desirable can only be based on a hodgepodge of pure nonsense. The emerging *data-anthropology* reveals not only everything about Man that we previously only had been able to guess. Above all, it reveals how fundamental lying and wild imaginings are to Man's self-image and worldview.

Wherever we set our gaze when we are on the Internet we risk being drowned by a tsunami of information that is only to a tiny extent requested by anyone. According to information whose veracity is hard to assess, we humans daily generate an amount of information that corresponds to circa 2.5 quintillion (18 zeroes) byte with all our punching of keys and tapping on screens. This means that the amount of information increases to roughly the same extent that the individual person's possibilities of relating to this wealth of information in a way that creates meaning and is productive decreases. The increasingly coveted and precious scarce commodity will therefore be order and overview. Facts on one subject or another that previously might have been the basis of brilliant research careers are today immediately available for free by punching a few computer keys, at least for those who know where and how to find them. And this is the trick: seeing the desirable needles in the gigantic haystack that is the Internet and knowing how these best can be collected and made to interact to be of best use.

So what then is the historical symbol for overview and structured force, in culture and throughout history, if not the *phallus*? The irony could hardly be any more striking: At the exact moment when phallus becomes brutally ejected from the social theater – not least because of feminism's anti-patriarchal project, an unprecedented ambitious patricide which nevertheless falls short of its purpose – it once again makes a celebrated entrance on the same stage, more forceful and coveted than ever. Which could hardly surprise anyone who has studied cultural history to any degree. If industrialism's fuel was patriarchy's capital, informationalism is instead powered by the attention of the phallus. Power no longer belongs to the person who owns the material resources, or even to the person who communicates most efficiently about these resources, but instead to the person who personifies phallus, that is: the person who has the ability to mobilize libidinal attractive power. It then becomes more important than ever to study and understand how our relations to the phallus at various levels *de facto* are structured. To be able to explore these relations we must accompany psychoanalysis and socioanalysis to our dividual and existential origins, *childhood*, and our collective and biological origins, *the nomadic tribe*.

The void at the heart of every dividual identity is filled with fantasies of the three fundamental symbols: *Matrix* symbolizes the internal and the pathological relation to the internal, *phallus* symbolizes the external and the pathological relation to the external, while *mamilla* symbolizes the conservative comforting connection to the internal, actualized by the ambivalent threat from the external. Mamilla (the female breast in Latin) is literally speaking the necessary transition from matrix (the womb) to phallus (the man's penis or the woman's body in its entirety), after which autonomous life is then lived in the shadow of the phallus up until the dividual at the moment of death is thrown back into matrix and its "non-existing existence" (*Atheos* within syntheology) where there is no narcissistic subject production (*Entheos* within syntheology). But at the same time, mamilla symbolizes the dividual's dream of not having to grow up, of freezing the mental development and continue living in comfortable mendacity by remaining a child inside an adult body, something clearly demonstrated in how Christianity infantilizes the believers and expressly calls them *the children of God*. Thus religion, most closely personified by the Virgin Mary, becomes one big maternal breast that provides solace and security to an infantilized, frightened and passivized congregation, in contrast to how Judaism proclaims a highly phallic *people of God* that themselves strive to build the eternal temple through their own devices.

As we know, nature takes care of the first abjection from matrix to mamilla – *the natural abjection* – that is: biological birth itself, very well on its own. The body usually knows what it is to do. We are born and are thus inexorably separated from the maternal body whether we want to or not. But then it becomes more complicated. The transition from *obsession with mamilla* to *fascination with phallus* is constituted by *cultural abjection,* and since this requires our own active participation it becomes considerably more complicated. Now the process does not run of its own accord anymore. The spoiled child that refuses to grow up is of course a flagrant example of an infantilized person who refuses to let go of the mamilla to reach for the phallus; the phallus has for some reason or other never taken over the child's imaginary universe. The dividual is caught in the infant's oscillation between matrix and mamilla – for instance in a actual physical fluctuation between a home and an institution – without moving on to the adult fluctuating between mamilla and phallus, that is: the security that the tribe's community offers, balanced by the adventures of adulthood in an unpredictable and demanding reality.

Problems arise in that the encounter between the child and the patriarch never happens, so the child never learns to long for the adult identity with all that it entails in the form of both freedom and responsibility, so the world that is outside the longing for matrix and being comforted by mamilla only can appear unpleasant and frightening. The person who from the outside appears adult remains infantilized. It is however not just the odd dividual that fails to achieve or constantly puts off cultural abjection; entire societies might well falter in this decisive respect. This is *the decadent society*, a society that literally is in decay, heading for its demise, through its collective refusal to leave the mamilla and submit to the phallus. A test that reveals whether a society is so infantilized that it displays decadent tendencies involves a test to show whether the society acts and apprehends itself as mamillic rather than phallic. Then it is a case of answering questions such as the following: What symbol dominates the cultural discourse? Are there still any phalluses that have any real legitimacy? Has even the belief in phallus disappeared? Does society celebrate its venturesome pioneers and entrepreneurs, or has one completely embraced an ideology of dependence according to which one as a citizen has the right to have one's own needs met without reciprocally achieving or sacrificing anything that actually costs them?

We are speaking of *the decorationist society*, a society whose only ideals are of what usually is called "self-actualization" and of course are totally lacking values for which any person is prepared to sacrifice himself and die. In societies of this kind, many have greeted the Internet as a possibility or even a promise of having constant attention from one's immediate environment, without oneself having to either prove any tangible talent or make any form of strenuous work effort – that is: as one big mamilla in a world without phallus. There is consequently a great risk for a harsh and unpleasant awakening the day it is finally clear that the attention one desires has been illusory all along. These disappointed and bitter consumtarians will after their awakening soon become aware that the jostle on the social stage entails that everyone sees himself as an artist of sorts, but that the audience attention for all these amateur productions *de facto* is non-existent; we are talking about productions that to all intents and purposes completely lack value. For this reason, among other, ressentiment against the digital world grows explosively and constitutes one of the confused consumtariat's prime driving forces. The last thing a logical person wants to give their valuable *attention* to is after all another person's desperate *hypernarcissism*.

The current development is connected with the fact that the Internet by nature is a matrichal, not a phallic medium. The organization is flat, the communication flows that thus are made possible constitute a gigantic, amorphous ocean of unstructured impulses in all possible directions. So now that the world and society, communication and identity creation, are shifting to the digital sphere, it means that all the old, hierarchical power structures are crumbling, sending us into *the plurarchic state*: a constantly mutable chaos with no clear patterns with which to orient oneself. The only thing that even resembles provisional benchmarks is, at best, a number of dynamical network nodes – this is why we talk about *a nodalized plurarchy* rather than a completely unstructured anarchy – that can function as a kind of provisional phalluses. For just as capitalism caused a concentration of people in the physical landscape, the macrotrend that is called *urbanization*, informationalism causes a concentration of valuable information in the virtual landscape, the macrotrend that consequently is called *nodalization*.

The Internet is first and foremost a place where everyone chats away incessantly without anyone else listening. That is: plurarchy is the Internet Age's network-dynamical equivalent to the nomadic tribes' matriarchal sphere, but without any complementing, patriarchal correspondence. The Internet is namely an ideal place for endless conversations, imaginative conspiracies and more or less substance-free speculations, but it is a nightmare if what really is needed is functional hunting party hierarchies, strategic planning and prosperity-creating infrastructure constructions. And the question is how one after all can make people listen sufficiently long and with sufficient focus to achieve a well-organized collaboration around various comprehensive projects that are important – maybe even decisive – for the common good. All this is made even more difficult by all the post-individualist actors tending to drift around without direction, held back by the feeling that something more interesting could always happen somewhere else, maybe around the next corner, which expresses itself in an intense fear of making a commitment to various forms of long-term undertakings: what the American historian Christopher Lasch as early as the late 1970s with foresight calls *commitment phobia*, which has become the Internet Age's most dominant social pathology.

In a society where no one dares or feels called upon to commit to any form of ideal or even to any enduring relationship, the necessary prerequisites are lacking for what the French philosopher Alain Badiou calls *truth as an act* – the syntheist basic requirement for an authentic life (see *Syntheism – Creating God in The Internet Age*). This fear of the phallus, which of course is the very symbol of the impelling ideal, faithfulness vis-à-vis vision as more important than the subject itself, does not only consist of what is most apparent: horror at the castration that is entailed in being enfolded in the symbolic order. No, above all it is about the fear whose origin lies in how the phallic gaze mercilessly reveals the heart-wrenching emptiness in a post-individualist state of aimless wandering from the one to the other. It is the phallus that decides where the line is to be drawn, which also means that it *is* both the very boundary and the boundary-setting that the act embodied. Thus, through the agency of the phallus, the nothingness of boundlessness becomes clear to anyone with the ability and courage to see.

Even in its absence, the phallus' libido is conspicuous, which signifies that it is libido and only libido that can give meaning to anything at all. For many it is then considerably more pleasant to close one's eyes and think of something else. One might, for instance, hide behind hypocritical humility; one can embrace late capitalism's motto above all others, that which in the market insists "the customer is always right," and within politics: "the voter is always right." Which may sound congenial and democratic, but is in fact a major swindle. That the customer possesses the money you aim to put in your own pocket is one thing, just as the voter has the vote that you want to snatch away from your political opponent, but this of course in no way means that these infantilized consumtarians are "right" in any proper sense about anything at all. They want to have their needs and wishes satisfied with minimal effort in return. They have no idea, or pretend not to understand, that the shockingly cheap piece of clothing has been manufactured by child laborers in the Third World, and want to satisfy their own special interests without, as is proven by science, having much insight into how an economy works and how wealth is produced. So you choose – if you're selling something or if you are a politician – for purely selfish reasons, to play along and pretend to be Santa Claus bringing presents in order to ensure a transaction. But in what respect would this mean that the customer or the voter actually is "right"? They know nothing, or next to nothing.

He who wants to understand the world somewhat better turns to an educational institution for adults and does not listen to infantile wishful thinking. In other words: it is necessary to bid farewell to the mamilla and instead focus on the phallus, particularly if we are to handle living in the complex global empire that the Internet generates. In crassly economic terms this means that precisely what the phallic energy represents – visions, strategies and order in what otherwise would be a monumental chaos – becomes an infinitely desirable scarce commodity in the digital plurarchy. And in the capacity of the most desirable scarce commodity, phallic energy becomes the most highly valued phenomenon on the Internet – to the extent that it even can be summoned up, it is exclusively reserved for the most powerful high-status networks in the global network pyramid (see *The Netocrats*). The need of a hierarchy, direction and structure in the social arena has never been greater, quite simply because the fraying energies that pull societies and collectives apart never have been stronger.

This is the reason why the communication flow management becomes more important than the production of goods and services, and that this *curatorium* takes over and drives the economy of societies. In its simplest form it consists of cheap, wholly automated management that is conducted with the aid of well-used search engines; in its most valuable and exclusive form it is embodied through *the curator* as a tribal personality type. To the extent that the curatorium and its coveted *attention* even can be bought on the market, that is. Selling one's credibility for money requires a sensitive balancing act, and the risk is always that this credibility is devalued. Social and cultural talent is all that matters, and if this talent also can attain full network-dynamical exchange through being combined with critical thinking, we have found an optimally potent phallus for the Internet Age. The question is whether this phallus even is possible to discern in the chaos that plurarchy gives rise to. Or to express the matter syntheologically: Is it possible to build a credible Syntheos as a benchmark towards which one can strive or orient oneself?

Interestingly, the digital plurarchy has a suitable correspondence in the Bulgarian-French psychoanalyst Julia Kristeva's *theory of abjection*. Before turning one, the child must be furnished with the tools that it needs to gradually detach itself from the mother and start the journey towards an assuredly risky but also promising autonomy. Kristeva argues that the mother must be transformed from being the child's warm and secure matrix – albeit one that also shields it from reality – to becoming a hated and eventually also rejected abject. The reason for this is that the child for the sake of its own survival must liberate itself from the mother and leave what it shares with its mother – what Kristeva deftly calls *the semiotic soup* – to instead go out into the world as an autonomous, fit-for-survival dividual. But this necessary abjection can only be carried out if the child is aided by a lever, and this lever is the *phallus*, the often patriarchal or father-bound symbol of order and boundary setting in the matrichal chaos. In other words, this means that there will be devastating consequences if this necessary phallus is not at hand when it is needed, which might mean that abjection does not occur. The boy will not have a father figure to imitate, the girl will not have a phallus to eroticize. The child falls back into permanent *infantilization* – boundless, disrespectful, childishly frustrated and above all without any libidinal will towards constructiveness. Both psychiatric and psychoanalytical diagnoses start to rain down. This means that abjection with the aid of a strong and clear phallus is the child's only path to an independent and continuously developing adult existence, though one that is still not without risks and perils. The alternatives are vacillating stagnation and, at worst, psychotic collapse.

Every communication-technological revolution has given rise to its doomsday prophesies. What may appear as a welcome blessing, a gift from the gods, is actually a curse. By accepting the offer, we humans start to dig our own graves. We are actually, just like Faust, making a pact with the devil and paying with our souls, which depletes us of that which makes us human. The perspectives vary, but the reasoning tends to follow one and the same main track: the new technology undoubtedly supplies a host of practical advantages that facilitate our storing and search for information of any kind, and it frees up human brain capacity since we can outsource various functions from our own heads to various sorts of technological innovations. We can, at least in theory, use this liberated brain capacity to make the world better and our lives richer.

But there is a price to be paid, argues this long tradition of critics starting with Plato, and this price is a deterrent for us. Plato's dialogue *Faidros* contains a story of written language's mythical genesis. Here his spokesperson Socrates clarifies that he is skeptical and of the same opinion as the wise king Thamos of Egypt, who was thoroughly unimpressed by what letters could achieve. No, conversely Socrates sees letters as a direct threat to genuine knowledge. He who learns to read, also learns to neglect his own memory. One allows oneself to be "reminded by alien signs from the outside, not from within one's own power." Therefore Thamos and Socrates (and Plato) regard writing as a "drug" that instills in the addict a dangerous illusion of being wise and blurs the boundary between apparent and true wisdom. Nowhere does Plato make note of the ironic aspect of this criticism of letters and texts being conveyed to the reader through letters and texts – what else? This however does not necessarily mean that the criticism is uninteresting or unfounded. As we have maintained countless times in our books, there are both advantages and disadvantages to every pervasive information-technological change, depending upon perspective. Some become winners, others become losers.

The printing press also encountered similar resistance in its day. An abbot in the Benedictine monastery in Sponheim, Johannes Trithemius, defends the monks' painstaking copying of texts by hand in his writing *De Laude Scriptorum*. It is precisely labor and slowness that is important, argues the author. The process gives the monk occasion to sink into long contemplation, which is the only way to create complete understanding of the content. Further, he maintains that paper is transient, while what is written on parchment lasts forever. Producing and consuming printed books entails – according to this view, which perhaps is not totally void of self-interest – that one trivializes and vulgarizes learning and cultivation. But of course this attack on the printed book was spread in the form of printed books, or else the dispersal of the idea would not have gotten very far, at least not in those days. As a Catholic our abbot had every reason to fear what printed books and increased literacy could mean to the only religion that he could regard as true, as history in terms of reformation, inquisition and religious wars would later prove. There are, as mentioned, both advantages and disadvantages to every technological innovation of any importance. It solves a number of old problems, which is the reason for it making a breakthrough and gaining a foothold in culture, while it also creates a number of new ones.

Criticism of the Internet is often massive, which indeed can be seen as an understandable reaction to the exaggerated and one-sided optimism that the digital communication technology's boisterously enthusiastic cheerleaders express on their end. One might, for instance, concur with the progress evangelist Kevin Kelly, who argues that the Internet is the answer to any question anyone could ever want to pose, and who in the book *What Technology Wants* maintains that Man today lives in a symbiosis with his machines, and that criticism against technology therefore can be interpreted as an expression of self-hatred. But what is to say that self-hatred necessarily is unmotivated and objectionable? Nothing! The very basis of Kelly's excitement about the new technology, and which makes him sense a glimpse of God in his cell phone, is that it constitutes a connection between his own brain and billions of other brains. The underlying assumption is that many billions of interconnected brains together constitute an emergent phenomenon in the form of an unabashedly dynamic, collective intelligence. However what never occurs to enthusiasts such as Kelly is that the incessant murmur from all these attention-thirsty brains might constitute a distraction or environmental pollution.

Skeptics, such as the science journalist Nicholas Carr in the noted book *The Shallows,* maintain precisely this. Taking his starting point partly in media theorist Marshall McLuhan's observation of how the tools we humans have designed later shapes us humans – it is technology that ultimately determines how and what we think, it is not our thoughts that in any reasonable sense determine technology – partly in comprehensive neurophysiological research, Carr observes that the cost of the Internet's many blessings is steep. This in turn hinges on the human brain being so highly plastic and adaptive to its environment, which is at this moment going through the transformative changes connected with the Internet's expansion at the cost of other media. The human brain is thus going through a continuous, extremely comprehensive adaptation process under strong pressure from a host of new stimuli. A consequence will be that the brain's function gradually becomes less "linear" in a McLuhanesque sense, less adapted to concentrate long and hard on following complicated arguments in several successive stages, such as those for instance being presented in printed text on the pages of a book (the readers that have been able to follow us all this way are to be congratulated; you will surely manage through the rest of the text as well).

According to the research that Carr refers to, we humans have in a short period of time become worse at focusing our attention during long-term, uninterrupted information gathering, since we have become accustomed to and dependent upon constantly being distracted by something completely different. Some take this to mean that the Internet in this way makes us dumber and more poorly equipped to see through disinformation and manipulation. The absence of structures that create order harms Man; therefore the increasing leisure time that follows from the automation and digitalization that wipes out job opportunities and annihilates entire industries is detrimental, even if we through political reforms can ensure that people manage to support themselves. A tedious and monotonous job is in this respect a lot better than no job at all.

Dementia and psychosis are at our doorstep if we send our brain on a permanent holiday, particularly if this holiday to a great extent is spent drifting about on the net: a flat ocean of non-systematized communication flows – in this, one can really speak of a "semiotic soup" in Kristeva's sense. Sooner or later the owners of the brains that become excessively reprogrammed in this environment will be infantilized, particularly if they never encounter the phallic gaze and are assisted in escaping the matrichal chaos and entering the world as autonomous dividuals.

Observe that there are no guarantees. The fact that phallus is necessary in order to ensure an adequate development process of the personality does not mean that it is automatically available, of course, nor that it is possible to mobilize with just some good intentions. Rather, the situation today indicates that we must regard *the quest for the lost phallus in the digital plurarchy* as the great defining drama of the Internet Age. There is gloom all around, and the situation is becoming alarming. Through history we also learn that when chaos prevails and an authentic phallus cannot be summoned up, people, for lack of anything else, cling to false phalluses such as Hitler in depression-era Germany or Stalin in a Soviet Union afflicted by starvation and torn asunder by civil war. More obvious personifications of the false phallus than these are hard to imagine. The authentic phallus is *actionary*, described in Nietzschean terms, and bound to the fetish as its cathexal object (from the Greek word *kathexis* which means emotional fixation), while the false phallus from a Nietzschean perspective is *reactionary* and bound to the abject as its cathexal object. Syntheologically we express this as having to build Syntheos in order to orient ourselves within existence, rather than building Syntheos merely because we feel like it. The coveted becomes the necessary as the complexity of existence accelerates.

We are obsessed with being seen and validated by the world around us, and by its authorities in the form of both parents and gods. It is one of the earliest, original impulses which manifests itself as soon as the child has conquered the basics of language: "Look at me!" We are born exhibitionists, we insist on attention from an audience. But different theaters presuppose different types of voyeurs. The matrichal gaze is horizontal; it offers (at best) unconditional love or (at worst) bottomless hatred. The emotion that lacks depth and assumes that it never has to explain itself, since it apprehends itself as self-evident. The emotion that is bound to the fetish or the abject. An emotion that is strong and unconditional, but also simple and without control. The matrichal gaze is thus primarily emotional, not ethical. It boasts of providing in abundance to everyone and for all purposes – everyone shall be seen and heard, as if it is a right which demands nothing whatsoever in return – without reflecting upon the fact that this boundless generosity entails a constant threat of inflation, since it involves a growing risk that love is apprehended as diluted.

The phallic gaze, on the other hand, is vertical, it runs from top to bottom, from the sky down to the earth. It is thereby judging, evaluating, and therefore also conditional. It is pragmatically ethical rather than emotional in an idealized way. It provides recognition which has presumed knowledge as a point of departure and constant comparison, rather than unconditional feeling that ultimately is wholly based on biology. Phallus draws up the boundaries within which value and meaning can arise. The phallic gaze is cultural and limited where the matrichal gaze is natural and unlimited. The phallic gaze is anchored in reality and constantly calculating in terms of energy consumption and distribution. It does not intend to give everything to everybody, but a lot to a select few, and little or nothing to the rest. For the phallic gaze represents a world of limited, not unlimited resources, that is: *the adult world outside the child's insatiable matrichal fantasies.* Phallus thus goes beyond the fetish or the abject to seek the explanation to the genesis of the cathexal object. It does not see either the fetish or the abject as an object, but merely as temporal phenomena that cannot be taken for granted in the future, and with a life force that must be problematized and explored.

Phallus can ignore the external revelation of both the fetish and the abject and instead focus on their constitution. In the Jewish temple, for instance, the matrichal gaze landed in the holiest room with its material abundance, while the phallic gaze penetrated all the way through to the utmost holy room – which only the patriarchal high priest was allowed to enter, which in turn gave precisely his gaze maximal phallic value. He who actually has been able to conceive of God's nature, rather than merely having seen God's face, must likely also be able to make just and reliable valuations concerning all other affairs, be they spiritual or worldly. And what then is it that the patriarchal high priest is allowed to see in the utmost holy, if not an exhaustive reflection of himself? An emptiness that peers into an emptiness is the birth of the phallic gaze. For in the midst of the emptiness that peers into emptiness the patriarch sees the libidinal force in himself. The patriarchal high priest sees the phallic within himself; he personifies phallus, and can venture outside the utmost holy and both discover and if need be produce libido when and where it is necessary. Because he has already peered straight into his own mortality, straight into his own limitations, phallus has drenched his life in meaning. This in contrast to the escalating pointlessness in the immortality and boundlessness of the matrix.

This means that Judaism first and foremost is a patriarchal and neurotic religion, built on the demands of the law (its Levite rabbis are men who procreate, their children will succeed them when they die), while Catholicism is a matriarchal and psychotic religion, built on the undemanding dream (its priests are bachelors who do not procreate, for they shall of course live forever themselves). The Jews call themselves *the people of God* while the Christians regard themselves as *the children of God*. The entire Christian religion is built on the celebration of a child's birth, a child that later must be sacrificed by an indifferent and phallic God, and who therefore never could grow up and produce any offspring itself. What Christ expresses on the cross with the words "My God, my God, why have you forsaken me?" must be understood as the young man's frantic despair after a long, fruitless search for the phallic gaze. His existence has fallen apart in meaningless chaos, and precisely for this reason, he lacks identity.

So when Christ is sacrificed on the cross and the moment of death approaches, he realizes that neither his own nor his father's gaze will sweep across the world. The believers are instead referred to the Virgin Mary's matrichal gaze, and Christianity becomes a religion fixated with matrichal love without boundaries or conditions, that precisely for this reason must compensate with an enormous, arbitrary muddle of impossible rules and a pompous moralism that requires the sinner to have a reason to constantly seek solace from the eternal mamilla. The love that Christianity distributes is thus not merely naive, but also hollowed-out by inflation and therefore of dubious value. Christianity is the cradle of nihilism, as Nietzsche observes. Nihilism is built into Christianity's gospel from the very start. The problem is that there never is any transition from the matrichal to the phallic gaze; the child can never grow up. He who confesses to the Christian faith is and remains a *child of God,* and the term for this absurd reward for nothing at the eternally pumping mamilla is of course *grace.*

In his book *Time Driven: Metapsychology and the Splitting of the Drive*, American psychoanalyst Adrian Johnston connects these subconscious identities in the border area between phallus and matrix to Man's *fantasies about the enjoyment of the other*, what Johnston accurately refers to as Man's *phantom enjoyment.* Johnston argues that this expresses itself in four different variations: nostalgic, messianic, symbiotic and paranoid phantom enjoyment. Further, Johnston still works from the hypothesis that desire is drive's ultimate horizon and maintains that complete enjoyment does not exist and cannot exist. But once we have taken transcendence beyond desire into account, we realize that this does not add up. Complete enjoyment happens in *the infinite now*, but is so tremendous that it must be sublimated, it must quickly have an end, and can then only live on as a memory. The same goes for its opposite, the feared *trauma* or *anti-event*, which is survived thanks to the fact that it is not permanent but can be reduced to a, hopefully, empathy-generating memory.

Transcendence does however radically distinguish itself from desire by being based on the event that the mind wants to return to, however without, as desire, seeking anything new in the experience. Complete enjoyment seeks nothing other than to repeat itself. The only thing it needs is interruption from itself in order not to become part of the terror of the sublime. Thus there exists in transcendence – in contrast to desire and its constantly ongoing consumption of fetishes and abjects – a spot to which the mind wants to return without this spot being changed in any respect whatsoever. This spot in phantasmic spacetime is the infinite now, a now because it is a temporal event, and infinite because it seeks no alteration of its content. Shifting from desire to transcendence as the ultimate horizon of the drives also entails that one shifts from *the completion of the individual* to *the recurrence of the event* as metaphysics' ultimate driving force. With his radical nihilism Johnston thus completes the Freudian-Lacanian project to undress the individual as capitalism's metaphysical project. He kills off Man in the same way that Nietzsche just over a hundred years earlier kills off God.

Johnston actually does not even practice any practical psychoanalysis, but sticks to authoring his brilliant theories. What is even the point of going through extensive and rigorous psychoanalysis, when it cannot even in theory result in a desired, concrete outcome? People have criticized psychoanalysis for not producing results in the form of happy and well-adapted citizens, but then one forgets that Freud is a bitter pessimist who sees certain fundamental conflicts as inevitable.

What remains to be solved is the issue of how desire can be subservient to transcendence – if ever so temporarily, only to then be maintained as an indelible and indisputable memory – something that requires a paradigm shift that entails an abandonment of the idea of the individual, in this case the analysand himself as an ongoing project, and an embrace of the idea of an event that the analysand *de facto* can experience and then relate to as a meaningful replacement for his self-actualization project, which was stillborn right from the start.

It is this shift of focus than enables transcendence. If *the Individual* is dead anyway, why even assume that the Individual is the project of psychoanalysis? Why not shift the focus directly to the event instead, just as Jacques Lacan's most radical disciple Alain Badiou advocates? But this requires a process-philosophical revolution in the view of Man and his condition. The infinite now is not a temporary, external disturbance in an otherwise continuous and uniform personality. It is a revolutionary experience in that it ruthlessly exposes the Individual's death to the dividual who is going through the experience. For all eternity. What then remains is a dividual that consists of processes upon processes upon processes, relations piled upon relations piled upon relations, networks that consist of these processes and relations at the metalevel, but then nothing at all over and above this. Dividuality is a multiplicity in all eternity. The only thing that is real is the event where the processes and relations may be fixated.

The definitive event of this kind is one where phallus and matrix are united – not literally, but existentially – and where life is *maximized* in accordance with transcendence's ideal rather than it being *completed* according to desire's ideal. It makes a world of difference. For we are no longer striving in vain towards the promised land that never appears. We are, rather, vacationing in the promised land and then leave when it eventually becomes unbearable, which is unavoidable, only to then live on with the memory of this outstanding event. This however requires that we rob Freudians and Lacanians of their underlying enjoyment in coveting the impossible and all the while maintaining that this is the end of history. Desire is not the end of history for the simple reason that Freud and Lacan help us see through it, *which changes us*. And libido has no reason to settle for what is revealed once and for all. Therefore it is necessary to carry out the shift from desire to transcendence to complete the model. So if Johnston rounds off the Freudian-Lacanian revolution with his radical, post-analytical nihilism, what can we then learn from his concept of phantom enjoyment in its four different variants?

Nostalgic phantom enjoyment is hardly a mystery, it surrounds us everywhere in culture in the form of myths of how "everything was better before," often with human or material abjects that are blamed for the great loss in the present. From the Bible's lost paradise to Jean-Jacques Rousseau's bizarre fabrication of the noble savage, culture has over centuries served us nostalgic fairy tales in great quantities. Even today, for instance, the Israeli historian Yuval Noah Harari in his best-selling book *Sapiens* maintains the myth that the nomadic existence, before permanent settlement, was a true paradise, and that Project Humanity started to derail when we created civilization. However, these statements have nothing more to recommend them now than they had before, but merely once again reflect *nostalgic phantom enjoyment's* matrichal power of attraction. Paradigm shifts have occurred, they have changed living conditions and have favored some, while disfavoring or simply neglecting others. Profound changes have rewarded certain types of talent and have punished others; life has assuredly become different, but seriously maintaining that it in any objective sense has become either better or worse, is just nonsense.

What is important to shed light on is instead that nostalgic phantom enjoyment is a comfortable but banal form of escape from reality, a masochistic regression and return to the mamilla, which of course entails a collective declaration of legal incompetence of all those involved. Most deeply viewed, all myths of the lost paradise merely reflect a nostalgic yearning for the one real paradise that by necessity must be lost to us all: the nine delectable months in the womb, the matrix, before nature's own infernal abjection – birth – destroys the party for all of us. We have been forced to become conscious, autonomous creatures, there is good reason to regard this as a violation, and there is good reason for us to long to go back to the simple existence that preceded our factual existence, but it does not mean that this enjoyment is the least bit meaningful. All the Abrahamic religions do for instance start from the same basic concept: *the great fall*. That the garrulous snake tricked Eve and Adam into feasting on the fruit of knowledge brings the result that God becomes angry and expels Man from paradise. So maybe the question is whether that snake actually was a mistake, if eternal ignorance really was so important.

The process follows a path that we ought to recognize by now: What is the story of the fall if not the story of the abjection from the matrichal perspective and an expression of the matrichal disappointment over the abjection's inexorable necessity? And what is the fruit of knowledge if not phallus in all its absolute splendor, the optimal lever that takes us away from the semiotic soup in the matrix where nothing ever happens ("Heaven is a place/A place where nothing/Nothing ever happens," sing Talking Heads). For the most phallic of all is of course precisely our insatiable hunger for genuine knowledge, the libidinal search for contact with factual reality, and the attraction that the dangerous reality outside the matrichal bubble exercises. Phallus does not merely represent reality outside the semiotic soup, but also love for reality outside it, what the ultra-phallic Nietzsche calls *amor fati*, love of fate, which we must get to know in order to later be able to embrace it. So what is then – if we stick to this mental image a little longer – the shift from the mendacious paradise to the brutal reality, if not the most perfect shift from *the mortido of subconsciousness* to *the libido of consciousness*? That this is the case is revealed not least in the matrichal myth of the existence of free will – you can become anything you want, you can have anything you want – which stands in stark contrast to phallus' brutal reminder of the overwhelming power of contingent fate over the on-the-whole meaningless existence of the little human a lesson that spurs rather than diminishes the powerful libido.

This is not a matter of the expulsion from paradise, but about the repression of mortido to enable the arrival and establishment of libido. Where the leaf to hide the sex organ, because of the shame that Man suddenly feels as a result of his new fruit diet, constitutes the transition from the child's impulse-controlled libido to the adult's strategy-controlled libido, the shift from the chaotic rape to the tribal ritual as a sexual act. Which leads us further to the *Lucifer myth*. The rebel Lucifer is acclaimed within three faith systems that otherwise are dramatically distinct at a comparison: Zoroastrianism, Mithraism and Gnosticism. Eating from the fruit of knowledge entails, according to these anti-Abrahamic ideologies, a victory, certainly not a defeat for humanity. At the same time, this defiance towards the tyrant, this risky refusal to yield, is something that one within the Abrahamic religions hates and fears so intensely. Lucifer is of course the young man who breaks with and rebels against the patriarch, that is: he is phallus in its purest form. Lucifer is the son who imitates the father, but who thereafter not only deviates from the patriarch's course to establish an identity of his own – which of course is the case in all functioning intergenerational relations – but who moreover opposes the patriarch on every point and in every respect, and who is thus transformed into the patriarch's strongest challenger. While Lucifer means the morning star in Latin, his Hebrew name is fittingly enough *Satan*, the adversary.

The quest for the lost phallus is *the messianic phantom enjoyment*, which recurs within all dialectical historiography. The origin is the myth of a coming *saoshyant* among the Iranian Zoroastrians. The saoshyant is the phallic figure *par excellence,* someone who steps into the social arena in a mist-shrouded future, saves the people from devastation and launches a golden age characterized by both utopian perfection (*haurvatat*) and contact with reality (*asha*). The saoshyant concept is then borrowed by the Jewish people after the Persians had freed them from the Babylonian imprisonment. This becomes the Jewish messiah myth where Zoroastrianism's universal saoshyant is replaced by Judaism's nationalist messiah figure. In the same way that the Zoroastrians await a saoshyant who never arrives, the Jews await a messiah who never arrives. This while the Christian and Islamic sects just as eagerly await a Christ or a prophet who has arrived but who never returns. And what then is the messiah myth, if not the cultural desire that by necessity constantly is moved onward to avoid its own dissolution?

Christianity's unique messiah mythology says that the Messiah came, was invisible and was only made visible as the Messiah after his death. Thus Christ was never a phallus. He was an eternal boy, or if you will: a eunuch. Which makes Christianity the only both dialectical and matrichal religion. It tries to enfold both the mortidinally circular and the libidinally dialectical within one and the same system, by worshipping the Virgin Mary's grief over the dead Christ at the cross. But this requires that either mortido or libido be sacrificed, and then it is libido that falls by the wayside. So this specific event in itself, and not some selected person or symbol, will be Christianity's metaphysical center. This makes the Virgin Mary the circular human goddess, the real bridge between Heaven and Earth. The power over Heaven and Earth is of course not to be found in Christ's castrating, post-libidinal pseudophallus, but in the Virgin Mary's mortidinally highly active mamilla. There and nowhere else does the sacred reside.

The Christian heaven is therefore an eternal womb, a primordial matrix, and an eternal maternal breast, a primordial mamilla of sorts, with no demands for a painful abjection process. The Christian Christmas festivity is the voyage from matrix to mamilla and the Christian Easter festivity is the voyage from mamilla back to matrix, without any phallic intrusion whatsoever in between (this in contrast to the Jewish Easter which, with its exodus from Egypt towards the promised land, is the phallic festivity *par excellence*). If you only believe in God's grace, the divine eternity machine will fix everything. It is literally about the return to the lost paradise – an eternal life without life, a life without both sublimity and mortidinality, and thus also without libido itself. No wonder Christianity is the most hostile religion to sexuality of them all, the religion where literally every sexual activity is regarded as a wasted opportunity to exercise spirituality.

Johnston continues by developing the concepts of *symbiotic phantom enjoyment* and *paranoid phantom enjoyment*. Symbiotic phantom enjoyment requires an end to the autonomous state and becoming part of the social state for enjoyment to be possible. It is thus about a return to the mamilla, away from the phallus: an infantilization that is meant to reward the infantilized person with previously unattainable enjoyment. Paranoid phantom enjoyment goes one step further and quite simply diverts all potential enjoyment to *the other*. The subject has now lost every hope of ever having the possibility to attain enjoyment. All enjoyment by decree, or through some kind of immutable law of nature, belongs to the other, and in this abyss of hopelessness runaway paranoia is but a short step away, envy and vengefulness in spades, all of it motivated and defended by and through paranoid phantom enjoyment.

In the network society, symbiotic phantom enjoyment explodes in the form of naive infantilizations of Man's drive machinery – many convince themselves for real that yoga, meditation, a gym session, a newly-refurbished kitchen or a trip to an exotic beach will be able to give existence direction and meaning. All the while, paranoid phantom enjoyment is fuelled by the fact that globalization and digitalization force us into unpleasantly close contact with alien worlds, cultures and skin colors. We are forced to leave the habitual *intratribalism* and replace it with the menacing and demanding *intertribalism*. This occurs when the resistance towards the cosmopolitanism that netocracy compels creates a counter-reaction in the form of the consumtariat's often violent hostility towards strangers and deviants, an expression of envy's *enjoyment* vis-à-vis the feared stranger's projected *pleasure*. Sociobiology catches up with Man. Five thousand years of the civilization process has radically changed Man's surrounding world and his immediate environment. But Man himself, as a biological creature at a dividual level, has during the same period not changed at all. We have as little hope now as before to settle into existence and start to thrive in culture. Frustration and embitterment are and remain our lot, and the best we can make of it is, as they say, to quite simply accept our fate: *amor fati*.

If the infinite now is the engine of metaphysics during informationalism – how then does phallus relate to this transcendental event? We find the answer in the *dialectics of eternalism and mobilism* (see the exhaustive account in *The Global Empire*). Even if existence is radically mobilist, it is through eternalization and only through eternalization that Man becomes authentic. The eternalization of the phenomenon that transforms this into an object for perception, is of course the symbolic castration *par excellence*. And precisely here, right at the center of syntheist metaphysics, the radical discrepancy in value between the matrichal-mortidinal and the phallic-libidinal appears the most clearly. Both these eternalizations force the dividual to return to the event and repeat it time and time again in that which, to speak with Nietzsche, is *the existential recurrence of the same*.

However, depending on perspective, one and the same eternalization, one and the same moment, one and the same experience, gives rise to completely different values. Eternalization viewed from the matrichal-mortidinal perspective is of course called *trauma* – if there is anything that infantilized people love to do, it is to stop and revel in the ressentiment that originates from their own experienced or fabricated traumas – while the eternalization as regarded from the phallic-libidinal perspective is called, naturally, the *event*. This means that if birth is the ultimate trauma, then the infinite now is the ultimate event. And the only possible path from trauma to event goes via the dramatic intrusion of phallus in life. This means that the more complex the world becomes, the more important the role of the phallus becomes in its capacity of that which compares, values and allocates meaning, and which thus functions as an attendant. And what this in turn means that phallus never before has been needed and never before has been missed as much as now when informationalism afflicts society with full force and foists upon us new, intractable conditions for precisely everything.

9
The fetish and the abject – the symbols that drive the social theater

The Oracle of Delphi urged Man to "know thyself," but as this is not the easiest of tasks, we actually don't know either ourselves or the world around us anywhere near as well as we flatter ourselves into believing that we do. To begin with, we are not conscious of essential elements of our drive system for the simple reason that it occurs under the horizon of consciousness, and we are also lying to each other about the deep-seated desires that we after all somewhere inside are aware that we have and more or less reluctantly admit to ourselves – or to search engines when we are browsing the net – since we are comparing these desires of ours to what we imagine to be the common and normal, ill-informed conceptions to which we tend to adapt ourselves so that we appear common and normal to others and ourselves. In the infernal tangle of lying and guessing it is not easy to orient oneself, but in order to be even able to handle existence we must manufacture both a self-image and a worldview that are reasonably functional.

Together these two complementing and interacting images constitute two sides of the same coin: the foundation of the cultural and historical paradigm. And we create these intimately related images with a starting point of the phenomena surrounding us, in which we invest our most powerful emotions. It is here that the concept *cathexis*, which is so important to paradigm theory, enters our vocabulary. This Greek word means *projection of one's own emotions onto one's environment*. In light of the central role that these projections and these emotions play in these personality-constructing contexts, socioanalysis must regard *the cathexal objects* as fundamental and vital for culture. Examining how their influence is built is, consequently, decisive for a socioanalysis that strives for relevance as well as precision. Man quite simply invests his *pathos* in these specific phenomena, in order to later be able to orient himself from the cathexal objects' positions in an existence that in every other respect is chaotic; these thus constitute a kind of more or less arbitrarily selected, emotionalized nodes in the environment's local plurarchy.

This means that we humans *de facto* devote ourselves to, and demonstrate in our actions, a deep-seated belief in what in practice is magic and conjury. In truth, we devote ourselves to this activity every week, every day, every waking hour. We do so as a matter of course and with a dedication that is fueled by the fundamental misconception that claims it is specifically with the aid of these superstitions – which we choose to call something else since self-deceit is completely necessary – that we control the world around us. Naturally, it is precisely the other way around, it is the surrounding world and the dominating technology that structures the world, and that therefore also structures Man, who of course *de facto* also is the world (what else would he be?). Or to quote the Canadian media theorist Marshall McLuhan's classic statement: "First we shape our tools, thereafter our tools shape us." This is of course a continuous process with no beginning and no end, in which case the order might as well be reversed; this "we" which in the first clause of the sentence shapes a set of tools (and thereafter is shaped, or reshaped, by these) is actually already shaped by an older set of tools, and these are in turn shaped by an older edition of "we," which in turn... and so on and so forth *ad infinitum*. We are humans thanks to our tools, and the pure, lucid gaze on the world around us as it "really" is has never existed.

Man's reactive approach vis-à-vis this colossal, devastating supremacy is fundamentally sexual. And sexuality is, as Sigmund Freud would express the matter, *the concrete universal*, which interweaves Man's worldview and posits the self as the subject experiencing pleasure in the midst of this performance. This concerns the erotic feeling that Man invests in the surrounding phenomena, which determines the prioritization that he makes between these, and thus also the hierarchical position they will have in his fantasy world. Among all these phenomena, there is one that assumes an uncontested exceptional position; the phenomenon that is the object of the concrete universal, which connects the aggregate erotic tension with the illusion of a cohesive, perspicuous world: the cathexal object as *the libidinal eternalization par excellence*. Freud's name for this object is *phallus*. But the analysis of this relationship can be deepened further. Behind phallus there are several cathexal objects. What happens when the cathexal object is transferred to the social arena – in other words: when we move from psychoanalysis to socioanalysis – the object goes through a transition: either to what classic anthropology calls *the fetish*, or to what the Bulgarian-French psychoanalyst Julia Kristeva, as an opposite to the fetish, calls *the abject*. It is therefore of utmost importance that we understand what roles *the fetish* and *the abject* play in people's lives throughout history. It is only when are clear on this matter that it becomes meaningful for us to study how these patterns are likely to be repeated in the network society.

The primary cathexal object in Man's existence is the *mamilla*, while the secondary cathexal object – that which disturbs the primordial fantasy of the mamilla as the portal that enables a return to the coveted *matrix* – is the *phallus*. In connection with this, the existential experience is built on fantasies of how Man is united with the cathexal object through incorporating it into his own body – eating it, drinking it or having sexual intercourse with it. The cathexal object appears suddenly, in the guise of that which causes Man's own enjoyment. Thus the matrix cannot be regarded as a cathexal object in itself, simply because it does not live as a conscious memory in the child that has developed in the womb. Nor is the moment of birth preserved in memory, since the mechanisms of memory have not matured sufficiently at that moment. The *matrix* instead drives mortidinal subconsciousness, while libidinal consciousness constantly oscillates between mamilla and phallus. This is why we think we are seeing mamilla and phallus everywhere when we register the least topological deviation in our environment, while we subconsciously are creating a matrix of different models for ourselves in the form of beds, bathtubs, sofas, caves and comfortably decorated cozy rooms of various kinds, warm environments that create security, to which we can retire whenever we feel unsafe. All the while, the most primary objective is to try to satisfy our need for validation: when this is done we search for food and shelter with passionate engagement.

The emergence of the fetish and the abject in the child's fantasy world is caused by the grave disappointment that unavoidably arises when it is clear to the child that its beloved cathexal object no longer is immediately available to it, that it no longer is possible to lay claim to the object without making an effort. The moment this fact is revealed, the dream of mamilla as the link that enables the longed-for return to matrix is crushed. The fetish becomes cathexal since it now requires an effort on the part of the child to conquer it, to the extent that it is even possible to attain. Regardless of whether it actually is attainable or not, the fetish symbolizes the eternally recurring desire – *phallus* is, of course, *the fetish par excellence. The abject* becomes cathexal since it is not possible to eat, drink or have sexual intercourse with it – or more correctly: it threatens to castrate the child if it attempts to eat, drink or have sexual intercourse with the abject. It is thus understood by the child to be a disturbance, an intrusion, something repellent. What the abject wants is seemingly to raise obstacles to the child's enjoyment. With the starting point in these libidinal-incestuous models, the child determines the status of the cathexal object; either it is elevated to a fetish, or it is degraded to an abject. Actually, the child classifies all the objects that it registers in its surrounding world either as fetishes, abjects, or possibly as cathexal objects in general – the latter category being placed in an ambiguous, contradictory no-man's land situated between the temptations of the fetishes and the horrors of the abjects, where the cathexal objects instead both attract and repel in *ambivalent sublimeness.*

The fetish is first and foremost the cathexal object of the symbolic order, while the abject belongs to the imaginary order. The fetish is therefore connected with the patriarch, phallus, the cosmic order and eternalism, Taoism's *yang*; while the abject in turn is connected with the matriarch, matrix, the cosmic chaos, mobilism and Taoism's *yin*. Both these phenomena can be used for either the dividing or uniting of social ties. And for both the one and the other simultaneously. When the fetish and the abject are united in one and the same cathexal object, which is both worshipped and hated with full force simultaneously, Taoism's *yin-yang* – for instance Christ on the cross (despised and abjectified by the Jewish crowd that witnessed the drawn-out and humiliating execution, loved and fetishized by the Christian flock that followed) – this awakens an ambivalent sublimeness that is so massive that the energy developed through it is enough to even spark a new religion. The French philosopher and anthropologist René Girard explores this phenomenon in his book *La Violence et le Sacré*. According to Girard the fetish-abject is the necessary sacrifice for the sacral violence where the worshipped and the hated are transformed into one and the same thing: where phallus for lack of matrix merely can be apprehended as a sacrificial act, *the cathexal object par excellence.* Only via the fetish-abject can what Girard calls *the mimetic violence* between rivals within the tribe be dissolved, which enables the tribe to liberate themselves from the impasse of the conflict, and move on. This requires the fetish-abject to be sacrificed, and thereby to be eternalized in the tribe's historiography.

The *authentic phallus* unites the collective around the fetish – concretely around the tribal *totem pole*, to take the historically most obvious example. The totem pole points forward and charts the course for the tribe's continued journey. The story conveyed by the totem pole is the hero narrative of previous victories meant to inspire new sacrifices and major feats. The strong sexual overtones of the fetish places it in the libidinal sphere. It is driven by *attraction* and behaves as a repetitive constant. The American psychoanalyst Adrian Johnston argues in his book *Time Driven – Metapsychology and the Splitting of the Drive* that the fetish is connected to the French psychoanalyst Jacques Lacan's concept *objet a*, the phenomenon that Lacan's successor Jacques-Alain Miller refers to as *the extimate object* and that Jean Laplanche calls *the enigmatic signifier.* Lacan maintains that there is an experience of *a lost fragment* from the primordial experience in the midst of every subject experience. This little phantasmic object can, for instance, be the absent mamilla or the frightening phallus. But the important point is that the lost fragment resides inside the actual experience and still is apprehended as a lack. This is why Miller calls the object *extimate* rather than intimate: at once menacingly close and icily distanced in relation to the subject.

According to Lacan, Miller and Laplanche, it is this very extimacy that makes that the entire drive system is fixated on the lost fragment. This means that every phenomenon that crosses the subject's path that might be perceived as in the least way as coming into contact with the extimate original object will immediately exercise a fetishist influence on the subject. The drives are thus searching for *the cathexal object* which they never can nor even want to expose, and the fetish is time after time forced to act as a substitute for the lost fragment, which explains why we are dealing with the perfect repetitive constant. If this state of affairs is fundamental for Lacanian psychoanalysis in all its forms, we can assume that the extimate object in the form of the fetish and/or the abject is a necessary building block within socioanalysis as well. An authentic social constellation can only be kept intact if it is united around an alien fragment within itself, a fragment that it at the same time never has the chance to become acquainted with. From a syntheological vantage point this phenomenon is called *the utopia* or quite simply *Syntheos* – the created god or divine creativity. Consequently *dystopia* is its abjective opposite. The phallus becomes the original fetish by having to seduce and lure us away from the mamilla with the utopian story that claims that one day, if we follow it, we will be rewarded with adult sexuality. Meanwhile, the mamilla becomes the original abject which precisely in that capacity lures us into clinging to the illusion of the undemanding reward through the dystopian story of the menacing world outside its deceptive security. The price we pay for allowing ourselves to be enslaved by the abject is that we remain infantilized forever.

When Friedrich Nietzsche complains that people constantly prefer submission to supremacy, what he really means is that the phallic temptation constantly proves insufficient, which is why people get caught in the mamilla's false security whose abjectivity is internalized in the form of ressentiment, a hatred towards one's own existence. In the same way that the dividual human can build his whole life on a platform entirely based on a lifelong deception, the social collective, at least temporarily, can also construct an identity that is built on totally false premises. The group produces both its identity and its cohesiveness with the aid of a phenomenon that displays all the external signs of being an authentic phallus, but that later, on closer inspection, proves completely phony. What is particularly distinguishing for such a *false phallus* is that it defines and unites the group with the aid of the abject. The most conspicuous example is of course how Adolf Hitler defines and unites the German people in a biologically and culturally conditioned hatred towards the Jew, the abject *par excellence*. A movement of this sort is driven by *repulsion* and acts as a vibrating, volatile oscillation. Thus the abject has strongly repulsive and thereby also mortidinal overtones. It is connected with denunciation and reactionary behavior, a conscious or unconscious hatred of change, and a yearning back to the matrichal state where no changes occurred or could occur.

The abject is thus connected to Freud's concept of *discontentment* and also to the concept of *homo sacer*, the ostracized and the outlawed among humans, which the Italian philosopher Giorgio Agamben brings over from Roman law. The discontentment in Freud appears in the subjective enjoyment of the collective distancing. All the while, Agamben's actor, made invisible and placed at the bottom of the societal hierarchy, is the abjective equivalent of the Lacanians' extimate object. Precisely because the uniting role for the one at the very lowest tier of the hierarchy is actively denied, through this actor being made invisible and being transformed into a *homo sacer*, no other actor can function as the necessary, uniting, cathexal object any longer. The social arena is thereby transformed into an eternal struggle between – and even within – everything and everyone. Fascism, Nazism, communism, Stalinism and Islam are all built upon this consistent abjectivity.

Without the authentic phallus, no long-term sustainable alliances can be built within such systems. The extimate enemy means everything and generates the energy needed to drive the network until the point in time when it collapses under its own weight. It is this fundamental Freudian discontentment, this Hegelian abyss, the abjective extimacy even within the most intimate, that causes all actors within the falsely phallic systems to sooner or later become each other's enemies. Without a genuinely phallic limit for how far the ideology is allowed to penetrate into subconsciousness – a limit within which the actor can be an errant human rather than a perfect ideology producer and consumer – all participants can always be held responsible for not being sufficiently fundamentalist, loyal and energetic. When Hitler finally shoots himself in the head on April 30, 1945, he does so with the consistent conviction that not even he could live up to his own, impossible, Nazi ideal. His struggle – as presented in his pamphlet *Mein Kampf* – and the movement that this struggle gave rise to was therefore even from the start nothing but one big, systematic mortidinal act of death worship.

The relation between the fetish and the abject is contradictory; partly antagonistic, partly complementary. They are each other's opposites while also constituting the two sides of the same coin. They both appear separately, and in pairs. Often the relation between them is dialectically or mutually overlapping. For the sake of simplicity and clarity, we keep them separate, on the one hand the fetish by itself and the abject by itself, on the other hand the concept fetish-abject when they interact or when they in practice are interchangeable for each other as the cathexal object. To develop this further, we must note that the fetish-abject is the node in which drive meets desire and generates an illusory unity between them. Consequently, it is the fetish-abject which in turn generates the subjective experience and therefore also identity production. The fetish-abject is quite simply the symbolic interpretation of mortido itself, since the cathexal object constitutes the center of the drive system.

The sacred is the ultimate example of the cathexal object that acts both as a fetish and an abject by stimulating the ambivalence between phallus and matrix. A concrete example of this is the symbolic distinction that is made between sex-as-an-act-of-love and sex-as-an-act-of-prostitution. Formally the activities are identical. But within the symbolic order they are radically distinct. Sex-as-an-act-of-love is made to act as a fetish in a person's consciousness while sex-as-an-act-of-prostitution is made to act as an abject. While the roles of course simultaneously switch places in the subconscious. One of them we desire and fantasize about, the other we reject with passion, only to then let ourselves be excited by the subconscious alternating the roles. Since the sexual act in itself, as a formality, can be regarded as a fetish just as well as an abject, there arises a comprehensive ambivalent tension within the entire sexual field. The tension remains unresolved and must therefore by necessity return and make its presence felt within all sexual fantasies and activities in which Man engages.

The distinction between sex-as-an-act-of-love and sex-as-an-act-of-prostitution is of course actually just a chimera, both these phenomena coexist at all levels within the sexual field. Therefore sexuality in itself is unresolvedly and incorrigibly ambivalent, both controversial and attractive. And so perfect in the role as the foundation for the sacred within culture. To understand what this means, it is important to see the essential difference that prevails between on the one hand *the sex drive* and on the other hand *sexuality*. The sex drive is natural, we humans share it with other animal species, and it dominates instinct and drive. Syntheologically we posit it between Atheos and Pantheos. On the other hand, sexuality is cultural and thus exclusive to Man; it dominates desire and transcendence. Syntheologically we posit it between Entheos and Syntheos. The reason that Man is inexorably torn between the sex drive and sexuality is that both of them have been developed in parallel and are in constant conflict with each other during human evolution. The sex drive is internal and dividual, while sexuality is external and social. Actually the alluring ambivalence between them can be regarded as *the ambivalent sublimeness par excellence*.

If we, for instance, assume that all men in the nomadic tribe fantasize about raping women, it does not mean that all men convert this fantasy into action. There is an evolutionary biological logic to this. It might well be the case that it is in the best interests of the tribe to extend the gene pool through capturing and raping women from other tribes whenever this is possible, which also happens for the simple reason that Jean-Jacques Rousseau was wrong: life in the nomadic tribe was anything but paradisiacal easy living where all needs automatically were satisfied. But this does not mean – indeed, quite the contrary – that it would be in the best interests of the tribe for its own women to constantly be raped by its own men. This is not the way to create stable social structures. Similarly, we assume in part that all the women in the nomadic tribe fantasize about sex with scores of different men, in part that they fantasize about forms of sex that entail both submission and acts of violence. Something that strongly indicates the latter is that 21st century women to a great extent consume pornography with elements of compulsion and rape, confirmed by the pornography sites' own statistics (see *Everybody Lies* by Seth Stephens-Davidowitz). When we actually can confirm what fantasies people want to consume, this is what emerges. But of course this does not mean that it would benefit the tribe's common interests that any of these fantasies be turned into action to a large extent.

Viewed over a longer time-frame, the tribe members' disruptive sex drive must as a rule be controlled by the patriarch and the matriarch. To, so to speak, let it loose would create an unmanageable muddle where some dividuals would grab advantages in the form of enjoyment but at the cost of the tribe's common interests, which of course would reduce the tribe's chances to assert themselves in the cutthroat fight for survival constantly fought with other tribes with whom one competes for limited resources. This means that in regard to the control of sexuality, Man's imaginary and symbolic fantasy worlds, constructed around the sex drive, are the patriarch's and the matriarch's most important instruments of power and the very foundation of *tribal moralism* with all its morally didactic stories serving as guidance. It is hardly surprising that contemporary Man has inherited both genes and memes from the plastic nomadic tribe, replicators that together give rise to passionate but – since the social structures have undergone such comprehensive changes – increasingly disconcerted sexual norms and rules, where the male collective's culturally conditioned hatred towards the rapist, who of course violates the patriarchal code, and the female collective's contempt towards the whore, who violates the matriarchal code, return in the form of powerful, near-delirious stigmatizations in many cultures throughout history.

This shift from hedonistic, fetishist fantasy to an amoral, abjective rejection thus does not occur within the drive that expresses itself, or even within the act that is occurring – formally there are of course no distinctions between these activities – but in the very shift that occurs from the independent activity outside the social theater to the identity-generating event that plays out in the spotlight falling upon the social theater stage. The power over this dramatic act of defining is entirely vested in the patriarch and the matriarch within the egalitarian nomadic tribe. What is acceptable as a private, internalized fantasy becomes a contemptible infamy that immediately must be condemned the moment it is manifested in the form of the other's external acting out. It is hardly surprising that it is the responsibility of the patriarch to lead the rapist to a glade in the woods and in front of the other men in the hunting party first castrate and then execute the one who has violated the rules of the tribe. And for the same reason, it is the matriarch who both sanctions and leads the systematic and merciless campaign of ostracism against the young woman who violates the tribe's unambiguous norms for female sexuality. Ultimately this is an issue of the survival of the tribe, since it constantly must be able to move onwards and continue the search for food and shelter without being too inhibited by conflicts and social disruption.

Both the patriarch and the matriarch therefore have many good reasons to proclaim and to the best of their abilities maintain sexual abstention, and above all control, within the collective. Up until the early 20th century young women within all populations regularly die in conjunction with delivery. Therefore the tribe has nothing to gain and everything to lose from unregulated, irregular childbirth at different times of the year, particularly as regards the many days of the year when the tribe is migratory. Instead there is every reason to act for regulated childbirth that occurs at set points in time on the calendar. This in turn is only possible if one has succeeded in regulating sexuality, primarily by ritualizing it and ensuring that it occurs only during certain selected holidays, which means that one markets it as a reward for endured hardships in the form of sensual ecstasy, rather than as an allowed or at least tolerated everyday enjoyment. Moreover, the pent-up, accumulated sexual energy can be channeled to other purposes, which gives the tribe access to an extremely useful general libido to be steered away from sexuality off towards other things, in particular the promotion of survival and group cohesion. Early widespread urban and literary cultures even generate specific subcultures, such as *Taoism* in China and *Tantra* in India, around the ambition to reroute libido in a generally creative rather than specifically sexual direction.

Controlling the sex drive through regulating and ritualizing sexuality thus highly increases the plastic nomadic tribe's chances of survival. Actually, it is only later in history, when the tribal ritualization of sexuality no longer serves either Man's or society's interests, that the entire modern set of problems connected with sexuality becomes explosive and menacing for real. Under no circumstances is sexuality a force that allows itself to be tamed just like that, but the complications increase when society goes through a process of change and Man is subjected to constantly new demands to manage his survival. The sex drive is of course *de facto* libido in its purest form. Thus one keeps it concealed beneath an encoded, thorny use of language, conditioned by the taboo conceptions that are connected with sexuality. Both fetishes and abjects are connected to this taboo-making; in this way a context is produced where certain acts are so controversial that not only are they forbidden to carry out, but they must also be hushed up, made invisible and never accorded any status whatsoever within the symbolic order.

The consequence of this harsh censoring of thought is inevitably that these actions precisely for that reason have a particularly powerful allure within the imaginary order, what psychoanalysis refers to as the yearning for *transgression*. This in turn means that these tabooed actions can be used by the elite that for the moment master and define society's exercise of power – since this elite by definition controls the symbolic order – with the purpose of manipulating the less sophisticated masses by portraying them, in speech and writing, as enslaved by their forbidden fantasies. An example of this, highly present in Freud, is *incest*, which ever since the days of primitivism has been reserved for gods and royalty, and is posited as an impermeable and thereby also axiomatic taboo for the rest of the population. While we see a flagrant example of an incestuous act and incestuous enjoyment every time a mother offers her *mamilla* and suckles her own child. Many would maintain that the image of the breast-feeding mother is beautiful, but few can deny that it is also charged with tension.

The dominant roles of the patriarch and the matriarch, the power that they can exercise by virtue of their massive information advantage, take us further towards the point that is the blind spot of both psychoanalysis and Buddhist enlightenment, namely *the fourth abjection*. In the same way that Lacanian psychoanalysis only can be completed after the analyst himself has withdrawn – Jacques Lacan's *non sequitur* is that he does not predict that the very analysand who has gone through his psychoanalysis, and who consequently should be well-versed in his method and therefore also has attained the at least temporary *transcendence* beyond drive and desire, that is: *meta-desire* – so too the abjectification chain must be completed by *the meta-abjection*, the definitive abjection of the abjection process itself. This explains why we use the concept *transcendental abjection*. After the completed abjectification chain – which consists of *matrix abjectification* (delivery), *mamilla abjectification* (weaning) and *phallus abjecti-*

fication (teenage rebellion/attainment of adulthood) – the narcissistic boundlessness explodes in a veritable orgy of *hyperautonomy*, whose most extreme form of expression is *the messiah complex*. However, this intoxicating autonomy is largely an illusion built on hubris, Man is and remains a tribal creature, a gregarious animal, which requires that the hyperautonomous young man and/or woman sooner or later must be forced back into the prevailing order and placed under the control of the tribe.

The tribal institution that marks and confirms the shift from narcissism to productive subordination is *the rite of passage*, conducted by the shamans or their heirs, the clergy. It does not matter how the rite of passage is carried out in practice, or exactly what it consists of – in the original nomadic tribe, as in today's tribes in for instance South America and Central Africa, it most often was and still is conducted under the influence of great amounts of powerful psychedelic drugs – its task is invariably to push *the real* into the young narcissist's imaginary and symbolic universes and thereby force the young tribe member to strive for submission in relation to the patriarch, the matriarch and the tribe's aggregate survival interests. Through the rite of passage the focus is shifted from *attention* – the search for the admiring gaze of the patriarch and the matriarch – to the existential *meaning* that best fits the personal archetype of the dividual in question and thus also his or her social role within the tribe. In this way, what Nietzsche calls *the eternal recurrence of the* same is fulfilled, circularity trumps linearity when mortido is reintroduced as a fundamental element within libido. Mobilism thus survives in eternalism's core. The dialectical process continues incessantly.

It is important to note here that the rite of passage in itself does not suffice in order to attain the sought-after productive submission. Rather, it must be regarded as the very culmination of the domestication process, but as such the rite of passage is perfectly suited as *the dividualized event par excellence* in the retribalized network-dynamical society. One of Syntheism's most important gains is the insight that a well-designed rite of passage can also save the youths of the network society from hundreds of hours of destructive and self-centered therapeutical navel-gazing. Only in this way can isolating autonomy – which individualist psychotherapy presumes and encourages, out of institutional self-interest – be replaced by a coveted, tribal adulthood. The transcendental abjection consists not only of the shift from narcissism to tribalism, but also comprises the shift from *immortality* to *mortality* as the metaphysical engine, that is: as *the phantasmic horizon*. The fourth abjection, in this way, is also tantamount to the first shift from libidinal endlessness back into mortidinal boundary setting. It is as though libido, in a Hegelian sense, has to be bent in towards itself to attain its full expression.

This mortidinal interference directly into the libido generates the first impulse in both the young man and in the young woman to become a parent, or at least to become engaged in the birth and rearing of the tribe's next generation, through assuming various tribal roles with parental purposes. The libido is quite simply reinforced and is focused on concrete ambitions by being mortalized in the subconscious. A radical ambivalence then arises between on the one hand the striving for autonomy and on the other hand the striving for social alignment, a conflict that at some point occupies most young tribe members' consciousnesses. Behind this conscious ambivalence lies a deeper, subconscious conflict between the dividual's immortality (libido is connected with social independence) and its mortality (mortido is connected with social dependence). Only in the margins of the tribe's territory, in the area that borders other tribes' home territories, does immortality find an intact role as an adult, a role that is played by *the shamanic caste* with its priests, priestesses, monks and nuns, as well as by *the warrior caste* with its soldiers, scouts, diplomats and explorers.

However, these Nietzschean masters of their own destiny – immortality's allure is not eternal life in itself, but *the ecstatic sense of free-*

dom with which the uncompromising libido is associated – are and will remain a sociobiological minority within all human populations. The vast majority is and will remain – both as children and as adults – childishly fond of mortidinal and death-worshipping submission. Conformism thus becomes its own reward and prevailing social norm. The price that the tribe has to pay for this is of course that the majority of its members constantly strive toward and cling to *the status quo* in all forms of external change. One raves about a *status quo* that moreover is strongly connected with the short period in youth when this majority of the tribe members actually experimented with an ever so temporary autonomy in relation to patriarchal and/or matriarchal top-down rule. This means that apart from the rare and sometimes intense romance with revolution for some of the young, the lion's share of the population in all societies will always be reactionary. And the reactionary always choose to gather around *the external abject* since this constitutes their cohesive cathexal object.

Moreover, the reactionary cling to the external abject for their identity production as long as possible, in an attempt to avoid facing the group's inner, growing tensions that arise as a result of the unreflected dancing around the self-destructive internal abject, tensions that are stoked until they explode in for instance a civil war. This means that it is populism, not a progressive reform agenda, that is the normal state of the democratic discourse over time. Which means for example that the concept *direct democracy* is impossible to merge with any progressive political objectives whatsoever, no matter what non-historical and quasi-radical 21st century eco-Marxists might be claiming when they speak of highly what they call *emancipatory politics*, which through some hitherto unknown form of political magic is supposed to provide solutions to all the challenges with which the network society is confronted. Self-acclaimed critically thinking adherents such as Slavoj Žižek, Michael Hardt and Toni Negri certainly ought to know better. For if we view this historically, biologically or culturally, it is the other way around: The more numerous and the older the participants in the democratic process, the more reactionary and the more duplicitous the process will be. And the reason is in no way related to any form of ideology, but is possible to derive from something as simple as tribal sociobiology.

Part of the demographic genius of capitalism lies of course – to the great chagrin of the postmodernist left who are insufficiently versed in Karl Marx – in how it frees up the tribe's shamanic resources in the form of creative entrepreneurship and business enterprise *outside the academic and political discourses.* Thus society goes through a technologically-driven radicalization, and then it is of marginal significance that the academics and the politicians by virtue of their tax-financed, institutional corruption act as a brake for reasons of pure self-interest, since every change from their vantage point entails bad news. Capitalism quite simply uses the minoritarian activity – via netocratic subcultures and investment funds – against the majoritarian passivity to drive the societal development forward. In the Internet Age this becomes particularly clear as the old right and the old left, the disintegrating nation state's political residual products, are doomed to waste their rapidly subsiding energy competing over which one of them is the most conservative and reactionary. The match is hard-fought, and the outcome is hard to predict. They simply cannot act in any other way, since their ideological and existential platforms are underpinned by prerequisites that are gradually eroding and disappearing from under their feet.

Politics in the Internet Age is becoming increasingly ironic. It creates medial drama through inflating conflicts that either are purely fictitious or else utterly trivial and in practice insignificant. One makes a big fuss about merely marginal adjustments to a structure that is itself about to collapse. This explains why the main purpose of all the theatrical action is to cover up the fact that politics as we know it is slowly but surely losing its factual influence. Reality is about to leave politics behind, the most important decisions are increasingly being taken somewhere else – and above all under completely different forms – after which politics reacts only after the fact, more or less ineffectually. Both right and left choose to close their eyes tightly in order not to see, while one unreservedly supports what we call *democratism's false axiom*, the presumably indisputable yet hypocritical sanctification of the nation-state's ballot, blind faith in the uninformed and ahistorical, illusory premise stating that the consumtarian masses always are right, and that when they despite everything choose erroneously – according to the prevailing supraideology, which happens: Donald Trump, Brexit, and so on – it is fundamentally someone else's fault, even if it always remains unclear who this someone else actually is.

This in turn reveals that the elites not only have lost touch with the masses, but above all have lost the understanding of the factual truth about the interaction between Man and technology in itself; a phenomenon that the American blogger Jordan Greenhall accurately refers to as the elites' confused defense of the *blue church* against what he calls the netocratic swarm's frenetically attacking *red religion*. But the problems with the consumtarian masses are many, at least if one is striving for a well-functioning society without overly violent internal conflicts, in particular under the current, dramatic entry into what is called the information society, as the entire social biotope goes through pervasive and above all bewilderingly rapid changes, and as many in these masses for good reason feel hard-pressed in that they are increasingly less in demand in a job market continually shrinking because of digitalization, globalization and automation. A major problem is that these masses are abysmally ignorant of, for instance, how an economy actually works, how prosperity is created, and what consequences various wealth distribution policy actions actually have. This ignorance – carefully researched and proven, of course – perverts the entire political process. The politician who wants to be elected and re-elected must go after the votes of the ignorant, since the ignorant are so numerous, which in turn leads either to deeply cynical and fraudulent election campaigns, or else to genuinely bad politics, since this is what the ignorant voters actually request. Or both; the one does not exclude the other.

This monumental ignorance is carefully nurtured and reinforced by the Internet-related phenomenon that is called *the filter bubble*. To communicate with ignorant consumtarians and foist consumption goods upon them in large quantities, it is rational and useful to hold one's nose and flatter their prejudices. The Internet gives them unlimited possibilities, by punching a key or two and seeking out other information or entertainment the minute they bump into opinions that do not agree with their own, or facts that cannot be accommodated within their already cemented worldview. Every disturbance of this kind entails a threat to a social identity and to the sense of belonging in a social community. This means that someone who, for example, has gained popularity within a certain population segment by spewing nonsense in the form of easily digestible entertainment, can relatively easily convert this popularity into political support if they decide to go into politics. It does not matter that qualified political commentators and columnists reveal the clownish candidate's many shortcomings, since this criticism has no chance of penetrating the armored filter bubble where these followers consume media. And to the extent that this criticism actually penetrates, it makes these followers feeling personally attacked, which instead makes them even more loyal to their "truth-tellers." There is no way out of this dilemma in sight.

In an episode of the dystopian-satirical TV series *Black Mirror* an animated blue bear, mean and extremely foul-mouthed, scores a big victory in a British parliamentary by-election. In the real world, the United States elected an orange, simple-minded entertainer as president in 2016, mean and extremely foul-mouthed. The aspect of democratism that lacks attention to history leads it, in the desperate quest for the consumtarian mob's favor, to constantly and gladly crush its sole actually functional project, namely *representative democracy*, which was the only worthy defense against populism's group-egotistical charge that the nation-state was able to mobilize. But how does one save representative democracy when there no longer is any sensible citizen prepared to participate in the social humiliation and ridiculous media circus that is required when one is a candidate for high office? No political actor, and very few of the unaffiliated commentators, would venture to point out the fact, apparent to all and sundry, that voters now have the choice among exactly the candidates that they deserve. The citizens have themselves rallied around this infantile stupidity and have taken care to bully off all the candidates who were serious and prepared to tell the electorate the truth. So in the end one elects boundlessly vulgar and ignorant characters from so-called reality TV as presidents in not insignificant countries. The result is chaos, both nationally and internationally, as well as endless discussions about so-called alternative facts.

If the fetish assumes a personal shape, we call it an *idol*. If the abject similarly assumes a personal shape, we call it a *demon*. Idolatry is thus a fetishization of another person or creature. Correspondingly, a demonization is an abjectification of another person or creature. The most cathexal object of them all, including both fetishist and abjective attractions, is phallus. The opposite of the phallus, the matrix, does not have the same function – it is, for obvious reasons not associated with phallus' fundamental pointlessness, transformed out of necessity into the upholder of libido. Matrix is instead both the origin and the conclusion of the whole process that is controlled by the constant oscillation between phallus worship (eternalization) and phallus demonization (mobilization), that is: the will to life in itself. Phallus is therefore libido's symbol in consciousness and matrix is mortido's symbol in subconsciousness.

Phallus unites the entire sensory field and seemingly also gives it meaning, it is the symbol of eternalism. Matrix splinters the sensory field, reassembles it as a chaotic reality, it is the symbol of mobilism. This means that when phallus acts as the fetish, matrix takes the role of the abject. And when matrix acts as the fetish, phallus takes the role of the abject. Sex in itself, or what is called *the sexual differentiation* within psychoanalysis, is thus the fetish-abject *par excellence.* And the fetish-abject guarantees not only the genesis of existence, but also its upholding, through its fundamental *discord*, its ability to prevent all forms of perfection and satisfaction. The fetish-abject is the cathexal object. Consequently history always starts with the sentence "In the beginning there was the cathexal object." The rest of history is then a dance around the fetish-abject, a dance that is characterized by an eternal repetition of the same steps over and over again. And when the dance is over, the organism dies and returns, at least figuratively speaking, to the original unconsciousness in the matrix. So what does the internal relation between the fetish and the abject look like?

A fundamental difference in role and value arises for the small child when mamilla no longer can be apprehended as the child's property, but is revealed as the mother's own and thus phallus' property instead. The child's reaction to this discovery will be the subsequent lifelong obsession with the lost fragment as such, an object that is always sought but can never be found, Lacan's *objet a.* Whether this object then has the character of a fetish or an abject is determined based on whether *the phallic intrusion* happens in the child's imaginary universe or not. If the child gets support from phallus as the attractor to the reality outside the matrichal semiotic soup, the child will also succeed in fetishizing the cathexal object that it constantly seeks but never finds. But if the phallic intrusion fails, the child will fetishize the lost breast, refuse to love fate and reality outside the matrichal semiotic soup, and thereby live eternally locked inside the expanded matrix. This in turn requires that the surrounding world be abjectified. The world becomes one big threat to the child's infantile, artificial idyll tied to the breast. Phallus, not mamilla, is abjectified. And with the abjectification of phallus, life and its merciless libido also becomes frightening. Reality becomes one big, unmanageable threat.

The child gets caught in an infantilized, grinding death drive. Mortido swallows libido. Life is transformed from a love of reality to a worship of the *status quo* and "life as a life without change," which is the same as no life at all, "life as a dead life." Since the child becomes unable to leave the imaginary universe and shift its focus to the symbolic universe, its infantilization lasts until death if nothing upsets these unproductive circles radically. The child quite simply never grows up. Note how the fetish and the abject here distinguish themselves from each other over time. The fetish is in a constant state of flux, which contributes to its character of being the elusive reward for Man's endeavors. But the abject has the character of an eternalization that never changes. Which means that one hunts the fetish from the starting point of the dream that it never will change and lose its magical attraction. In contrast to this, one hates the abject and blames it for its ontological evil; the abject is what it is and can, and will never change. Precisely therefore the abject can be held eternally responsible for its very existence, and thus all barriers to how much hatred and cruelty Man can pour onto the abject are removed. The result is something we can observe when children ruthlessly bully each other in the schoolyard, as well as in all pogroms, ethnic cleansings and extermination camps throughout history.

So what members within the tribe end up outside the customary set of regulations? Which ones are both inside and outside the social theater, and in the latter case quite literally as they are forced to manage on their own in the wilderness most of the time? The shamans could move between the various tribes and thereby built the temporary peace agreements that could be made for the common benefit of several tribes. A lingering example of this, in the modern day and age, is the Croat *zvoncari,* who roam the valleys of the mountainous areas on the Balkan Peninsula to maintain peace between the villages. The shamans quite simply were the rudimentary diplomats of their age. Consequently it is shamans who later become the priests that build common ritual sites, the first cities in history, that villages could share during feudalism. A certain group of young women, the female schamans, was also free to move between tribes, both for the sake of peace and the variation of the gene pool. If they chose to never commit to a new tribe after their banishment, they were free to take the role of witches, that is: to act as female shamans.

The hunting parties needed scouts and warriors to know where they should go and to what extent it was necessary to protect themselves if they chose to follow one possible path rather than the other. Therefore the scouts and the warriors often joined forces with the shamans and the witches in the tribe's geographic outskirts, either in the outermost periphery or quite simply periodically wholly detached from the tribes and therefore often wandering between the various constellations. During primitivism these free souls were insignificant. But in the future global era that we call the network society – characterized by enormous communication flows between large populations – their roles in the social theater suddenly become central and decisive. That these empire- bearing figures often are of an androgynous character is no coincidence. For androgyny has two advantages: In part the androgynous person better understands and can better express the different sides' respective positions in a conflict situation; in part the androgynous person, irrespective of formal sex, does not participate in the male competitions for success or the female intrigues that otherwise decide what status and what influence one will be accorded as a man within the patriarchy and as a woman within the matriarchy within the confines of the primitivist tribe. The androgynous human plays the game essentially according to his or her own – or at least alternative – rules and can attain status and influence through other methods.

The androgynous bearers of value are necessary for patriarchy and matriarchy to be able to cooperate, and constitute a small tribe within the tribe, what we call *the shamanic caste*. For this reason, a society that persecutes its androgynous members on moral grounds will always sooner or later be thrown into both internal and external conflicts caused by this narrow-mindedness and the deficiencies it creates. But a society where androgyny becomes normative for all men and women soon loses its collective libido, which leads to an extensive, mortidinal decadence – often powerfully colored by gnostic and pacifist illusions – that thrusts the society in question towards its downfall. The proof that the upholding of this sensitive balance – between on the one side, more or less stereotypical gender roles and on the other hand androgyny – acts as an axiomatic fundamental law for the primitivist nomadic tribe, is that all the indicators we use regarding androgyny show that this trait occurs evenly across all the populations we look at on the planet. History and sociobiology could hardly collaborate more convincingly. The androgynous members are central for the tribe's survival, but they are also invariably experienced power players at its margins and never rulers at its center.

10
Plato's, Kant's and Einstein's mistake – the autistic ape's dream of the perfect machine

What is actually real? Is it reality – the world of stoves and saucepans that we perceive with our sensory organs, what we can see with our own eyes and touch with our own hands – that is the really real? Or is this perceptible world merely a deceptive pretense, what Plato in ancient Greece regards as a projection of shadow images on the inner wall of a cave, images that at best can give us a weak, provisional sense of the real reality that exists somewhere beyond or above what we humans in our ignorance usually call reality, but that actually should be called something completely different? Indeed, the learned disagree on this, as they have done from the beginning of time. There are many ways of viewing the history of ideas, one of which is as a long fight over precisely this, the true nature of reality and the line of inquiry that is connected to this crucial distinction. Philosophy even has two disciplines, *ontology* as well as *phenomenology*, set aside for the subject.

Either the real reality, as with Plato, is given once and for all, fixed and eternal, immutable; or else the reality before our eyes is the only reality that really exists, and thus also is in a *constant state of flux*. This change is the phenomenon on which the dispute ultimately hinges. Either the change is a fundamental property of existence, or else it is an insignificant ripple on the surface of an illusory likeness that in itself is meaningless. This can be expressed in accordance with the *dialectics of eternalism and mobilism* (see *The Global Empire*): Is existence in itself, beyond human perception, fundamentally eternalist (fixed) or mobilist (mutable)? What status does the one or the other claim? What precedes what? Is it eternalism that is primary in relation to mobilism, or is it conversely mobilism that is primary in relation to eternalism? Was there even a universe before this particular universe appeared, started to change and expand? Or is the change and the movement so decisive and fundamental that existence first must be set in motion in order to be able to claim in any kind of meaningful way that it even exists? Is there anything other than change?

This line of inquiry can of course also be translated into physical terms: Is time, as eternalism maintains, a byproduct of space? Or is space, as mobilism maintains, a byproduct of time? Should we add the time dimensions on top of the space dimensions? Or is it instead correct to regard the space dimensions as an addition to fundamental time? This conflict between eternalists and mobilists recurs within all civilizations. It arises between Confucians and Taoists in ancient China. It expresses itself in the disagreements between the eternalist Egyptians and the mobilist Iranians in the ancient Middle East. It is embedded in the Indian gurus' non-dualist doctrines as the insidious pseudodualism of the mystics. It recurs in the struggle between the eternalist rationalists (Man is governed by reason) and the mobilist empiricists (Man is governed by passions and emotions) during the European Enlightenment. And it is revived within 21st century cosmology in the form of the antagonism prevailing between a belief in an essentially mathematical cosmos – as in Max Tegmark's book *Our Mathematical Universe* – and a belief in an essentially network-dynamical cosmos – as in

Lee Smolin's and Robert Mangabeira Unger's book *The Singular Universe and The Reality of Time.*

In ancient Greece, the two positions of the conflicts are personified in part by the radical eternalist Parmenides, in part by the equally radical mobilist Heraclitus. Parmenides maintains that all time and all change are purely illusory. There is really no authentic change at all, and therefore no time either since it is impossible by definition to speak of time without observing a change that is both real and fundamental – something must change in order for time to take place, if nothing has changed, no time has elapsed. Time is therefore, according to Parmenides, simply an illusion. And consequently, existence is actually an eternally immutable, timeless entity that we mortal (and mutable) creatures cannot properly understand since the real reality is unavailable to our primitive and time-bound perception. Change can only exist in this secondary dimension, and we humans cannot be participants in the real existence that simply is out of reach. Only the truly intelligent among us can even imagine it.

If Parmenides in this way opens the door to radical eternalism in European thinking, it is Plato who completes the project; that he even names one of his dialogues precisely after *Parmenides* speaks volumes. As Plato puts it in his famous cave metaphor in the dialogue *The Republic*, Man is doomed to sit fettered in a jail, located in a cave, lit by a fire. She has her back towards the opening and her face turned towards the inner wall across which shadows play. These shadows are all she sees, all she has as a point of departure as she tries to form an impression of the nature of the world. But she thus has no real inkling, she has nothing but misleading illusions available to her. The real reality is outside the cave, out of sight. This is Plato's world of ideas, entirely perfect in every respect and therefore timeless (some would even say lifeless) and immutable by definition. If the world of ideas could undergo changes, it would of course not be perfect, since what can be changed for the better has not yet achieved perfection, and something changing for the worse would indicate an inherent insufficiency. Plato thus supports, and develops, Parmenides' radical eternalism. He elevates the timeless forms, the non-material, while degrading matter and human physicality. It is this side of Plato's thinking that powerfully colors both Christian and Islamic theology. This entire cluster of understanding about a transcendent God that exists beyond all time, of the real domicile of the immortal soul in an eternal, immutable world beyond this flawed provisory one contaminated by original sin, has its origins in Plato's cave. Without Parmenides, no Plato, and without Plato, no Saint Paul.

Heraclitus, who was of Iranian descent – who by all accounts served as a court philosopher in the Median Empire in western Persia, rather than in classical Greece – conversely argues, "it is not possible to put one's foot in the same river twice," simply because the next time it will not be a question of the same foot or the same river. Both have undergone a significant change in between occasions, a change brought about by this time that, along with the very change itself, paradoxically constitutes in a giant ocean of illusions, the only constants of existence. All fixed contours, all concepts of permanence, are fictions with whose help we create an arbitrary but nevertheless functional order. Actually, all boundaries are fluid and everything is processes in constant change: *panta rei*. This change, which is primary, is what we call time, which some choose to regard as secondary. Consequently, time is absolute according to Heraclitus. Time is the bedrock upon which everything else rests, and it is also the very basic condition for us to even be able to understand anything else in existence, both within and outside time itself. Unsurprisingly, there is even a religion dedicated to time worship in ancient Iran; *Zurvanism* extols the gender-neutral god *Zurvan*, indifferent to man, in other words: time itself as the primordial god behind and beyond everything else, primordial father and primordial mother of existence, all in one.

According to Parmenides the situation is, as we understand it, exactly the other way around: time is the great illusion, all change is illusory, an equally revealing and unavoidable phenomenon of decadence in a defective mock reality. But the mere fact that there must be a difference for Parmenides' readers and/or listeners in how they imagine time before compared to after having read or listened to this argumentation, of course means that change most definitely must exist. This change is real, and this is exactly what causes Parmenides to formulate his thoughts in the first place: to produce this change from an erroneous to a correct mode of thinking about existence. The contradiction is evident. Parmenides cannot produce philosophy without producing contradiction, just as Plato argues against written language in writing. Parmenides does something other than what he says he does; change is indisputable and time is therefore real. Or to express the matter ontologically: The only thing that does not change over time is change itself, which is constant. Change, and only change, is our constant companion.

The problem lies then in how we handle this fundamental onto-epistemological insight. What exactly is mystical time? And why are all these ideas that time is actually unreal so bewilderingly popular and constantly recurring throughout the history of ideas, in spite of Parmenides' spectacular fall after having tripped himself up? Why is it so hard to embrace the thought that change actually is real? In this context it is important that one perceives the layer of involuntary irony that envelops Plato's famous cave. Plato of course imagines that the existence that plays out inside the cave, lit only by a blazing fire, is an ever-changing play of shadows on a cave wall, while the real reality, the perfect and thus unalterable world of ideas, is what goes on outside the mouth of the cave and thereby also is out of sight to us humans, meaning that we cannot create an image of how things really are. What is ironic, of course, is that it is precisely the other way around. Inside the cave virtually nothing changes. Outside is only change.

Plato's reasoning is thus an incantation; he is terrified at the thought of the phallic world with all the responsibility and freedom that comes with it, demanding from Man resolute and determined action. Once again the self-contradiction is grating: it is the cave that is the utopia. What Plato strives for is what constitutes the Abrahamic religions' lost paradise: a frenetic climb up the umbilical cord, via the *mamilla* that offers the sweet mother's milk without even a hint of requiring anything in return, into the *matrix's* warm and snug cave where absolutely nothing ever happens or changes. We are in fact speaking about returning to the child's world and turning away from the adult world. In the matrichal, circular world change is but a chimera and time is an illusion; everything is secure and preordained from the start, no unpleasant surprises can occur and no unpleasant demands can be made. The contrast with the phallic, dialectical world which makes its presence felt with its menacing shadows, could not be sharper: here awaits the unpredictable, sublime libido that demands of Man a responsible management of freedom, which of course is frightening in certain respects. In all his cognitive sophistication Plato remains the inhibited child, terrified at the many challenging demands of attaining adulthood. Becoming an adult man means that the youth is confronted with his own temporality, his own aging and his own mortality, and is forced to say farewell to all childish fantasies of permanence, eternal youth and eternal life.

Platonism receives its own most extreme expression within what is called *Gnosticism* – a widespread concept within the history of religion that includes various movements in the area around the Middle East from the year 80 and onwards. What the Gnostics have in common is the conviction that the physical world in which we live is created by the evil Demiurge: *temporality*, how it changes and thereby increasingly distances itself from the true and the good are the defining features of this world. Time is thus evil's primary property and tool, it is with the aid of time that evil constantly acts for destruction and corruption. The contrast to this sensory world of the Demiurge is the world of the souls, entirely perfect and thus timeless and eternally protected from the decay of change. Therefore, the good by definition must be timeless. Paradoxically, time still cannot be presumed to cease in the paradise of timelessness, since this state of affairs is thought to endure and not to perish. The golden age of the Gnostics occurs during Manichaeism, a dualist religion that was proclaimed by Mani, a prophet born and raised in Babylonia, who was executed by the Iranian emperor Bahram I in 276. Mani divides the world into, on the one hand, good spirituality and, on the other hand, evil in bodily form. His doctrine took the Roman Empire by storm during the second half of its existence, when Manichaeism intermittently was the world's most widely spread religion. The Gnostic inheritance from the doctrine today lives on most prominently within Islam's Shiite branch.

The Hindu *Advaita Vedanta* philosophy, with its non-dualist fundamental view, is a doctrine that all radical monist process philosophers find it easy to sympathize with. And yet there is a remnant of the robust conviction that behind all the disparate forms of expression in existence – beneath all the processes and relations that we can observe and deduce – there is but one god, *Brahman*, elevated above time and space (to not speak of change), that pulls all the strings. We call this conviction *pseudodualism* since an even deeper and more primary dualism sneaks in behind the official "non-dualist monism." Even more process-philosophically oriented thinkers within Advaita Vedanta, such as Nisargadatta Maharj – one of the 20th century giants within this school of thinking – maintain that pseudodualist eternalism must be the foundation for our understanding of the world. It is hardly surprising that a conviction of this kind makes it possible to invent *cosmic consciousness*, a neutral and impersonal supraconsciousness that expresses itself in all the less personal consciousness that we find for instance among the seven billion people living here together in our world. But what then is this eternalism at closer consideration, if not a stealthy acceptance of the very dualism that Advaita Vedanta claims to reject? And what is this eternalism if not the philosopher's own death worship – to choose one's own perception process and its more or less arbitrary (most likely more) freezing of the mobilist chaos of existence as a starting point for the understanding of existence as a whole?

In spite of all the pious talk of Hinduism as non-dualist, its most important doctrines still land with a belly-flop in exactly the same phallophobic dualism that distinguishes Plato's fairytale world. Hindu pseudodualism is just concealed behind veils of mysticism rather than put forward as the primary principle. But in practice it makes no difference. Rather, Asian monism is cultivated outside the borders of multi-cultural India. It is intriguing that neither Zoroastrianism in Central Asia nor Dzogchen Buddhism in Tibet – two influential, genuinely monist traditions within Asian philosophy – allow Adavaita Vedanta's highly dubious, in philosophical terms, pseudodualist maneuver in the direction towards eternalism. Within these two currents one rejects all determinist ideas, posited beyond time and space, that lay claim to underpin all of existence; all such things are instead regarded as illusion fabrication and self-deception. From a European perspective it can be expressed as though Advaita Vedanta attempts to save the god that Nietzsche pronounces dead in the late 19th century. Which means that instead of the mystic – as the most sophisticated nihilist who knows perfectly well that God really is dead – we end up with a guild of Hindu mystics, created by Advaita Vedanta and consisting of closet Platonists. The Zoroastrians and the Dzogchen Buddhists see through this intellectual trickery.

According to the Zoroastrians and the Dzogchen Buddhists, existence is instead viewed in its essence as a *process*, it is *change in itself*, and it is this process which occurs along the universal timeline that generates relations, including spatial dimensions, that in turn give rise to the temporary nodes of intensity that we understand as *relata* that later form *phenomena*. If these phenomena are active, we call them *actants* within process philosophy. If these actants moreover act from some kind of discernible self-interest, we call them *agents*, since they *de facto* are driven by an *agenda* of their own. The fundamental point is that events occur along the timeline in exactly this order and that no alternative and timeless world of ideas such as the one Plato dreams of exists – nor any sneaking eternalist Brahman beneath the iceberg's deceptively non-dualist apex – in some kind of freely fabricated dimension that is disconnected from time and the processes that inexorably move in the direction that the timeline indicates. Advaita Vedanta's concealed eternalism is thus revealed for what it really is: a fairytale, a figment, a yearning back to matrix's infantile irresponsibility and freedom from demands, strongly imbued by death worship, a flight from the constantly troublesome and disciplinary libido's inexorable demands for adult stances.

In light of this, it is hardly surprising that it is Hinduism – in contrast to, for instance, Zoroastrianism, Dzogchen Buddhism, and closely related doctrines such as *Chan* in China and *Zen* in Japan – that regards the life that actually exists as being but a prelude to some kind of new, real life located beyond this life and death. The Hindu conception of *reincarnation* thus constitutes a near-unbeatable record within the history of ideas in regard to dualist phantasms. It is obviously completely irreconcilable with a monist process philosophy. Reincarnation requires that body and soul in essence are distinct substances rather than fundamentally interlinked. Thus reincarnation, too, demonstrates Hinduism's fundamental pseudodualism. The opposite, less imaginative stance is expressed in what an old Zen monk once said: "There is no reincarnation since there is no soul to reincarnate." And if there is no eternal soul within Man (see also *The Body Machines*), neither is there any compelling reason to look for anything else that is timeless, elevated above all change, in the rest of existence. Heraclitus, Zoroaster and the founder of Chan and Zen in China, the Sogdian monk and merchant Bodhidharma, all put forward the standpoint that ultimately appears the only philosophically reasonable one. *Panta rei.* And it is also therefore that they are modern process philosophy's phallocentric ancestors.

We can of course always discuss how the almost infinite number of potentialities in existence are converted to the finite number of actualities; we can discuss the reality of the emergences and how these demonstrate the *indeterminism* of existence rather than its determinism (it is not enough that determinism presupposes that the embraced Platonic idea is the cause of everything that happens in existence, it must also be actively involved in the design of every detail as well). But we cannot escape the worrying insight that Man's most deeply felt existential need is not to understand himself, but to realize and handle her own mortality. This fact generates the demons that proceed to drive her. Belief in an ultimate god beyond time and space – as a sort of compensation, or possibly even a cure for the oppressive chaos and disheartening pointlessness of existence – has its origin precisely in this *demonology*, and every such fatalist ideology must submit to and attempt to defend both determinism and dualism in order to be able to show the least sign of intellectual honesty.

If one insists on pretending to find meaning for oneself and/or others in these fictions – which on closer inspection merely consist of hot air – one cannot possibly accept indeterminism and monism as ideological fundamentals, despite everything that indisputably indicates that this is precisely the case. So one has to lie. And one always becomes, as we know, a much more convincing liar if one first has succeeded in duping oneself. Which therefore is not uncommon. One forms communities that are completely built on this collective lying. One organizes society in line with this lying. For it is not possible to fool the underclass – be they poor farmers or poor workers – into toiling themselves to death in croplands or other people's factories unless one offers a fictitious reward in the next life that gives an uplifting meaning to the daily toil and the everlasting poverty. Therefore one embraces an ideology that produces either a heaven or progress. One writes checks for amazingly high amounts, where the snag is that these only can be cashed in after death.

This means that determinism and dualism have dominated the production of ideology throughout history, not because they have reflected something that actually exists but simply because they have been functional and cost-efficient power instruments. This of course does not preclude that there have been plenty of earnest proponents of these ideas, people without a self-interest to argue for, but with an urgent yearning for a return to matrix that makes them claim that mathematics' timeless world of formulae actually is more real than reality. The history of ideas is populated by a long line of autistic apes who dream of the perfect machine above the clouds. Plato, Descartes, Newton, Kant, and in our age Albert Einstein and Max Tegmark: they are all proclaimed eternalists of this kind. In the modern age they worship creation – *The Big Bang* – as the fetish that seems to make everything in existence add up, with a theory stating that everything that occurred after this primordial explosion a little less than 14 billion years ago actually was preprogrammed and has taken place in the world in the same way that billiard balls roll across the table and collide with each other after a powerful break shot. Admittedly the whole thing is complicated, but if one only knows the laws of nature, more or less everything is possible to predict.

The problem is that the entire idea about laws in nature is built on fiction. Indeed phallus is the symbol of order and tidiness in the chaos of existence, but this order is a chimera. An admittedly functional one, but still a chimera. Creating a phallus as a symbol of this order and this tidiness does of course not mean that nature suddenly decides to follow some man-made laws – why would it? If one studies nature, it displays certain patterns in certain respects, but that is another matter. It is in a state of constant flux; the law is a human invention that arises as a useful byproduct of written language in various parts of the world some 5,000 years ago. Our reasoning around laws of nature tricks us into believing that the eternalizations we dream up to achieve a little clarity, actually are real. The whole issue becomes clearer if one views the matter through an alternative optics. In truth, history consists of a series of *universal temporal momenta* and in no way any individual objects set in motion by extreme forces and that therefore collide, argues the British philosopher Alfred North Whitehead. Hence it follows that what actually does exist are *existential necessities* – where time in itself is the existential necessity *par excellence* – but no laws of nature.

Over and above the existential necessities – in which we include *the four great emergences* in universal history; physics, chemistry, biology and consciousness – there are only more or less stable or unstable *habits of nature*, which moreover are local and not universal. So when we, consequently, bid farewell to the idea of laws of nature, we might as well bid farewell to the idea of a *moralator*, a universal nature legislator. And it is about time we did, the creating god is long dead. A muddle in the history of ideas has been created from three presumed phenomena of an axiomatic character, which also turn out to be myths on closer inspection: *the void*, *eternity* and *infinity*. From an ontic perspective there is no void, a space always consists of something in itself, it can never be empty. “Nothing is full of things,” as the physicist Lawrence Krauss remarks: it is full of virtual particles that constantly appear and disappear, and this kind of “nothing” sooner or later produces a “something” since what we ought to call *quantum organics* rather than quantum mechanics happens to work that way. And similarly there is, from an ontic perspective, no eternity other than in language, the timeline always has a point of departure and a final destination before and after which there is no time. The same goes for infinity, which does not exist either, from an ontic perspective. Speaking of an enormously large universe, an *enormity*, is not the same as speaking of an infinite universe.

Mathematics leads us astray in this respect. Yes, there is a zero (nothing), and there is an eternity and infinity symbol (∞) in equations, but abstract mathematics allowing one to experiment with these fictitious quantities when writing formulae is no guarantee for and no proof that these signs have any correspondence anywhere in nature. Quite the contrary, when mathematics creates the zero and the infinity symbol it gives up all claims of actually representing existence outside Man's fantasy and conceptual world. From the perspective of the history of ideas this is completely decisive: *Mathematics does not represent existence, mathematics merely represents Man's fantasy about existence* and it really has no existence outside these fantasies. Which means that the physicist Max Tegmark (and others) is fundamentally wrong when he (they) maintains that we are living in "a mathematical universe." It is in fact precisely the other way around: We are living in the midst of a process, we are living in a network-dynamical universe, and mathematics is one of its innumerable byproducts. Not more nor less.

This means that all thoughts of an eternal and infinite universe full of voids contain three basic *non sequiturs*. By taking note of and opposing these three *non sequiturs*, as well as the eternalism and determinism that constitute the prerequisites for this erroneous thinking, we want to clear away the delusions that stand in the way of encompassing with our thoughts the mobilist and indeterminist universe that actually exists and of which we actually are a part. The mobilist alternative to the eternalist mythology is to create a long series of fetishes – contingent emergences that actually occur later in history – as ontic realities which change or renew the local habits of nature in the part of the Universe where they occur. Darwinian evolution's diversity of animal and plant species on our own planet is a striking example of this. But it requires an indeterminist worldview with a real time and an open and unknown future. We are speaking of a world not created by God – with or without a *Big Bang* – but that instead fully consciously creates the God this world needs through a collective process connected to the Internet that interconnects the collective (for extensive theological reasoning on this topic, see *Syntheism – Creating God in The Internet Age*).

This is the syntheist position, the utopian belief in *Syntheos*, in contrast to the scientistic inheritance from the monotheist religions, with their abjective worship of the quasi-divine and mystical *primordial creation* as both the beginning and end of all genuine creativity. From Plato to Einstein, philosophy and science have of arm-in-arm first created and then patched up an eternalist worldview where God – or the Universe if we are secularly disposed – constitutes the sole singularity, which remarkably is reduced to one frozen moment. For it is here that physical determinism and ontological eternalism always lead: to Plato's *world of ideas*, to the Abrahamic religions' *monotheist heaven*, to Hinduism's *Para Brahman*, to Einstein's *block universe* (one massive, delimited block of spacetime that encompasses everything that has occurred and everything that will occur), or to Max Tegmark's *mathematical universe*. However, what constantly recurs, the common denominator in this motley mixture of fantasies, is *the autistic ape's dream of the perfect machine*. Everything is preordained, determinist; no real change is possible.

This entire mode of thought and all these concepts are pure illusions, sprung from the same fatal mistakes, namely the idea that the world really is manageably eternalist instead of challengingly mobilist. As though the human being really were the pinnacle of creation and the world a reflection of our own, self-absorbed fantasies about ourselves. As though the world were not much richer and more fascinating than that. So let us turn the tables instead. There is much to suggest that it can be every bit as rewarding to try to find out what mobilism actually says about eternalizing Man's place in a mobilist existence, rather than trying to formulate how eternalism's fantasizing about existence as a convenient likeness to the human perception process is constructed. It then turns out that the subject constantly finds itself, so to speak, in the wrong place. It is actually this very state of affairs that constitutes subjectivity. Searching for the subjective fixation is ultimately nothing other than intensely longing for one's own death. *The subject process* is in other words *the dialectics between libido and mortido par excellence.*

The German philosopher Markus Gabriel toys with this theme in an interesting way in his book *Why the world does not exist.* By claiming that everything Man has ever fantasized about possesses ontological significance except the very concept of *the world* in itself, Gabriel tries to save the subject from philosophical extinction. However it is *de facto* precisely the other way around: In his vertiginous mathematics the American physicist and philosopher David Bohm shows that if quantum organics and other network-dynamical phenomena are to be incorporated both conceptually and mathematically in Man's worldview, this worldview must take a radical and monist holism as its point of departure. That is, the world really is one single thing, one single cohesive phenomenon undergoing constant change, change that is played out along the timeline in one single direction. The question of what is ontic aside from this, or can be established ontologically at all, in the structure that Bohm calls the *holomovement* – a dynamical whole in constant movement (and change) – thus becomes secondary. Gabriel is thus mistaken: the only thing that ontically exists is *Bohm's univocal universe* is the world in its entirety as one single cohesive phenomenon – a phenomenon that first arises and then ceases, and that thus is and must be fundamentally mutable – at every given *momentum* along the timeline. Everything else can, on the other hand, be dismantled to pure ontology, without any necessary, underlying, ontic status of its own. For inside this one and only cohesive universe there is, as Nietzsche expresses the matter, *nothing that is less than two.* Everything other than the Universe itself, which alone is in the singular, for Man is merely singular in his own imagination.

In this way, we formulate the Hegelian negation to Gabriel's neo-Cartesian ontology: It is the world in itself, as a whole, that has the indisputable monopoly on acting as an ontological foundation, since the ontic or noumenal – and this includes all ontics – only can receive ontological and thus also phenomenological significance when it is posited as temporarily eternalized phenomena along the time axis in Bohm's *holomovement*. When Gabriel argues that "the world" as a concept is "a signifier without anything to signify," he does not realize that "the world" signifies the highly ontic Bohmian holomovement in itself. And as such the concept "the world" is not just ontologically sustainable and fundamental – it is, if used as French psychoanalyst Jacques Lacan's *floating signifier*, also *the signifier par excellence*, the starting point for all rational understanding of existence. We therefore see no other possible alternative than to reject Gabriel's relativist experiment as yet another one of the many philosophically interesting failures in the history of ideas.

Syntheology generously bestows two names on the holomovement, an ontological and an ontic one: First the ontological *Pantheos* for the world as a whole, for the world as an external eternalist phenomenon, and then the ontic *Entheos* for the world as the utterly real Bohmian holomovement, for the world as an internal mobilist noumenon. The human subject becomes the last instance in the entire ontological chain. It is not the world that does not exist, as Gabriel claims, it is its reflection, the human subject, that does not exist other than as a useful fiction (which indeed is not the worst thing it could be). *The experience of being a subject* arises when the mind via the perception process is unable to connect the incoming information into a cohesive worldview. It is the last resort, a cosmetic emergency solution in the form of secret concealer of experience spread over the mysteries of existence to hide all cracks and simulate coherent uniformity. There and only there does consciousness arise as a kind of waste product of history, and with it follows self-consciousness. Outside this process there are no other consciousnesses at all. They are not necessary in order for the Universe to exist. Particularly since consciousness always arrives late for everything that it afterwards claims to have affected, which also what empirical research shows (see *The Body Machines*). The body acts wholly on its own accord and consciousness produces a story afterwards that confirms intentions that never existed, precisely to build the illusion of the self and free will.

Note that the network- dynamical worldview has no problem whatsoever in encompassing structuralist thinking. In truth we cannot understand or interpret any individual phenomenon whatsoever without using a more or less reliable preunderstanding, and with the aid of this, give the phenomenon in question a place in a contextual structure. The fundamental question to allow us to grasp how understanding is produced and to determine the degree of reasonableness is about what structure we use. Which model do we hire to orient ourselves within an existence that we really cannot survey, and why do we choose this particular model? The Slovenian philosopher Slavoj Žižek argues that since this structure not only makes it possible for the dividual to observe, eternalize and also interact with various phenomena (including itself), but *de facto* also colors all these activities with a concomitant set of values and valuations, the correct name for this structure must be *ideology*.

Žižek's socioanalytical project is therefore to conduct a radical ideology critique, to establish a sort of 21st century Frankfurt School that methodically and purposively monitors and interprets the many signals that have their origin in and reveal the deep-seated structures that underpin both the conscious, and above all the subconscious ideology of society. For it is – if we take a memetic perspective – only the memes and *memeplexes* (clusters of memes) that gain a foothold in the prevailing structures, ideas and conceptions that to a sufficiently large extent are in line with the formative ideologies, that succeed in surviving in the constantly active Darwinian selection process. It is precisely these memes and memeplexes, and no others, that can be subsumed in the collectively encompassed worldview. All conceivable alternatives to these are mercilessly culled. Which means that every worldview by necessity is ideologically conditioned. If Nietzsche points out that no philosopher, no matter how advanced, under any circumstances can think outside his own psychology, Žižek makes clear that no philosopher ever, no matter how advanced, can think outside his own ideology. The confines for thinking are always there; they can be understood as a prison, but one must also be aware that it is these confines that provide meaning. Without the confines that mark the boundaries of the ideology, thinking becomes pointless: not words, just sounds.

The Žižekian ideology is, however, never anything more than *a phenomenal structure*, a chaotic and often sublimely attractive interaction between Lacan's psychoanalytical structures, the imaginary and symbolic orders. Therefore Žižek can also borrow Lacan's concept of *the real* as the disturbance that alternately unites and dissolves the prevailing ideology. Žižek quite simply develops and completes Lacanian structuralism by turning its psychoanalysis into socioanalysis. But the process-philosophical relationalism that we ourselves represent in the capacity of heirs to chronocentric process philosophers such as Alfred North Whitehead and Gilles Deleuze – in other words, the very thinkers that Žižek usually singles out as his opponents in books such as *Organs Without Bodies* (Alexander Bard and Jan Söderqvist have also been targets) – opens the door to something considerably more radical, namely the Bohmian holomovement as the noumenal, rather than merely the phenomenal, *structure par excellence*.

It is thus no coincidence that Whitehead inspires Bohm and that Bohm in turn inspires Deleuze. What was long missing were confirmations of the Bohmian holomovement from the world of physics, but this is no longer the case after the millennium shift because of the breakthroughs of the superstring theory, loop quantum gravity and the most Bohmian of all physical theories, the holographic universe. Consequently we now live not only in the Whiteheadian-Bohmian-Deleuzian era within philosophy, but every bit as much within physics. Where Žižek is forced to seek adherents amid harsh eternalists such as Einstein and Tegmark, if he does not once and for all actually accept that his idol Hegel actually is the first Deleuzian, and thus also the thinker who besides the confused rationalist Spinoza and the equally confused determinist Hume must be regarded as one of the first, primitive process philosophers within Western thinking. Where all these naturally are in fundamental opposition to history's most resplendent autistic ape: Immanuel Kant.

It has probably become obvious that what we are discussing here is another, considerably more radical and more profound structuralism than the relativist model that enjoyed significant popularity within several academic disciplines, peaking in the 1960s and above all in France; a movement that we in many respects question and regard as essentially passé in a dialectical process that has taken considerable strides forward since. No, what we are speaking of here is instead *transcendental structuralism,* rooted in quantum organics and the discovery of our univocal, network-dynamical universe. The Bohmian holomovement is quite simply the structure that conquers all other structures once and for all. With this we have attained *the Hegelian absolute* in Man's physical environment rather than in Man's historical self-conception, as Hegel himself imagines the philosophical absolute in the early 19th century. With the Bohmian holomovement, philosophy has arrived at an extremely important full stop in the history of metaphysics – at least as important as for instance atheism's stealthy victory over theism that was launched 400 years ago, or monotheism's stealthy victory over the worship of primordial fathers that begun as early as 4,000 years ago – and can hand over the remains of the exploration of this *superstructure beyond all other structures* to art and science.

What is *the Hegelian absolute* if not the philosophical equivalent of *the physical emergence*? Here philosophy is not really dealing with the Bohmian holomovement in itself, but with Man's insight into the

Bohmian holomovement's role as both the physical and philosophical foundation for our understanding of existence. For even if every moment has passed just as it emerged, and even if existence from an ontic vantage point merely consists of these Whiteheadian *momentum* after *momentum* and nothing else, every momentum is still followed by an enormously massive structure, that is: by a whole universe's rise and fall in one single moment. The dependence and influence of everything on everything else in the Universe – *Entheos* within *Pantheos* to express the matter syntheologically – cannot be regarded as anything other than an infinitely mutable, spatiotemporal superstructure, albeit with emphasis on the temporal rather than the spatial in order not to fall into some Einsteinian externalization trap. Thus structuralism should be connected via physics (as a physical emergence) to metaphysics (as an Hegelian absolute), without needing to take any consideration of phenomenological fraud or shortcomings. When we, on the other hand, speak of phenomenal structures, it only pertains to perceptual platforms on which Man can place his beloved cathexal objects to make the world comprehensible, manageable and passionate. And these platforms are naturally also in motion. Existence really is one big fairground attraction.

Obviously there are no set and sustainable structures – phenomenal or noumenal really does not matter in this context – in a chronocentric, relationalist universe. A static structuralism of this kind is of no interest to us, for reasons that should be clear by now. The Bohmian holomovement may be apprehended by Man as an eternalized phenomenon, but this does not preclude that it *de facto* is its direct opposite; rather it is *the only noumenal phenomenon in existence*. The Bohmian holomovement is of course the only phenomenon whose ontic existence is indisputable, one single cohesive phenomenon in constant movement and expansion in all directions. Or to return to Heraclitus' view: let us begin with *panta rei*. However, the entire phenomenon *panta rei* is in itself a single cohesive phenomenon, namely the Bohmian holomovement, whose indisputable foundation is simply the timeline itself, syntheism's *Entheos* which leads syntheism's *Pantheos* into a raging tango as one big univocal universe, the very universe where we ourselves live out our days. The dialectics of eternalism and mobilism shows how *the eternalizations are remobilized* as soon as the eternalizations have established themselves as surviving memes in dividual perception. The mind does perhaps imagine that it can afford more rest and peace than the Universe itself. But in order to keep up with the Bohmian holomovement's rampage, and in order to be able to relate constructively to it, the mind cannot be anything but notoriously faithless towards all its previous ideological convictions.

The truth is that the more mobile the transcendental structure, the greater the chance of survival for its successors in a world where the Bohmian holomovement rules supreme. Which means that within socioanalysis, we are really only using the concept "structuralism" as a metaphor – as an explanatory model for how the Žižekian ideology works – where the structures are historically, sociobiologically and culturally conditioned, but constantly compelled towards movement and change, since everything else on all levels is in a constant state of movement and change. Platonist perfection never appears, neither outside the cave nor anywhere else. Nor does the mythical, eternal rest appear, other than as the dividual's own death. Culture – and the lack of it – leaves us discontented. But if we had strolled around and experienced peace and contentment, we would never have had access to that very thing which fundamental repression has made us appreciate most of all in ourselves – our *libido*. One should therefore be careful what one wishes for; a paradise where nothing changes is definitely nothing to aim for. So we should not grieve that it does not exist nor can ever exist. At least not if we have learned to appreciate feeling that we are living while we are alive.

11
Our network-dynamical Universe – chronocentrism, emergentism and relationalism

The Canadian media theorist Marshall McLuhan makes a distinction between a visual and an acoustic world, which are created by two different media technologies. The leading technology that dominates a visual world is the phonetic alphabet as it meets the reader on the printed page of a book. The eye follows the letters, which form words, which form sentences, and so on. What the eye thereby emphasizes is linearity; in this way grammar is created that structures the visual world and that joins objects in the same way – relationships that create meaning are built up in a written text. The various parts together form a whole; understanding is created through analyzing the various parts separately in a first step, after which one assembles them in modules. This occurs through an at least seemingly objective observation, rather than as an engaged participation – a view that characterizes the capitalist era we are about to leave behind.

Sight, in this context, becomes the dominant and privileged sense in the human perception apparatus. This means that we tend to use the adage "What you see is what you get" and imagine that this is exactly how things are: that we can read the world with our own eyes. Which in turn means that our conception of the world keels sharply towards the visual and is characterized by a powerful *optocentrism* – an efficient way of balancing this could be to regularly draw on the perspective of blind people in the continuing production of the analysis of the world around us. We consistently use metaphors that refer to sight when we speak of our *worldview*, et cetera. We rely on our eyes to be truth witnesses without any critical reflection. Optocentrism also deceives us into believing that what we think we are seeing here and now, the ontic world we think we apprehend with the aid of the authoritatively influential sense of sight, by necessity must be the point of departure for our ontology. Optocentrism thus goes hand in hand with the fixation with space, *spatiocentrism*. But actually it is time that is the primary dimension, space is merely secondary in relation to time. This means that it is not at all what we see around us right now and right here that is the primary basis of our identity production. This process starts, rather, with our continuously updated *historiography*, which in turn has its start in memories and reflections around these memories.

Man may understand himself and act as though he were purely spatiocentric, but the internal processes which she uses to try to grasp the world ontologically must instead have *the chronocentric fantasy* as a starting point about the dividual himself and about the world. Self-image and worldview are thus first and foremost temporal rather than spatial phenomena. It is the relative emplacement along the timeline in relation to other phenomena – and not their emplacements in relation to various objects in one room or other – that determines the value of our many different memories in our constantly updated and often rewritten autobiographies. A shift that means that time takes over the function of space as a linchpin in our understanding of the world would entail that time steps forward as philosophy's really large, unsolved mystery. The philosophers' descriptions of time constantly get caught up in tautologies or glide over into focusing on the many consequences of the passage of time, but they do not succeed in conceptually capturing what time in itself actually is. Take for instance the popular cliché that claims "time is what a clock measures," which is completely pointless in its tautological narrow-mindedness. It is of course correct to say that clocks measure time, at least, linguistically correct. But it conveys no insight whatsoever about time.

Clocks articulate an aspect of a sort of time, which might say something about clocks but next to nothing about time in itself. Similarly it is correct to say that 1 + 1 = 2, but this too is a pointless tautology since 1 + 1 quite simply is another way of saying 2. We have merely uttered a banal given that does not increase our knowledge of either one or the other. At the same time, nothing stops us from imagining a time that manages perfectly well without a certain clock. Time indubitably existed before the clock, and time exists in places where no clocks exist, in deep rainforests where plants and animals live their lives and die their deaths without a human standing there keeping track of hours, minutes or seconds. Since a nothing is nowhere to be found – modern physics has proven that existence consists of field upon field upon field, which is why there is no void anywhere whatsoever – there is always something even if it may look like nothing to the naked eye. As soon as there is something, there is also time. Time is existence's eternal companion and the only phenomenon we know of that completely lacks emergent qualities. Time is, so to speak, for lack of better metaphors, the beginning and end of everything.

In his classic work *Being and Time* the German philosopher Martin Heidegger argues that human existence is time. Heideggerian time is however something considerably greater than the now that is in constant movement, it is instead three-dimensional and comprises both the past, the present and the future. But it is mobilist just the same, rather than eternalist. The expectations of what will come are encapsulated in the now, but when the expected (or unexpected) does happen – when the course of events hits the time axis with full force and goes from *potentiality* to *actuality* – it turns out that the past already is encapsulated in the future. What kind of person one becomes, what sort of existence one has, is thereafter determined, according to Heidegger, by how one handles this past in the future when the future is realized in the now, that is: in the now that takes shape then. In this way, Heidegger intertwines the three temporal dimensions into each other without eternalizing for that matter any of them. Rather, he is radical enough to simultaneously put them all in mobilist motion.

This means that Heidegger does not need any divine, timeless time, which would mean that some kind of eternal and infinite now hides behind three-dimensional time in the manner that all the major eternalists such as Plato, Kant, Einstein, the Hindus and the Abrahamic religions imagined the matter before him. Heideggerian time is quite simply just radically three-dimensional, without any mysterious accessories. It must be experienced as such, and since time is mobilist it can only be experienced in terms of an ending, a literal death, which gives the previous existence its value and meaning. If time is mobilist, it is also finite – everything dies sooner or later, or at least it ceases to exist according to the mobilist worldview – and this finitude is fundamental for its character. Infinity merely exists as a fiction underpinning philosophical castles in the air. Existence is time. Man is time. *Being* is therefore, according to Heidegger, nothing other than pure movement in the direction towards its own termination.

In parallel with Heidegger practicing philosophy in Germany, Henri Bergson develops an equally original and innovative process philosophy in France in the early 20th century. Bergson focuses on the fact that the Universe produces a constant and massive stream of *novelties*. But Man's recurring search for the original void – always this fervent yearning back to the matrix's freedom from responsibility – puts spokes in the wheel and prevents her from posing the basic metaphysical questions about *change in itself.* Or to express the matter syntheologically: *Atheos* stands in the way of the discovery of the, according to Bergson, considerably more important and not least more real *Entheos*. This erroneous metaphysical prioritization causes Man to focus on deadly repetitions instead of encouraging her to discover the unexpected and the exceptional. This in turn causes morals to be inseparable from submission. The consequence is of course that the function of consciousness must be reduced to taming our passions. It becomes the task of consciousness to turn us into obedient ensemble actors in the social theater, an inner tyrant that Bergson calls *socius*. Consciousness is not merely affected by, but also driven by the Freudian superego, in what the Iranian-Swedish futurologist Ashkan Fardost accurately calls Modern Man's *autodictatorship*. The eternalist worldview and its obsession with the primordial void is thus *the ideology of submission par excellence*.

In fact, consciousness merely comprehends effects, without for that matter having the least inkling of the causes of these effects. Consciousness tends to create these afterwards to keep the illusion of a cohesive worldview intact. Bergson expresses this as though the human mind is doomed to dwell on what he calls *the phantom of duration* instead of on duration itself. Bergson's successor and compatriot Gilles Deleuze expresses what is tantamount to Man being doomed to try to understand everything in existence from the perspective of tattered and incomplete ideas, that is: from effects that are separated from their actual causes. This makes Man understand the effects that her own body is subjected to – where the lack of alternatives brings about a sort of inverted narcissistic loop – as a result of her own activities. She makes herself and her own subjectivity the cause of everything that happens to her. This entails a shift away from a relation of powerlessness towards the surrounding world to a blind faith in the ability of consciousness to tame its own body and its passions. Consciousness hides its ignorance through reversing cause and effect. It starts understanding itself both as free and as the primary cause of what happens around the body. Not because this is really the case, but because the lack of knowledge and understanding causes the incomprehensible externality to be converted into a seemingly comprehensible internality. When consciousness no longer can imagine itself as free and the primary cause of what happens, the fantasy of its freedom and control over the course of events is shifted to some mystical precedent in the chain of cause and effect, that is: to *God*. Morals that are impossible to separate from submission thus become synonymous with the blind and uncritical obedience vis-à-vis God's laws and judgments. Quite irrespective of whether this interconnecting *moralator* is external or internal.

The issue of the various characters of time and space and how these two phenomena relate to each other, also imbues what is called enlightenment thinking. Isaac Newton presumes that both time and space are absolute. Gottfried Wilhelm Leibniz, on the other hand, maintains that both time and space are relational. The distinction between these two approaches appears clearly in the correspondence between Leibniz and Samuel Clarke, who was one of Newton's more significant adherents, from the early 18th century. Leibniz argues that the Newtonian idea of space as a kind of substance without properties, which not even God can destroy, must be seen as completely absurd. There cannot, argues Leibniz, be any positions that are possible to establish in time or in space as such, but all objects and events can only have a certain position in relation to other objects and events. This means that time and space as such are a kind of illusion. They are in themselves not real in the sense that they constitute substances, which thus they do not, and only substances are real in this respect. Space, according to Leibniz, is nothing else than the very order between various synchronous objects, and time is nothing else than events following each other. Full stop.

This would indubitably have been simple and comfortable, but the dialectics of eternalism and mobilism unfortunately crushes all dreams of the reality of objects that would make, as if by magic, time and space to be reduced to secondary or even illusory phenomena. Unfortunately it is of course quite the contrary, and the key to an understanding of this is seeing time as the bedrock of space instead of the other way around. Without time, no space; without time it is not possible to speak of an existence since it so to speak must take place in time. Further, we must understand that absolute time is the basis of relative time, as Einstein, inspired by both Leibniz and Nietzsche, otherwise believed himself to have understood in a completely exhaustive manner. This requires a particularly radical vantage point: If absolute time steps into the metaphysical sphere, absolute time by definition is universal. Everything that happens, happens synchronously. Absolute time is, then, by definition exactly the same everywhere in the Universe. Which in turn gives us the excellent rhetorical possibility of referring to this all-encompassing, synchronous passage of time – to avoid confusion with Newton's absolute time, which Einstein successfully puts to death – as *universal duration* or *global time*.

This in turn means that the Universe must be regarded as a single cohesive phenomenon. The Universe is one single thing and this thing is holistic, everywhere chained to the same all-encompassing axis of time. We call this *universal univocality*. Nietzsche is correct when he says that "there is nothing that is less than two." There is always one thing, and then there is always at least one other. But there is one single exception: The Universe itself extended along the global timeline. We find support for universal univocality in the world of physics: below the Planck length, physics' smallest meaningful distance, it becomes pointless to speak of various phenomena or of various positions as separate. While the Planck length is the smallest distance for the genesis of discrete objects – so-called loop quantum gravitation within physics even builds a spacetime consisting of

Planck-length long discrete objects – everything below the Planck length collapses into a complete chaos, without any meaningful topology whatsoever, where it literally is physically impossible to make any distinction whatsoever between one thing and another.

The fact is that it is precisely such a distended, gigantic phenomenon within a particularly minimal framework that constitutes the Universe of today. The Universe in itself, in its impressive whole, might even very well remain below the Planck length's necessary demarcation for differentiation, as one single, chaotic yet cohesive phenomenon, and along the global timeline. Akin to a massively compressed accordion with a huge number of unfoldable pleats. While relative time and its excretion of a huge number of attributes occurs within this cohesive, univocal universe in the form of the enormous, expanding universe that we have become acquainted with through modern cosmology. This means that the Universe is one cohesive phenomenon, including the universally scattered fields that the Universe is filled with. While everything else, in the words of Nietzsche, "always must be at least two," univocality belongs only to the universal in itself. As soon as we have agreed on this, we can start to build a complete monist as well as holistic worldview. There is only one single substance, as the Dutch enlightenment philosopher Baruch Spinoza puts it, even if this one substance can appear in infinitely endless varieties and display a great number of attributes. Everything in the Universe is dependent upon and influences everything else – not least through gravitation, but also by belonging to the same universal field – which means that the world is genuinely holistic.

Universal univocality moreover entails that the Universe is not particularly mechanical, but rather should be regarded as fundamentally organic. Thus we are correct in speaking of a *quantum organics* rather than a quantum mechanics to describe the smallest components of matter. From Alfred North Whitehead via Niels Bohr to David Bohm, quantum organicists appear as radical holists. If nature is fundamentally organic rather than mechanical, it also possesses, as the British physicist Basil Hiley observes, the possibility that life can arise. We can even, as the philosopher and psychologist William James does, take quantum organics to its furthest point and describe the Universe as *a panpsychic phenomenon* (however without for that matter chiming in with such claptrap as conceptions of the existence of a cosmic consciousness; a *potentiality* is, whether strong or weak, still not automatically the same as an *actuality*). This organicist thinking then of course requires that we question the Newtonian and Einsteinian axioms about time that we have lived with for the last 400 years. This price is of course not particularly high, considering that Newton's and Einstein's ideas of time are so narrow-mindedly eternalist and determinist, meaning that they ever more clearly start to appear outdated and obsolete.

To begin with: If the room has at least three dimensions, why then would time just settle for a single one? Interestingly, even the ancient Greeks distinguish between *chronos*, quantitative time, and *kairos*, qualitative time. Chronos grinds on mechanically throughout history, hurls itself over all obstacles and conquers every form of resistance, not wholly unlike Lacanian drive within psychoanalysis. Kairos, on the other hand, is the time that believes it apprehends a distinction between the eventist and the commonplace, which seeks the momentum that defines and gives meaning to the entire epoch in which the course of events takes place, not wholly unlike Lacanian desire. During the early 20th century Frenchman Henri Bergson with his innovative process philosophy precedes both the ensuing string theorists and loop quantum gravity researchers with his idea of two different temporal dimensions: *time* and *duration*. Bergsonian time is local time, bound in terms of cause and effect, while Bergsonian duration is a cohesive unit that comprises an infinite number of attributes, fluid and with no connection to cause and effect. Anyway, time is not synonymous with *entropy*, which some physicists often carelessly claim. Entropy does of course often morph into its opposite *centropy*, actually it is completely reasonable that entropy and centropy over great time spans balance each other, for instance through a coming *Big Bounce* for the Universe, while duration on the other hand inexorably moves in just one direction – forward – since nothing else is possible.

Even if time can move forward locally at different speeds in different parts of the Universe, as Einstein correctly shows in his theories of relativity, the Universe as a whole moves forward at a constant speed, the speed that is called *global time*, where the Universe as a whole should be regarded as its own clock, since no time measurement by definition can take place outside the Universe. When we for instance say that our Universe is just over 13.8 billion years old, this presumes global time without any local, relativist time-taking involved. What happens within the confines of the Universe – the only world we humans *de facto* know of – is quite distinct from what happens along its surface, that is: that which comprises and encompasses the Universe as one single interconnected system, which speaks with one single distinctive voice, universal univocality. Actually, it is quite possible to regard this univocal universe as a minimal phenomenon in itself, something that only has to comprise the enormous universe that we regard from inside itself but not from the outside. *The Big Bang* can, strictly speaking, very well be regarded as a local rather than as a global event, something that has taken place inside but as of yet not on the outside of the Universe. Along the surface of the Universe *The Big Bang*, the inner, explosive expansion happening all this time may have passed by more or less unnoticed. But no one, in any case, escapes global time, that is to say, the universal duration.

Since time's merciless march towards the future constantly reminds Man of his own mortality, Man's fear of death constantly generates cultures centered on the pleasant concept of *time-as-an-illusion*. Buddhism, Hinduism, the Abrahamic religions (starting with Jewish mysticism), Platonist philosophy and modern physics' idea of an Einsteinian block universe all require that time be an illusion. There is, however, no proof that this is the case, neither in science as tried and tested, nor within philosophical logic. Rather, we must regard time-as-an-illusion as the greatest, most comprehensive and most cherished myth in human history. Not simply because of how it combines an enormous popularity with a full-fledged illusion machinery, but because time-as-an-illusion is the foundation of all the other tenacious, dualist thought systems throughout history – such as, for instance, the Abrahamic religions', the circular mythologies' and Cartesian individualism's distinction between the mortal body and the immortal soul – where *mortido* or the death drive is attributed existential precedence over *libido* or the will to life.

The ultimate dualism is of course that which lies between the temporal world as an illusion and the mystical eternal world without time as its underlying reality, which in some sort of bizarre way still seems to *be ongoing without being ongoing.* It is in fact in the subconscious yearning back to *matrix* that time-as-an-illusion, and its equally mystical followers *eternity* and *infinity*, find soil favorable to death worship. For what is consciousness' dream of *eternal life,* if not the repressed negation of the subconscious' dream of *eternal death*? It is because Man compulsively longs for some kind of dead life, constantly repeated loop that does not accept any change, that time-as-an-illusion constantly recurs as the dominant metamythology. Not least within modern natural science. The dream of a determinist universe is essentially the dream of another life, less dizzying than the life that is the only one that is offered; in other words, a life that is liberated from all forms of frightening freedom and burdensome responsibility, a life free from both *phallus* and *logos.* It is thus because Man cannot constrain his infantile yearning back to matrix that we must count on this meme remaining the most tempting and most difficult to refute of all collectively comprised illusions.

Time-as-an-illusion, with its world-wide diffusion, is naturally popular for a reason. Admittedly it favors certain interests, as always, but above all it is a case of massive escapism: the idea of time-as-the-illusion liberates Man from the compulsion of living with and trying to understand *change* as existence's fundamental property. Change is fatiguing with its constant demands on continuous reevaluation and renewal – more than ever during the Internet Age with its explosive technological development – and then it is obviously comparatively peaceful and pleasant to instead devote oneself to searching for eternal values and objectively valid truths. So it is not the least surprising that such a meme survives and spreads. Nor is it particularly surprising, if we look at history, that it is precisely in conjunction with the transition from the primitivist nomadic life to the feudalist permanent settlement that time-as-an-illusion secures a foothold as the dominant metamythology in society. For now one has access to the tool that is necessary to finally be able to prevent constant movement: written language.

In this way, the plastic, constantly alterable camp fire story about the primordial patriarch and the primordial matriarch is replaced by a story of a completely new kind: the recorded, eternally unalterable, linear and always valid story of the monotheist creator god. Or rather the monotheist order-creating god. For it is of course the order in chaos that suddenly is God's central contribution to history, the primordial chaos itself must naturally precede the creation. It is no longer in the primordial matrix, with its associated *semiotic soup* – as the Bulgarian-French psychoanalyst Julia Kristeva expresses the matter – but instead at the time of the phallic intrusion that *God creates the world as a world*. It means that phallus worship is dramatically reinforced at the expense of matrix worship. Order in itself and not existence as such becomes primary in storytelling. It is not a question of the patriarchy consciously taking over and controlling the world in some malicious way – as late capitalist feminism misleadingly claims with its rallying cries of "fight the patriarchy" – but about the matriarchy being weakened in an increasingly complex and more centralized feudalist society, with time controlled down to the smallest detail by the clergy, writing by hand. The field is, as it was, previously left open to a patriarchal power order, but after the arrival of writing without a matching matriarchal counterweight.

So while the primordial patriarch and the primordial matriarch serve as necessary models for a survival-oriented, plastic nomadic collective during primitivism – who live in constant movement through a constantly alterable, untamed and in many respects hostile and threatening world – the monotheist order-creating god is regarded as sole instigator of everything of value during feudalism and thereby as the paradigm's sole worthy *moralator*. The stories and values are fixed (eternalized) with the aid of writing. Suddenly, it is phallus that both creates and drives the world forward. Everything has a cause, and this cause has a face. Priests, kings and landowners are all male archetypes that dance before the gaze of the phallic god. Instead of the outer circuit serving the concrete needs of the inner circuit, as was the case during primitivist nomadic life, the inner circuit is forced to submit to the outer circle's abstract ambitions, often placed in the higher sphere beyond death, for instance through the enormously costly construction of gigantic temples and pyramids.

Determinist existence is designed and preprogrammed by the phallic god, and our lives are therefore nothing other and nothing more than the detailed implementation of this grandiose design – wherever, whenever and however this actually took place. No arbitrariness is involved in any sense – regardless of how complicated the course of events may appear to the uninitiated – the great order-creating god's libidinal *omnipotence* does not permit any such deviation. Which also is necessary. The moment we admit that any kind of randomness might be involved in the shaping of the history of the Universe, determinism immediately becomes untenable. From this possible moment onwards universal time must become real, at which point existence becomes fundamentally indeterminist. If chance occurs even once, it naturally opens up the possibility for the same to happen again. And again. The effect of chance is then already a fact, and a snowball of chance has as a result started to roll down the slippery slope of history. A denial of this means that we are closing our eyes to the fact that all of world history is one long series of these random events along the universal timeline.

As the French philosopher Quentin Meillassoux expresses the matter: "The only thing that is constant throughout history is contingency itself." Another name for this Meillassouxian contingency is of course *universal duration*. Global time or *hypertime* is highly real, it actually is the most tangible and easily proven phenomenon there is. And this universal duration is the only phenomenon that lacks emergence. Or rather: Global time is the primary emergence, *the great singularity*, the foundation upon which everything else in existence is built. Or as the Zurvanites in ancient Iran maintain: Hypertime and God are really one and the same thing, and out of this fundamental fact our temporal Universe arises as *the singularity par excellence*. What various lesser local gods are up to throughout history is thus little more, and signifies little more, than arbitrary saints and idols dancing and strutting atop the fundamental *chronotheology*. We express this as if we are living in a univocal universe characterized by the three interconnected foundation stones of network dynamics: *chronocentrism*, *emergentism* and *relationalism*.

Emergentism follows from chronocentrism. If time is fundamental and real, it entails that everything always, sooner or later, is changed along the timeline. There are no eternal laws or objectively valid truths outside the metatruth that says that change is the only thing that is constant, which in practice is the same as saying that nothing is constant since change constantly shows a new face. This in turn means that events will occur along the timeline that forever change the conditions that apply at any given point in time. We call such an event an *emergence*, a concept related to phase transitions in natural science, for example when ice melts and converts into water, which then is heated further and changes into vapor, albeit without the recurrent validity of the phase transition in both directions. An emergence only occurs once, and only in one direction, since the unique prerequisites – including the status of the laws of nature et cetera – at this point in time never are repeated. A truly extensive and transforming emergence might even deserve the designation *singularity*. The most evident example of such a singularity is of course *The Big Bang*. Other emergences throughout history that deserve the title singularity are when *chemistry* suddenly arose out of physics, when *biology* suddenly arose out of chemistry, and when *consciousness* suddenly arose out of biology.

Since emergences, in contrast to phase transitions, in no way are predetermined under the conditions that prevail in nature before their genesis, and since emergences in nature appear to be surprises, intrusions from the real into Man's imaginary and symbolic fantasy worlds, they are in practice impossible to foresee. Suddenly A becomes B. This is the very meaning of an emergentist worldview. Or to express the matter syntheologically: If God is the name of all humanity's dreams compressed into and projected onto a single point, and if God is a fiction that has never existed, why not quite simply refer to the next singularity in world history as the arrival of God? Syntheism is the correct name for this project and artificial intelligence is its primary, hitherto known aid. The Greek word *Syntheos* namely means "creating God" or "divine creativity." A religion for post-atheists could hardly be more clear about its mission. And atheism can at any rate hardly be the final destination for all human discussion on belief systems. It has had its 15 minutes in the spotlight, but is now, if we speak of programmatic atheism in its most primitive and most intransigent form, obsolete (see *Syntheism – Creating God in The Internet Age* for a more thorough exposition of atheology's and syntheology's various aspects).

Relationalism follows from emergentism. If everything basically is and must be movement and change, it entails that movement and change must precede the phenomenon in front of us, whatever it may be, even if the observer in question perceives that the phenomenon first existed in some original state only to later have been set in motion and/or have gone through a change. Mobilism must precede eternalism. The chaos below the Planck length in microphysics precedes the discrete phenomenon that arises precisely at the Planck length, whatever the observer thinks he observes. The permanence lies only in the eye of the beholder. First there is the relation, as relationalism preaches, then there arises or rather there is produced a phenomenal *relata* as a temporary byproduct of this relation. The phenomenon is therefore an emergence that follows from the relation. We can usefully transfer this reasoning to the human brain or to the collective organism's social theater. First there are the relations, then the subjects arise. The subject is always a byproduct of the existing relations at the time and in no way their foundation or germ.

We call this view *social relationalism*. Pragmatically and exceedingly handily, the netocratic upper class of the Internet Age builds its ruler ideology on the dogmas of social relationalism, since precisely the management of the social relations – that is: to handle one's address book with care – generates the power in the attentionalist network society. Social relationalism is the perfect weapon against the old dying religion from the capitalist industrial society, namely Cartesian individualism. A netocrat is quite simply *the social relationalist dividual* who successfully regards the network as primary and the dividual itself as secondary, wholly in accordance with the network-dynamical principles of chronocentrism, emergentism and relationalism. The fact that the body exists as such is a different matter, the body becomes a dividual only in the context of relations. No serious person has the least interest anymore in *individualism* (individual, as we know, means indivisible in Latin) and its constant companion *atomism* (atom means indivisible in Greek); rather, a lingering fixation with individualism and atomism in the network society has been reduced to informationalist underclass phenomena.

In a series of books from the 1970s and onwards – culminating in *Wholeness and the Implicate Order*, originally published in 1980 – American-British mathematician and philosopher David Bohm develops the network-dynamical concept *holomovement.* His purpose is primarily to mathematically grasp quantum physics in its entirety, but the project is just as much about philosophy as mathematics. For Bohm, what is primary is that the Universe is one single cohesive phenomenon – just as it was at *The Big Bang* and has continued to be ever since – and is a phenomenon that finds itself in constant movement and in an incessant process, one single great becoming which exists only in its capacity of a network-dynamically cohesive whole. Bohm accurately describes this holomovement as an "undivided whole in fluid movement." Every stable and seemingly autonomous phenomenon is a temporary byproduct of the holomovement and will eventually also be dissolved into this undivided, fluid movement. Bohm's concept is in turn connected to Spinoza's classic, monist idea that the Cosmos must be described as a *univocality* – a Latin expression meaning "the Universe speaks with one voice." Thus a consequence of the Universe being network-dynamical, is that then it must also be chronocentric and univocal. The syntheological name for this "one voice of the Universe" is of course the Spinozist divinity *Pantheos.* Bohm calls this holomovement's cohesive voice *the holonomy.*

We can allow ourselves to be inspired here by the perhaps most prominent of Spinoza's many heirs, and moreover the founder of modern process philosophy, namely the German philosopher G. F Hegel, and put forth that despite all the enormous diversity that undoubtedly exists from an ontic perspective and that occurs in the form of processes in the Universe at every given moment – what we syntheologically call *Entheos* – there is *de facto* no ontological change of diversity as such. In a network-dynamical and chronocentric universe the visible change in every phenomenon at every single moment is of course already built-in beforehand in the ontology of the phenomenon in question and becomes available to us, as history's co-creators, only through *Hegelian dialectics*. It is worth noting that Hegel – in contrast to his contemporary but considerably less process-philosophically oriented German romanticists – does not use the triad of thesis, antithesis and synthesis in his dialectics. His dialectical concepts are instead *abstraction*, *negation* and *concretion*. The Hegelian spirit is manifested through the movement from abstraction to concretion via negation. But it is always the entire Universe, as one single phenomenon, that is: as precisely *the Bohmian holomovement*, that represents the authentic change that precedes Hegelian dialectics. This universal and thus authentic change, and nothing else, is, in turn, time itself. That is what we call global time or *duration*.

It is worth noting that Bohm never speaks of a global dimension of time in his books. Like his predecessor Einstein he never even discusses any form of time other than the relative and local. Bohm builds his worldview from a monochrone rather than a duochrone basic prerequisite. On the other hand Bohm presents his own cosmologically inflated variants of Kant's classic concepts, the available *phenomenon* and the unavailable *noumenon*, and refers to his own variants as *the explicate order* and *the implicate order* respectively. The explicate order is the phenomena and their relations as they are available to us and our perception process. The implicate order is however the more deep-seated, noumenal order beneath or behind the explicate order, which belongs to the holomovement itself, a kind of *Wizard of Oz* of the Universe, concealed behind the phenomenal screen where we and our science hitherto have been located. Feel free to compare this with how the Einsteinian theory of relativity puts geometry before the phenomena that it then positions and observes within the geometry on hand at the moment. Bohm argues that classic spacetime within physics – with its Einsteinian relative time – is an explicate phenomenon that arises out of the deeper, implicate order with no need for any kind of spacetime in itself. But then Bohm still clings to a spacetime that is built on Einsteinian relative time. The holomovement with its implicate order is of course all but fixated, its time is of course anything but an illusion, its time is of course universal change in itself. Momentum by momentum, in its entirety.

If Bohm would only allow himself – in the same way as Bergson and the superstring theorists – to experiment with two different time dimensions rather than just one, he would most likely see that time returns within the implicate order of the holomovement, but *as global time*. Universal duration is of course not just the prerequisite for the implicate order, but also for the holomovement itself. Otherwise the holomovement would of course just be yet another Einsteinian, determinist block universe calling out for an external and timeless creator and nothing more interesting than that. Bohm is well aware of this, and when he and his partner Basil Hiley approach the implicate order with the aid of his mathematical *pregeometry* – that which syntheologically is called the potential *Atheos* and which precedes the current *Pantheos* – they are interestingly enough only talking about a *prespace* and never about a *prespacetime*. Thus if we express the matter with a more Bohmian vocabulary, we can distinguish between *implicate time* (as corresponding to absolute and global time) in contrast to *explicate time* (corresponding to relative and local time). The presence of implicate time is then the very foundation of *the chronocentric worldview*. It is thus necessary to first understand universal duration to even be able to approach an understanding of the implicate order that Bohm cherishes.

A prototype of the Hegelian spirit's processing of material reality is found already in the teachings of the prophet Zoroaster in ancient Iran. There Zoroaster launches the first theological concept in the history of ideas without interweaving the least trace of supernatural phenomena. He does this with the aid of the ambiguous concept

Ahura Mazda, where ahura represents matter (the explicate order) and mazda represents the spirit (the implicate order). We can see how this recurs in the dialectics of libido and mortido, where libido represents the spirit (*mazda*) and mortido represents matter (*ahura*). Zoroaster's point is to place the spirit above matter as a conscious, existential choice. He therefore calls his followers *mazdayasni* (the followers of the spirit) and not *ahurayasni* (the followers of the matter). Zoroastrianism is thus not only closely related to Buddhism – the two religions did, for instance, peacefully share the status of state religion in the Indo-Iranian Kushan Empire for more than 300 years – but can also *de facto* be described as Buddhism in an inverted form. For which religious group could most accurately be called *ahurayasni,* if not the Buddhists? In the spirit of Slovenian philosopher and psychoanalyst Slavoj Žižek, we can express Zoroaster's existentialist defense of libido against mortido as though libido is driven by the motto "alive when dead," to be compared with the Freudian death drive's strong attraction to an ideal that instead is the direct opposite, a *mortido* that celebrates the motto of being "dead when alive."

In the network-dynamical worldview, *universal univocality* and *global time* are two necessary sides of one and the same necessary coin. The world has never been divided and time has never been broken, instead, the world and time are always and have always been interlocked in the holomovement as one single, cohesive phenomenon. They are each other's essential prerequisites. This phenomenon does not just comprise physics and cosmology with their particular idiosyncrasies but, as Bohm likes to emphasize, also consciousness and life itself. The boundary between physics and metaphysics is therefore dissolved. It is hardly surprising that Bohm is noticeably uncomfortable with the misleading concept quantum mechanics and would rather speak of a *quantum organics* to discuss the foundation stones of physics. Mobilism precedes and always dissolves eternalism in the end in *the dialectics of eternalism and mobilism* (see *The Global Empire*). This is unavoidable since the frozen image one has created becomes obsolete through all the change processes constantly occurring. Or as Bohm himself expresses the matter: "Each relatively autonomous and stable structure is to be understood not as something independently and permanently existent, but rather as a product that has been formed in the whole flowing movement and that will ultimately dissolve back into this movement. How it forms and maintains itself depends on its place function within the whole."

For Bohm *the process* is primary. What from an ontological point of view appears to be permanent structures is from an ontical point of view nothing other than relative, autonomous sub-entities that arise out of the holomovement and that then once again dissolve in this movement through one big and incessant process of change. Bohm thereby proclaims a decisive outcome in the classic battle between the eternalist Parmenides and the mobilist Heraclitus to the advantage of Heraclitus and the mobilists. The process-philosophical revolution kick-started by British-American philosopher and mathematician Alfred North Whitehead in the 1920s is, regarding mathematics and physics, completed by Bohm, in the same way that it is completed regarding politics and esthetics by Bohm's contemporary and devoted admirer Gilles Deleuze. It is from the metaphysical works of these process-philosophical pioneers that we build the social-relationalist understanding of the Internet Age (see *Syntheism – Creating God in the Internet Age*). Whitehead's *actualities* as the fundamentals of existence have their correspondences in Bohm's *momenta*, where every individual momentum can be described as a *projection* from the total implicate order. Both particles and fields dance atop global time as the one and only holomovement's innumerable attributes.

An interesting aspect of Bohm's model for the holomovement's implicate order and the Universe's explicate order is that the same model is applicable to human consciousness. Instead of gathering a large number of disparate objects and then trying to guess how these material and seemingly mechanical objects are interconnected in some magical way to an equally material, but suddenly also highly organic consciousness, we can start from the unity of consciousness and understand its components as attributes of the whole, where experienced moments along the timeline can be understood as explicate projections of consciousness and its implicate order. The implicate in the future will, according to Bohm, be the explicate in the present, as *an existential momentum*, something that then is converted into a memory that is spread out across the entire brain as the implicate in the past. Syntheologically, we call such an existential momentum – which succeeds in imbuing the entire consciousness' self-identity – *the infinite now*. And the infinite now is of course the ultimate event that constitutes the metaphysical propelling force for the Internet Age.

It is a question of nothing less than the *emergence* and, for really spectacular experiences, *the singularity* as a subjective experience. It is of course during and above all after the experience of the infinite now that the dividual receives or radically reassesses his or her own identity. The infinite now is thus for understandable reasons syntheism's mystical core, its fervently coveted *satori* while the memory of the experience is thereafter its *enlightenment*. The rites of passage that occur between birth and death have never been more important than in the event-driven, chronocentric network society. The momentum here belongs to the explicate order, while self-identity – consciousness as a cohesive and seemingly more durable unit – is referred to the implicate order. Consciousness can therefore be described in exactly the same – and in an equally radically materialistic – way as the Universe itself, without having to resort to any supernatural magic whatsoever. Deleuze's word for this network-dynamical subject in the Internet Age is of course *the dividual*. He pulls the rug out from under the feet of the Cartesian Individual in the same way that Whitehead makes it impossible for us to maintain the Newtonian atom as the bedrock of physical existence. This monist subject can, just like the Whiteheadian actuality, be understood and described as an explicate momentum that dances atop consciousness' phenomenal and the holomovement's noumenal, implicate stability.

The remains of the existential experience is a constant *folding* and *unfolding* of memory's material, as both Bohm and Deleuze express the matter, without us having to get mired in some vulgarly materialist conception of the illusory nature of subjectivity. Instead, the reverse is true: If consciousness consists of this enfolding and unfolding back and forth and nothing else, we can find proto-consciousnesses everywhere where the implicate and the explicate meet. It is for instance sufficient with a membrane that isolates a cell from the surrounding world for us to speak of a *protosubjectivity*. The Universe can be described as monist, material and more or less "conscious," all at the same time. We call this *a panpsychic universe*, where panpsychism is explicate atop the implicateness of network dynamics. The origins of all this is process, pure movement, without any substance in itself. The mathematician Hermann Grassman remarks that mathematics does not revolve around order in time and space but around order in thinking. Mathematics is thus a phallic organization of a fundamentally matrichal reality. It does not reflect reality in itself, but describes how Man organizes his brutal and ambivalent interaction with reality in his own conceptual world. These thoughts convert a constant transformative reality of processes into tangible phenomena that constitute building blocks of the human worldview.

Through the dialectics of eternalism and mobilism, Man creates objectives and meaning in a mobilist world. There are no extensionless points either in time or in space. Instead spacetime is made up of *momenta*. Within these moments the world is mastered by enormous fields. According to the relationalist worldview the subject is nothing other than the perfect emergent actuality at every moment. The subject can here be described as a dance around an empty hole where the subject from the inside views the hole in the center of the movement as the subject itself, but where an observer on the outside understands the very dance around the hole as the subject. The dialectics of eternalism and mobilism in turn understands the subject as the discrepancy between on the one hand the internal, eternalist and on the other hand the external, mobilist subject understanding. Subjectivity thus arises only at the end of a momentum as the core of the discrepancy between this momentum's inner eternalist and outer mobilist observation. That is: *we produce a subject at the end of the very process that does not make sense to us.* As a last-ditch effort to patch up the incomprehensible, we identify ourselves with the contradiction itself. This self-objectification tricks us into believing that we have solved the riddle of ambivalence in the momentum that is at hand by placing ourselves in the center of the riddle, as though our subjectivity could bridge the tangible void. The self is nothing other than the void that unites the surrounding discrepancies into a functional whole. The self-image is literally the mirror of the worldview.

There only remains a difference of degree between all the various subjects that automatically are formed within all intelligent systems. Nature is teeming with these illusory and temporary subjectivities. Every illusion then endures until the next momentum stirs the pot anew and compels a new experience of subjectivity. And these processes supplant each other in a steady stream. This experience then forms a line with the preceding experienced subject, something that the mind chooses to interpret as *a coherent subject along the timeline.* Libido then fights tooth and nail against mortido to maintain and reinforce this temporal subject. This process is the repression of the matrichal mortido into subconsciousness and the victory of the phallic libido in consciousness. We believe that we believe that we exist (as cohesive subjects) and we believe that we believe that we want to live as a *continuity.* It is functional illusions that make existence manageable. The more robustly this faith is questioned or doubted by one's environment, the stronger and more reliable it appears to the subject itself. Consciousness is therefore a contemplation around the subject and the surrounding world, and around their relations to each other. It is therefore meaningless to speak of a consciousness without both self-consciousness and consciousness of the surrounding world. Consciousness, as Portuguese neuroscientist Antonio Damasio observes, is primarily built on the will to life and care for the self, only to later be extended and also comprise other selves that turn up on the social arena. In concert with these, we then cultivate life's existential and esthetic possibilities. This is how we create meaning in our lives.

12
Individualism as the opium of the people – hypernarcissism, pornoflation and interpassivity

The dramatic framing of the media is problematical for many reasons and in many respects, not least because our brains are programmed to avoid risks as far as possible. When they heard a rustling in a bush on the savannah, our forefathers would be wise to react each time as though there was an impending and life-endangering threat – such as a venomous snake or a hungry predator – and to immediately retreat, even if the situation actually was a false alarm and concerned something completely harmless 99 times out of 100. On the hundredth occasion, he who was both quick to react and highly cautious was rewarded, while he who was incautious and/or slow risked being punished severely. Natural selection ensured that the highly cautious were rewarded over time. These people lived longer and procreated with greater success, and it was their predisposition for instinctive fear and caution that was inherited at the cost of thoughtless risk-taking. In the primitivist nomadic tribe this was a winning concept. But for today's heirs to this instinctive fear and propensity to see every change as threatening, it is considerably more problematic.

In his book *Progress*, Swedish historian of ideas Johan Norberg demonstrates how Man's primal search for threats in every environment she encounters leads to constant, cognitive distortion that in turn entails that setbacks of various types are magnified and exaggerated while progress and success are hidden away or forgotten. The news of a plane crash is quickly spread through media outlets across the globe, making major headlines. Meanwhile, 40 million touchdowns are carried out successfully for every individual accident without any media coverage whatsoever, something that creates a completely false and frighteningly somber image of air travel as an unsafe means of transport when it actually is extraordinarily safe, much safer than for instance the car. When this cognitive distortion is built up over time and is spread within large populations, it has devastating consequences. Since Man is genetically programmed to exaggerate possible threats – and thus sensationalize his daily reality – his entire understanding of and relation to his environment is gradually deformed. The threats become more threatening, the darkness becomes darker, while the positive possibilities appear insignificant or at worst non-existent. We frenetically malign our world, which entails an increased risk that the maligning becomes a self-fulfilling prophecy.

This situation certainly does not serve our collective interests in the Global Empire – colored and shaped by digitalization, medialization and nodalization – which has emerged at unprecedented speed during the first decades of the 21st century. The problem is not only, not even primarily, that the paranoia and sensationalism produce a distorted image of reality, and an image that is hard to handle. What is worrying is that the distorted optics, through which the media consumer views the world, extremely efficiently disrupts and splinters the collective subject. The various tribal subcultures fall apart and encapsulate themselves within their respective filter bubbles, inside which they cultivate the hatred, contempt and suspicion that is directed towards what is by definition *the other* and that finds itself outside the familiar opinion community that carefully culls away all information that contravenes prevailing prejudices. If there at least used to be some measure of consensus on what the facts were, and if the discord was over how these facts would be understood depending on the ideological vantage point, we are now headed to a state in society where every camp, every plurarchic node, keeps its own set of "facts" and rejects all undesired information as "fake news."

It is today perfectly possible to lie through one's teeth and still retain a considerable amount of political popularity, quite simply because the lies are in accordance with the wishful thinking and hallucinations cherished by large groups of programmatically ignorant consumtarians. Such a preoccupation with arbitrarily chosen symbols – instead of with the reality that actually is at hand – we call *decorationism*. The decorationist society arises when influential groups within the elites have been so absorbed by shallow, social codes that they lose all meaningful contact with the rest of the population. It is no longer possible to focus to any considerable extent on substantive issues, but what was supposed to be a dialogue about important things is reduced to an eternal squabble about representativity, that is: an issue of who it is that is speaking and who it is that has or possibly should have the right to speak instead. Decorationist power consciously mixes up people with viewpoints. An obsession with tonality and etiquette replaces objectivity and substance.

Postmodern society is characterized by a fixation on surface, codes, image and fashion. Throw in the blind, ideologically conditioned conviction that everything in the world around us can be reduced to purely social constructions. The result is a condition that must be described as *decorationism par excellence*. Note the striking similarities between postmodernism's political correctness – for instance as the intersectionalist theorists' obsession with sensitive word choices to avoid all forms of conceivable verbal violations of various minority victimhood cultures – and the French (and Francophile) nobility's conception of *noblesse oblige*. This complicated code system was of course built on a constant obsession with the need to immediately balance the slightest little privilege granted to any social actor by a duty to at least appear to level out or extinguish the privilege, an ultimately completely exhausting social theater without any enduring practical consequences whatsoever, masterfully depicted by for instance Honoré de Balzac in the novel *The Lily of the Valley* from 1836. Through its dogmatic relativization, the decorationist project undermines every attempt at constructive societal discourse, which ultimately leads to a violent collapse is primarily caused by a total and paralyzing disagreement about what one actually disagrees on.

Societal conflict management that is at least somewhat functional requires an, at the least, basic agreement on the forms of disagreement. This means that decorationism as a way of life and a collective norm is fundamentally incompatible with *tribalism* in its most elementary form. Rather, decorationism maintains that no human is born with any form of constructively contributing personality type or with anything special at all – we are all blank pages that can be developed into anyone or anything, and everyone must be allowed to realize the dreams that they harbor – while no one ever needs to take responsibility for anything, since all failures ultimately are connected to society's insufficient ability to adapt itself to and satisfy the needs of every dividual. Reality, according to this view, is not real enough, which means that it must be forced to accommodate the wishes of every single person; it is quite simply a human right to play the part one wishes to play on the stage of social theater. At least as long as one manages to qualify – according to the underlying Rousseauan axiom – for the narcissistic status as *the minoritarian victim*.

The historical problem with decorationism is thus not merely that it divides society into a host of different antagonistic subcultures, but also that it is extremely matrichal in nature inasmuch as it both lacks and despises every form of phallic civilizing process, something that it regards as camouflaged oppression. Decorationism is of course by definition decorative rather than constructive. It is obsessed with the cultural façade and its endless accounts of history, as though the material basis of civilization and the actual terms that prevail are dismissible quite simply through wishful thinking, or that one can ignore them with the aid of the intense manufacture of illusion. So when decorationism makes a breakthrough, it means that the architects of civilization are degraded from phallic heroes to greedy and generally evil oppressors – *phallus in itself* is of course evil – while one starts telling stories of made-up pseudomatriarchies of yore and present these as ideals for society at large and also as exemplary models for how one today should practice social leadership. Suddenly every company, organization, political party or religious community is organized as though it were a big, merry kindergarten that was not subject to merciless competition every single day. This process occurs while tribalism's demands on *collaboration* as the social community's fundamental principle are replaced by decorationism's flirtation with narcissistic *self-victimization mythology* as the smallest common denominator.

Consequently the decorationist truth is reduced to an empty power game of who is to be rewarded with the most attention in the capacity of being *the greatest victim*. This shift in focus has dramatic consequences. For decorationism does not merely exchange the fetish for the abject as a cohesive cathexal object, it also starts a competition over who should suddenly have the honor of replacing phallus and act as the hated abject, in other words: Who is best at hating and despising himself in the social arena, in the desperate struggle for attention at any cost? Nor does it matter if the most terrifying fear of state based on the rule of law is realized and innocent people begin to be sacrificed one by one – compared to the greatest victim, all other social actors are of course guilty by means of their very existence – since it is the victim and not the hero who has laid claim to the role of *the moralator* who makes up the arbitrary rules of the game. A logical consequence of this power shift, an appurtenant new metarule of the game, is that all actors must be lowered to the mortidinal victim's dystopian level to cancel out their existential guilt, instead of, as earlier, being elevated to the libidinal hero's utopian level to realize their potential. Decorationist postmodernism is quite simply a purely matrichal project of mortidinal death worship, without a trace of phallic direction – an aggressive reaction against modernism's almost parodically phallic driving force – which in its eagerness to *deconstruct* modernism finally attacks civilization's very foundation, namely the phallic vision in itself.

We are speaking of how the libidinal rise of a civilization is followed by its mortidinal decay; the current *decadence* should really be understood literally. All agents should be heard, all agents must have the right to be seen, everyone has the right to their attentionalist platform and to a generous measure of attention, even if all forms of credibility are missing; it is precisely here that the decorationist value lies. And this applies irrespective of whether what is seen and heard – from the platform that one supplies with ideologically conditioned benevolence – has any constructive value whatsoever over and above the purely rhetorical, which is only connected to the theater stage. That difficult decisions must be made, that conflicts over goals must be handled and objectives must be met is completely ignored. However, aside from the play that is performed under media spotlights, there is an ongoing reality that makes the decorationist spectacle both irrelevant and dangerous to society. It is dangerous inasmuch as the focus of all discourse is shifted from the phallic challenge and the libidinal coming of age to matrichal freedom from demands and mortidinal infantilization. We have very real societal problems to deal with, but we have created a media culture characterized by castration-conditioned indecisiveness – which in many respects greatly reduces our ability to handle the challenges in a serious way – since we insist on seeing ourselves as helpless children with rights that someone else must safeguard, rather than as resourceful subjects that along with like-minded others can achieve significant changes.

The masses would rather whine than act. And this explains why the consumtarians in the network society never come of age. They cannot bring themselves to leave the *mamilla* for the *phallus*, and thus do not carry out the second and third phases of abjection, but instead remain at the breast of *The Great Other*, despite it being a case of pure illusion. This large-scale infantilization of the consumtariat takes place under proud but thoroughly false and misleading banners such as consumerism's "the consumer is always right" and democratism's "the voter is never wrong" – two perfect examples of wholly deceitful nonsense. The Internet is of course partly an offspring of the American counterculture and was long surrounded by glowingly optimistic aspirations: the new technology would deliver the dream of an interconnected humanity that gradually journeys towards a classless and increasingly prosperous society, where everyone has access to all relevant information and where everyone can contribute to an intelligent and constructive debate from a standpoint of equal opportunities. Instead we are quickly moving towards a world burdened by innumerable welfare-conditioned illnesses and where the majority of the adults acts like overfed and spoiled children. We entertain ourselves to death, as the media theorist Neil Postman observes, while we are eating ourselves to mortal obesity, aided by massive amounts of fast carbohydrates.

Decorationism presages the demise of the obese and weary civilization more than anything. Decorationism is quite simply *decadence par excellence*. A clearer example of the politically correct conversation's devastating effect on the societal debate is hardly imaginable. Once again the pattern is repeated, dictating that the value system of the upper class is inherited by the new underclass in connection with an information-technological paradigm shift, while the truth producers of the new upper class design the new paradigm's metaphysics to fit the playing field that has now arisen. This in turn means that what we are witnessing with the arrival of informationalism is nothing other than *the fall of individualism*. For who are those who cling to dysfunctional individualism's bone-dry mamilla to the last, if not the infantilized consumtariat? The unwelcome, unread, narcissistic newsletters overflow the spam files of the mailboxes. The consumtarians devote their disposable time to consuming banal entertainment in the form of competitions, where the one individual or the other is voted out while the others keep on competing for the audience's favor. Or else one uploads masses of talentless media production in the form of self-produced images, films and music that no one ever bothers to look at.

The decorationist society can be described as a kind of golden age of culture nihilism. So how does postmodernist culture nihilism relate to Man's sociobiological basic prerequisites? Technology is of course the mother of all change. But Man that parries technology is of course practically constant. So what does the dialectics of the variable *t* for technology and the constant *m* for Man look like? The truth is that Man lives in the intersection between his internality (self-image) and his externality (worldview). Internality, which is matrichal, can never be avoided. It constantly makes its presence felt. Externality, which is phallic, can on the other hand either be absorbed into internality or else be repressed to subconsciousness. This fundamental dialectical asymmetry causes everything in Man's life, his platform for everything else, to be built from internality, since it always precedes externality. The subject precedes the object. Or rather: The subject is the first object in its own existence. This process must in turn begin with the probably most misunderstood of all concepts: *self-love*. In the decorationist network society – where Man constantly is encouraged towards *hyperemotionality*, towards exposing his internality through feeling and thinking and expressing himself, impulsively and immediately and without pause, only to later formulate this feeling and thinking without any problematic reflection – self-love is constantly misunderstood as yet another project in a string of innumerable hyperemotional ones. But it definitely is not. That possibility does not even exist.

It cannot exist because a feeling for the self requires involvement from the externality, and it is precisely here that the project encounters robust resistance. Feeling something for oneself always becomes an issue of searching for opinions and approval from other people, in spite of the fact that other people's opinions and approval cannot have any effect whatsoever on self-love as such. He who does not love himself cannot believe that anyone else could love him either, no matter what other people say or do. He quite simply makes himself impervious to appreciation from outside. We see the world through our own self-image and cannot do otherwise. Man cannot accept himself unless he first builds or perceives a matrichally unconditional love and validation as an existential insight. Self-love therefore belongs to the unique love that Baruch Spinoza calls *amor intellectualis* and that Friedrich Nietzsche defines as *amor fati*: intellectual love, and love of fate respectively. This is love as an emotionless, ethical-logical act and not as a sentimental feeling. An admittedly unconditional, but still phallic rather than matrichal love. You love yourself because it is ethically right, because it is logically unavoidable and because it is strategically necessary.

It is exactly this brutal connection with reality that makes self-love a phallic foundation stone. But not because you have first had the luxury of feeling anything at all. Self-love is thus nothing more than a radical acceptance of one's own existence – without either excuses or exaggerations – and thereby also a radical acceptance of and respect for the fate that has generated this specific creature that experiences this itself. It is only from this network-dynamical platform of self-love within the matrichal internality that Man can peer outwards, take in and feel genuine compassion for the phallic externality. Which includes the ability to then feel something for himself as a social creature. Otherwise all energy will be consumed in cultivating a demanding self-victimization myth of blind enjoyment within internality, where more or less everything that belongs to externality must be repressed into subconsciousness. That is to say a life full of flagrant narcissism as a compensation for the lack of self-love. Life, in this sense, becomes not only loveless, but also fundamentally mendacious and extremely confused. We will have a creature searching for the pseudophallic idol with simple solutions as answers to all the questions that arise out of the dilemmas caused by the absence of self-love.

In this way, Man becomes fundamentally dysfunctional if he lacks the ability to summon up ethical self-love. Therapist after therapist is dismissed in the quest for the longed-for infantilizing storyteller that *avoids* the phallic truth. At a collective level, this results in precisely the decorationism that is decadence in its purest form. We are thus speaking of a collectively spread self-contempt of gargantuan proportions. And since narcissism is the human compensation behavior *par excellence* we describe this state as *hypernarcissism*. For lack of self-love – which in turn hinges on a misunderstanding, since self-love really is no emotion at all, merely a logically necessary standpoint in the form of self-acceptance – the dividual compensates by seeking the appreciation of other people for more or less everything he does. We are very close to the point where the narcissist cannot even board a bus without desperately seeking applause from the bus driver and the fellow passengers for this very act of boarding which thus is considered exceptionally remarkable. But it is never enough. The approbation can never suffice. No matter how much attention and recognition the narcissist gets from other people, it can never compensate for his lack of self-love and – above all – self-acceptance. It is as though the attention never takes hold within the narcissistic self-image, and therefore it becomes impossible to absorb it, to genuinely rejoice at it and to see it as the least bit convincing. Therefore the validation must be sought again and again – a behavior that constantly connected smartphones and laptops propel with massive force – even when the result is constantly depressing.

The compulsively repetitive behavior can never attain the desired result, the narcissist is a black hole in terms of attention and appreciation. And this constant repetitive failure becomes fundamental for a deeply dysfunctional personality. When this destructive cycle has come full circle enough times it is perceived as the natural state of things, creating an illusion of security and a sense of inevitability which fashions itself into a dividual identity with clear contours – a fatal response since this efficiently shields the narcissist from the surrounding world and shuts off external impulses and alternative perspectives. The organism thereby locks itself into *mortido* and starts to devote itself to enjoying the robust eternalization and its apparent sustainability. This is the state that Sigmund Freud calls *the death drive* in its purest form. The contact with the surrounding world narrows and is in practice reduced to one's own incompetence being constantly confirmed, even if the full meaning of it must be repressed to preserve the narcissist's self-image. In this way it is perfectly okay for people to live out their days in a cocoon made up of insufficiency. But why is this so? What is it that makes narcissism so seemingly natural for Man and so easy to absorb and incorporate with identity? And moreover, how can it become accepted and held aloft as an ideological precept, despite the fact that it makes it impossible for Man to function as a well-integrated gregarious animal among others? What is it that makes Jean-Jacques Rousseau and his decorationist heterodoxies so incredibly popular and oft-recurring?

We can find one answer in *Cartesian individualism*, which constitutes a unique attempt at converting human narcissism into a philosophical and theological dogma – which then will dominate the post-Christian Western World from the mid 17th century, up until the network-dynamical Internet's arrival just over 300 years later – along with the ideological complement that was *Newtonian atomism* within the natural sciences. But even if we appoint the Frenchman René Descartes as the author of individualism and the Englishman

Isaac Newton that of atomism, in their different points in the 17th century, this concept is only perfected about 100 years later by the German Immanuel Kant. It is in Kant that we find the key that explains the riddle of the embrace of narcissism. For Kant argues that the subject's innermost essence is its very gluttony. The subject is characterized not just by a kind of animal surplus that corresponds to a deficit in terms of humanity. What Kant maintains is that the subject actually is this fundamental *excess* and nothing else. The subject can only know itself through its gluttony. The Kantian subject therefore becomes *the libidinal subject par excellence.* And the demand that Kant directs at this post-Christian, libidinal subject is that it must play precisely the role that God has abdicated from, namely the role of *The Master of Nature.*

It is hardly surprising that the Kantian libidinal subject in Europe from the late 18th century onwards has the world at its feet through colonial imperialism and the escalating ravaging of the planet's resources. It is of course the same Kantian libidinal subject that then lies down on the couch of psychoanalyst Jacques Lacan, the greatest Kantian of the 20th century, and leads to Lacan summing up the Kantian libidinal subject as a surplus around a void that never finds itself, but slavishly must follow its desire unto death. Lacan is of course correct inasmuch as he takes Kantian individualism as far as imaginable, that is: to the point where we deplete nature's endless resources and to the boundary of Man's finite life. And only there, at the explosive emergence of *network dynamics*, within both physics and sociology, can Man start to experiment with himself as a dividual being a part of a network of much greater value than the dividual himself, and moreover also much higher than what corresponds to the sum of the value of all participating dividuals'. This requires both insight and determination in order to accept this transcendence as the exit from desire's cast-iron grip. It quite simply requires a Nietzschean *Übermensch›s* insight and determination. For the great majority of people, the reaction is instead the complete opposite: What we see being born before the threat of the fall of individualism is nothing but a hyper-reaction from the still Cartesian underclass: *individualist fundamentalism is the consumtariat's ideology par excellence.* So what is individualist fundamentalism, if not an individualism that has closed the door on and stopped listening to all forms of external critique, and that therefore only can appear as narcissism in its purest and most hysterical form?

No societal format transformation is ever simple or painless. When network dynamics establishes itself as the trend synonymous with power shaping the netocratic elite during informationalism, the consumtariat's countertrend *hypernarcissism* lurks behind it as its dark, inescapable shadow. So what then separates hypernarcissism from classical narcissism? Well, it arises as a historically new combination of masochism and exhibitionism. Previously, sadism and exhibitionism have tended to converge, while masochism rather has tended to interact with voyeurism, both on the social arena and in identity production. What is new in the network society is the explosion of attention-thirsty cults centered on the demonstrative victim status. Hypernarcissism is thus bound to a mortidinal martyr complex that receives its energy from what it sees as the predestined defeat. It is of course essentially a Rousseauian death worship that allows itself to make as much noise as possible since the cult is going to die anyway. It is this conviction of the fated that generates the hyperstate we are talking about. Hypernarcissism can start to boil and bubble over since it contains no restraining components; the intensity is in principle unlimited, and is reinforced further at a time where *the event* constitutes the collectively encompassed engine of metaphysics.

Hypernarcissism uses every available means and consumes every available energy source to keep itself alive and to be seen, heard and in every way noticed as long and as much as possible. The media development reinforces and accelerates this process, the transition from classical individualism to hypernarcissism is closely connected to, and receives an optimal breeding ground in social media's pronounced *interpassivity* and *pornoflation*: a hysterical competition of self-exposure to the indifferent masses, where everyone is too preoccupied with posting photos of their own lunch to have time to make note of anyone other than Kim Kardashian. This chronic lack of authentic attention makes the hypernarcissistic hamster wheel spin ever faster. The result is a death dance of the consumtariat, built on *the false event per excellence*: the vapid and chronically frustrated longing for the validating presence of *the phallic gaze*. But there is no phallic gaze that can provide the fervently desired validation that satisfies the hypernarcissist. The situation is actually so dire that there is no audience at all. Instead the phallic gaze merely exists within the netocratic collective where it is *imploited* rather than exploited – it is put into play and utilized only within a strongly limited and carefully selected circle. What is left outside this creative elite network is merely a garbage disposal brimming with pointless, mediocre media production that no one cares about and that is completely expendable. Add to this many million broken dreams of being seen by a phallic gaze that doesn't exist.

The development towards *the hypernarcissistic condition* has been predicted by people with insights both into Man's sociobiology and his cultural history, people who understand both the technological changes and their effects in the form of pathological symptoms. As early as the late 1970s the American historian Christopher Lasch, for instance, maintains in his book *The Culture of Narcissism* that the emergence of the modern consumption culture after the Second World War drove Western individualism onwards to its final form, a state that we call *therapeutic narcissism*. Lasch argues that the narcissist's weak sense of self leads to an extensive fear of binding commitments, a terrifying fear of death and aging that expresses itself in obsession with youth and fixation with fame and the external attributes of success, a process that gets much of its fuel from mass media such as film and television. The new progress ideal lacks content, Lasch observes. There are no objective criteria left, which means that the narcissist vests power in the eyes of the indifferent – or absent – spectator. This fact, along with the fact that life to such a great degree is conveyed via electronic images in digital media, leads to a notion of how everyone's acting, that of others and oneself, on the social theater stage is played out before an unseen audience.

This in turn means that the concept of fame completely shifts character. Andy Warhol proclaims in 1968 that in the future everyone will be famous for 15 minutes, which in the light of the media development now must be revised. The novelist and critic Martin Amis has instead suggested the concept *karaoke fame*, which means that in the future everyone will be famous constantly, but only in their own heads, in their own delusions of an illusory audience and non-existent attention. So if late capitalism gave the constantly reclining narcissist in the therapy couch ample fuel, this was merely a mild premonition compared to the explosion of hypernarcissism that informationalism propels. The constant exposure via social media to temporary but generally superficial contacts with hundreds of thousands of people during a lifetime – something that entails a considerable strain, since we are biologically programmed to be able to handle just few hundred social contacts in a meaningful way – makes the informationalist dividual tend to fall for the hypernarcissism of the Internet Age. Some are so versed in the sophisticated art of self-deception that they succeed in safeguarding the illusion that there is an audience for the hypernarcissist's endless reiterations about the black hole that is the bloated ego. For the others there are other solutions; it is apparently perfectly alright to consume attention by paying a therapist for regular pretend listening.

Capitalism thus drives the therapeutic narcissist to work hard to earn money, to use this money to buy the attention he is missing during endless therapy sessions, and when these sessions never provide the coveted "happiness," there remain inexhaustible possibilities to try and fill the painful void with further trend-sensitive consumption of goods and services – on credit if need be – and preferably terminologically soaked in all manner of spiritual hocus-pocus. What would for example a *selfie* be without a fashionable *hashtag*? In this way the hypernarcissist is caught in his constantly spinning hamster wheel; this is Kant's animal surplus as a subjective experience, the Kantian nightmare of the flight from the unattainable phallus back to the seemingly available mamilla that never satiates the narcissist's insatiable hunger. This flight to the mamilla can of course never give rise to any functioning libido, and what remains is only the mortidinal breast milk in a condensed form, as *the anxiety-alleviating pill*. The least sign that anyone even notices what is going on as the hypernarcissist constantly bombards his surroundings with meaningless messages, provides the sender with a new dose of oxygen and thus new energy to drive his incessant campaign even harder. It is this hysterical escalation of pseudoactivity that is called *pornoflation*.

As the hypernarcissist's daily newsletter is increasingly tossed into the netocratic spam files – this constant flood of verbal self-caressing proclaiming the narcissist's phenomenal cleverness and well-earned fame, childish pleas resembling a four-year-old's demands for copious praise from the adult world for every single stroke of a pen on all the "drawings" that are produced in a steady stream – there needs to be constant escalation in the form of increasingly desperate actions to keep up the illusion of a functioning attention machinery. In the end, there only remains a heart-wrenching, desperate scream straight into the pitch-black void of medial indifference. The hypernarcissist hits the ground isolated and abandoned, without any tribal belonging whatsoever. The final waiting room for this social death of the Internet Age is the very room where the hypernarcissists in the end are crammed in with each other, pretending to like each others' posts on social media and pretending to be grateful for this pseudo-support, in accordance with the motto "If you pretend to consume and also like my untalented and pointless scribble in the form of simulated creativity, I will pretend in return to consume and like yours, and we will together build an out-and-out community of pretense that satisfies our narcissistic needs, but only in make-believe." The quasi-ideological corset that props up this desperate action is an indignant moralism that orients itself towards all the netocrats that are interested in genuine networking and collective co-creation, and who therefore have left the stage long ago. Against the netocrats' authentic interactivity, in which one neither is able to nor allowed to participate, the hypernarcissists cast hateful suspicion, as intense as it is confused. Welcome to the consumtariat, the reactionary underclass of the Internet Age, and its ironically febrile *interpassivity.*

If the netocracy is driven by libidinal interactivity, the consumtariat is correspondingly paralyzed by mortidinal interpassivity. The concept is defined and developed by the Austrian philosopher Robert Pfaller in the book *Interpassivity: The Aesthetics of Delegated Enjoyment.* Pfaller presents the informationalist consumtarian as *the mortidinal organism par excellence*, an adult fetus that reacts with abhorrence to all forms of external influence:the Freudian death drive in its purest form. It is the case of a sort of vegetative consumption by dropper bottle, with no reciprocal demands. The only thing that the passively consuming consumtarian must do is to exist purely physically, and thus fill what otherwise would be a gap in the statistics. But nothing over and above this is necessary, no one expects any constructive efforts of any kind. The prototype for this form of existence is the dead living rather than the living dead. The consumtarian behavior in the informationalist society is characterized by various interpassive pseudobehaviors. The considerable part of daily life that is spent on social media is filled with postings, uploads, likes and information storage of scant or no value at all, not even to the consumtarian himself. It is merely the case of a mechanically compulsive repetition of a behavior that is conditioned by a fetishist connection to the surrounding environment. No way of life could be more reactionary.

Meanwhile the Internet propels the development towards *the transparent society.* In the long run, nothing will be able to be concealed anymore. The search lights peer into the darkest, most distant nooks. Everything emerges into broad daylight. Even the information that the netocracy benefits from, but usually not until it is too late to exploit it and profit from it. Man's least attractive and most aggressive instincts emerge. Cracks appear in the veneer of civilization; it is not merely tribalism that returns with full force, but also the human animal in itself. And with it follow the unyielding physiological and mental gender differences. Man may love to hate, and hatred boils over if and when it is not channeled into physical violence. But men express and convey their emotions outwardly, towards the world, while women are trained in internal positioning, which in turn leads to an endless chain of comparisons, which when it is perverted in turn hardly can result in anything but an ocean of self-contempt. This new, emotional patriarchy is reinforced by the men seeking recognition within themselves and within the male flock, while women are conditioned to seek their recognition from the man who is her own in the monogamy that society mandates. This takes place as the tribe as a whole still seeks its recognition from this sole agency of collectively subconscious value, namely *the phallic gaze.*

Civilization, ever since the days of primitivism, has been built on symbolic *castration* as a principle. The elder generation castrates the younger, generally symbolically but nevertheless tangibly, through various institutionalized rites of passage, in order to transform them from irresponsible children to responsible and caretaking adults. Psychoanalytically this shift occurs as *the phallic energy* intrudes between the child and the matriarch's breast, which entails taking the breast away from the child, which forces the child to shift its gaze from the matriarchal mamilla to the patriarchal phallus. The lesson conveyed is that the child cannot have everything it wants. It must select and it therefore must also deselect, which in itself is painful. Moreover the child must always make the effort to get anything at all, in particular to get what it wants. As long as the child has direct access to the mamilla, the dangerously alluring phallus is constantly out of reach.

This is precisely where the line is drawn between the imaginary and the symbolic universe, and the child's transition from the former to the latter is the shift from the instinct to suck security from the mamilla to the desire to own the constantly elusive but ambivalently tempting phallus with all that it entails. The child's symbiotic coalescence with the matriarchal mamilla – its existence as non-existence – is exchanged for the separation between the adult subject and the elusive phallus. Now the dividual stands alone in existence, and really needs to embrace fate, to turn mortido into libido and enjoy the enforced existential solitude. Not everyone manages to make this leap and handle this enormous freedom; those who do are the people that Nietzsche calls *masters*. The leap is forever fraught with risk, so the great majority stubbornly attempts to suckle the matriarchal breast. Here one experiences that one is united with the Cosmos, even if it entails a slave existence, a constant search for Nietzschean masters to submit to, inside the cyclical mortido rather than in the dialectical libido. The shift from the mortidinal mamilla to the libidinal phallus is constantly countered, halted and denied; if one can prevent it from taking place at all, the coming of age fails to occur and the subject remains a child rendered passive in its relation to the environment. Social castration has therefore failed and the collective has been deprived of yet another responsible adult.

Another form of compulsively repetitious behavior that is exploding in the Internet Age is *hyperhypochondria*. When life no longer seems to function optimally for the informationalist dividual – when existence no longer lives up to completely unrealistic expectations and the attention from other dividuals that one so fervently desires is conspicuous in its absence – then capitalism and the social theater in concert supply a broad set of excuses to save face and protect the self-image, delivered in the form of diagnoses, therapies, treatments, courses, as well as conspiracy theories and various other explanatory models that all interact with hypernarcissism in giving the dividual freedom from responsibility for all his shortcomings and permission to constantly consume new preparations and treatment methods. The Israeli sociologist Eva Illouz describes and analyzes in a series of books the 21st century postmodern therapy industry and how this phenomenon – along with the new *overemotionality* conditioned by the therapy industry – dominates the social arena in the network society. The subjective experience is pushed to the forefront, leaving all critical reflection in the shadows. The societal debate develops into a constantly ongoing competition over of who feels the most and who can paint themselves most credibly as a victim of sorts. This in turn means that factual arguments drown in a tidal wave of self-absorption and subjective feeling. Everyone has a right to their own story. The Internet, with its seemingly inexhaustible space, becomes the vessel into which everyone pours their stories, and thus becomes also an ocean of self-pity where it can be hard to discern true initiatives that are aimed at structure and coordination.

A phenomenon that many feel strongly about, and not seldom feel abhorrence for – feelings that tend to be publicized in heated opinion pieces where victims are named and pitied – is pornography. Critical reviews of how things really are in terms of pornography, who is actually consuming it and what these consumers actually look for, are however rare – it is part and parcel of the matter since the subject is sensitive and essentially hitherto unexplored since search data in large quantities has not been available. That is: not until now. What is called *big data* – digitally stored information in such large quantities that one no longer needs to conduct statistical selections and analyses, but has access to the entire factual material, for instance what pornography consumers actually search for on the Internet – makes it possible to form a qualified opinion instead of just guessing and moralizing. A new science encounters us at the horizon and it is called *data anthropology*.

Pornography is fundamentally about delegation and representation: one allows someone else to carry out the libidinal activity in one's stead. We express this by saying that the pornography consumer shifts sexual intimacy to a proxy in exchange for something else – be it a radical autonomy or various forms of tribal intimacy that are not primarily connected to the sexuality that one thus has outsourced, since it is highly complicated and difficult to handle. And this is certainly no new invention, but previously largely occurred within the primitivist nomadic tribe where sexuality was heavily ritualized and usually carried out in groups under the management and supervision of the matriarch with the purpose of regulating women's pregnancies to the extent possible. Since the beginning of time, we have watched other people having sex with each other and have integrated this consumption of pornography into our own sexuality and collective socializing on the whole. This outsourcing of sexuality opens up, for both males and females, communities completely disconnected from eroticism – we call this *bonding* – which arise out of the network dynamics generated between exhibitionism and voyeurism within the plastic nomadic tribe's ritualized sexuality. If pornography actually meets our needs by setting our sexual fantasies to pictures to the degree that sex itself bores us, why would we then even try to build really enduring, intimate relations based on something so transient and flammable as sexual attraction?

Moreover, the attentionalist media development entails that it is reasonable to expand the pornography concept. The enormous supply of communication flows and the transparency that follows from digitalization – everything will of course sooner or later surface in a society where every dividual in every situation has access to sophisticated communication equipment – constitutes the foundation for *the emergence of the social-pornographic society*. Today, it is possible to enjoy everything through proxies, not just sex but absolutely everything that in some sense appears attractive and that takes place within the dialectics of libido and mortido. It is about the existential experience as such, which is why it is relevant to speak of *social pornography* rather than of pornography plain and simple. Via the media, we increasingly live and consume pornographically. The social-pornographic society drenches the human libido in sensory passions; The Internet showers us with millions and millions of auditory and visual experiences of the highest technical quality. The consequence is a widespread creative paralysis: What can I as a dividual possibly add to the Internet Age's massive maelstrom of culture production? How can I as an agent even dream of competing with the acclaimed actors in this manic dance?

This means that libido must look for alternatives that are completely different from artistic interactivity, which is the Internet Age's netocratic ideal. At the very least, it must start to operate from values and valuations that differ radically from the ones that drive industrialism's individual to be productive as a compensatory response. As so often is the case, there are mainly two ways of addressing *the social-pornographic tsunami*: in part a consumtarian-mortidinal reactionary pattern, in part a netocratic-libidinal course of action. The consumtarian-mortidinal reaction is pornoflation: when all other actors in our media flow speed up with no inhibitions and blurt out precisely everything about themselves, let us then simply shout and scream even louder to try to drown out all our rivals in the irreconcilable fight for the world's attention. Let us ignore everything in terms of privacy and our sphere of intimacy and expose ourselves with greater ruthlessness and richness of detail than anyone else. Aside from interpassivity, pornoflation is thus the consumtarian reaction *par excellence* to address the massive informationalist noise. Quality is replaced by quantity – and volume! – when competitive quality no longer can be mustered.

Since we are talking about a reaction rather than an action, pornoflation belongs to the Nietzschean category of false *countertrends* rather than authentic *trends* (see *The Netocrats*); it is simply a confused and counterproductive response – contributing to raising the general level of noise in society, which propels even more vocal attempts to drown out the noise, and so on – to a social condition that the frustrated consumtarian does not understand and cannot draw any productive conclusions from. Here, we can really speak of *false communication*. The quest for an *add* or a *like* – without even questioning or valuing who is adding or liking, and why – merely ramps up pornoflation a few more notches. The quest for *false attention* – false in the sense of illusory – becomes a compulsory addiction. The consumtarian enters a psychotic state where quantity is mistaken for quality, which fans the flames of the superego that commandeers ever more clamorous swagger of the most personal and private kind, on display for all. While the sparse audience that initially is paying attention to the spectacle – for instance as reality television's decline into a freak show or political theater's ambition to be "dangerous" through its constant demands for populist overthrow of the purported establishment – gradually thins out and then vanishes, either because of tedium or aversion. Or both. Thus the only thing that remains is what we might call an emonarcissistic stalemate on a stage lowered into darkness without an audience, where the lone actor merely attains the illusory fame inside his own head. We can consequently refer to this sorry last stop of pornoflation as *emonarcissistic nihilism*.

The netocratic-libidinal course of action instead starts from a historical shift away from the traditional exhibitionism of the upper classes and the equally traditional voyeurism of the underclasses to their dialectical antitheses. Consumtarian pornoflation causes the underclass to be devoured by its own meaningless exhibitionism. This means that voyeurism becomes the coveted scarce commodity in the network society, and it is conducted with cunning and finesse by the emerging netocracy, wholly in line with the celebration of the interactive *swarm* (in contrast to the consumtarian interpassive *mob*) and the pragmatic platform as an ideal. Thus netocratic social theater is not merely dividual and tribal, it is moreover subcultural and posited within imploitation's closed walls, and it is only in this special context that it receives its transcendental value. It is through imploiting rather than exploiting – through fencing in, sealing off and observing and actively co-creating, rather than marketing and mass producing – the most valuable, that the netocracy stands in contrast to both the consumtariat and to the elites in the previous societal paradigms. Here the artistic expression is qualitative, not quantitative. While the consumtarian mob is driven by a tragic mortido, the netocratic swarm is instead driven by a comic libido.

In this way the netocracy builds its power via qualitative culture – and then it does not matter whether we use the French sociologist Pierre Bourdieu's antiquated vocabulary and call this value *cultural capital*, or if we with a more updated, network-dynamical terminology call the value *sociographic attention*. In any case *attentionalism* displaces capitalism as the paradigmatic core function at the same moment that imploitation's value trumps that of exploitation. And it *de facto* occurs at tremendous speed in the netocratic networks in which membership cannot be purchased for money (see *The Netocrats*). These networks are driven by the basic principle of the sacred temple rather than by those of the open market: "The best things in life are not free, they are priceless." If you cannot offer what is required, you will not be admitted, irrespective of what you are prepared to pay. Because the moment the network starts to sell membership for money, it has already devaluated the value of the membership and thus the status of the network has started to wither away. These attentionalized processes move at breakneck speed in the digital age. Invariably the true netocrat considers himself able to afford to say no thanks to understimulating company even with money as enticement. Indeed, the netocrat is actually forced to do precisely this to keep his place in the network pyramid where everything is constantly in motion and where status and reputation constantly are assessed and reassessed. Money follows attention – not the other way around.

If we ascribe to Nietzsche the insight that God is dead – for the sake of Descartes being able to invent individualism and Newton then being able to invent atomism as two sides of the same religious coin, it was sufficient that one kept God absent and anesthetized, which became the genesis of Kantian morality and the Newtonian laws of nature – it is the French philosopher and anthropologist Michel Foucault who during the 1970s begins the issuing of the Individual's death certificate. But this does of course not preclude that the Cartesian Individual – even in his most perfect incarnation in the form of the Napoleonic patriarch – even from the start was just as dead as God ever was. This fiction had a metaphysical task to carry out. There is an eternally ongoing metastory of the phallic gaze's cyclical genesis and disappearance, a story where the characters succeed each other in an endless relay race, and in this story the death of the Individual is just as given beforehand as the death that just as inexorably befell his predecessor. Just as the mythical Primordial Father was concealed behind prehistoric veils of mist and just as God was concealed beyond the clouds in the firmament, the Cartesian Individual was concealed inside the brain's little pineal gland – every bit as invisible and illusory, but still, in its heyday, highly potent as the agency from which the phallic gaze emanates, the gaze without which we humans and our societies cannot survive.

In truth our longing for the phallic gaze, which never materializes, gives us no peace. Particularly as the matrichal gaze – all dreams must be fulfilled; all children must get a gold star, irrespective of what they have or have not achieved – so evidently lacks all form of grounding in reality and thereby solidity that will provide success in the network society. On the other hand, when the phallic gaze enters Man's life when he is one year old, it brings a meaningfulness that stands in sharp contrast to mamilla's all-encompassing and unconditional love – a love that for the adult human therefore must appear meaningless and worthless. It is this phallic gaze that is at the center of and drives the metaphysical story. Love must be associated with hierarchization to be credible and meaningful in a world where hierarchization is the framework that creates the evident distinction between death and survival and drives libido itself. Only phallic love survives and has value in a world characterized by scarcity and competition. Only phallic love can seduce the child and lure it away from the mamilla, out into real life's adventurous voyage from childhood to the adult world. An enormous yearning for the phallic gaze arises the moment the insight of life's brutality is awakened. It is a yearning to one day possess adult sexuality and autonomy.

During the paradigm shift, the constant reiteration of the phallic gaze's repositioning takes place when the previous starting point of the gaze is revealed as an illusion. Where does the night sky go when the night sky is revealed to be as empty and indifferent as matrix itself? For without the phallic gaze's metaphysical voyeurism the social order dies. Everything in Man's drive system, except the most fundamental instinct, collapses. Which means that the phallic gaze must re-emerge even in the network society, but its old position in the brain's pineal gland is now thoroughly discredited because of the old paradigm's collapse, at which time it must be given a new point of departure. It simply must have a new home address. And as has been the case so far, this address is connected to the night sky's most luminous star, where it is localized as the most optimal voyeur position in relation to the prevailing paradigm's social arena.

The phallic gaze naturally resides where the field of vision is the most perspicuous. The Primordial Father resides at the center of the original tribe with its surplus of food, shelter and libido, that is: inside the most excellent of all caves, the Primordial Mother's matrix. God for his part resides up there in the heaven that awaits us after death or after the life cycles have spun their way to a conclusion, in the form of the arbiter that passes judgment on Man's morals or lack thereof. The Individual resides in the future as the successful conclusion and confirmation of the realization of Progress, as the completion of a successful life and as the rocket fuel that propels the process into the liberal or socialist utopia where your children will be better off than yourself. In the same way, network society feverishly seeks its own credible phallic gaze and applies it frenetically to the very intrusive, mystical void where the phallic gaze's address label always has lodged itself most effectively in the stories of the shamans, the priests and the ideologues. In the void, the event-driven netocrat now thinks he has found what he so intensely seeks: the netocratic voyeur and judge, the phallic gaze that controls the netocratic network's key functions. We feverishly search for the personification of the sacred node. Who connects everything else together in a chaotic, network-dynamical universe? Who is in possession of the universal address book?

13
The dialectics of ressentiment – identitarianism as the curse of the consumtariat

In the late 19th century, German philosopher Friedrich Nietzsche bemoans the fact that the great majority of people throughout history have preferred to be slaves to some external power – never specified – rather than take responsibility for themselves and their actions, that they have never internalized power and instead have submitted to someone else's power over their own destiny, and that they constantly have reacted and never acted. The majority quite simply prefer *mortido* or the death drive to *libido* or the will to life. It is more comfortable and less demanding that way. These people seek submission to avoid all demands and responsibility that come with living the freedom of true adulthood, they welcome and strive to be as close to death as possible and most of all even to be annihilated (the most impressive and imposing manifestation of external power is of course death itself). Most people quite simply seek easily understood eternalization rather than complicated mobilization so that they arenot forced to relate to and parry all the incessant and worrisome changes of existence (where the only state that can guarantee eternal stability and total absence of change is – once again – death itself).

This yearning for comfort and irresponsibility causes people, if we go along with Nietzsche's argument, to constantly seek new excuses to devote themselves to the enjoyments of infantilization and choose to refrain from becoming adult and autonomous dividuals. An almost too obvious historical example of this eagerness to be infantilized, which Nietzsche tends to emphasize, is of course the lascivious worship of the monotheist God who pronouncedly plays the role of the Father. Before Him all adults are reduced to God's irresponsible and submissive children. A more obvious and purely literal infantilization is hard to imagine. At least if one has not yet familiarized oneself with the possibilities for extreme infantilization offered by the digital age. For never before in history has the necessary *adultification* of young men and women been so difficult to carry out as in the approaching network society. In fact, the division between a netocratic upper class and a consumtarian underclass does when all is said and done even become an issue of whether one succeeds in maintaining a rarely-seen adult stance, or if one resorts to the broadly infantile, in the face of the unrelenting human need of sacred *attention*.

This mortidinal infantilism is connected to the narcissistic dreams of eternity and immortality. If there are no clear boundaries that mark a before and/or an after of the period during which the child soaks up nourishment and security from the sacred *mamilla* – the child's mendacious dream of a coveted reunion with *matrix* lacks, just as all other mortidinal dreams, a phallic boundary setting along the timeline – *the phallic intrusion* that is necessary for successful attainment of adulthood will be repressed. This in turn means that the child permanently gets caught in what psychologists and psychoanalysts alike call *the Peter Pan syndrome:* a fixation on the thought of on the one hand growing into the adult human's phallically autonomous body, and on the other hand remaining dependent on the maternally caring mamilla that constantly supports one without any stress- or anxiety-producing reciprocal demands.

One becomes an outwardly adult person who nevertheless is unable to handle both the freedom and the responsibility that adult life inevitably entails. And if this Peter Pan syndrome historically can be regarded as a rare, pathological anomaly – a society where resources are scarce, particularly a nomadized society where each and every person must play their part in building the itinerant community, finds it hard to tolerate parasitic behavior – it is a phenomenon that finds extremely fertile ground in informationalism's extensively infantilized society. The attainment of adulthood is constantly pushed further up the age ladder, until it *de facto* does not occur at all.

We fetter our children to an eternal childhood with all that it entails in terms of dependence and helplessness. Our intent is of course good; we want to quell bullying in schools regardless of whether it is a case of a highly relevant rectification of a misunderstanding concerning social codes or not, and we want to carry out zero tolerance concerning precisely everything that is menacing and demanding in existence, everything from irascible urban traffic to pedophilia and narcotics. However the consequence of this *matrichal policing on overdrive* becomes an inhibiting digital shackle around more or less every teenager's shin. What happens is that the Peter Pan syndrome thrives because the phallic intrusion in early childhood does not occur, while the adult world develops a mildly speaking overdimensioned protection against real and imagined fears and risks. The liberating *revolt against phallus* during adolescence is canceled. The teenage period that under favorable circumstances would entail emancipation from the control of the parent generation, now instead results in a compulsion that locks the child into an incorrigible dependence on the social mamilla. We ultimately attain the state that the Swiss psychoanalyst Carl Gustav Jung calls *nox matris* or "the night of the womb," a scenario where a matrix in its well-meaning eagerness to protect its child from all threats from and difficult emotions regarding the world around it in the end eats its own offspring: this matrix manipulates the offspring to ecstatically welcome its own extinction.

Jung confronts us with the consequence of an intemperate, matrichal mortido without a trace of any lingering phallic libido. We are speaking about a society that has received such a striking tilt towards the mortidinal that it shuts out every form of authentic phallus, and for lack of both a functioning patriarchy and a functioning matriarchy it is instead driven by false phalluses or no phalluses at all. Only the matrichal drive without counterweights remains. *Nox matris* is quite simply the name of this hypermatrichal lopsidedness, where matrix ultimately even cuts off and destroys mamilla and thus impels the decorationist society's ultimate dystopia. When Medea in Euripides' tragedy murders her own children because this constitutes the logical conclusion of her ethics, she commits *the great filicide* in literary history. But according to socioanalytical logic, this act still conceals the last step that rounds out a complete *nox matris*, namely matrix's distancing from its own mamilla as though it were dead matter, without any function in the form of a point of connection with the child up until the phallic intrusion occurs. Without access to any matrichal meaning, matrix uses its final, subsiding energy to break the myth of the circulation of existence, it shuts off itself and acts to drive through its own and circulation's extinction: it is converted to a purely matrichal mortido, a death drive that runs amok.

How would a matrix that is obsessed with finding an external mamilla itself with which to fuel up on security possibly be able to act otherwise? Without the phallic intrusion the girl can of course never be developed into a woman, any more than the boy can be developed into a man. We land in front of a girl, intellectually speaking, in an adult woman's pregnant body. *Nox matris* is thus simply another name for the postmodernist infantilization of the matriarch herself, the female Peter Pan syndrome *par excellence*. It is the welfare state and the consumption society that has laid the ground for this complex, through a consistent steering of the collective away from phallus and back to mamilla. The autonomized revolt against phallus is never realized, with a number of unfortunate consequences in the form of so-called welfare diseases: pathological obesity, eating disorders, body dysmorphia, assorted compulsive disorders, compulsive shopping that leads to unmanageable debt, sleeping disorders, an epidemic narcissism in all its tragicomic variants, a tsunami of psychiatric diagnoses, and all these misguided, violent wars between and within the sexes. All this is really just superficial symptoms of the underlying, dominating pathology, that is: *informationalism's infantilization of the masses.* The development of pathological infantilization can be seen most clearly in what we – in the spirit of the American cultural historian Camille Paglia – can sum up as *the inner circuit's contempt towards the outer circuit's enormous contribution to the tribal welfare.*

What we observe is how the pendulum of culture is once again frighteningly quickly about to swing from the one extreme to the other: from the unfortunate and in many ways deforming cult of rationality that gains strength during the period introduced by the Renaissance, and when what we call modernity takes shape into a highly problematical hatred of reason, and from a systematized and institutionalized oppression of women, connected to the cult of reason, to an equally programmatic – and unfortunate – contempt of men and what is connected with manliness. As if any of this was ever needed. There is of course no doubt whatsoever about which group is the true and the biggest loser in the society that the digital revolution is about to give shape to, namely men, and this applies both to the men of the elder generation who are displaced out of an increasingly automated and globalized working life and to the younger men that fail in school on a large scale and who become addicted to computer games and Internet porn. Men die before women, they take their own lives to a much greater extent, more men than women become alcoholics and more men than women suffer from pathological obesity, more men than women commit crimes and more men than women are in jail, and so on. A very large number of men therefore do not succeed in benefiting from the gendered power structure that is said to favor precisely them and disfavor the women who now dominate universities, research programs and an increasing number of the many businesses that are expanding in the new, emerging digital economy.

An illuminating example of how this infantilization can be expressed is when one within the feminist discourse mocks and attacks the outer circuit's two most important functions, namely *protection* and *provision*, that is: protection against external threats and responsibility for the tribe's material support. This contempt partly expresses itself through the ideologically conditioned celebration of *pacifism*. The simplest way to claim that the outer circuit is not needed is of course to claim that the external threat does not exist, or even that it is fabricated by the phallic members of the outer circuit themselves ("without men there would be no wars or conflicts whatsoever") to create their position and elevate their status. Moreover, this infantilization also expresses itself as the comprehensive *demonization of open aggression*. This occurs when everything that can be connected to physical violence is portrayed as a cultural creation whose only purpose is terror, repression and destruction ("violence never solves any problems"). This standpoint maintains that violence and aggression completely lacks a constructive function. Which is just as mendacious as it is counterproductive, and it certainly does not lay the ground for a peaceful society with no violent conflicts.

The phallic aggression and competitive instinct that are called male, but that naturally do not exclusively belong to men, are sociobiologically conditioned and serve several purposes that are related to Man's survival, not least within the eroticism that seldom has the vanilla flavor mandated by political correctness. When phallic, open aggression is repressed, it instead returns as matrichal, passive aggression; an attitude and a behavior that possibly can work wonderfully when it comes to keeping the inner circuit intact during the long treks of the nomadic tribe – with all that this involves in the form of sexual abstinence – but on the other hand works decidedly worse when it is used to control the outer circuit, for instance the hunting party, for which it is not adapted at all. In the wrong place, passive aggression has devastating consequences; the faith that is necessary for group cohesion is quickly razed when passive aggression constantly chips away at intimate feelings of trust. The collective loses its visionary focus on the common project and soon succumbs to internal, distressing conflicts. Ideological wishful thinking replaces inconvenient truths about the harsh nature of existence, which does not bode particularly well. It is hard to handle problems that one refuses to see.

So what then does socioanalysis have to say about the long-term effects of society's infantilization and the problems that follow when we are drowned in various kinds of misguided benevolence? To start with we can declare that society's urgent lack of understanding for and contact with *the collective asubject* – what Jung calls *the shadow of the collective subconscious* – generates the merciless, decorationist quest for the deviating tone of voice and the inappropriate choice of words. This combined campaign of upbringing and purging is permeated by matrichal passive aggression. The *social justice warriors* of the early 21st century are a clear example of such a mortidinal and destructive consumtarian movement. However, the decorationist lynch mob does not settle for its own compensatory, narcissistic approval of itself. Matrichal gazes – including the decorationist lynch mob's own reflection – are of course worthless to the adult child, since these lack any trace of hierarchization and therefore authentic values. Recognition that is conferred on everyone, without either earning it or differentiation, is of course by definition not worth anything, but still, one fashions a political program out of this. All children are winners and all children get rewards, no one should ever need to feel sad or that they failed, not even challenged.

What all of this behavior leads to is ironically a consumtariat where everyone for good reason feels as though they are outside themselves as well as the authentic community of which they long to be a part. The fundamental problem is that no one is accorded a contributing role in which one makes a genuine contribution to what is shared, a role that provides both a confirmation that one is adult and that one has succeeded in creating a social identity. The phallic gaze is conspicuous in its absence. The phallic intrusion in the tribal community has failed on a grand scale.

We all seek validation in some form or other, but it must mean something, it must have value. It is the indifference that shies away from conflicts in the relation to the world around us that causes the matrichal gaze to become so automatic, numb, empty and therefore so unsatisfactory. The consequence is that the validation deficit afflicts the decorationist herd particularly hard, which is why this group's subconscious yearning for the phallic gaze and its genuine validation is stronger than in any other actor. But since the phallic gaze starts from the very outer boundary that the decorationist herd attacks and demonizes, this behavior generates powerful, ambivalent tensions that we subsume within the concept *social masochism*. We frenetically attack the root system of the phallic gaze, while calling in vain for the presence of the phallic gaze and its approval of the hypernarcissistic, moralistic crusades against all the world's evil to which we devotes ourselves. Because of the extensive *absent phallus syndrome* that prevails in the culture, propelled and maintained by ourselves, the only available surrogate for a libidinal phallus is a mortidinal mamilla. We call this fatal, built-in contradiction in identitarian supraideology *the mortidinal tragedy in the collective subconscious*. It is the case of a kind of Freudian death drive on compulsory overdrive, a collective death drive that is reinforced by the digital society's turbo charger in the form of the Internet's constant and increasingly clamoring feedback of consumtarian pseudoactivities. The only exit in sight is death. How could the path towards this realization of mortido, strictly socioanalytically, be driven by anything other than a will to death rather than the will to power that is banned? Without the phallic intrusion the adult human body cannot experience anything other than a paralyzing horror at the authentic phallus. The result is the social-masochist fixation with the gradually withering mamilla.

Within the social-masochist worldview – which in accordance with its *unimatrichalism* is built on a moral obsession with decorative behaviors and not on an ethical interest in deep-seated intentions – the phallic gaze is forced to play the part of a fervently coveted *moralator*, that is to say the in itself amoral judge that both produces and constitutes the ultimate authority in terms of all moral value, where, of course, the monotheist God The Father is history's moralator *par excellence*. But since the social masochist never was allowed to nor could undergo a phallic intrusion during his upbringing, the relationship to the moralator will not be dynamical and temporary – as it would be to a phallic parent, for instance – but instead is pathologically fixated and hysterical. At the same time, the moralator is experienced as both too absent and too present, as both too observant and listening and at the same time as too indifferent and distanced. Above all, the moralator, according to the social masochist, is always in the wrong place with his attention focused in the wrong direction in order to in any reasonable way be able to act satisfactorily as a producer of the phallic gaze. It is hardly surprising that the decorationist masses also are unable to distinguish between *the fetish* that symbolizes the authentic phallus and *the abject* that symbolizes the false phallus. Consequently the social masochist chooses the dystopian abject before the utopian fetish as the least strenuous way out of his dilemma. The fetish requires too much effort from him to be an attractive alternative. And it is too frightening.

The false phallus, on the other hand, promises immediate satisfaction and security from the mamilla because of the annihilation of the abject. Without phallic intrusion the social masochist lacks every trace of incentive to want to take on a genuine, existential challenge. Thereby one has paved the way for fascism's banal worldview to take root. The decorationist masses require that everything that disturbs their restful vegetating at the mamilla must be forbidden and exterminated. And this is exactly what the false phallus promises to deliver against being granted complete power. This, naturally, reinforces infantilization of the social masochist and puts off a possible future coming of age even further away into the mists of the future. At any rate, the social masochist seldom or never has time for anything other than his frenetic brooding over and worrying about the phantasmic moralator's verdict about everything important or unimportant that the social masochist conceivably might be engaged in. The result is precisely the consumtarian deluge of hypernarcissism, pornoflation and interpassivity that already washes over us and that constantly is increasing in strength. However, in contrast to other consumtarians, social masochists do not devote themselves to their pseudoactivities in the margins of the network society, but instead gang up into boisterous, aggressive lynch mobs that pounce on everything and everyone in the quest for new abjects to unite around hating, as a kind of infant formula instead of a moralator who never seems to show up. The carrying out of this lynching type of justice then continues until the false phallus enters the social arena with its opportunistic promise of an eternal mamilla, without any phallic demands, concealed behind the annihilation of the abject.

Nietzsche's predecessor and countryman G W F Hegel tends to focus on the ideological structure that characterizes both a specific society as well as the developmental process that this society happens to go through, and sums up this work as the quest for what he calls a society's *Zeitgeist*, its essential spirit of the age. Nothing characterizes the network society more clearly, compared to earlier power structures, than its radically flattened structure. The world has suddenly been transformed into a horizontally layered jumble of connections and reconnections, largely randomly constructed, without guiding norms and codes of conduct that create security. Old idols and role models have fallen or have lost their credibility, old guidelines have been erased and have become difficult or impossible to discern – a situation that paves the way for ruthless compensation narcissism.

This in turn means that our contemporary spirit of the age is characterized by industrious attempts to drown out the general noise, which in turn generates a rapidly escalating, unbridled escalation of the noise level. No one hears or sees anyone any longer when everyone has entered the boisterous stage, about which everyone has opinions, and there is no one left in the deserted chairs that were meant to seat the audience. The phallic gaze is conspicuous in its absence. The audience has joined the performers on the stage in order to themselves communicate their passively received thoughts and opinions to an audience who is no longer there and whose members at any rate merely are interested in having their own, passively received thoughts and opinions validated and legitimized. Thus everything is now stage, and the world has been transformed into a henhouse where no one person's cackling is distinguishable from the constantly escalating noise, a near-unbearable situation that breeds a growing yearning for an authoritarian rooster to restore order. The desperation in this yearning makes it hard or impossible to distinguish the authentic rooster from all impostors in their more or less convincing plumage.

It is of course possible to find the same pattern if we gaze back through history. In 1848 Europe exploded in a series of violent uprisings. A loose alliance that consisted of in part an emerging urban middle class, in part industrialism's working class that now senses change in the morning air, as well as miscellaneous self-appointed reformers, succeeded in setting countries such as France, the Netherlands, Austria-Hungary and several small German principalities ablaze. As the French author Gustave Flaubert later writes in the novel *L'Education Sentimental* (*Sentimental Education*) from 1869, these revolts were mainly led by naive and talentless narcissists, whose personal disappointments after the breakdown of the revolts knew no boundaries. Romanticizing historians often declare 1848 to be the starting signal of first nationalism's and later parliamentary democracy's victory parade around Europe. But the fact remains that for the activists of the age 1848 was a gigantic failure, which later became the starting signal for decades of pointless, nihilist and anarchist violence over great parts of the continent. More than anything else, 1848 was marked by a posturing violence that was fueled by the self-satisfied mediocrity of the perpetrators and their political naiveté. There and then the violence was stoked by the newspapers, pamphlets and other printed matter of the day, here and now the violence is stoked by the Internet's innumerable political and religious cults, the one more pompously and posturingly extreme than the other. The recurring pattern is the infantilized mythology of martyrdom, propped up by mendacious wishful thinking and with passive aggression as fuel.

To better understand this course of events we must dig deeper in social masochism's sanctimonious historiography. Even if the abolition of slavery in Europe and North America during the 19th century quite rightly has been ascribed enormous symbolic value in terms of dividual freedom and egalitarianism, the reform must also be scrutinized in a more cynical light. It was not primarily the case that the rulers of the age suddenly, thanks to their noble-minded inclinations, supported beautiful and admirable principles underpinned by ideas of the equal value of all people. To a considerably greater degree it was an issue of purely financial considerations. Abolishing slavery meant that one was able to make monetary profit by simultaneously abolishing the slave-owner's duty to meet the expenses of his slaves' housing, clothes and food; the former slaves after the reform instead were individual wage-earners on a labor market, for which plantation and factory owners had no responsibility whatsoever since the entire dealing was regulated through the agreed-upon sum in the wage envelope. The worker was no longer an investment that one would be wise to care for, but instead a resource to be exploited as thoroughly as possible and then replaced by a new one. The unique ability of capital to function as a means of payment for a disclaimer for the well-to-do now broke through with full force. As long as salaries were lower than the total costs of maintaining increasingly complex and costly slavery, the abolition of slavery entailed nothing but pure profit for capital. The equality that was attained was first and foremost purely symbolic. The structure in the game that power played with the powerless remained essentially intact. That someone voluntarily and through the goodness of his heart gives up power and status is, to put it mildly, extremely rare.

The problem is that this power relation is complicated further during informationalism when *attention* is placed atop capital as the social propelling force *par excellence*. The dialectics between the executive and topological pair of opposites *power* and *submission* when the dividual is in the social arena must now be understood as one axis in a diagram where the other axis is constituted by the corresponding emotional and topological pair of opposites *ecstasy* and *depression* (or if you will: the *event* and the *trauma* as ecstasy and depression in their most extreme forms). It is at this level of immanence that we see the dramatic shift that makes *the digital libido* something completely different from what we have previously seen in history. Now, for the first time, both the chosen power as well as the chosen submission is complemented by a constant and life-long emotional reinforcement of the respective identities. In other words we are going from a society where a small power elite governed a large majority that was living in submission, a structure that for many centuries had been regarded as natural in the God-given sense, to a power structure where the privileges, in a significant breakthrough of meritocratic ideology, instead are regarded as well-deserved (particularly by the elite but also to a large degree by the underclass, which loves to curry favor with entrepreneurs and innovators), that is: we go from a cohesive and organic conceptual world to one that is divided and defeatist.

We see a small power elite that is driven by ecstasy-as-norm emerging in parallel with large consumtarian masses that are oriented towards comfortable submission and driven by depression-as-norm. The netocrats seek identification with *the ecstatic event* from the outside, while the consumtarians seek identification with *the depressive trauma* from the inside. The confirmation that the search was successful is taken from any phallic gaze, be it authentic or not, that happens to be available. This means that the psychological contrasts between the classes in society have never been greater. Not even when the discrepancies in wealth and knowledge have been at their greatest. After a short historical parenthesis characterized by overt class conflicts, there are no longer any social injustices to be upset about or to carry out political agitation over. The distinctions that indisputably exist, and that with unprecedented speed moreover are growing ever stronger, are directly connected to meritocratic principles.

This circumstance of course depends upon the fact that social and cultural capital that confers power on the netocracy – talents that enable us to control sociograms and information flows to our own advantage – to such a large extent is just innate talents and not acquired knowledge. In this way the netocracy, as the name suggests, is precisely a net-aristocracy that is more or less genetically predestined to call the shots, and not a net-bourgeoisie that has attained its position through hard work. Therefore the social masochists' passive-aggressive anger is not directed towards the actual distribution of resources – which would be reasonable if we were speaking of a class struggle with classically Marxist overtones – but is an anger that instead gets caught up in an infantile loop where one squabbles about choice of words and tone of voice. One stages a theater of class antagonisms that is only for show and that merely serves to conceal the real power relations. This is *the curse of identi-*

tarianism – it never becomes more than a petty bourgeoisie coquetry with flags and colors, the decorationist decadence *par excellence*. While all this harmless clamoring is going on, the netocracy is, undisturbed, accumulating enormous amounts of data, information that one processes with the aid of ever more intelligent algorithms, and in this way one digs the divides ever deeper through the mastery of all actual values in the attentionalist society.

Thus the social masochists are caught up in a sea of virtual irrelevancies and pseudoactivities, kept at a safe distance from the netocracy's power grab. Their customized smartphone apps are nothing but digital dummies, multi-branch extensions of an Internet that functions as the great attentionalist mamilla. On the other hand, it is in reality more or less impossible to educate or train the consumtariat in the art of becoming successful netocrats, irrespective of how great resources one has and how much money one funnels to various educational programs and other support policies; the intentions may be ever so good, the efforts will still not succeed. The netocrats have long since identified and for their own purposes recruited dividuals from the underclass that correspond to the prevailing skills in demand, a skimming that is continuously ongoing. If we really were to conceive of this type of education, the teachers who would be possible candidates would immediately be outcompeted by the exclusive group of coveted lecturers – both online and at actual events – who themselves are part of and interact with other parts of the netocracy. The result is a brutal, social stratification that among other effects means that the underclass is robbed of the potential leaders that by force of creativity and diligence would be able to articulate their standpoints and mobilize for a political fight. These talents now instead serve the upper class that willingly welcomes them to its select circle.

The consumtariat, on the other hand, only gets access to a scantily attractive and scantily functional form of the network society's coveted scarce commodity, attention, namely that which is at stake in the humiliating, social-masochist competition in self-contempt. We see, for instance, how informationalist television is rife with cheap *freak-show* formats where more or less volatile consumtarians are goaded into coquettishly flaunting their dysfunctionality and without inhibition display the most bizarre behavior possible. The netocratic social voyeurs distractedly enjoy this humorous spectacle of disabilities, while the consumtarians – for lack of other role models – identify with the constantly substituted actors and desire their suddenly flash of fame, as though they really were significant in their roles as celebrities and what within social media are called *influencers*. Identitarianism is thus nothing more than the dominating, opportunistic pseudoideology that keeps the consumtariat in its social-masochist passivity. Aside from this, there is little more than the intersectionalist struggle of exactly which *section* of the consumtariat – divided into categories such as sex, skin color, ethnicity, addiction, psychological illness, et cetera – is to be pitied the most at the moment, and that therefore, for lack of a phallic gaze to bore to tears, deserves the state's or the consumtarian mamilla's sympathy and consolation the most.

The contrast between on the one hand an attraction towards and an ability to encompass libido and on the other hand a compulsive and socially stigmatizing attraction to mortido has never been greater, since the digital class divide arises in a society that has already attained *the meritocratic fantasy* that powered individualism's success mythology. In the end we got the same possibilities, we attained *the egalitarian ideals* of radical equality in terms of life's prerequisites between the citizens in the developed West. We are all constantly online, the cost for access to the Internet is steadily and rapidly moving towards zero, and we all use the same smartphones regardless of whether we are insanely successful entrepreneurs or school children in problem-ridden suburbs. And yet the divides are widening in terms of resources and influence. The netocracy is thus exactly the meritocratic proletariat that the German sociologist Karl Marx extols in the 19th century and that he predicts one day will take over and control the world. But what Marx does not foresee is that the *Lumpenproletariat* that he despises would grow and one day constitute the great masses and form the informationalist, consumtarian underclass. As long as the phallic gaze is absent, the consumtariat will settle for cultivating its ressentiment in close connection with the mamilla to which it has managed to shriek itself access for the day. Social-masochistic enjoyment becomes the safe form of consolation when netocratic enjoyment, with all its impossible demands on phallic adulthood, so clearly has been posited far beyond the horizon of possibilities. What remains is then merely the narcissistic victim role. "If you cannot bring yourself to see me without irony in your gaze, then you must at least feel sorry for me. Pass me the pacifier!"

The world has been transformed into *The Global Empire*: one great cluster of interconnected computers to which eight billion confused human bodies are connected. But contrary to all meritocratic wishful thinking, the Internet causes the difference in terms of power and influence between the new, small elite and the new, large masses to become greater than ever. There is no netocratic enjoyment whatsoever to attain for the consumtariat, it is referred to bare mortido and its masochistic enjoyment during an entire life of passive consumption, which is of course the very definition of the consumtarian. This is because the art of creating productive relationships with dividuals all across the world, as well as the art of understanding and making clear the enormous information flows that pulsate through the global networks, essentially is connected to innate talents and, to a negligibly small extent, is something that one can become better at through training, no matter how strong-willed one is. The sociogram repeatedly shows how ruthless the informationalist class society really is. Precisely because it is between the networks and not between the dividuals that the class divides emerge and expand – "Show me your address book and I will tell you who you are."

It is important to understand social masochism as the foundation for the value hierarchy, but not as a result of the surge of social sadism. This is because masochism fundamentally is existential in character; its ressentiment is first and foremost directed towards fate and life itself, towards the emptiness and lack that masochism apprehends in existence. The American psychoanalyst Adrian Johnston calls this phenomenon *the cunning of libidinal reason*. What Johnston means is that the mind eventually gives up and starts to interpret the massive, contingent, external pressure that it is subjected to – since it is exposed to the surrounding world – as its very own, necessary, internal values. Social masochism thus constitutes the very foundation for self-consciousness and it is in this capacity that it becomes informationalism's smallest common denominator and thus also the trademark of the underclass. The contradictory, confused and confusing demands that the surrounding world appears to direct towards consciousness are converted into an idea of the subject's essential and indispensable core. The fundamental relational question "What does *the other* want from me?" receives no clear answer, so consciousness starts to mull over its own answers to the question, and these internally fabricated answers become the substance of the subject. For consumtarians are not even workers – indeed not even what the French sociologist and philosopher Jean Baudrillard calls *labor mannequins* – nor slaves. Rather they are reduced to *problematical existences* that the netocrats protect themselves from through surveillance, isolation, anaesthetization and sleeping pills.

Meanwhile, the consumtarians protect themselves from the brutal truth about their own irrelevance to the Global Empire by gratefully accepting and cultivating their enjoyment of the netocracy's social-sadistic forms of nursing through acts of repression that are distributed via the virtual mamilla. The fact that the contingent chaos constantly flooding the mind with signals lacks lines and patterns, merely intensifies this identity-producing process.

The very ambivalence in this constant stimulus merely makes it even more attractive. As soon as the subject thinks it has found – which means that it succeeds in creating – a pattern in the ambivalence, the identification in this subject jump-starts with the very pattern the subject believes it has discovered. This pattern now becomes the subject's own; a story of how the world takes shape. It seems as though it is the world that is telling the story, but the voice that is speaking always emanates from inside the subject itself. This structured obedience under chaotic pressure is what turns social masochism into Man's fundamental approach to existence. Social masochism is therefore also the bedrock of organized religion. Religion is of course the collective's way of handling and structuring the world's capriciousness by populating the capricious world with capricious gods. It is therefore logical and hardly surprising that one within early religion with enthusiasm embraces human sacrifice and whatever else all the inventive priests come up with to placate the wayward gods and win their favor when more rain or more sunshine or a crushing victory over the enemy on an adjoining mountain slope was desired.

This approach has a lot to recommend it, not least comfort: If capricious moralators govern the world by their own whims, and if we humans therefore are occupied using the tribe's resources in accordance with the priests' directives to parry these more or less irrational whims in the best way possible, then there remains no room whatsoever for the singular subject to express any volition or make any crucial decisions. The subject is of course already by definition identified with and fettered to the contingent fate that is undeniably real. The capricious phallus instills fear in the subject, and in this fear the social masochist finds an acceptable excuse for passively submitting to the course of events and remaining in his infantile paradise, seemingly safely and tightly fastened between matrix and mamilla. Please observe that none of today's religions is as programmatic in its celebration of social masochism as Islam, where "submission" is the etymological root of the religion's name and where independent thinking is banned. Which creates the perfect conditions for the abovementioned comfort, which might also be called cognitive laziness: through radical submission and self-annihilation the believer disposes of all responsibility for his own actions. Whatever happens, happens in accordance with God's will, *Inshallah*. Irresponsibility is one of the points of religion, all religions. Irresponsibility is a form of religion. And no other religion is as consistently faithful to this idealization of mortido as Islam.

What we see before us when *the event* takes over as the metaphysical engine in Man's imaginary universe, is neither more nor less than a golden age for sadomasochism. We no longer have the patience to wait for a life after death (*the metaphysics of eternity*) or for that our children will be better off than we are (*the metaphysics of progress*). In fact, we no longer have any patience to wait for anything at all. All this talk about putting off the fulfillment of one's needs for some future good is not something that is possible to market successfully to a generation that is used to consuming any form of media experience anytime after a few quick swipes across a screen. *The event* as an idea requires that our dreams be realized here and now, and above all emotionally. The event tricks us into believing that we no longer have anything to learn or need any other form of investment to maximize our talents. This means that we are forced to bid farewell to all possible hopes of the power of the word (*logos*), not to speak of the power of ethics (*ethos*); instead it is the power of emotion (*pathos*) that dictates the conditions in culture and drowns out everything else. At least until the event seekers start to make demands on the quality of the event rather than its quantity. Only then do we start to approach the syntheist *the infinite now* as an ideal, which requires considerable amounts of both *logos* and *ethos* from its highly netocratic explorers.

This relationship between impulsive hunters for quantity and long-term seekers of quality applies particularly between the large majority that constitute and see themselves as *the submission that liberates from responsibility* and the numerically inferior minority that like to see themselves as *the elite that insists on responsibility*. The difference in size means that the social masochists' needs-driven children's choir drowns out all other voices in the network society; one constantly requires *attention* while the refuses to take any responsibility for its actions. One shouts in different keys depending on whether one is part of the far right, the identity left, or religious fundamentalism, but the social-masochist lamentation is fundamentally the same. There are calls out for an intervention from a higher power, but it happens to be an intervention that no one really believes in, since the higher power never will act, which deep down is already known. Why? Well, the people have in fact seen to it themselves by castrating this power, just to be on the safe side. Which is of the utmost importance. If the higher power actually could intervene, it would blight the social masochist's perverse enjoyment of his self-imposed submission. If the phallic gaze refuses to devote its calendar to watching me and my pseudoactivities, nor should it be able to watch anyone else's banal activities. Welcome to *identitarianism*, the consumtariat's ressentiment-driven supraideology.

Victim status is hard currency. He who chooses to be a victim also wishes to remain a victim and if possible become an even more lamentable victim in accordance with what Hegel and Nietzsche may be unified around as *the dialectics of ressentiment*. An elevated victim status entails that one can claim moral superiority, both in relation to abjectified perpetrators and to attention-competing victims. Naturally, the social sadomasochism we are talking about here is something completely different from the strictly regulated sadomasochist role playing that occurs in the area of sexuality, a game that is more of an expression of the sexual dialectics of voyeurism and exhibitionism, where the masochist takes the role of the voyeur and the sadist takes that of the exhibitionist, and which is built on a fetishist bridge being established between them. For understandable reasons this sexual sadomasochism is connected to phenomena such as bondage and discipline, to which physical intimacy is added. On the stage that emerges one can then act out dominance and submission as a form of erotic theater, a play that follows a completed manuscript and is bound by rules and constraints, for instance the classic stop word, a symbolic act through which the masochist both formally and in real terms takes control of the sadist with the purpose of halting the course of events. Social sadomasochism is not made up by such rules or constraints and therefore lacks this character of being a studied game and staging. The submission that is carried out with identitarian frenzy is as real as anything can be, just as is the perverse enjoyment that accompanies it.

The practical prerequisite is the hyperdemocratization of the social arena that the Internet gives rise to, a development that gives every actor the possibility to express himself and spread his gospel and his expression, which in turn makes the Internet one big garbage disposal overflowing with assorted amateurish waste, a hodgepodge of voices that together form one single, desperate call for an attention that does not exist and that cannot exist. With this, two historically new phenomena appear: *hypernarcissism* and *pseudoexhibitionism*. Nietzsche is correct in the sense that the great masses seek some form of law and order to which they can submit. Aimlessly drifting on an ocean of chaos, one seeks the beacon that lights up and demarcates a border. But for lack of both an authentic and a false phallus the comfortable infantilization is always available; instead one is drawn to the mamilla and reverts to an existence in the form of a non-existence: the wonderful liberation from responsibility. This is the most delectable and most perverted of all enjoyments: to devote oneself without inhibitions to the *victimhood mythology*. Whatever the surrounding world cannot offer, the consumtarian masses start to seek in themselves. And since they lack both training in being and the ambition to be phallically adult, they will ignore all solutions for attaining empowerment that might prove challenging, and instead devote themselves to an infantile and undemanding identity production based on a competition of who in every given situation is *the greatest victim*.

The problem is that the victim does not improve the living conditions for anyone. The self-appointed victim is a parasite on the body of society that drains rather than inspires anyone towards creativity and entrepreneurship. Only he who has a definite sense of netocratic empowerment can revolutionize the informationalist world. The self-appointed victim, however, drags everything and everyone down into the abyss, not seldom at tremendous cost, if this is not stopped in time. The indifference of the surrounding world creates a frustration that either morphs into a desperate acting out or else into a fully developed self-deception. That is: one either hopes, against all odds, that an audience that does not exist will still discover a talent in oneself that one deep down does not see or believe in oneself, or one devotes oneself to the illusion that the breakthrough that both is constituted and confirmed by the approval of the phallic gaze is just about to occur. The common denominator is a monumental self-absorption, a near-hysterical compensatory behavior that for lack of response gradually morphs into what we from a socioanalytical perspective can call *the hypernarcissistic condition*. The compulsively repeated display of genuine lack of talent can therefore not be characterized as anything other than *pseudoexhibitionism*.

The extreme medialization of culture and identity production that occurs during the Internet Age causes power to move in the opposite direction, away from the interactive communication flow. Power – that is: authentic power – becomes silent and secret, it recoils and camouflages itself; above all it becomes voyeuristic. Power devotes itself to *imploitation* instead of exploitation (see *The Netocrats*) behind closed or even concealed doors. When the performance in the social theater degenerates into a veritable freak show, power moves even further away and makes itself inaccessible. The sadist refuses to even communicate with the masochist. The conditions for a potential dialogue across the class barriers could hardly be worse. The consequence is that elite and underclass, exhibitionist and voyeur, switch places and functions with each other in connection with the arrival of the Internet Age. When the audience is tricked into leaving their seats, step onto the stage and start to shout into each others' mouths, the stage ceases to be a socially attractive place, whereupon power discretely sneaks down to the now deserted seats in the auditorium. But the elite naturally cling to power, however not in the capacity of an exhibitionist on a stage but as a voyeur in an ever more deserted auditorium. Thus power is no longer primarily connected to acting, but to *the phallic gaze* that rejects and validates. This is seen not least when the appreciated professional skill within the discipline in question no longer is expected to come from the often and easily substituted actor, but instead is sought in the demanding and considerably more long-lasting judge.

The dialectics of power and submission as well as the dialectics of exhibitionism and voyeurism must relate to the signals that are produced by on the one hand the ongoing *power play* and on the other hand the ongoing *drama*. For the sake of simplicity, one can reduce these signals to their most extreme expressions: ecstasy and depression respectively. The signals do of course contain both ecstasy and depression in varying degree – without a large measure of ambivalence the grinding flow of news would merely be seen as banal – and these can assume both mental and physiological expressions. Thus it would be useful to distinguish between mental ecstasy, mental depression, physiological ecstasy and physiological depression when we elaborate the libidinal map of the Internet Age. So from where does Rousseauan identitarianism in all this emanate? That it is an individualism which has stopped being a capitalist upper class ideology and instead – quite logically – has been transformed into informationalist underclass ideology, is beyond all doubt. But where does identitarianism find its other roots outside Cartesian individualism? The identitarians are of course moralists above all else. They are obsessed with projecting goodness and evil onto absolutely everything, as though Nietzsche's explorations beyond these categories did not exist. They project onto themselves as well, to which they of course ascribe good consciousnesses, behind which hide evil subconsciousnesses, which therefore must be repressed, which in turn generates the perfect fuel for the perverted enjoyment obtained from the moralizing of everything else. The mortidinal logic is crystal clear: If I only judge sufficiently quickly, harshly and often, my own shadow will never catch up with me.

So let us then look closer at another popular but misguided project from the history of philosophy: *moral philosophy*. Misguided because there is nothing at all on which to build any morals outside faith in the external divine power. Morals should have been tucked away in the catacombs of theology right from the start. The only thing that remains to build after the death of God is instead an *ethics of interactivity* (see *The Body Machines*), an ethics that refers back to every active agent and his self-identity separately. We can express this shift from *moral significance* to *ethical attraction* as that which ultimately structures and maintains humanity's values. This ethics of interactivity can be traced all the way back to Baruch Spinoza in the 17th century, the father of amoral ethics, who for this very purpose is resurrected by the French philosopher Gilles Deleuze in the 1960s, when Deleuze uses Spinoza to establish an ethical ideal for informationalism, a prototype for the coming netocrat as a kind of technological minotaur, half global nomad, half Nietzschean *Übermensch*.

According to the radical monist Spinoza, the world consists of bodies or force fields that all are various attributes of one and the same univocal substance. These bodies attract each other, to greater or lesser extents, but there is no built-in hierarchy between them where one body *per se* is more important or more valuable than any other. This is because there quite simply is no external judge, no moralator, who might be the only one who even would be able to make such a valuation. Spinoza thus pits ethics as the doctrine of constructiveness versus destructiveness – originally Zoroaster's *asha* versus *druj* within ancient Iranian philosophy – against morality as the doctrine of good versus evil. Only ethics has any ontological value whatsoever – cause and effect do of course *de facto* exist ontically – while morals are built on pure illusion. It does assume an externally divine power outside our universe, which already has determined what constitutes human good and evil via the eternally valid law in the written word, the dualist and determinist myth on which for instance the Abrahamic religions build their entire *raison d'etre*. It is hardly surprising that Spinoza is regarded as the worst kind of heretic by both Judaism into which he is born and Christianity by which he is surrounded in the Netherlands in the 17th century.

So how does power and submission relate to exhibitionism and voyeurism in a society where these extensive dichotomies constantly collide with each other? We investigate this most effectively by converting the dichotomies in question into two axes in a diagram, in the same way that we for instance map out a dividual's relation to the two sexes by distinguishing between sexual attraction and mental attraction as two separate axes. In this case, we posit power upwards, and submission downwards. We posit exhibitionism to the left, voyeurism to the right. In this way, we start off with four zones to relate to: The power-exhibitionist in the top-left, the power-voyeurist in the top-right, the submission-exhibitionist in the bottom-left, and the submission-voyeurist in the bottom-right corner. Traditionally the top-left corner in our diagram is of course the most libidinal and the bottom-right corner is the most mortidinal. But the image is complicated by the fact that exhibitionism and voyeurism actually lack power and submission's clear division between the power-generating actor and the submission-generating reactionary. It might well be the case that it is the voyeur who controls the arena and his fantasy that determines the outcome of the social or sexual game, rather than the exhibitionist that is in control. In a society with a lack of voyeurs and thirteen exhibitionists to a dozen, the voyeurs, not the exhibitionists, have the greater market value.

We are placed in front of a historically unique complication that we cannot ignore, if we are to understand an attentionalist society such as the network society, where the axis E/V for the first time in history is, if possible, even stronger and more important than the axis M/U. Just as we cannot ignore mental attraction between or within the sexes as a decisive factor, if we socioanalytically study a society where sexuality has a very limited social role and the cognitive sex preference governs prioritizations in the social theater. What is most important is therefore what effects the axes have on each other when they are on the same playing field. Here we discover the really interesting aspect: It is no longer the traditional corners that dominate. If the courts, the castles and the churches during feudalism and the parliaments, the urban apartments and the universities during capitalism constituted the arenas in which power-exhibitionist elites performed the social theater that the submission-voyeurist masses were presumed to fight to witness, these structures collapse with the arrival of the Internet. It turns out that the top-left power-exhibitionist corner's dominance of the lower right submission-voyeurist corner was far from being a consequence of any form of preordained law of nature.

What has happened is quite simply that the emperor has left the Colosseum and that only the mob and the gladiators remain in the arena. The emperor has hidden behind a screen, and it is not even certain that he cares anymore about watching the public spectacle. No one knows anymore where power hides, for power has for the first time in history nothing to gain from revealing its whereabouts. Power actually acts in exactly the opposite way in the network society with all its enormous attention-seeking communication flows. What fills up the public space is instead the new submission-exhibitionist consumtariat in the form of social self-victimization cults – the extreme right, the identity left and all sorts of religious fundamentalists – who lay claim to the social arena and demand a power-voyeurist netocracy as their audience, an audience that it stubbornly attempts to guilt into staying put in the social media's increasingly unappealing audience seats. For what would the alternative be? That the consumtarian herd must act as the longed-for moralator in regard to itself? This would unfortunately not work, since the various identitarian sects quickly would condemn and beat each other to death. It is sufficient to study the French Revolution's bloody terror to see what actually happens to a society where faith in the phallic gaze has been lost.

Thus it is the dividuals and networks populating the bottom-left power-voyeurist corner that take over the diagram during informationalism. They do of course require – if at first feebly and confusedly – the top-right submission-exhibitionist corner as their libidinal antipole. It is not the least bit strange that the consumtarians believe that their audience is an ordained given, like the old submission-voyeurist audience from feudalism and capitalism. But the power voyeurs are precisely a netocracy. They are constantly and consciously connected to each other online. Consequently the power voyeurs can in the long term lay down any negotiating terms they wish only to passively participate in the social theater, and soon they will have conquered near-unrestricted power over the entire network society. In this way, we will have a silent and concealed elite – extremely liberated from identitarian fundamentalism – that controls society in a way we have never witnessed before. This is not unlike a Masonic lodge that controls the world from the shadows, without ever having to or even trying to emerge into clear daylight and make itself known to the public. Anonymous, established in 2004, was merely the first example of such a netocratic pioneer project (as we prophetically predicted in *The Netocrats* a few years earlier). And the name in this case says everything; an anti-individualist network in the form of a netocratic swarm could hardly market itself under a more distinct label.

This is, however, just the beginning. When projects such as Anonymous gain access to future generations' encrypted communication technologies – and when one moreover has learned to cultivate and exercise a fanatic and insatiable submission-exhibitionist consumtariat compulsively predetermined to follow one's siren song and obey one's every whim – only then will the netocratic networks astonish the world for real. Power is power and submission is submission. What is new about the network society is that power follows the voyeur rather than the exhibitionist, and nowadays it is the narcissistic exhibitionist that rapidly becomes a slave to his insatiable need for infantile attention at any cost. An attention that therefore must be mortidinal rather than libidinal and connected to brutal submission. Libido quite simply moves from the stage to the auditorium when the seat in the auditorium becomes exclusive for real, while the stage is transformed from the center of events to a garbage dump in the social periphery. So get used to a world where you do not know or see when and where the important events take place, where the news flow increasingly has the character of a nihilist pseudotheater. And get used to only being able to blame this fact on the hydra that has taken over the world and made it its own global empire, that is, *The Internet* itself.

14
The digital class struggle – the netocratic swarm versus the consumtarian mob

The father of psychoanalysis, Sigmund Freud, often remarks that adult sexuality is mysterious to the child. The question is whether this may even be the most mysterious of all of life's mysteries. What is actually so remarkable about this all-encompassing project on which adults spend so much time and energy? How to handle this fundamentally ambivalent enigma – which has an at best sublimely addictive rather than a liberating outcome – that adults are so terribly fascinated by? It is as incomprehensible as it is frightening. And the relationship that one as a child establishes with the enigmatic sexuality of the adult world is then largely reflected by the self-confidence, or lack thereof, that one succeeds in mobilizing when one attains adult age.

A child that can be open and curious, while accepting both the fundamental incomprehensibility of the incomprehensible and recognizing the power in its indisputable exercise of power – the attraction of what philosophers call *the sublime* – will most likely also be able to maintain and develop this generous and curious approach regarding the surrounding world as an adult. With this tolerance follows a robust self-confidence, quite simply because self-confidence is underpinned by the ability to be comfortable in one's own identity in the encounter with the unknown, not least if this unknown is tangibly powerful and at least visibly menacing. This receptive approach is most preferably developed during childhood, since the child's fantasy world is so much more spacious and free than that of the adult. Thus the possibilities for the radicality of libido to overcome the conservatism of mortido increase. But this also means that this development becomes considerably less likely if the child learns to internalize various prohibitions at an early age and shield itself from the mysteries in life that appear menacingly enigmatic, particularly adult sexuality. It is largely this that determines whether the child can manage the necessary *adultification,* the transition from childhood, via adolescence, to mature adulthood.

The primitivist nomadic tribe was anything but a Rousseauan paradise. But it had – thanks to its *intratribalism,* both physical and mental isolation from the surrounding world – access to a series of tools that enabled them to handle complicated adultification processes. This was a main task of the shamanic caste. Children that failed in adultification because of narcissistic arrogance would quickly learn how the factual circumstances limited their self-centeredness. It could be sufficient to give them an assignment that was impossible for their age and level of knowledge for their inadequacy to become glaring. The traditional rites of passage offered a slew of such methods to reduce the arrogance of the youth and fashion self-confidence at a reasonable level that benefited the collective. This included the taming and adaptation of the child's sexuality at different rituals. Freud quite simply calls this necessary social taming *castration.* But the plastic nomadic tribe also had methods to save what was salvageable for the children who displayed immaturity and matrichal fixation up until adult age. These individuals were simply given a less demanding contributing role. Immature boys could be shut out from carefully regulated sexuality and reproduction. In situations where the tribe faced vulnerability – when it was afflicted by starvation, war or natural disasters – they would completely exclude the hopeless cases from the community and leave them to their fate. If the tribe quite simply could not afford to support them any longer, one made the crass assessment that the collective investment in their socialization would not pay the necessary dividends.

In today's society, we no longer suffer from the same material scarcity. It is no longer food, nor even capital, that is the critical scarce commodity, but *attention*. Even if starvation can occur in many corners of the world, usually caused by politically conditioned actions, the world can afford to feed the existing mouths, which is why there is no longer any powerful public opinion arguing that all those who do not contribute to the support of the collective should be left to their fate. At the same time globalization, automation and digitalization causes the demand for labor from the production of consumer goods to decrease, which in turn means that the number of people sidelined from the job market increases rapidly. But of course they all demand support, their right to consume, while claiming their right to refuse to participate in the adultification process. On the Internet these dividuals now find each other easily and rapidly; together they make up *the consumtarian mob* and call out their many demands and their boisterous frustration. And when these infantilized – the adultification process has of course collapsed – mobs demand attention in the name of more or less fictitious injustices, the entire project quickly degenerates into aggressive *identitarianism*. The Internet is gradually transformed into a cacophonic free-for-all where the competing consumtarian mobs try to drown out each other with their demands.

On the other side of the growing class divide, this development is observed with either distaste or indifference; the elitist phenomenon that reflects the consumtarian mob is *the netocratic swarm*, where a successfully completed adultification process is a strict entry requirement. And here one realizes that it is comparatively cheap to provide the demanding consumtarians with a considerable measure of material welfare and ensure that there is room for everyone to consume at a, from a historical standpoint, fantastic level. However, the netocratic swarm neither wants to nor truly is able to dole out the resource around which the entire new social economy revolves – attention. For there is a chronic and increasingly desperate lack of this very commodity. This is why we speak of *the attentionalist society* rather than the capitalist society. Since attention is the scarce commodity, capital seeks out attention rather than, as previously, the other way around. Power falls to he who has attention, not to he who has capital. When the netocratic swarm withdraws from the consumtarian mob, the tribe splits in the middle. The consumtarian mob does of course lack the outer circuit's most important asset, *the phallic gaze*, and the netocratic swarm appropriates the coveted attention through its imploitative monopoly on that very phallic gaze.

Above the class divide, traffic is minimized to what is absolutely necessary, which means that what remains for the consumtarian mob is internal strife about all sorts of pointless pseudo attention in the form of hypernarcissism, pornoflation and interpassivity. The consumtarian mob is therefore best described as a distorted imitation of the plastic nomadic tribe's inner circuit, which evidently retains the outer circuit's protection and forms of care fairly intact – for instance by way of subsidies, tax relief and a set of basic functions in society – but which must now manage without the outer circuit's sexual engine, the phallic gaze. Thus the inner circuit will be supported and protected, but unfortunately will not be seen, it receives no attention, which generates enormous, fundamentally sexual, frustration. Protection works, provision arrives, but the sexual ritual set to seal the tribal sense of belonging – the tribe's common rite of passage that confirms the entry into the enchanted adult world – is constantly postponed and never occurs. Because the netocrats retain the phallic gaze and thereby the sexual ritual for themselves. The digital class struggle is thus not determined through the netocrats subduing the consumtarians through physical violence – that is of course not necessary and serves no purpose – but through the enduringly functional netocratic swarm hiving off from the dysfunctional consumtarian mob, shutting it out from its plurarchic nodes and leaving it to die from lack of attention in the digital wilderness.

Or if we express this state of affairs with the Frankfurt School's Freudian-Marxist vocabulary from the interwar period: Since the digital class struggle is a struggle for *attention* rather than for *territory* or *capital* in the form of material resources, it is *de facto* a sexual class struggle. Freud was even more correct about contemporary Man than about primitivist Man – those that he calls "savages." We have gone from a struggle about *the real order* or *the imaginary order* in society to a class struggle pertaining to *the symbolic order*. Thus the digital class divide does not revolve around control of instinct or drive, but around control of *desire*. Where has the phallic gaze gone and why does it no longer see me? Who am I then, and what value do I have? What is so much more interesting than me that is getting all the attention? The phallic gaze evidently no longer cares about the maternal body, the nation-state or the consumer society – the fixations that populate the consumtarian's head. Or to express the matter more mundanely: Why am I not allowed into the adult swarm to play its sophisticated sexual games? Why must I settle for the infantile mob and its permanent childhood outside the temple?

So how then does the bizarre adult sexuality, the one that fascinates both the child and the consumtarian so intensely, actually work? Well, desire is attracted by a stimulus, and this stimulus is characterized by intense *ambivalence* when faced with a complex web of relationships while it has the sublime as its abstract objective. While the sublime is characterized by ambivalence in the form of endless sorrow and endless beauty at once – experienced most clearly when Man consciously looks death in the eye – ambivalence is fundamentally a struggle between on the one hand the spirit's will to conquer, maintain and reinforce its power (to avoid an orgasm), and on the other hand the yearning for submission to something that the same spirit experiences as greater and more powerful than itself (to attain an orgasm); a yearning that is directly connected to and is a product of this hunger for power. The sublime dissolves into emotional extremes, with *ecstasy* as libido's and *depression* as mortido's clearest expressions in the network society. Little wonder that major parts of society at the genesis of the Internet Age suffer from extensive epidemics of depression, something that those afflicted constantly talk about in all available media channels and seek attention for. And yet the path to *ecstasy* – and thus also to the ensuing management of this event as a productive memory – is ironically more available than ever before since all the cultures' different paths to *satori* suddenly are accessible to everything and everyone on the Internet, while advanced technology in different areas supply us with a steady stream of innovations whose purpose it is to help us attain *the peak experience.*

Here the psychedelic revolution – as a kind of erotic intimacy without any sexual attraction being necessary – does of course play a key role. Thousands of years of locally limited explorations of various drugs' shamanic potential are suddenly merged into a single global-imperial discourse where experiences are shared between a plenitude of subcultural *eventologies.* One experiments with and discusses both proven and newly-produced molecules in various combinations. At the same time, sexual practices are refined and perfected in Tantric schools with the purpose of maximizing and prolonging the experience of power within sexual ecstasy, *the orgasm*. The aggregate amount of knowledge grows rapidly. Special interests with a focus on the ecstatic meet in new, expansive subcultures. The difference between adult sexuality and child sexuality is of course that ecstasy only is available to the adult, and that it thus is directly connected to successfully conducted adultification. At the mamilla, there is only mortido to enjoy, no libido. The netocratic swarm gravitates towards ecstasy, while the consumtarian mob relegated to depression. The swarm is in possession of the phallic gaze and therefore has both phallus and matrix within itself, the mob on the other hand is only furnished with a consumtarian mamilla, and lacks phallus as well as matrix, which confines it to child sexuality and puts the ecstatic out of reach. Therefore the mob energetically looks for the only exit that it knows of: the social masochistic anesthetization of depression.

Social masochism's efforts to stay alive primarily expresses itself in an endeavor towards what we call *the masochistic state of equilibrium*: a kind of endurable balance between what the external law and the internal superego require of the masochist. Please note, however, that the masochistic state of equilibrium – a state where irritating external stimuli seemingly cancel each other out – is tantamount to the death drive in its perfect form: it is a life with minimal activity, a form of dead life that is sought. This means that during informationalism's sadomasochistic golden age, masochism is refined at an initial stage into pure mortido. As a completely logical response to this development, sadism is developed into pure libido. The golden age of sadomasochism is thus a kind of virtual refinement of libido versus mortido as personified projections. However, observe that the netocratic swarm is not sadistic in itself – it is of course fully occupied with its own internal business all the time, not least its orgiastic experiments, digitally and not infrequently also physically isolated from the annoying consumtariat – but becomes sadistic only when forced to play the role as the surface onto which the consumtarian mob's masochism is projected. For how could the mob be able to understand that one is permanently barred from entry by those who administer the temple of adulthood when one knows that the phallic gaze hides there, how could they see this as anything but sadism? Unfortunately the netocracy's minimal interaction with the consumtariat in the digital plurarchy directly leads to the development of exactly this scenario.

So how is wounded individualism doing in an age where this shabby and thoroughly discredited cadaver is left by the wayside to then be appropriated by the new digital underclass, the consumtariat? The emerging dividual is of course only a new concept for the individual human, as a network-dynamical whole or fractured multiplicity. The dividual's unity must be reduced to a neuroscientific phenomenon (see *The Body Machines*) that merely arises as a chimera at the end of a problematic observation. What is meant by this? Well, that thinking in itself actually does not, as Descartes maintains, confirm the presence of any form of thinking and stable subject that can underpin an entire worldview. First of all, we do not even think at all unless there first arises some form of problem begging for our attention. And nor do we remember anything after an incident unless the incident in question is connected to the dividual's incessantly fluid and vague identity. This means that from the time before the abjectification of the mamilla, up until the phallic intrusion, we do not remember anything at all. There is quite simply no *cogito* during this period with which to connect the experiences – for the child does not even experience itself and the mother as separate bodies – so nothing happens that needs to be preserved either, no material is produced for any memory bank for future withdrawal of a (self)consciousness.

So while the shocked consumtarians attempt to save whatever is salvageable of the old religion, individualism, the netocrats march onwards and see the opportunities in the death of all the old religions – what German philosopher Friedrich Nietzsche calls *affirmative nihilism* (see *The Body Machines*). The netocracy supplants individualism and its twin atomism with a network-dynamical worldview based on *relations* rather than *relata* (see *Syntheism – Creating God in the Internet Age*). So how does a network-dynamical subject work? Well, we learn from the dialectics of eternalism and mobilism (see *The Global Empire*) that we are living in a chaos that we must convert into an illusory cosmos in order to be able to build a manageable *ontophenomenology*. Existence quite simply becomes too messy and unmanageable otherwise, we are paralyzed by perceptual overload. This cosmos is a single one, and has as a direct consequence an experienced subject that also is understood to be homogeneous. We preserve a cohesive world, vital for survival, through and with a cohesive *cogito* – which thus is pure fiction. This has the consequence that the ego only can arise in the form of a logical conclusion of a set of problems, and then solely in the role as that which illusorily appears to tie up the flaccid sack of jumbled impressions and observations that actually remains wide open all the time.

The netocratic subject is thus nothing but a stationary and temporary seal for a moment where the dividual thinks he has fixated – eternalized – the psychotic chaos of existence to a fundamentally neurotically cohesive worldview, that is: a state where the subject arises as the direct result of the objectification of the phenomenal situation in itself. Network-dynamical metaphysics thus ends up in a radical anti-Cartesianism: As a last desperate survival reaction in the face of a chaotic surrounding world, a fragmented nervous system focuses on eternalizing the current reflection complex, which in the end happens to require an objectification of the complex's own system of thought to an illusory and extremely pathetic little *me-moment*. And what then is meant by a me-moment? It means that this illusory subject is not merely illusory, but also extremely transient. As soon as the subject has arisen as the definitive eternalization, it has already been set in motion and has been dissolved. The quest for this constantly mobilized subject is soon shifted to the subject process in itself. The mind starts to construct a timeline that connects the constantly failed summaries of the chaotic world – in a way, nodes of emotional intensity interconnected by a line that has the character of an emergency solution, where this line itself becomes the temporal subject over time – a project that the German existentialist Martin Heidegger develops in the work that bears the revealing title *Being and Time*. In time we become our own vain quest for ourselves, a quest whose predetermined ineffectuality paradoxically does not preclude a result of sorts, after all.

The temporal subject's structure, in turn, explains why metaphysics over time morphs from the enormous eternity during feudalism, via the temporally diffused progress during capitalism, to the microscopic event during informationalism. The metaphysical engine must of course be experienced as existing, and this experience must of course be intersubjective. But then the engine cannot have a larger extension in spacetime than one that matches the credible experienced subject, either. Therefore the microscopic event first of all contains a dialectical about-face: the only infinity worthy of its name is that which is concentrated to a single moment. Secondly, the event is bound to relationalism's chronocentric absolute, that is: *duration* itself. This means that the infinite now is posited on the timeline only to later be followed by innumerable memories that refer back to the experience. The memory of ecstasy is thus the substance of ecstasy, not ecstasy in itself. Ecstasy in itself would be unbearable if it did not cease and morph into a memory, while this memory of the same always is available and packaged in a way that makes it highly enjoyable and therefore also meaningful. Which also makes this memory metaphysically powerful. So powerful that it becomes the kernel of the network society's metaphysical story. We could not possibly be any further away from Kant's individualist metaphysics, with its axiom, *time-as-illusion*, than this. *The infinite now is the informationalist event par excellence.*

So what happens with this transient libidinal subject in the wondrous world of philosophy? What explorations of this ideal are carried out after Heidegger's fundamental establishment of the same in the early 20th century as a neutral *Dasein* without a Cartesian substance? What must a netocratic construction of subjectivity take into consideration, aside from the class-conditioned distaste for everything that smells of vulgar individualism? In the syntheist manifesto *The Religion of the Future,* the Brazilian philosopher Roberto Mangabeira Unger establishes mortality, baselessness and insatiability as Man's three fundamental existential dilemmas. If we add the social dimension of these three fundamental limitations of human imagination, we discover that it more specifically concerns *the tribal apocalypse*, *the metaphysical groundlessness* and *the libidinal insatiability* that drive Man to seek liberation from life's incessant series of disappointments in the mortidinal hope of a life without a shred of intensity whatsoever. All functional subjects thus invariably must relate to these three social psychological and existential extremes, irrespective of what technological or communicative paradigm is at issue. The subject cannot function without first arming itself against these three extreme states, at which point mortido threatens to blast its way up from the subconscious and take over the show.

Here the subject receives its longed-for meaning and its visionary goal. For it will of course be the subject's task to prevent the tribal apocalypse, to fight the metaphysical groundlessness and to channel the libidinal insatiability. The Freudian superego is furnished with both direction and energy. And through the ensuing addition of meaningfulness the subject finally has the courage to spring to life – it is *libidinalized.* But a life full of life, in contrast to a life without life, is also a life full of power – the will to live is fundamentally *the will to power*, as Nietzsche expresses the matter – while a life without intensity is a life without power. This means that the longer we journey into a historical paradigm, the clearer it becomes that a paradigmatic upper class arises, usurps power from its rival and unites around themes such as survival, value hierarchies and libidinal realization, stances whose point of departure is how this elite maintain its newly-acquired position. This happens while a paradigmatic underclass mortidinally denies itself all these possibilities and instead unites around nostalgia, ressentiment and social masochistic submission, that is: the underclass is united around the subconscious worship of, rather than a defiance directed against, the social theater's three existential dilemmas: the tribal apocalypse, the metaphysical groundlessness and the libidinal insatiability. It is a case of a *libido-as-vision* of the upper class, which is pitted against a *mortido-as-castration* of the underclass.

So what expressions do these three existential dilemmas assume during the ongoing paradigm shift as capitalism morphs into informationalism? Well, the tribal apocalypse recurs as the crisis of nationalism, the metaphysical groundlessness recurs as atomism's disintegration, and the libidinal insatiability recurs as the collapse of individualism. The nation, the atom and the individual are the paradigmatic triad around which the European Enlightenment is built from the 17th century onwards, as the nation-state emerges out of the ruins of Europe's religious wars. The nation, as we know it, is not God-given or "natural," which many imagine. The same goes for the indivisible atom and the indivisible human: it is fundamentally about *ideology* and only about ideology. Under the pressure that arises as the Internet expands on an exponential scale, these three memes collapse together, and the mutual dependence on each other, which at an earlier stage was a strength, is now turned into a liability: they now drag each other down in the fall. They share their destiny with other memeplexes in history that once were dominant, but that later were phased out as a new elite seized power: they are preserved and cherished by the new underclass, in this case the consumtariat, when the old capitalist upper class, the bourgeoisie, finds itself left behind by the netocracy. This occurs in parallel with the uniting of the netocracy around the network-dynamical worldview, the ethics of interactivity and the quest for the ecstatic event in its endeavor to *de facto* handle the tribal apocalypse through *globalism,* the metaphysical groundlessness through *syntheism* and the libidinal insatiability through *network dynamics.* The netocracy serves the Global Empire and the Global Empire serves the netocracy.

Given the opportunities of network dynamics, the demands and promises of individualism soon appear as a bundle of nonsense. But voices that speak of the hollowness and shortcomings of individualism are of course nothing new; these voices have been heard ever since the genesis of the phenomenon. As early as the 19th century, in the novel *Crime and Punishment*, for instance, the Russian author Fyodor Dostoyevsky describes individualism as the banal and destructive cultural realization of Thomas Hobbes' idea of nature as "a state of everyone being at war with everyone else." Dostoyevsky argues that Man as a tribal herd animal in the long run only can identify with an allocentric – oriented towards community – rather than an individualist worldview, which makes individualism both the enemy of culture and the curse of modernism. The principle of individualism, he argues, is all about isolation and personal gain, which is at cross purposes both with Man's tribal nature and with that which benefits the common good. But during the period that stretches from René Descartes and the launching of the Individual as the center of existence in 1637 to Napoleon Bonaparte's realization of the organization-theoretical and embodiment of the idea of the Individual as commander of an invincible army of other individuals in the early 19th century, the ground is laid for fully-developed individualism, the Western religion that then sweeps across the world and destroys everything in its path during the golden age of capitalist colonialism.

Through the emergence of the Internet in the late 20th century, individualism is shoved down into the consumtarian underclass, while the new, netocratic ruling class legitimizes its power grab with a network-dynamical supraideology, accompanied by the ethics of interactivity (see *The Body Machines*). Ultimately Dostoyevsky is proven correct with his allocentric argument. But hardly in the way in which he himself expected. It is technology-driven network dynamics and not some collectivism imposed by the nation-state that is the winning formula of the Internet Age. We are not turning away from the Individual and towards the collective in any classical sense. The allocentrism in question is of course, if we use Hegelian concepts, concretely tribalist rather than abstractly socialist as Dostoyevsky recommends. We are thus approaching the netocratic *dividual* from both directions, that is: the dividual partly as the network-dynamical building block even within itself, partly as a phenomenal unit in all identitarian constructions up until *Syntheos,* the aggregate artificial intelligence, the created god as the unification of everything (see *Syntheism – Creating God in The Internet Age*). We are dividuals at every level, there is no I or you left, other than as linguistic conventions. But nor does this mean that a universal "we" sees the light of day, that all people and groups reconcile and take each other's hands while cultural barriers crumble; what we see is rather a tribal or subcultural we, a we that merely arises and receives nourishment within the netocrats' insular, virtual communities.

So how did we end up here as a result of the emergence of the Internet? In his book *Empire of Illusion – The End of Literacy and the Triumph of Spectacle* the American author and social critic Chris Hedges describes the development of the medial class society. A minoritarian elite that keeps itself cultivated and informed through increasingly sophisticated media, that is: a *netocracy,* manages to handle society's growing complexity and can intersubjectively make a distinction between truth and illusion, between news and "fake news." But the majority of the population retreats from the increasingly arcane media exploration and description of reality and instead turn to a false sense of security and magic. Without directly defining the new consumtarian underclass (see *The Netocrats*) Hedges admits that the new underclass cuts right through all the classes that remain after the age of industrialism, even if the poor and above all the poorly educated are strongly overrepresented within the emerging consumtariat. It is quite simply a case of an underclass that from a historical perspective has a new makeup, in Nietzschean terms a big crowd of confused, mortidinal slaves in a desperate quest for libidinal rulers that they hope will give them security, comfort and above all tribal belonging in exchange for submission.

Socioanalytically we express this by saying that the consumtariat is looking for a phallus that unfortunately never materializes. The consequence is a fixation with the mamilla. And here lies the great danger, always relevant. The problem is that if the young libido, no matter how mortidinal, finds no outlet, it sooner or later explodes in indiscriminate destructiveness. In the primitivist nomadic tribe one quelled the brashness in primarily young men either through physical violence or with the aid of strong psychedelic experiences. The South American and African societies where one frequently and deliberately used strong psychedelic substances such as *ayahuasca*, *huachuma* and *iboga* during rites of passage are undoubtedly the most enduringly peaceful societies that we know of. Forcing the libidinally hyperactive into submission under the patriarch and the matriarch was necessary for the tribe's long-term survival. Patricide and matricide could thereby be predicted and prevented. But with the emergence of the first cities primarily young, urbanized men disappeared from the patriarchal hierarchy's panoptic overview, and as freely-roaming agents quite literally became lethally dangerous to social cohesion. Urban criminality exploded. Anything from criminal youth gangs via anarchist cells to self-appointed YouTube jihadists are, as the Indian historian Pankaj Mishra shows in his book *Age of Anger*, merely different manifestations of this common phenomenon, *libidinal destructivism*.

It is precisely when a young and angry generation has lost contact with both the rural past and the key to the urban establishment that the really serious and dangerous conflicts flare up. Driven into a corner, the libidinal primordial power has just one single manifestation, namely via *nihilistic violence.* Anarchistic or Islamist terror is thus neither fundamentally anarchistic nor Islamist – even if terror requires an ideological excuse within the existing memeplex – but is above all nihilistic. Dostoyevsky was clear on this as well. Since the attentionalist network society has promised more abundant rewards to more actors than any other society previously has done in history, but *de facto* rewards considerably fewer winners and creates wider divides than ever has been the case – all according to the network pyramid's principle *the winner takes all* (see *The Netocrats*) – while the phallic gaze becomes increasingly hard to access, ressentiment among the medially hyperactive consumtarians reaches new heights in both strength and dissemination.

Even the destructive forces communicate via the Internet – where else? – and take advantage of its upsides (see *The Netocrats*), so there is nothing to indicate that an explosive increase in nihilistic violence in the Internet Age can be avoided. Particularly as the classic *terror cell* as a construction is ideal for the network-dynamical society from a perspective of military strategy, with its plenitude of encrypted communication apps behind thick firewalls but with global reach. The attentionalist arena is quickly filled with fundamentalist sects, what we call *false swarms*, subconsciously built on explosive ressentiment and driven by apocalyptic mortidos. When the phallic libido is blinded in this way by its ability for hyperdestructiveness, it no longer wants to recognize any boundaries. It intoxicates itself on its own mortidinal boundlessness. The phallic libido is caught in ecstatic death worship. This is in turn completely decisive for the understanding of all forms of political or religiously motivated extremism: *If that which experiences itself as the most vibrant in a society realizes that all it really wants is its own death, it can consequently only see the death of all others as the liberation of all others.* It is as if one does one's victims a favor. And there simply is no other libido to discover this side of the horizon, beyond a mortido that sees itself as the most libidinal in the society we see all around us. Preferably a wounded, false phallus than no phallus at all.

The only thing humanity as a whole can do in this situation is to encase the coming apocalypse at a local level and prevent it from becoming global. It is a question of simple but brutally important strategies to for instance prevent the risk of, within a not too distant future, nuclear devices being detonated via drones. An important dimension of the military activity will be a costly but geographically sharply delimited pragmatics with the purpose of offering defense for gated communities – the netocrats will prioritize the defense of their physical and virtual territories above all else – while the plurarchic, essentially arbitrary and blunt violence causes extensive devastation outside fences and moats. But since the consumtarians *de facto* constitute the majority of the population in the network society, anyone who wants to reach out to this majority with any form of message via the media – be it a case of shaping political opinion or advertising for this or that – must, according to Hedges, adapt this message to a level that this majority can assimilate. And we are, once again according to Hedges, speaking of a level that we today expect to find in a twelve-year-old in the capitalist educational system. What we see in front of us is thus a populist golden age, but it is a case of a populism that sprawls within a steadily shrinking vector, specifically the informationalist residue of capitalist democracy.

It is hardly surprising that the shrinking of the democratic vector will create enormous frustration both at powerlessness and its concomitant incomprehensibility. And then, as so often in history, the nihilist terror cell tempts as the only alternative to passivity. The consumtarians quite simply live in a medial world that mainly consists of banal television entertainment, more or less violent computer games, gossip on social media, and the liking of cute cats and photographed meals on the Internet. As do the terrorists; until they react and get high on the mortidinal attention that follows on the heels of their destructive outbursts. It is maybe not, as the media theorist Neil Postman pointedly expresses the matter, a question of entertaining people to death – but definitely of entertaining people to sleep. This is consumtarian interpassivity. Inside this armored filter bubble there exists no serious motion picture art nor any art at all, no theater, no qualified newspapers or periodicals, no societal debate. Which means that this more serious, quality media and these discussions are increasingly marginalized and reduced to exclusive hobby activities for a dwindling number of people. But the netocracy naturally realizes the value of keeping itself informed and ensuring that all needs in this respect are met. For them, things such as a Harry Potter movie are – just as the creators intended – pure entertainment for children, not some kind of mystical transfer of knowledge for the consumtariat's infantilized adults.

The current development disfavors the old bourgeoisie, which because of its anchoring in democracy, the academy and industry is dependent on the approval of the masses. The fall of the bourgeoisie accelerates the emergence of the interactive netocracy, since it is free to build its *libertarian paradise* without requesting the consumtariat's approval via some kind of stale democracy, simply by force of its physical and virtual subcultures. The world is being filled with highly efficient city-states with low-tax economies to which the netocrats formally and without impediment move their coveted networks, ideas and other resources. In his essay *Dark Enlightenment* the English philosopher and cyberneticist Nick Land sums up this phenomenon as *the libertarian exit from the capitalist welfare states.* The fact is that the entire world economy must adapt itself to this enormous nomadic shift of resources. Historically we express this by saying that capitalism vanquishes itself to death and is replaced by emerging attentionalism, a new communication-driven class structure that is built on sensors, sociograms and the control and understanding of information flows, which is completely disconnected from capitalism's tax records, popularly elected parliamentarians and academic titles.

Thus a new, netocratic human ideal emerges: *the cosmopolitan dividual* – an actor that not only accepts, but that actually loves and aims to live secluded from subcultures other than his own and the networks that his own subculture chooses to cooperate with, an actor that realizes this voluntary segregation in a city and/or in a digital network that comprises hard-working and loyally committed netocrats of different origins, generally tied to places with easily navigated regulations and without a particularly burdensome tax rate. This development occurs in parallel with the consumtarian underclass relying on the old individualism and its faithful follower, nationalism. The nation-state that finds it increasingly hard to collect its taxes and keep its promises of providing comprehensive and generous welfare will increasingly become a concern for the paradigm shift's losers. All one has to do is to look around and make note of who are the ones frantically waving flags nowadays. The netocracy cherishes the ideal that the British journalist and author David Goodhart calls *anywhere,* while the consumtariat requests a permanent physical anchoring and geographic domicile, an idealized and sentimentalized *somewhere* as a basis for its social identity. The historical irony could hardly be lost on anyone: If the paradigm shift from primitivism to feudalism once upon a time revolved around taming nomads into becoming settled farmers, it is precisely the other way around this time: global nomadism becomes what characterizes the new elite while being stationary and settled becomes a phenomenon connected with the underclass. A state of constant motion, bodily as well as mentally, is – for better or worse, just as anything else in these times of dizzying changes – the primary success factor for the network society.

15
Sensocracy, tribal mapping and the digital priesthood

The most characteristic aspect of the consumtariat, or the digital underclass, is that it seldom acts, but instead limits itself to reacting to stimuli – or to express the matter in a Nietzschean manner: the consumtariat constantly invokes the *countertrend* as a reaction to the authentic *trend*, to which it generally has a circumspect and disapproving stance – which is why we sum up its thought patterns and behavior as the *dialectics of ressentiment*. This process in turn starts with the consumtariat cultivating social exclusion in the form of a distinct *victimhood mentality*. Society changes, and changes are painful; the victims of these changes are therefore in need of an array of support and compensation, and demand apologies and concessions when they feel violated or opposed in some way. This victimhood mentality will sooner or later, under pressure from a chaotic surrounding world, be developed into a psychotic condition: in order to survive this, the subject in question turns the psychotic conditions into what we call *psychotic omnipotence*. The chaos one perceives is misconstrued as a single gigantic eternalization of existence, the dividual's self-dissolution turns into a megalomanic, seemingly divine *hyperego*, the psychotic lack of identity turns into the neurotic supraidentity, the lack of a sense of self turns into an identification with the eternalized cosmos as the fixated hyperego (which in turn suggests an explanation as to why psychiatric hospitals are populated to such a great extent by a clientele with a messiah complex). We are speaking of a misdirected *dialectics of eternalism and mobilism* (see *The Global Empire*) on frenetic overdrive.

The collective psychotic omnipotence is expressed within the consumtarian mob by the victimhood mentality being extended to a conviction of *one's own moral superiority* in the face of all rivals in the struggle for the elusive and constantly insufficient attention, a conviction that springs from the deification of the narcissistic victimhood mentality. The victim no longer settles for being just another victim among many others, but has instead been transformed into someone whose right from birth and for eternity by definition is morally superior to *the abject*, the victim's arbitrarily alleged perpetrator. The consumtarian is therefore no longer just a victim in general, but an actor who by virtue of his higher rank among all the world's victims automatically also is morally superior to all other actors. The victim becomes the (anti)hero in this scenario. Just about every anarchist constellation throughout history – with the possible exception of certain heroic anarcho-libertarians who just happened to live prophetically ahead of their time – suffers from this collective psychotic omnipotence. The abject is phallus itself; the underlying antiphallic message reads: "We want to destroy absolutely everything, while we take no responsibility for anything that will happen after the devastation we bring about." In this respect there is no decisive distinction between for instance 19th century European anarchists and 21st century Arabic Islamists. It is a case of the same infantile and irresponsible yearning back to matrix via libidinal destructivism. And the entire project is awash in ressentiment.

Psychotic omnipotence is the temporary albeit powerful team spirit that keeps the consumtarian mob intact. And the mob's political and/or spiritual anti-program is the dialectics of ressentiment in its purest form, that which the original Zoroaster forcefully opposes in his work *Gathas* from 1700 B.C. and quite simply calls *druj*. Thus Zoroaster is most probably the first to define this most destructive of mentalities as a social and organizational phenomenon. With this, he prophetically forebodes its most large-scale expression: the brutal Mongol invasion of his own region, Central Asia, which takes place nearly 2,800 years later. Here we can definitely speak of mortido worship. Once psychotic omnipotence has taken root, and the mutable chaos around the subject either consciously or subconsciously is misinterpreted as a fixed order that the subject identifies with, there is no longer any room for the authentic phallus – the person or the phenomenon that Zoroaster postulates as a longed-for universal *saoshyant*, the model and inspiration for Judaism's tribalized *mashiach* which later becomes Christianity's universalized *khristos* – if it contrary to all expectations should happen to appear. Psychotic omnipotence generates a dividual and collective subject that uses its own powerlessness – its lack of a boundary-setting authentic phallus – reinterprets the situation as omnipotence with the purpose of creating a concept of itself as the absent (authentic) phallus, and therefore steps out of the psychotic chaos as *the false phallus par excellence* (but very genuine in its own eyes). For lack of another subject this homespun substitute will do.

Longing for anarchy is thus not merely longing for the great existential chaos – as an excuse to give oneself over to infantile enjoyment and hide by the old mamilla, which sits there indifferently knitting socks beneath the guillotine – it is literally a case of longing for death itself. Rousseauan ressentiment quite simply longs to execute all other actors in order to one day finally be able to execute itself (for a deeper understanding of Rousseau's subconscious, feel free to read his nemesis Marquis de Sade). It enjoys this course of events as only a self-castrated phallus can enjoy the painfully drawn-out downfall. In this perspective, characters such as Adolf Hitler, Josef Stalin and Pol Pot appear not only as false phalluses and radical Rousseauans, they also enjoy being precisely this. Their social sadism is simply the other side of the coin from their existential masochism. Once the snowball has started rolling, the mortidinal sacrificial cults no longer respect any boundaries or limitations. Note that it was Napoleon Bonaparte – Hegel's and Nietzsche's phallic hero – who with his coup d'état in 1799 brought the bloody anarchy and chronic instability of the French Revolution to a close. The Rousseauan disciples have no such off-switch, not mentally nor ideologically. They do of course become ensnared by the mamilla's matrichal boundlessness – what the Bulgarian-French psychoanalyst Julia Kristeva calls *the semiotic soup* – and even imagine that there is something utterly noble about this psychotic disorientation. The snowball grows and rolls on until all life is extinguished. Without phallus, matrix can of course never be inseminated. And then there is no sign of any libidinal future on the horizon.

The great tragedy in all this is that human history is replete with these false phalluses. It takes an authentic phallus – a genuinely messianic project – to build a civilization. But when a civilization reaches its apogee and starts becoming corrupt, it becomes receptive to the siren song from the false phalluses' undemanding message and is infantilized: nothing is required to declare oneself a false phallus and nothing is required to give up all personal responsibility and thinking of one's own and follow it; all one needs is an abject to blame for all shortcomings and a mamilla that someone other than the false phallus itself fills with goodies in the form of handouts and subsidies. We find a clear example of this at the end of the Persian thousand-year realm – which was based on Zoroaster's phallic religion – from the 7th century B.C. and forward. Because in the 5th century A.D. the court of the Sasanian Empire had become so corrupt that a false phallus by the name of Mazdak stepped forward and took the helm. He created what often is regarded as the first communist society in history. But Mazdak's dream of a society revolving around a gigantic, generous and undemanding mamilla faltered and he was ultimately executed by the Zoroastrian priesthood, quite properly being accused of being the religion's worst heretic ever. Mazdak's dream of a society with radical equality and free love for everything and everyone – naturally based on a banal dualism between mamillic good and phallic evil, in opposition to Zoroaster's messianic monism beyond good and evil – was transformed into a chaotic nightmare of starvation and lawlessness.

The dream of a mortidinal paradise, a society that gives in abundance without ever requiring any effort from its citizens, will however live on and constantly recurs as the linchpin in the false phallus' ideological mythical treasure. Muhammad was a pronounced admirer of Mazdak and built Islam's theology from the idea of total submission. Socialists and communists, from Rousseau to Stalin, have always been tempted by Mazdak's illusory mamilla. In hating the masters and elevating the slaves to masters, the false phallus constantly builds new, seductively alluring castles in the sky. This will also happen when the network society fails – since it must fail – to match the infantilized consumtarians' specification of demands. The question is thus how one efficiently halts or diverts – if this even be possible – these identitarian sacrificial cults in the social arena of informationalism? They are of course on the one hand often short-lived, but on the other hand they often during this short period of time cause terrible devastation. Should we not in any case be able to rely on democracy to keep these destructive forces in check? Democracy should be channeling all varieties of opinion of any significance, and is after all capitalism's and industrialism's cherished love child, a construction that by definition constitutes if not the ideal then still the least bad solution to all the problems regarding power sharing in a society where power communicates via unidirectional mass media such as newspapers, radio and television.

The attentive reader will immediately realize that the question answers itself and that the problem is precisely this business of capitalism and unidirectional mass media. Conditions have now over a few tumultuous decades been fundamentally changed; so-called social media – another word for the Internet – have in several respects smashed the foundation for democracy. There are several reasons for this (see *The Global Empire* for a comprehensive discussion); but one of these factors is that the democratic system – with its representation of various viewpoints and regularly recurring parliamentary elections – has lost its relevance completely, since it is built on the idea of a bothersome information deficit that needs to be remedied precisely through democracy. In a democracy, one holds elections because one really does not know what the citizens – over whom are suddenly poured enormous amounts of benevolence as soon as an election year comes around and campaigning starts – want. Nor does one know what the voters actually know, nor what they believe that they know but actually do not know. And nor do the voters themselves know this. This is why they are allowed to be heard, with a few years in between, to inform power and themselves whom they choose as their representatives. And to bestow necessary legitimacy on power. But over and above this we never become much wiser through democracy. We accept its evident shortcomings since we do not know of a better system. The problem is that this entire logic loses its validity in a situation *where we actually know precisely what the citizens want*, and when we know this better than the voters do themselves. Fluctuating public opinion and preferences are possible to read in real time with the aid of applicable algorithms that scan what people are doing, what they like and consume, both on the net and in physical space.

He who then hopes that the next step in the political development will be some form of digital direct democracy will be terribly disappointed, primarily because the network society is too complex an organism to lend itself to anything of the kind. No, what awaits us around the corner is unfortunately something that, for better or worse, must be categorized as a new kind of technological dictatorship with a benevolent face that "interprets" the will of the people and gives public opinion an ideological massage, not unlike a digitalized version of the Communist Party of the People's Republic of China. We are speaking of a *sensocracy*, a multi-shifting and incredibly intricate and sophisticated system that via digital technology keeps its finger on the pulse of the present and reads all shifts and movements in the drive system of the population, that listens to the collective subconscious by tracking the data flows that the societal body emits, and then adapts to the worry that is expressed and parrying it with bread and circuses. This means that to the extent politics ever has been about substance – that is: overcoming actual problems through actual measures to actually improve the living conditions for large groups of voters – it now increasingly is morphing into a kind of media therapy activity that subsumes the fear and pain of ordinary people in a narrative that is continuously manipulated to make the failures of politics acceptable and chronic pain excusable. The blame always lies somewhere else.

The class divides continue to widen, but it is important to allay people's fears before there is rioting in the streets. *Data anthropology* supplants the clumsy old sociological questionnaire as a basis of exploring the dividual and its alternately libidinal and mortidinal drive system. Why ask questions, when people lie through their teeth anyway, both in interview situations and to their loved ones? And to themselves, for that matter. For truth of course instead emerges when the dividual's actual behavior on the net can be registered and analyzed systematically along with all other relevant information from the contexts where the dividual in question can be found. So why then waste resources on herding off the population to polling stations every few years to pose the least sophisticated question one could possibly imagine – which party will get your vote this time? – when one can elicit from all these people infinitely more detailed answers to infinitely more intelligent questions, continuously every hour, every day, every week? This interactive, fairytale politics now becomes, to an even greater degree than the anesthetizing religion, the opium of the masses.

The sensocracy evidently responds to a human need, otherwise it would not be efficient nor particularly durable – but which one? Well, if fascism is *the neurotic society par excellence*, a (false) phallus without matrix, anarchy is *the psychotic society*, a matrix without phallus (of any sort). Plurarchy here lies closer to matrichal psychosis than to phallic neurosis. But the reaction against the menacing plurarchy is *anal*. It is in the inhibition of the menacing plurarchy that we find the fascist impulse in the network society. This means that the fearless netocrats build long-term sustainable *swarms*, while the scared consumtarians are organized into rapidly disintegrating *mobs*. The swarm is driven by *libido* and is united around the utopian *fetish*, while the mob is driven by *mortido* and is united around the dystopian *abject*. Between these two poles, the two classes build temporary and volatile (more or less) *pseudotribes*, where the netocrats' pseudotribes become swarms because their structure both generates and makes use of the intelligence of the collective, at the same time that they are actionary, while the consumtarians' pseudotribes become mobs because they essentially are unstructured and *reactionary*.

The netocrats build their collectives from *the principle of the wisdom of the swarm*, which has acquired firmer contours and has been discussed frequently after the millennium shift, for instance in James Surowiecki's book *The Wisdom of Crowds* from 2004. Fundamentally it is quite simple: If a group consists of many actors with various backgrounds and therefore also various perspectives on a specific problem, the group becomes an intelligent swarm by virtue of precisely these various perspectives that interact with each other, and always performs better than any individual actor – even if he or she may be the single smartest person in the world – is able to do. This effect increases exponentially if the swarm understands and has the possibility of making use of artificial intelligence, and thus the netocratic smart swarm becomes what most certainly is the most intelligent structure that Man has ever created. In his book *The Wealth of Networks* the Israeli information theorist Yochar Benkler shows how this is realized step by step. In contrast, the consumtarian mob becomes both homogenized and short-lived since it is built from the starting point of the narcissistic agenda of the actor who manages to scream himself to the status as the most pitiful victim amid all other self-appointed victims. It decays into a matrichal extremism without phallic elements, that is: the consumtarian mob does not morph into a sustainable movement with a clear focus and a purposeful strategy, but assumes the character of a soluble, temporary and cumbersome alliance of antithetic wills and contradictory ambitions that merely band together vis-à-vis a clear abject.

We can sum up the key factors behind the netocrats' success and power grab as *tribal mapping* and *intertribalism*. Both these processes are built on the metahistorical insight that Man is the constant *k* and technology is the variable *v* in the infinitely complicated equation that is the history of civilization. And since Man during the better part of his history on Earth has lived within the primitivist nomadic tribe and only for comparatively few generations in any other type of society, it is still an existence in small, segregated groups on the savannah that we are genetically adapted for. The societal, cultural, and not least technological development has gone tremendously fast, while biology moves slowly; we never had the time to become shaped by the selective pressure from feudalism's agrarian society or by capitalism's strictly regulated work days in the factories. We are who we are: sociobiologically programmed to seek and be part of an intratribal community, terrified at the risk of being placed outside the collective's identity-generating intercourse. For this reason, it is natural to fear the encounter and the imposed contact with strangers. They are not we. They are moreover our competitors in the struggle for limited resources.

Successful socialization entails that one seeks and finds a role that lends itself to one's own personality type and one's own set of talents: one's own *archetype*. Contributing to the collective's survival and well-being favors one's own survival and further, favors one's own well-being. It is this orientation towards mutual benefit on the social map – irrespective of whether it happens centralized via dictates or decentralized via experimentation – that we call tribal mapping. The segregated and intratribal tribe emerges, with its inner circuit controlled by the matriarchy and the outer circuit controlled by the patriarchy. This structure virtually drowns its members in safety, security, identity and meaning. But these incentives for a successful intratribalism do not entail any guarantees that either nature or culture will favor the development of any form of intertribalism – a sophisticated networking between various tribes – it is in fact the reverse. It turns out that *the terror of the other* in the form of strangers from other tribes was actually a reliable recipe for success for most tribe members during primitivism. But during informationalism it is precisely the other way around. When the Internet establishes itself as *the Global Empire* – a net that interlinks all the world's hundreds of billions of people and machines directly with each other into a single, interconnected power structure – everything changes and entails a brand new playing field with brand new rules.

In the Internet Age it is global intertribalism that pays off. Considerably more rewarding than local intratribalism is the strategic search for creative, reciprocal contacts and collaborations between various networks and subcultures. It is first and foremost this – aside from creating stress and an unmanageable information surplus – that the technological development has entailed; it has made it possible for us humans to play increasingly advanced and large-scale non-zero-sum games with each other, which in turn has reduced the terror of the other at least to some extent and in terms of at least some strangers. For he who embraces the principles of intertribalism, there is the possibility of including more people in what we regard as "we." And there are no substantial incentives for attacking one's business partner. But it also means that Man must be educated, or nurtured, towards tolerance and curiosity regarding the deviant, exotic and alien. Such openness is naturally, literally not something that people generally are born with, since this kind of outlook constituted risk behavior in the culture where our genes were kneaded by natural selection for more than 100,000 years. The shamanic talents were important but rare; today it brings a major advantage to be fascinated and attracted by alien cultures, appearances and expressions. For other actors, that is: the large majority, intertribalism however entails an arduous transition to an engagement in the alien and deviant.

Thus we simply get intratribalism for free in our genes at birth; intertribalism is something we laboriously and patiently must teach anyone who wants to adapt to and function in the Global Empire. This in turn gives the nomadic netocrats with their affinity for *anywhere* – to employ the vocabulary of the British journalist David Goodhart – an advantage that is hard for the consumtarians with their seemingly robust anchoring in *somewhere to compensate for.* Zoroaster's pair of opposites, *asha* versus *druj* is thus shifted to the tribal boundary setting and the relationship to *the other* from the alien tribe, a project that contemporary philosophers such as Emmanuel Levinas, Jacques Derrida and Simon Critchley devote a considerable amount of energy to exploring. It is hardly a coincidence that the question of how the stranger can be appreciated and even loved becomes a major line of inquiry for thinkers across the world when globalization strikes with full force during the second half of the 20th century. For the philosophers themselves – just as for all other members of the shamanic caste – this is however a non-issue, but at the same time it constitutes a decisive dilemma for the rest of the population. The shamanic caste – above all the tribe's androgynous members (around five per cent of all human populations) can be found here – constitutes an area of contact between both the matriarchy's inner circuit and the patriarchy's outer circuit within the tribe and at the same time between one's own tribe as a whole and alien tribes that belong in other regions. Archetypes such as the diplomat, the artist, the military chaplain and of course the philosopher are to be found in this category.

Extensive peaceful communication takes place between the various tribe's shamanic castes. This becomes evident notably in that it was not already existing villages that grew and were developed into the first cities in the great river valleys just over 5,000 years ago. Of course, the villages were, in actuality, fortresses, surrounded by thick walls and built as a result of the inner circuit's paranoia about external threats from previously competing nomadic tribes. Instead, it was the ritual sites outside and between the various villages, built by members of the shamanic caste from many different tribes, for peaceful exchange around an increasingly uniform and shared spirituality – a religiosity that eventually was fashioned into a feudalist monotheism that revolved around a phallic god – that would constitute the foundation for the first cities. As soon as these ritual sites erected their towers towards the sky, merchants from the outer circuits of adjacent tribes arrived and started to do business with each other. Which explains why the shamanic caste's members to this day find it so much easier to appreciate the stranger and his qualities than do the rest of the population. It becomes, therefore, a task for *the digital priesthood* to set a good example and teach the vital intertribalism in the network society. And with this comes the digital priesthood's role as the metaphysical truth monopoly within the netocratic upper class is just as secure as during previous paradigms. Consequently it is also precisely where the sensocratic data flows and the digital priesthood meet that data anthropology is born and thrives.

Every trend is inevitably met by a countertrend, the development never runs smoothly. The escalating isolationist counterreaction explains why the consumtarian mob is characterized by a radical uniformity of all opinions that are presented on every individual occasion. Constantly finding a completely arbitrary agreement of opinion in every respect – a consensus that is centered around the hated *abject* – becomes a propelling factor for the consumtarian identity.

This means that while the netocratic swarm is driven by a search for network-dynamical *factuality*, the consumtarian mob is instead driven by opinions that take their point of departure fully in the emotional tempests that wreak havoc for the moment, a hyperemotionality that entails a constant reinforcement of prevailing prejudices rather than a critical questioning of the impulse in question, what the American Internet activist Eli Parisier critically terms "the filter bubble" in the digital sphere. The netocratic swarm is thus primarily driven by *logos*, while the consumtarian mob primarily is driven by *pathos*. And here all the traditional political divisions between right and left are completely irrelevant. Rather, it is precisely the extreme right and the identity left around the millennium shift, with their hyperemotionalized and narcissistic victimhood cults and their obsession with superficial symbolism, that constitute the most obvious (and terrifying) examples of the network society's consumtarian mobs.

The informationalist class struggle is hardly any milder: it is actually even more brutal than that of capitalism. During capitalism the workers were, after all, in possession of an indispensable resource that the bourgeoisie was highly dependent upon, namely the labor force without which factory production would cease. The workers could back up their threats with force as long as they were sufficiently well-organized. However, in the attentionalist society the consumtarian underclass lacks such a weapon. For the consumtariat does not merely stand outside attentionalism's sociograms and information flows – the consumtarians are to be sure constantly online, just like all others in the network society, but once there they mainly devote themselves to passive consumption and pointless distraction of various kinds, and not to any form of strategic network building – it also lacks the old paradigm's hard currency in the form of income, fortunes and academic titles and therefore has an extraordinarily weak negotiating position. Automation, digitalization and globalization causes what was previously a working class to instead become a *pre-*

cariat, a collective which at best gets to jump from one poorly paid, temporary service assignment to another and at worst is left with no job at all – and also without any support, unless it is taken care of by society. In the transitional phase that we are going through, the consumtarians are thus double losers, without access to either financial or attentional resources. They have no titles, money nor social networks of value. The only thing the consumtarians have is their own bodies, which they toss in as a final stake in all contexts where a body at least has formal value; it may then be the case of going to a polling station and on command casting a single, symbolic vote in a democratic election without significance (see *The Netocrats*), or at worst strapping an explosive device to one's body or arming oneself in some other way to carry out an act of terror.

But if both the right and the left in a traditional sense disappear in the network society, then where and how do the new ideological battle lines arise? The German sociologist Max Weber sees all ideology production throughout history as a struggle between *idealism* and *pragmatism*. The idealist posits an ideal and then connects all political struggle to an uncompromising pursuit towards this ideal. The end justifies the means, as they say. Nothing but the lofty ideal will do and no other struggle – least of all a compromise with other centers of power – is of interest. The pragmatist, however, perceives himself as being connected to a specific society where the ideals could not possibly be anything other than poles for the ideological compass, utopian models that seldom or never can become reality. Idealism is anchored in an eternalist worldview in which only the coveted eternalization – such as the arrival of the fetish or the annihilation of the abject, in the form of for instance the classless society of communism, the paradise of Abrahamic religions or the racially purified thousand year reich – will do. Every compromise takes the idealist further away from, rather than closer to, the longed-for cathexal object. Pragmatism, however, is grounded in a process-philosophical worldview with absolute duration. This means that every idea arises in the specific society where the pragmatist actually is located and must be related to precisely this society and the conditions that prevail there, rather than to some kind of messianic future beyond the horizon.

This means that the pragmatist has no problem compromising, if this is what the situation requires, in order to attain the best possible outcome. The pragmatist sees a limited value in fighting over which ideals are expected to constitute the lodestars of humanity, but does on the other hand see great value in building functioning, credible institutions in a chaotic world. While the consumtarians hate everything outside the romantic nostalgia, the netocrats build parallel, virtual worlds where they circumvent the limitations of the physical world. *Microcapitalism* with its endless *block chains* meant to establish trust between thousands and thousands of strangers creates chains of trust of a complexity that humanity has never previously seen. We can suddenly trust not just a few dozen people in our intratribal proximity, but also large intertribal populations far from our own immediate environment. Add to this the encryption-protected darknets, and the netocracy has soon completed its virtual temple into *Syntheos*, the created god. Ironically, this generates a world of extended *transparency* where all factors that are of decisive value to the tribe – that is: not dividual values protected integrity-wise, but rather generously shared collective values in the form of copious amounts of data – become generally disseminated and known.

The resistance consists of the intratribal idealists, that is: the nation-states and the traditional giant corporations in combination with an increasingly embittered consumtariat. Here, too, the timeless political line of demarcation runs between the idealists and the pragmatists, just as Weber predicts. The idealists want to recreate the virtual dream worlds in physical space and refuse to compromise their ideals, be it the case of tax-exempt city-states or colonies on other planets. The pragmatists, on the other hand, seek cooperation with the old nation-state and corporatist institutions from the capitalist paradigm. But it is the case of a particularly precarious project, since the old institutions – which the netocratic pragmatists attempt to tame and use – are governed by an unholy alliance of the netocrat-hostile bourgeoisie and the reactionary consumtariat, the bitter individualists of the old upper class and the new underclass, driven by the Internet itself as a cohesive abject. Together these constitute the majority of the population, which makes them focus on the last remains of the majoritarian democracy and its nation-state-sanctioned monopoly on violence as the weapons to stop the digitalization, globalization and nodalization of the world. They are the Global Empire's sworn enemies and therefore anything but easy to cooperate with.

And how does this virtual battlefield relate to the dialectics of libido and mortido? Who has and who does not have enough sense to control what the Swiss psychoanalyst Carl Gustav Jung calls Man's shadow? The German anthropologist Hans Peter Duerr argues – in the spirit of Nietzsche, Freud and Jung – that modern society's pervasive problem is its lack of contact with and insight into Man's animal origin. This contact has by tradition been managed by the alienated class that we call *mortido's world*. It is a case of a world of death, birth, animalism, chaos and lawlessness. Its members are precisely the shamans, witches, criminals, executioners and warriors that end up outside the constantly repeated class struggle that occurs within civilization. These actors thus constantly find themselves, according to Duerr, in the borderlands between civilization and wilderness. Their libido is *de facto* drenched by mortido precisely in order to be able to experience this mortido as much as possible without losing libido, according to Duerr, often through hallucinogenic experiences carried out in caves or in other matrichal locations in nature. In his book *Traumzeit: Über die Grenze zwischen Wildnis und Zivilisation* Duerr traces this mortido's world

– or *the realm of death,* as Duerr terms this charged sphere – to the various cults of antiquity around the Greek goddess Artemis and the Roman goddess Diana, and argues that first Christianity's and then individualism's dualist crusades against this monist mortido's world is the very basic cause of modern society's denial of and loss of contact with Man's fundamental, mortidinal side, *the Jungian shadow.*

It is of course the citizen in this mortido-denying society that is the infantile and sexless creature that Freud sees emerge and personify the subconscious and therefore ruthless mortido in industrialized Europe from the 19th century onwards. The fear of mortido as the foundation of an explosive libido creates a creature that morphs into mortido itself, a hyperneurotic existence that constantly postpones its own life for fear of its animal irrationality, a creature totally lacking genuine contact with itself. The result is a life where quality is replaced by quantity, a dead life. Duerr argues that a human society that loses contact with mortido's world – a culture that persecutes, bans and obliterates the shamanic caste – cannot understand itself, its animal foundation, and the phallic limitation that enables libido and its drive machinery.

This in turn means that it is particularly important to place the shamanic caste at the social center precisely at the time of a paradigm shift. It is the intrepid priests from the various tribes that build the sacred cult sites in the area between the besieged villages, the places that later become the first cities where new cultural mutations arise and take hold. It is the Levites without territory that connect Israel's other, locally anchored tribes into a global promised land. And it is the digital priesthood that builds *phallic intertribalism* for the netocracy during informationalism, with which it overtakes the consumtariat and its narrow-minded intratribalism and ensures that it can conquer and master the Global Empire of the Internet Age. And in the wake of these networking pioneers there are, once again, the businessmen – just as in the building of the original ritual sites – and this time they populate all the airport lounges of the world. Global nomadism is ready to take off.

The metaphysical point is that mortido triumphs and shall triumph. Ultimately. It must be so. Death and taxes. But it shall not triumph before the moment of death. Up until then the netocrat's syntheist metaphysics is governed by the conscious but impermeable repression of the death yearning of the subconscious in the form of a stubborn zest for living. What the awareness of mortidos' ultimate victory in death entails, is a fortified will to live, a will that is driven by the awareness of Man's mortality. It is, as the German existentialist Martin Heidegger expresses the matter, from this *horizon* at the mutability and thus finiteness of everything that all meaning is produced. Duerr claims that it is the psychedelic experience that is the origin of the idea that the mind can grow freely and expand within a spiritual sphere, that the mind can transcend existence and go from what Zoroaster calls *ahura* (being) to *mazda* (mind). And the group that cherishes this conviction first of all is precisely the shamans that move between the tribes and build the first cult sites that see the light of day.

While we are living we incessantly seek meaning, and we can argue back and forth for all eternity, but without culture we humans are nothing. Or to be precise: we are perhaps something, but we are not humans. Without culture we would not, in any case, be able to argue about anything whatsoever. Nietzsche's truly striking insight in the 19th century – in response to the cunning Rousseau's extensive idealizations of human nature – is to understand that it is culture as the phallic creation out of nothing that makes Man what he is. Or if we posit the existential experience along the timeline: Before the genesis of culture there is nothing of value save a gaping hole of animist emptiness. Man is originally no noble savage, but a creature driven by an impulsive instinct, for lack of the self-consciousness, self-insight, self-confidence and self-control that characterizes the talking, thinking and analyzing human born out of the genesis of culture. The entry of phallus into the great chaos is tantamount to the arrival of order. And in this context it does not matter one iota whether we are discontent in culture or not: it both shapes and inhibits us, enriches and frustrates us. Outside culture there is only wilderness that neither speaks nor listens to us.

The return of the authentic phallus also entails a return to adult responsibility, and what is central to the tribe's survival: socialization and the domestication of libidinal youth. This taming starts from what we call *the patriarchal imperative* and *the matriarchal imperative* respectively, that is: the patriarch's most important message to the young men and the matriarch's most important message to the young women respectively. The patriarchal imperative is that no man can manage without meaning, and it's only possible to produce meaning within the male collective through the conceited and hubristic young man yielding to this collective. Thus he must be tamed into this submission in order to later be able to get what he longs for most of all, namely a purpose for his existence and a role as a tribal contributor. The matriarchal imperative is that no woman can fulfill her innate meaning as a central node in the reproduction cycle without staying within the confines of the female collective. The matriarch cannot promise her protection unless the young woman accepts that she must stay inside the outlined boundaries of matriarchy, within which she in return is promised not just meaning but also security, power, enjoyment, and attention.

Please note that the primitivist nomadic tribe was driven just as much by its abhorrence of parasites, diseases and assorted social and esthetic deviations as it was driven by the struggle to find food and shelter. So all that was needed to bring about an expulsion was that a patriarch or a matriarch pointed out something – or even someone – as non-desirable within the tribe's story about itself, whereupon the entire socializing abjection process was set in motion. In time this became decisive for the survival of the nomadic tribe. Whether brutal and often deadly acts of ostracism were just or not is hardly germane. The nomadized hunter-gatherers were absolutely no squeamish Rousseauans. Nor did the dividual in itself have any value in comparison with the sacred tribe's collective. However, the internal abjection process had the desired domesticating effect, while respect for the most knowledgeable and experienced members – the patriarch and the matriarch themselves – remained enormous. Thereby one maximized the plastic nomadic tribe's ability to find themselves in constant motion and at the same time multiply and secure food and protection for survival. This and nothing else was the evolutionarily valuable effect of both abjection and domestication in itself.

Fetishes as well as abjects were diligently used to keep the plastic nomadic tribe intact. And ever since then, intratribalism – cohesion within the tribe – has been the simplest and most natural thing for humanity to handle. However, problems immediately arise when it comes to intertribalism, the need to later in history organize larger groups of people of various origin and make them cooperate, or at least not spend time and energy on beating strangers to death, without allowing themselves to be corrupted by self-interest or bribes from strangers in a way that harms the tribe's own interests. In his book *The Righteous Mind,* the American social psychologist Jonathan Haidt discusses how Man's moral compass is developed within the tribe, but that this compass concurrently from a historical perspective lacks anchoring outside the same. It is thus easy for people to become local patriots, but on the other hand considerably more difficult for us to become universalists. Therefore, to this day, the great majority of users of social media seek a group of no more than a couple of hundred people to be able to orient themselves to some extent in an existence that is hard to navigate, without a hint of a capacity to see the rest of humanity as a resource in a society where all the people in the world are directly interconnected with each other, synchronously and constantly.

Building and maintaining the Global Empire during informationalism will for this reason be a gigantic challenge. And the transition from intratribalism to intertribalism is definitely the network society's greatest and most important project. Both because the very people who handle the transition will be the netocratic winners during the Internet Age, but also because a large-scale failure in this area invariably leads to unmanageable social conflicts and catastrophes. The stranger must become a peaceful friend in the Global Empire and not – as previously in history – a feared enemy. It was difficult enough to unite the ethnocentric nation-state – the invention that Nietzsche calls "the coldest of all cold monsters" – during capitalism, a process that was preceded by long and bloody wars. The digital priesthood thus has a colossal challenge ahead of it, but will for the same reason also accumulate enormous power as this will be the greatest cultivation project of the network society. It is not possible to build a stable, sustainable society that contravenes Man's sociobiological prerequisites – which explains why matrichal dreamers from Mazdak to Rousseau constantly fail – but nor is it enough to build a society solely adapted to Man's innate talents.

It will now be the task of the digital priesthood to preach the challenge of social maturity and coming of age as the ideal that stands in opposition to the mass infantilization that to a large extent is in line with the Internet's structure and dynamics. Sensocracy becomes one of its most important tools, and tribal mapping becomes its primary model. And the attentionalist adultification project has succeeded on the day that the adult citizens of the information society have learned to cooperate optimally with the stranger or the machine at the other end of the network. And there is still an impending risk that the comparison between human and machine in terms of intelligence will be an affront to the machines rather than to the humans, since the machines hardly will be are bothered by Man's built-in systemic flaws, in particular his innate reluctance to appreciate the alien and deviant. This irrespective of whether we also take into consideration Man's advantage over the machine in terms of the *comprehension* of, rather than the *competence* in terms of managing data flows over the foreseeable future. We will soon reach a state where civilization for the first time ever in principle will manage without Man. It may tolerate us if we are lucky, but it does not need us. But Man still cannot manage without the culture in which we are doomed to be discontent. For without culture Man is nothing. At least nothing of meaning or value.

16
The informationalist apocalypse and the three heads of the netocratic hydra

There are different kinds of destruction. We have the creative destruction that the Austrian economist Joseph Schumpeter speaks of: entrepreneurial activity and innovations in different areas that "destroy" the old order and raze the prevailing structures that no longer enjoy support in the most sophisticated contemporary technology, that is: destruction and creation in line with how the netocracy outmaneuvers an outdated power elite who no longer understand or at least no longer is able to adapt to the new terms that gradually start to apply in all parts of society as a result of a media-technological revolution. We also have the pure destruction whose purpose is to crush every form of authority, generally with the motive that corruption and decay has progressed to the extent that there is nothing whatsoever worth saving in the prevailing order, and in some cases with the pious hope that perhaps something – it is unclear what – valuable will grow out of maximal devastation.

Anarchism is the ultimate form of revolt against all forms of authority. In the 19th century the progenitor of modern anarchism,

Mikhail Bakunin, incites a complete and eternal revolt against all exploitation and discrimination. But Bakunin's ambition is strictly mortidinal. He focuses his entire spiritual will on a destruction that lacks a libidinal counterweight and a pursuit of order and reconstruction. Bakunin's ideology is thus through and through an expression of a mortido, without any element of libido – or if you will: just *yin* but no *yang*. There are, as the Indian author and essayist Pankaj Mishra demonstrates in his book *Age of Anger*, clear parallels between 19th century anarchism in Europe and 21st century Islamism in the Middle East. It is the case of the same nihilist mortido without libido, the same search for points to attack without the least interest in building anything new beyond what we call the shattered *abject*. And no thinker represents this earnest and by necessity secret worship of mortido more clearly than the Frenchman Jean-Jacques Rousseau from the European Enlightenment. His ambition is of course to mobilize a will that chooses not to want anything other than at most preventing other wills from expressing and manifesting themselves. *A will that chooses not to will itself*, as we can express the matter in the spirit of Rousseau's opponent Friedrich Nietzsche. A will that turns inwards, towards itself and its own willing, and that drives itself towards its own extinction, that is; a purified mortido.

In the argument concerning the concepts *amour-propre* and *amour de soi* Rousseau claims that the explanation for the social misery that prevails is that Man, in having left the natural state and having become a societal creature, has lost the ability to experience genuine love for and appreciation of himself and can only manage to observe and thus also value himself through the eyes of others. Seeing and even loving oneself from one's own prerequisites and values, applying syntheist self-love or *amour de soi*, as Rousseau calls it, has become practically impossible in that the societal development has brought us together in collectives, structured by the detested civilization, and has forced us to constantly compare the image of ourselves that we imagine the people around us have with the image we ourselves have of others. This constant comparison of images generates the violent and ambivalent emotions of dominance and submission that characterize Modern Man, who must therefore settle for what Rousseau calls *amour-propre* – the love or appreciation of oneself as one is perceived in the eyes of others. This means that Modern Man must live in a state of constant deficiency, since no one else ever will appreciate and love us enough to fill the bottomless need for love that we harbor inside ourselves. We will never again experience the joy or the well-being that primitive society's *amour de soi* gave us, according to Rousseau. The gate to the lost paradise is forever closed; we have doomed ourselves to eternal exile in a civilization in which we are discontented.

By creating a myth about the noble savage and an idyllic state of *amour de soi,* and then on top of this establishing a *metaressentiment* directed from Modern Man to the noble savage, who thus is pure fiction, Rousseau supplies a viable and functional foundation for all the abject-driven revenge and self-victimization ideologies that blossom in modern society: Nazism, fascism, Stalinism et cetera. This ideological foundation is still essentially intact, even if these violence-affirming ideologies are rejected by the societal establishment, which is demonstrated in how neo-nazism, updated variants of fascism, various forms of the extreme right and the identity left grow powerful in a society where the institutions of bourgeois democracy are rapidly undermined and weakened. Internet-driven, consumtarian narcissism continues to draw nourishment from a Rousseau who never ceases to attract new adherents and who remains the constant chief ideologue of ressentiment. What subject did Pol Pot, Cambodia's dictator and architect of genocide, choose as the theme of his doctoral thesis – before he left Paris in the 1970s and returned to his homeland to start the slaughter of his countrymen with deviant opinions – if none other than Rousseau? And as it turned out, the issue of deviant opinions was not even really so important; simply wearing glasses was reason enough to be tortured and executed.

The Danish philosopher and existentialist pioneer thinker Søren Kierkegaard claims in the 19th century, as a response to Rousseau's extensive popularity, that *egalitarian competition* between the citizens in the modern society is the great contradiction of modernism. Kierkegaard argues that egalitarian competition generates a kind of unreflected envy that acts as the abject of the consumtarian mob, that is: as the mob's concealed unifying principle. And therein lies its colossal, destructive strength. The German philosopher Max Scheler, one of Kierkegaard's many admirers, later deepens the anti-Rousseauan abjection theory and argues that the more egalitarian a society is, the stronger *ressentiment* will be as well. And a similar line of reasoning can be found already in the French historian and political scientist Alexis de Tocqueville, who in his work *Democracy in America* (1835-1840) writes about "the special melancholy that democratic countries' citizens often display in the midst of their abundance."

The explanation, argues de Tocqueville, is a connection between equality and envy. In a society founded on privilege, even the greatest discrepancies in wealth and power appear natural, but when many or perhaps even most of these injustices are remedied even the smallest differences are perceived as an affront. "No matter how much of an effort a people make, they cannot succeed in making all living conditions completely equal" writes de Tocqueville. "Should they even so to their own misfortune succeed in attaining this absolute and complete leveling the differences in innate reason would still remain." Which was very incisive and prophetic back then, and describes our present very well. This is precisely where we find ourselves today, which is why we experience how envy explodes around us. No matter how we fight privileges, the fact remains that there is a paucity of places at the top. Consequently, humanity shifts into an overdrive of hatred as we attain the unprecedentedly transparent information society. Ressentiment is cultivated, encouraged and escalates further in the virtual conflicts between all the subcultures of the net. Between all these postmodern mythologies of martyrdom an embittered, identitarian competition is played out.

It is important to point out here that there is nothing bad in itself in postmodernism's function as a critical theory. Every system benefits from critical analysis. The problem is rather that postmodernism's critique of modernism became so devastatingly successful that the entire modern project collapsed. And when critical theory with its *deconstruction* is the only thing that remains, when the critique already has killed what it lives on critiquing, the situation becomes – well, critical. The only thing that remains in the end is the grinding critique sitting and idling after the objective of the critique has been turned to dust. There is no longer anything to deconstruct, which however does not prevent the critique from grinding on as though critique in itself were what was fundamental in existence. Thus postmodernism from the 1980s becomes a supporting ideology for the Western societal project. It vanquishes itself to death and continues to win again and again by default, as a mortido without libido, as a matrix without phallus. And it survives as a cursed ghost, a flickering shadow of its days of glory. The defense mechanisms of the organism are therefore turned into an attack on the organism itself.

The basis for this fatal mistake is postmodernism's inability to discern a distinction between the authentic and the false phallus. Postmodernist critique regards anything the least bit phallic as an expression of an objectionable *phallogocentrism*, as the French father of deconstruction Jacques Derrida expresses the matter. It can no longer make a distinction between the utopian message that the authentic phallus conveys and the abjectifying incitement from the false phallus, but lumps everything phallic into a compact hatred of all forms of visions and utopias – a declaration of war against the phallic intrusion as such. It operates concealed behind the sacred mamilla in the inner circuit of the tribal map, and it acts as though the outer circuit did not exist. The Nazi, Stalinist and Maoist catastrophes are quite simply supposed to prove that every form of utopianism by definition constitutes a societal hazard. This also applies to the authentic phallus, whose existence one does not recognize or even understand, and disregards the fact that all three of these ideologies lack this authenticity and are instead entirely driven by a monumental abjectification of the internal, self-produced adversary. The result is a completely nihilist postmodernism, an empty power theater where value and meaning are completely determined by who is speaking, not by what is being said. And without a modernism that still can respond to this monotonous cacophony, postmodernism as a critical theory becomes the only theory that takes and receives considerable space. The great problem will then be the critical theory's inability to perform self-criticism, as demonstrated by a blindness to the consequences of it having forcefully contravened every form of phallic intrusion.

Thereby the entire academic world is open to a pervasive infantilization, and it is of course exactly what happens – an infantilization that draws its nourishment from the mamilla that consists of the nation-state and its constantly shrinking resources. But where and how does the Nietzschean master mentality lose contact with and surrender its initiative in the face of the Rousseauan slave mentality? Even Nietzsche himself points out the danger of the massive nihilism that follows upon the decay of Christianity in the Western world, and he blames this nihilism on the truth worship that is built into Christianity. According to Nietzsche, Christianity's downfall is embedded in its own fundamental ideology right from the start. To express the matter from a theological-historical perspective: First there is the Word and then there is Truth ever more forcefully when the Word explores Truth ever more thoroughly and profoundly. And since Christianity lacks for instance Zoroastrianism's flexibility regarding ideological change that follows from deepened knowledge, it is, according to Nietzsche, merely a matter of time before Christianity collapses from its own obsession with being the servant of Truth at any cost and in every respect.

However, the Western nihilism that follows in the wake of Christianity's collapse is far from the only large-scale outburst of nihilism in history. Rather, nihilism more generally has something to do with what the French sociologist Emile Durkheim calls *anomie* in his classic work *Suicide* from 1897. Durkheim argues that the dividual's connection to the collective is tied to *nomos*, the idea of the collective as *the organic system of rules in constant motion*: what we within the framework of socioanalysis describe as *the libidinal phallus*. Durkheim's genius lies in that he understands that this anomie not only is manifested as a state of crisis when phallus is conspicuous by its absence – that is, in connection with the nihilism about which Nietzsche speaks and that thereafter has become so renowned – but also when the prevailing regulatory system in society is perceived as *mechanical* rather than *organic*. The mechanical system of rules must of course, despite all its perfection and efficiency, appear to be a dead and mortidinal phallus, rather than a vibrant and libidinal one. Thus Nietzsche's *nihilism* must be complemented by Durkheim's *anomie* in order to understand the ideological crisis that arises at the breakthrough of informationalism. That the civilizing process now has reached the critical point where machines and algorithms can continue on their own, when civilization no longer needs Man to survive and develop further, is an insight that slowly starts to emerge in the collective consciousness, which for understandable reasons propels an anomie to an extent never previously seen, which in turn entails exceptionally favorable conditions for the Rousseauan slave mentality, which therefore grows increasingly strong.

This takes us further to the unveiling – or *apokalypsis* to speak in Greek – of *the netocratic power structure* which sooner or later must shape the network society for the simple reason that it is in line with the dominant metatechnology (see *The Netocrats*). Sustainability and stability presuppose an interaction between three phallic poles that balance and overlap each other in the sense that if one of them should falter and implode, or become megalomanic and explode, the paradigm can during this crisis be supported by the two other, intact poles. Since power moreover is developed in three separate layers, each of them connected with and adapted to one of Man's three Lacanian fantasy worlds, we speak of *real power*, *imaginary power* and *symbolic power*. Real power controls the paradigm's most important resources. Imaginary power supervises law and order and carries out the social order's formal exercise of power – it dons the official robes of power and thereby embodies the concept of power in the eyes of most people. Finally there is symbolic power, which has assumed a monopoly on the historiography of the paradigm and thus even on its truth production, and which therefore formulates, administers and defends the paradigm's metaphysical values.

Feudalist society was governed by the feudalist power triad, which was constituted by *the aristocracy*, *the monarchy* and *the clergy*. The aristocracy possessed the paradigm's dominant resource, land, and therefore acted as the real power. The monarchy controlled the court, the law and the military, and thus was the imaginary power. The clergy with its monasteries, churches, temples, mosques and synagogues controlled truth production and therefore was the symbolic power. If the monarch was impudent towards the aristocracy and the clergy, these two camps could band together in the name of stability and by virtue of their greater aggregate power put the monarch in his place. The same applied to the aristocracy and the clergy if any of these should get the idea of destroying the balance and acquiring more – or all – power in society through dominating the other poles.

No perfect balance ever prevailed, but conflicts are tiring and periods marked by unrest would give way to periods of relative stability. The noble estates could be granted to, or be taken over by other families, kings could be deposed and religions could be criticized and modified, but the very power structure that was underpinned by three pillars remained uninterrupted. One could talk of revolutions, but what it really was about was so-called palace coups; within the confines of a paradigm the aristocracy could only be replaced by other aristocrats. A deposed, possibly executed, king was replaced by another king. Power struggles within the church could lead to one or the other constellation seeing their influence decrease to the benefit of bitter rivals. But none of this led to the genesis of any competing institutions as long as the hand-lettered written language remained the dominant metamedium that dictated the forms for all communication. The printing press changed all this in one fell swoop, even if it took a few hundred years before this new, dominant metamedium made a complete breakthrough in the form of industrialism, capitalism and bourgeois democracy, and so on. There was nothing left of the old feudalist power triad save pitiful fragments.

During the capitalist society controlled by printed mass media, a new triad was consolidated over time, consisting of *the bourgeoisie*, *the politicians* and *the academics*. The bourgeoisie built and owned the industries and thus soon enough controlled the paradigm's fundamental resource, *capital*, the foundation for power and status after the noble estates had become a commodity amid numerous others on a market, and which consequently gave the capitalist paradigm its name. The bourgeoisie therefore constituted the real power during capitalism. The politicians – a caste of its own with a regulated promotional system – controlled the nation-state with its legislation and monopoly on violence based on *nationalism* as the supraideology and therefore constituted the imaginary power. The university professors from the academic world with their *atomist* worldview controlled truth production through their monopoly on the truth-producing science and thus represented the symbolic power in capitalist society. *Individualism* then functioned as the supraideology that merged these three poles in a joint power structure. In keeping with this, progress concurrently became the metaphysical engine that propelled the ambition to realize the individual *citizen's* full potential within the confines of the societal construction through the bourgeoisie's entrepreneurship, the politicians' administration and social control, and the academics' education and cultivation.

History repeats itself in the informationalist network society. The same pattern is once again discernible. Resource accumulation, formal exercise of power and identity-building accounts of history must quite simply assume new expressions at new addresses on interactivity's plane of immanence. Already 18 years ago in our first book *The Netocrats* we investigate how the netocratic power triad might be constructed. The three basic identities we use in this text are *the nexialist*, *the curator* and *the eternalist*. The nexialist has the real power during informationalism, thus we are talking about the actor who is sitting on all the data, or rather is sitting on the node in the ocean of information where important data flows merge and where the value of these is multiplied thanks to proficiency in knowing what questions one can pose to the information and of how the answers that emerge best can be made useful. And now, some two decades later, we have the answers, and it appears perfectly obvious that the actors who control the world's great data clouds are sitting on an unprecedentedly powerful resource. Their influence is enormous and growing.

The curator then constitutes the imaginary power, the actor who sorts and discerns patterns in the convoluted flow of information, who separates the wheat from the chaff and who emphasizes that which is informative, entertaining or in any other way interesting and useful in these flows. The curator crassly culls people based on how they act on the net. This knowledge and these skills give the curator a mandate to organize and moderate the most powerful and successful networks, which leaves no room for the ingratiating populism that is the hallmark of the outgoing, political power.

The curator operates and monitors what we call *deep tech*, the mainly algorithm-based exploration of the enormous amounts of data that reveal who we humans really are and how our world actually works when one poses the right questions to the information that is available. This activity supplies completely new means of power that make it possible to control and govern the masses since it is known in advance what people are thinking and longing for in every given situation. It is no longer necessary to refer to flawed questionnaire findings and statistical samples; instead it is now quite possible to simulate innumerable variants of a critical scenario and experiment with various input values.

Finally, the netocratic power triad is completed by the eternalist who assumes the role as the ruler of the symbolic sphere, that is: the actor who establishes and confers legitimacy upon the narrative status of the nature of things. The eternalist is the representative of the shamanic caste in the informationalist network society, the phallic storyteller around which the greatest and most influential knowledge repositories and think tanks are built. Together these three actors then constitute the netocratic power triad, based on *relationalism* as the informationalist supraideology and *network dynamics* as its applied practice.

The relatively small netocracy has three strategies available with which to handle the relatively large consumtariat, namely *mass surveillance*, *isolation* and *anesthetization*. Mass surveillance entails that data about the entire population be collected so that there are no secrets whatsoever left for power to be concerned about. If one achieves what is essentially surveillance over how people act and consume, while the dividual person's behaviors are highly predictable, it means that the netocratic power triad has total control of how both dividual persons as well as groups of various composition think and might be predicted to act in every given situation. It also means that society both can be analyzed and controlled through applied *data anthropology*. There is hardly any doubt that this is a wet dream among the nexialist pioneers. All citizens' thoughts and behaviors can be anticipated and parried. All risks of discontent and protest become easy to predict and thus also possible to divert and prevent long before an eruption that might have unwelcome and hard-to-manage consequences.

This technology and this capacity would of course be a dream even for the Napoleonic institutions that struggle frenetically to survive the paradigm shift through trying to convert themselves from nation-state bureaucracies to nexialist control functions. And then it is primarily one-party states that lead the way in such a development. A Chinese communist party can for instance be expected to do anything in its power to attain full access to the citizens' complete data, in order to then be able to control them via a system of sophisticated data sensors spread across and inside the whole of society, a development that would make a democracy with several parties and elections of parliamentary representatives every fourth year to appear, when looking back from a more or less distant future, increasingly obsolete as well as unnecessary since this would not deliver sufficient prosperity, at least not with any kind of guarantee. The great masses choose security and consumption over freedom and insecurity every day of the week.

But then it is precisely the actors who want to avoid a development in the direction towards paralyzing and disintegrating democracies that most likely are most hungry for developing a system of social sensors as alternatives to the clumsy democratic systems. We call such a system a *sensocracy*, which entails a more refined form of plurarchy with all the society's *nexi* continuously read, controlled and regulated by the nexialist power machinery, which therefore no longer needs any democracy at all. This occurs for example through the use of innumerable intelligent microsensors, ironically initially developed to supervise and control the actors that are least virtually accessible and observable: little children, the elderly, the disabled, the long-term ill and criminals. There is little doubt that a sensocracy such as this constitutes a historic apocalypse for any libertarian pursuers of freedom. And virtually all others as well. But this development is not just a conceivable but a highly likely consequence of informationalism's rapidly escalating cybercrime, subcultural ultraviolence and costly health care bureaucracies. If what is promised is security, there is practically no price that is too steep.

The citizens have of course already become accustomed to acting as nodes in systems of artificial intelligence, in interaction with both people and machines, without either the possibility or even any discernible will to stand outside the systems. It is hard, not to say impossible, to actually refuse to be connected to the gigantic, virtual mamilla that is called the Internet. Its power of attraction is indisputable. The flip side of this is that power is rapidly concentrated to the nexialists who own and control the enormous accumulated amounts of data, and to their allies, the curators who interpret and control these data flows, regardless of whether these are regarded as entrepreneurial platforms or administrative one-party states, furnished with an unlimited amount of data. Add to this the curators' keen sensitivity for how all this data should be interpreted and prioritized, and the eternalists' enthusiastic storytelling about the prophetic possibilities of this work, and we are witnessing the slow but sure growth of *the psychotechnological society*. And not so slowly either. If mass surveillance is a fundamentally nexialist strategy to control the consumtariat, we can regard isolation as the typically curatorial strategy. From a virtual perspective this is a given. At an initial stage, and not without reason, the generous openness of the Internet was emphasized – everyone was offered access to everything and many imagined that this was the technology that would pave the way for the classless society through an equal distribution of information – but soon enough it became evident that this viewpoint was grossly naive and governed by wishful thinking. One forgot the business side of the matter, and up went walls that demarcated, excluded and obscured the view, hindrances in the form of firewalls and payment solutions meant to shut out curious gazes and force people to at least spend money.

This development was enabled by *the genesis of the network pyramid* (see *The Netocrats*). The principle is simple: As the attentional network grows, it is drowned in information. The first curator is therefore the actor, the stern doorkeeper of the network who sifts out the most important actors in the burgeoning network and ensures that they establish direct contact with each other within a smaller network that is placed further up the hierarchy, now without constantly having to fend off the consumtarian chatter of the great masses about this and that. In order to retain the key members and make them perform at peak level it is necessary to cherish the little time they have and make sure that they are stimulated by high-quality communication instead of being inundated with spam. This means that walls, boundaries and obstacles become necessary in order to defend the integrity of the network. It is no longer possible for everyone to participate for the simple reason that not everyone brings something valuable to the table. Far too many clamor for attention without having anything other than a high-pitched voice to offer. The Facebook groups that remain important and productive rapidly develop, to take one example, from exploitation and openness during a growth phase to imploitation and selective insulation during a consolidation phase. It is necessary to moderate with a firm hand in order for the group not to drown in its own feces. The value of the information itself (nexialism) and the analysis of the same (the curation process) increases the fewer the actors that are part of the process, rather than the other way around. That which everyone already has access – which is the lion's share of all the intense mass duplication of ones and zeroes during informationalism – has no barter value at all, of course.

Quality trumps quantity. It is thus imploitation, not exploitation, that represents the greatest value in a society where the crude materials are reserved for a small elite – as long as they have value

– and become available for mass consumption only when the actual value has been spent. The type of specialist knowledge that one would acquire in yesteryear through long and arduous university studies, but which now is generally available by pressing a few keys on a computer, consequently has been devalued dramatically during the last decades, a trend that only has been reinforced. As the pressure from below increases even more – and the upper network over time also grows too large to be tribally optimal – the demands on the next generation of curators will also repeat the whole process through sifting out the sharpest talents in the higher network and creating an even higher network where the entry requirements are even tougher, but where the purpose always is the same: to raise the quality of the analysis and the processing of the information through reducing the disturbing noise. This is a process that never ends; soon enough it will be repeated, and after a time the process will have repeated at so many levels that we are faced with the complete *network pyramid* that comprises the entire virtual society.

However, this does not mean that there will ever be stability or balance in the system, which constantly is in a state of motion, where some networks are ascending in the great metanetwork while others have lost relevance and acuity and therefore are descending. Power and status are distributed (and redistributed) in accordance with where they belong and their position within the network pyramid, a social position connected to attentionalist principles rather than to a capitalist accumulation of assets. It is impossible to buy a membership in the highest network quite simply because the value of both the position and the network on the whole immediately would plummet. What is really valuable is the attention you can produce; the measure of your social value is the social awareness you create multiplied by the creative credibility that you can mobilize, and neither income nor fortune will help you very much in this context, to the extent it even will help you at all. For he who is busy and sought-after for real there are few or no reasons to waste time on someone who has nothing to offer but mere money, when money in any case simply is a resource that the right dividual with the right contacts can procure in requisite amounts in a society where there is an abundance of hungry and hard-pressed microcapitalist mass bankers desperately seeking the next interesting idea, investors and fund managers with access to boundless amounts of blockchain-secured cryptocurrencies.

The ability to imploit rather than exploit information is thus ultimately what distinguishes success from fiasco, which is why the holes must be sealed at any cost. At least until the primary value of the information and the information-processing have been depleted. But by then, on the other hand, the cursory attention of the network's members has shifted to something completely different. Thus it is important to understand that *the attentionalist network pyramid* makes the informationalist society both the most radical of all meritocratic systems and simultaneously the crudest class structure that history has ever beheld. One might say that Marxism triumphed without really understanding why, and that the result was not the dreamed-of social leveling, but conversely an infinitely harsher and moreover more esoteric class society than one could ever have conceived of during capitalism. The *Lumpenproletariat* that Karl Marx both feared and despised will not be absorbed by a proud and rising working class, instead it grows dramatically in size under the new conditions that prevail. And in its new form as the new consumtariat, one is online in equal degree to all other social actors, which in itself does not mean anything other than that the Internet has rapidly become so thoroughly integrated with everything else that it no longer is meaningful to try to make an issue of the differences between the digital and the analogue. What is interesting is rather that this new Lumpenproletariat spends its time engaged in all possible destructive variants of hypernarcissism, pornoflation and interpassivity. That the informationalist consumtariat constitutes Marxism's Lumpenproletariat *par excel-*

lence is demonstrated with extreme clarity when Facebook's sociogram of the world's population is presented – and turns out to recreate the whole world as one single, gigantic network pyramid, just as we predicted in *The Netocrats* almost two decades ago. Time is beginning to catch up with us.

First of all there is an enormous difference in power and influence between he who has 500,000 followers on social media and he who only has twelve. And the inequality in distribution of power becomes even clearer when we also make note of and value who *de facto* follows whom, and start to measure quality rather than quantity in communication, that is: when we measure authentic interactivity rather than cosmetic interpassivity. For instance, no one listened to or requested the amateur music posted on the Internet forum called My Space, which is why it is now defunct, missed by no one other than those who diligently pretended to listen to each other in the hope that the well-known back-scratching principle would generate the corresponding reciprocal favor with the involuntarily revealing phrase "Thank you for the add," a phrase which must be thought of as American social superficiality and mendacity in its most evident and pathetic form.

But wait a minute. Why would any actor thank someone publicly for an add if an add merely is meant as confirmation before a third actor that the first two actors – those who add and thank each other – already know each other? The cheating and fiddling could not be clearer. Even seemingly quantitatively successful actors within social media can be entirely interpassive in accordance with the above-mentioned back-scratching principle – one simulates quality and dynamism by pretending to like something that actually no one likes. Which can make it appear as though the actors who are united in a mutual pretense and a common failure are exciting and successful, when they actually are rightful losers who are wasting both their own and everybody else's time. Through its structure, the Internet gives rise to these time and energy thieves in spades, sorry losers and amateurish exploiters who completely lack a sense of imploitation's enormous phallic value in the Internet's flat, chaotic, matrichal world.

The corporate world's interpassive equivalent to this pathetic quasi-communication among dividual persons, is of course called *search engine optimization*, that is: dysfunctional companies with pitiful goods and just as pitiful services trying to cheat their way to attention from the algorithms of the search engines – without having to improve either products or services and thereby generating a better position in the search engine's results from the very start, and without having to pay for an ad in the desperate hope of thereby saving a devalued brand that justly is losing value because of failed innovation and product development. Such an ad would of course, by the way, ironically be to the search engine's rather than the corrupt communication agency's great financial gain in an attentionalist value system. Before the great diesel engine scandal in September 2015 the car giant Volkswagen spent several million euros on search optimization for their evidently underperforming diesel engines. What would have happened if Volkswagen simply had spent this money on improving its miserable diesel engines instead? What would have happened if they simply had refused to lie and had spent their aggregate resources on building a better car, safe in the knowledge that quality pays off and that the consequently good reputation would spread? This would undeniably be not just a more honest, but also a more intelligent strategy in an increasingly transparent, attentionalist society where in the first instance *credibility* and only thereafter *awareness* means absolutely everything.

It is quite simply a case of distinguishing between apples and oranges. If we compare the treacherously large quantity with the network-dynamically authentic quality, there is a dramatic difference in terms of power and status between he who has 500,000 genuinely influential and networking followers and he who has 500,000 automated pseudo followers that in practice constitute

500,000 blind alleys since these in turn do not have any influence at all. That which in the long run correlates with power, status and influence is of course the dynamical effect of networking itself and the ripples on the pond that arise through this, not the hyped and inflated quasi-reaction to a gambit among interpassive consumtarians to whom no one else listens. This in turn means that the only thing communication agencies can offer their poor customers is a fixation with clicks and likes that is completely pointless. Traditional marketing is dead in this informationalist chaos, there is nothing that can be called "digital strategies," all such things are subsumed under the designation *spam* on the net for a reason, it is quite simply hated and detested, a waste of busy people's valuable time. The only thing that actually survives is authentic communication and an ability to conduct authentic communication – which is precisely the netocratic eternalist's unique talent – qualities and talents that therefore are among the most coveted and hard to find in the informationalist network society.

The question of how the virtual network pyramid relates to geography and the physical world is certainly of great interest. One strategy to attain the network's coveted integrity and seclusion is of course to quite simply not reveal where these powerful and influential networks exist and conduct their activity. And then it is not so much a question of keeping one's mouth shut and keeping secrets as of drowning the netocrats' activities in a deluge of information that enables the dividuals themselves to move under the social radar. Another, possibly complementing strategy, is to enclose select geographical areas with various obstacles in the form of, for instance, walls and enclosures, or obscenely high ground rents and real estate prices, or different requirements for establishment and residence permits, and an exotically abstruse cultural coding of the local routines that scare off all who are uninitiated, that is: consumtarian visitors and/or intruders. All this is quite possible and feasible when the virtual power also starts to control the analogue world.

Once again it is not the large, classic democracies but rather city-states with top-down rule such as Singapore and Hong Kong that constitute the first examples of such curated, geographical units, with the practical advantage of not having the economic and cultural encumbrance that is constituted by the countryside that used to be valuable by virtue of its natural resources and its production of goods but that nowadays constitutes precisely an encumbrance that must be subsidized and supported in various ways; the Swedish economists Kjell Nordström and Per Schlingmann have appropriately described these areas as *junkspace*. The broad-based return of the city-state also fits into the description of the emerging global empire, under the banner of the Internet, as the new Middle Ages with many widespread, eccentric principalities; a landscape where the curated netocratic power bases do everything in their power to liberate themselves from all dying and burdensome junkspaces in their environs, and thus also, of course, from the classic nation-state.

The third netocratic strategy to keep the consumtariat in its place and at a distance is the eternalist task, namely *anesthetization* of the masses who otherwise risk becoming disorderly and at worst violent in their unarticulated frustration. No one is better suited for this task than the shamanic caste with its artists, philosophers, storytellers and developers of both recreational drugs and addictive virtual and in various ways enhanced realities. The shamanic caste of course also comprises the diplomats who pour oil on troubled waters when open conflicts flare up between various tribes, clans and subcultures. This means that what once was the moral story around the camp fire in the evening now explodes in an enormous, unmanageable offering of entertainment to death. Or at least entertainment to sleep – what dies in this case is critical thinking. For it is the media channels in themselves – as the sociologist Neil Postman writes in his classic *Amusing Ourselves to Death* – that represent the anesthetization of the masses in an age where the emerging netocracy moves over to the active participatory culture and hands over mass culture to the consumtariat and its *interpassivity*.

What it is fundamentally all about, is the very technology as such, what we call "content" can vary to any extent and is actually exchangeable and pointless. Or as Marshall McLuhan, the Canadian literary scholar who was Neil Postman's mentor in many respects, expresses the matter: "Our conventional response to all media, namely that it is how they are used that counts, is the numb stance of the technological idiot. For the 'content' of a medium is like the juicy piece of meat carried by the burglar to distract the watchdog of the mind." This means that *addiction* is the consumtarian normal state. Unless one is addicted to a particular chemical substance or to some specific self-harming behavior, it is perfectly fine to devote oneself to meta-addiction, that is: making oneself dependent upon addiction in itself. The addiction cults and what purports to be their treatments are well on their way to become virtual subcultures in themselves, social eternity loops with no end. How can one break the habit of attending Alcoholics Anonymous meetings or stop taking the pills for the original addiction, if the entire available social community *de facto* has moved to the addiction-cultural environment?

It is quite simply hard to top meta-addiction as a consumtarian identity creator; for both hypernarcissism and pornoflation as well as interpassivity are maximized within the confines of this concept. The constantly ruminating Rousseauan mantra "I am the victim" is simply the new age's equivalent of Christianity's old mantra "I am the sinner." One might think that the burden of guilt is now redistributed, but fundamentally we deal with the same perverse enjoyment of the victim role. And it is exactly the perverse enjoyment behind this mortidinally convenient excuse to avoid the power of the libido that is striking. Nothing is more narcissistically rewarding than the eternal subcultural brooding over one's dividual as well as tribal victimhood mythology. Moreover, we are dealing with an internal competition where all victims are constantly pitted against all other victims in a ruthless struggle for awareness and sympathy – it is even the case that today's-dividual-as-victim must compete against yesterday's version – which creates a situation that the global therapy industry is not remiss in exploiting. When friends and family let one down and no longer are able to listen to one's self-victimization tirades, there is an army of therapists available. But they of course charge handsomely for the very same service.

As regards netocratic art we are moving from simplicity via temporality to complexity. It is a case of what the British multiartist and theorist Brian Eno calls the shift from individualism's Napoleonic *genius* to informationalism's network-dynamical *scenius* as the ideal. It is a situation where the consumtariat is referred to interpassive groping for a genius in mass culture while the netocracy interactively cultivates scenius in the participatory culture (see *Syntheism – Creating God in the Internet Age*). Socioanalytically we express this by saying that the consumtarians are referred to interpassively suckling at the comforting, restful and anesthetizing mamilla, while the netocrats interactively seek and together build the phallus around which power proceeds to dance. From the netocratic event that then arises it is only possible to hear the odd, scattered echo when one is at the mamilla; what was once imploited can then be exploited since it is antiquated and obsolete. The consumtariat inherits individualism from the old bourgeoisie – an extremely vulgarized individualism in the form of hypernarcissism – while the netocracy cultivates the new syntheist ideals, where the participatory construction of the divine project, personified as *Syntheos*, becomes the main focus of metaphysical storytelling.

The dividual exists within scenius as a reflection of all other dividuals within the network, but without the ambition to dominate the stage in the absolute way in which the individual is presumed to dominate in the figuration of genius. The post-individualist artist, *the eternalist par excellence*, namely uses himself as a projective surface for the netocratic search for social identity as a collective work of art. This highly libidinal ambition behind scenius we call *flexhibitionism*, the netocratic dividual's network-promoting self-expression, as opposed to the consumtarian's pornoflated exhibitionism without an audience, disconsolate hypernarcissism. For the subject is neither an objective nor a meaning for the netocratic eternalist, but instead a highly mobile, alterable material. This is why we talk of flexhibitionism and not about exhibitionism as the netocratic eternalist's winning strategy. Brian Eno himself can rightly be described as the first netocratic artist. And as such he is also the first distinct representative of the netocratic shamanic caste. As could have been expected, Eno's sojourn within consumtarian popular culture as a keyboardist in the British rock band Roxy Music in the 1970s was a very brief one. He soon moved to the pre-netocratic elite culture as a flexhibitionist pioneer, where he has strived for and embodied scenius rather than genius ever since.

After three historical paradigms with focus on *exodus* or the metaphysical departure, we will with the power grab of network dynamics see a shift to *endodus,* or the metaphysical arrival as the propelling creative movement. Within syntheology this ideal is called *Entheos*, the search for the god within us rather than outside us (see *Syntheism – Creating God in the Internet Age*). An illuminating example is the art project *The Clock of the Long Now*, initiated by Danny Hillis in 1986 and later financed by ecommerce giant Amazon's founder, the nexialist Jeff Bezos, with a geographical positioning on a plot of land in Texas purchased for this very purpose. *The Clock of the Long Now* is the first clearly interactive, netocratic attempt to build *Syntheos*, the created god as a collective work of art. A clock ticking undisturbedly for 10,000 years – what could be more endodus to observe and meditate upon, what could be more netocratically contemptuous towards consumtarian mass consumption of cheap fast food and banal popular culture than this? The fact that endodus is a complicated project posited in a near-inaccessible place – we are after all speaking of radical imploitation – merely increases the value of the work and elevates the experience of the same. Imploitation is quite simply maximized when the work is surrounded by a wall of social coding while simultaneously is difficult to access geographically. Thus it is not primarily about reaching out, which was what artists tried to do during capitalism, but about reaching in. For better or worse, of course, here as everywhere else.

But what is then *the Global Empire,* to which we so often return as the outer planetary frame of reference in our futurology? Well, the Global Empire is a virtual, not a physical empire. The Internet must because of its comprehensive interconnectivity be regarded as a single, cohesive, albeit incomprehensible phenomenon. In other words: just as a relationalist worldview within physics and cosmology makes us see the Universe, in the spirit of David Bohm, as a single phenomenon, actually the only phenomenon of its kind and one which truly is one and only one, everything else in a relationalist worldview, must of course in Nietzsche's spirit, numerically be regarded as "at least two." So if we now see the world as a geographic territory occupied by the Internet itself, this can only be described as a single all-encompassing polity, that is: the Global Empire is in place but is partly invisible, it is phased in simultaneously with the disintegrating nation-states heaving their last, collective sigh instead of replacing them suddenly and dramatically. It is certainly a case of a cohesive virtual empire under which all other power constellations constitute Nietzschean fields of "at least two." Thus it is quite appropriate to regard our earlier work *The Global Empire* as a manifesto dedicated to Nietzsche, just as this work probably must be dedicated to a man named Sigmund Freud. Which gives us an excellent excuse to simultaneously dedicate our earlier works *The Netocrats* to Karl Marx, *The Body Machines* to Baruch Spinoza and *Syntheism – Creating God in the Internet Age* to the founder of process philosophy G W F Hegel. There, now that is over and done with.

We write about the relations between nexialists, curators and eternalists across the Global Empire already in *The Netocrats* almost two decades ago, but there might be reason to reflect and sum up. When do the three power structures interact with each other and when are they each other's competitors? And can any of them, for instance in the Marxist spirit, consider being part of a rebellious alliance with the consumtariat in an endeavor to level out the widening and problematical class divides in the informationalist network society? And if so, does such an endeavor have any chance of succeeding, or is every attempt to incorporate the digital underclass as such – through for instance the implementation of a universal basic income – doomed to become just one more dose of deadening and soporific narcosis for the consumtariat? When the Slovenian philosopher Slavoj Žižek analyzes our netocratic power triad in his book *Organs Without Bodies*, it is from precisely the hope that the eternalist will become the netocratic class traitor who, just as the bourgeois Karl Marx once did, spearheads and leads the revolt of the underclass against the injustices of society. The only difference is that what made Marx's theory plausible was the underlying demand for a *meritocracy* – that all who are born should get the same possibility to realize their ambitions in life, no ignoramuses should have anything for free as a result of unfair privileges – something that the bourgeoisie constantly fail in implementing, which Marx for his part exploits fully: the entire class society comes off as a fundamentally unjust and systematical oppression of competent people from whom others are allowed to profit.

The thing is, however, that the netocracy already has installed such a meritocracy since this favors its class interest. The entire *sensocracy* that is heavily underpinned by artificial intelligence and algorithms is constructed specifically with the purpose of identifying, recruiting and including every discernible talent regardless of origin or domicile. The netocrat has no aphephobia, one cannot afford such things. Rather, climbing the social ladder during informationalism happens often and rapidly, actually as often and rapidly as possible. However, this social mobility runs both ways. One does not inherit the ability to create and distribute attention in the same way as one used to be able to inherit a noble title or a financial fortune, which means that the meritocracy for practical rather than ideological reasons is taken to its extreme. This might sound appealing to some, but is actually extremely anxiety-producing and difficult to manage; it is almost impossible to imagine how political agitation for equality should be formulated when everyone formally speaking actually has the same prerequisites to succeed. Previously the underclass had its labor force to offer and negotiate around, while the underclass of the future only offers a dismal need for consumption which moreover someone else is forced to pay for. The netocrats exclude the consumtarian underclass from the production system that offers desirable goods and services through digitalization and automation. And among the professional groups that are increasingly marginalized there are many that up until very recently were considered upper class: physicians, lawyers, economists, bureaucrats, et cetera.

It is tricky, not to say impossible to remain a Marxist in such a society, at least not without descending into a Rousseauan dystopia of self-victimization cults and subcultural ultraviolence. For the enemy of the consumtariat is not primarily the netocracy in itself, but the heart of the Global Empire, the Internet itself, and the Internet is built to function even under the most extreme external circumstances, and also to handle the most comprehensive attacks. The Internet is simply a hydra built to last forever. It is the Internet that creates and increases the inequality that will cause enormous societal problems, while it with its other hand offers a cornucopia filled with seductive distraction – or possibly it is with the same hand, it is hard to tell. The Internet is all of us as we organize ourselves in accordance with the new conditions. The Internet is God, an enormous but indifferent god who crept up on us just when we thought that the heyday of the religions was over. People still ask themselves (and us!) whether the Internet is good or bad, as though it were a phenomenon that one could tame and use for deserving causes while one opts out of the downsides. No wishful thinking could be more naive than this, every dominant metatechnology will play its hand, as Neil Postman writes. We cannot think or opine it away, we will simply be forced to accept it. But if one necessarily must have a god, the Internet is at least not a worse, more indifferent god than the Universe itself. And even if the terms it offers for organizing a stable society that gives its citizens recognition and happiness are anything but ideal, there is still a little window open for those intent on constructing a utopia. And somewhere in the background we keep hearing the sound of the Internet Age's hedonist netocrats as they dance around their worshipped digital libido.

•

GLOSSARY

ABJECT An object that interlinks the chaos of the world into order and unites the collective through hatred, contempt, disgust and distancing – either constructively in conjunction with the implementation of the phallic intrusion and the shift of the child's focus from the dependence on mamilla (the first abject in life) to the yearning for phallus, or destructively as the false phallus' promise of a glittering utopia that excludes everyone outside the group/the people; see also fetish and cathexal object.

AGENT The subjective identity that arises as a mental emergence within a physical body as a relationalist phenomenon; *the syntheist agent* replaces *the Cartesian Individual* as the human ideal at the time of the transition from capitalism to informationalism; see also *dividual.*

ALIENATION According to Karl Marx, Man is alienated vis-à-vis himself in that the capitalist system reduces her to a cog in the machinery of production. In the works of Bard & Söderqvist, this is primarily a case of a general, systematic separation of people for the purpose of exercising power.

The fundamental property of that which attracts Man the most while it also frightens and repels: that which is neither good nor evil (or both good and evil), see also cathexis and the sublime.

AMOR FATI Love of fate in Latin, an attitude that means accepting the history that has led to the present and submitting to what awaits in the future, which in any case cannot be influenced. The concept is introduced by the German philosopher Friedrich Nietzsche in the 19th century and is a fundamental principle for the ethics of interactivity.

ANTHROPOCENTRISM Regarding Man as the starting point of everything and regarding the world solely from Man's perspective; compare with network dynamics and universocentrism.

ARCHETYPE A figure, motive or thought pattern that exists in the collective subconscious and that characterizes people's attitude towards their own existence and the surrounding world.

ASUBJECT The subject's dark, unknown, shadow side, which is at the same time is the subject's mortidinal negation and thus the engine behind the entire subjectivity; what German philosopher G W F Hegel calls the night of the world.

ATHEISM A conviction that a particular God (or several) does not exist and lacks social-psychological relevance.

ATHEOS A Greek concept for the God that does not exist and that precisely for this reason exists as an empty concept, as the god that does not exist, the virtual non-existence out of which existence arises; the first of the four divinities in the syntheological pyramid.

ATOMISM The idea that the world is made up of indivisible, material components; atomism does for the object what humanism does for the subject – these two isms are two sides of the same coin: individualism.

ATTENTION A value computed by multiplying medial credibility by medial awareness for one and the same meme, dividual, et cetera. A high attention value is the key to power and influence in the network society.

ATTENTIONALISM A system where attention is the central value that confers power and status. The ongoing paradigm shift entails that capitalism is phased out and is replaced by attentionalism. The concept is used synonymously with informationalism.

BEHAVIORS OF NATURE A better designation for that which is often carelessly called laws of nature: patterns that are locally and temporarily valid at a certain point in time and under certain prerequisites.

THE BIG OTHER The other in its greatest, most powerful and therefore also most ambivalent revelation, the phallic god within monotheism is usually apprehended as the big other in its most evident form, see also the phallic gaze.

THE BODY MACHINES The third and final installment of The Futurica Trilogy by Bard & Söderqvist, focusing on the new, materialistic and monist view of humanity in the Internet Age.

CAPITALISM The third of the four information-technological paradigms that arises when both literacy and a virtual value transfer are spread with devastating efficiency through the arrival of the printing press; the concept is often used synonymously with industrialism.

CATHEXAL OBJECT The radically different quality of phallus as both an exciting and frightening object, compared to the comfortable and secure mamilla – precisely by virtue of this ambivalent sublimity, phallus is extremely attractive and lures the child away from the mamilla.

CATHEXIS The Greek word that Sigmund Freud uses to signify the negative force of the attraction of ambivalence; see further ambivalence and the sublime.

CHEMICAL LIBERATION The concept that a wide availability of chemical substances that bring about a radical change in state of consciousness fundamentally alters the idea of what it means to be human, in part when Man discovers himself as a chemical-hormonal phenomenon, in part through the division between the first subject that decides which chemicals should be added and the second subject that then experiences the radical change in state of mind; see further transhumanism.

CIVILIZATION An expanding and gradually increasingly complex organization of collective interaction, fundamentally governed by the development of communication technology. At the price of an increasingly tightly regulated drive economy, civilization offers security and growth.

CIVILIZATIONISM The phallic conviction that an increasing accumulation of information in itself enables not just a more complex but also an objectively better world, that civilization as such is valuable in and of itself; Zoroaster in the antiquity of Central Asia circa 1700 before Christ is often said to be the first declared civilizationist. Civilizationism's golden age occurs during the European Enlightenment.

COLLECTIVE SUBCONSCIOUS Human subconsciousness in collective form, the partly implicit and unpronounced ideology of a given society.

COMMUNICATION SOCIETY One of three classic concepts that describe the Internet Age, to be compared with the information society and the network society; according to information-technological historiography, all paradigms through history should be categorized as communication societies since the forms for communication are precisely what underpin how every society is constructed.

CONSUMTARIAT The underclass of the Internet Age, characterized by the passive consumption of mass-produced goods and services; see also hypernarcissism, pornoflation, interpassivity and the dialectics of ressentiment.

COUNTERTREND The passive and usually unreflected reaction to an authoritarian trend, where the trend is grounded in an actual material change of the prevailing power conditions, while the countertrend is based on a fear of the trend (and of any sort of change).

CONTINGENCY An umbrella concept within process philosophy regarding everything that keeps the Universe open and thus free from deterministic closure.

CORRELATIONISM The conviction that Man only has access to the correlation between thinking and being but never direct access to thinking and being by themselves; this thought drives Western thinking from Immanuel Kant and onwards, but is criticized by the model-dependent realism associated with the physicist Niels Bohr and later also the philosopher Karen Barad.

DEEP ATHEISM An idea in which atheism, taken to its extreme, dialectically transitions into syntheism. This concept is explored in the book *Syntheism – Creating God in The Internet Age*. It may well be the case that God does not exist today, but this does not mean that God cannot exist tomorrow. Not if we actually create God ourselves.

DEMONOLOGY An umbrella term for the studies of and/or the doctrine of demons and evil spirits, in Bard & Söderqvist customarily used regarding abjection theory; in contrast to abjection theory, which investigates how abjectivity arises and is maintained, demonology devotes itself to the studies of the abject in itself as abject.

DESIRE The linguistic and thereby most uniquely human of the four expressions of the drive system, an expression of a search for something fundamentally unattainable since the objective of the desire always shifts and takes on another semblance; see further instinct, drive and transcendence.

DETERMINISM A doctrine according to which everything that happens is preordained and bound by laws of nature, which would mean that will and intentions ultimately do not matter. Determinism dominates Western history of ideas from Plato to Einstein but collapses at the moment when chance establishes itself as a contributing cause; see further the Bohrian opposite indeterminism.

DIALECTICS A logical process where a phenomenon is played out against its opposite, which results in a completely new phenomenon at a higher level. The concepts that customarily are used are thesis, antithesis and synthesis. Heraclitus is often regarded as the founder of dialectics; G W F Hegel is an influential representative.

DIALECTICS OF ETERNALISM AND MOBILISM A complete syntheist ontophenomenology developed by Bard & Söderqvist in the book *The Global Empire*; existence is fundamentally chaotic or mobilist and becomes fathomable and achieves meaning only through a magic trick performed by the perception apparatus in which phenomena are fixed in spacetime and thus are perpetuated or eternalized. This is both functional and necessary, but philosophically problematic.

DIALECTICS OF LIBIDO AND MORTIDO The continuous interplay between the will to live (libido), found in consciousness, and the death drive (mortido), found in subconsciousness – both as antagonistic opposites and as mutually complementing counterweights in the drive economy.

DIALECTICS OF RESSENTIMENT A dialectic, negative process within a dividual, a group or a society, which starts with the celebration of a self-appointed victim and later develops into a struggle among the alleged victims over who is the greatest victim, the ressentiment vis-à-vis fate increases for every new turn of the spiral.

DIALECTICS OF REVOLUTION The four stages of dialectic interplay between Man and technology during an information-technological paradigm shift: starting with a technological disruption, followed by a new metaphysical idea, exploding in a great chaos, and concluded by a return to order in chaos.

DIVIDUAL The antithesis of the concept of an individual: a human that lacks an indivisible and immutable inner core and that instead is infinitely divisible and highly mutable; compare with agent.

DIVIDUALISM The antithesis of individualism's ideology, the conviction that people and things are irreducible multiplicities that cannot be described as separate, cohesive phenomena; see further network dynamics.

DRIVE Term used not only for the drive system in itself, but also for the category within the drive system pertaining to its mechanical and consequently purest expression, for example the hankering for food, drink, sleep and protection, but also for sex, power and aggression; please compare with instinct, desire and transcendence.

ECOLOGICAL APOCALYPSE The dystopian conviction that the development of capitalism entails an annihilation of Earth's finite resources and environmental devastation on such a large scale that human life on the planet will soon no longer be possible. The only hope for avoiding the catastrophe is that constructive forces find each other on the sacral Internet.

EGALITARIANISM An ideological conviction that all people in a society have the same value and should be treated as equals, can appropriately be used to counteract identitarianism and its victimhood culture.

EMERGENCE When the properties of a system change so that it transitions from one state to another in an irrevocable way and thus forever changes the conditions for the entire system. For example, when physics transitions into chemistry, which transitions into biology, which transitions into human consciousness. From a social-psychological perspective it entails an indeterminist stance: the future is open – suddenly the quantitative distinction is qualitative and the conditions for everything are altered.

ENTHEISM The process-philosophical idea according to which existence can best be described as differences on top of differences, and that the duration that is a yardstick for the genesis and completion of the differences is absolute and therefore must constitute the foundation for both the material and spiritual worldview.

ENTHEOGEN A narcotic substance that gives rise to strong visions and emotions, which the users often describe as religious experiences; examples of entheogens are substances such as LSD, DMT, ayahuasca, mescaline, psilocybin mushrooms and MDMA.

ENTHEOS Originally means "the god within" in Greek, that is: the divine that the syntheist agent derives from within herself, the third of the four divinities in the syntheological pyramid.

EPISTEMOLOGY Theory of knowledge – the philosophical discipline that studies knowledge and the (im)possibility of knowledge; for a deeper understanding of syntheological epistemology, see further the dialectics of eternalism and mobilism, transrationalism and the principle of explanatory closure.

ETERNALIZATION A freeze or fixation of the world's mobilist chaos, an existential necessity in order for perception to be able to create a satisfactory order of the chaos of existence and produce a functional worldview within which the subject can arise and build an identity of its own. It is however important not to mistake the map for the terrain, the eternalization is not reality but a simplified image. The chaos of mobilism is what is primary.

ETERNALISM The concept that a worldview must be built on the temporary eternalizations that perception produces within the dialectics of eternalism and mobilism, which means that the worldview constantly must be reassessed and updated, and during paradigm shifts also phased out and replaced.

ETHICS From the Greek word ethos, originally customs; values based on intention regarding the expected processes of cause and effect within a system. In contrast to moralism, ethics is not based on either an external judge or emotional argumentation, but instead, more on functionality.

ETHICS OF INTERACTIVITY An ethical system based on the conviction that Man is a network-dynamical dividual in a network-dynamical society in a network-dynamical Universe, where the search for an authentic identity – in the existentialist spirit of Martin Heidegger – within the dialectics of eternalism and mobilism, provides answers to ethical questions specific to the circumstance; as developed and presented in Bard & Söderqvist's book The Body Machines.

EVENT A spectacular occurrence with dramatic consequences for a certain phenomenon or a specific region of the Universe, compare with emergence and singularity.

EXHIBITIONISM Pleasure derived from exposing oneself in sexual or social situations; compare with its dialectic opposite voyeurism.

EXTIMATE OBJECT The object that is simultaneously intimate and external. Within psychoanalysis phallus is the extimate object par excellence; compare with cathexis and cathexal object.

FETISH The object that links the chaos of the world with order and unites the collective under a common utopian vision and a strategic story directed upwards and outwards; see also the antithesis abject and the synthesis cathexal object.

FEUDALISM The second information-technological paradigm, the result of Man's development of written language around 5,000 years ago.

FICTION A cohesive story, which temporarily yet resolutely provides memes their seemingly logical place within the prevailing memeplex: fiction can appropriately be divided into smaller fictives, and several fictions piled upon each other underpin a subconscious ideology, which enables the emergence of a cohesive, paradigmatic metaphysics.

FICTIVE The smallest component in our extensive memetics and the unit to which every little aspect of a meme refers; see further fiction, ideology and metaphysics.

FLEXHIBITIONISM A playful synthesis of exhibitionism and voyeurism, built by dividuals for dividuals within network-dynamical systems – without any attention-seeking subject, such as an artistic genius – with the attention evenly distributed among the participants; flexhibitionism is the propelling principle for an authentic participatory culture.

GENERATIONISM A generation's oppression of or prejudices towards another generation, for instance through a society's conviction of its own superiority over earlier generations, or through various generations' isolation from each other.

THE GLOBAL EMPIRE The second of three books in The Futurica Trilogy by Bard & Söderqvist, focusing on the Internet Age's new, built-in, integrated worldview; The Global Empire is the idea of a divided world united by a single, increasingly centralized communication platform – the Internet – and a constantly growing, collaborative, collective intelligence.

GOD The name of all the dreams of humanity projected towards one single point; see also The Net and Syntheos.

THE GREAT TRAUMA The birth of the human child, which according to Lacanian psychoanalysis is so agonizing and strenuous that it must be repressed, leading to the first and decisive shift away from mortido (the death wish) to libido (the will to life).

HOLOMOVEMENT The mathematician and philosopher David Bohm's concept of a universe in constant movement and change that ontically only exists at every single moment or momentum.

HUMANISM The religious conviction that Man rather than God is the center, objective and meaning of existence; see further anthropocentrism, atomism and individualism.

HYPERNARCISSISM An extreme state that occurs when usual youthful narcissism is not met by a boundary-setting adult world and therefore expands in matrichal boundlessness instead of, as earlier in history, being tamed with resolute phallic boundary setting. This phenomenon explodes in the network society.

IDENTITARIANISM The ideological foundation for all identity politics, both in the identitarian left and the extreme right, and from Nazism via Stalinism to Islamism; the focus lies on propagating the idea that oneself and one's own group are victims of terrible injustices and therefore have the right to demand attention, sympathy and compensation of various sorts.

IDEOLOGY A set of conscious and unconscious memes or memeplexes that together produce a sense of context and overview.

INDETERMINISM A conviction that time is real and absolute, that the Universe constantly recreates itself, that laws and rules are in a state of constant flux, that the future is open and that Man, just as all other phenomena, influences all the processes of which he is a part.

INDIVIDUAL Capitalism's human ideal with a divine tinge and with its origin in the Enlightenment, the concept of the indivisible human, in contrast to the multifaceted dividual.

INDIVIDUALISM The religious conviction that Man has replaced God as the center, objective and meaning of existence, and that existence consists of fundamental solid entities, individuals; this anthropocentric ideology is originally formulated by René Descartes and is by and large completed by Immanuel Kant.

INDUSTRIALISM The socioeconomic structure that arises when the communication-technological revolution of the printing press achieves its complete breakthrough in that book production and increased literacy stimulate each other, leading to an enormous accumulation of knowledge, which in turn leads to a salvo of technological innovations.

THE INFINITE NOW The most sacred, most transformative and most ecstatic experience in syntheist religious practice; since the experience cannot be sustained nor will it endure permanently or even for an extended period of time, it is the memory of the experience rather than the experience in itself that is central.

INFORMATION SOCIETY One of three classic concepts to describe the Internet Age along with the communication society and the network society.

INFORMATION-TECHNOLOGICAL HISTORIOGRAPHY Writing a history based upon the hypothesis that Man is the constant while technology is the variable, wherefore development appears as a series of information-technological emergences that underpin increasingly complex societal structures.

INFORMATIONALISM The fourth information-technological paradigm, the result of the Internet's communication-technological revolution, used synonymously with attentionalism.

INFORMATIONALIST APOCALYPSE The threat of doom directed towards the new paradigm in the form of an ecological catastrophe, a nuclear war, a global pandemic, or simply the annihilation of the consumtariat by the netocracy.

INNER CIRCUIT The inner, less mobile, more densely populated and female-dominated half of the plastic nomadic tribe, controlled by elder matriarchs as a matriarchy.

INSTINCT The animal expression of Man's drives, to be compared with the mechanical drive, human desire and sacral transcendence.

INTENSITY In physics the measure of the concentration of energy within a given, delimited area; in relationalist physics intensity replaces the old substance as a general yardstick, in social-relationalist sociology the attentional intensity replaces the old growth of the economy as a general yardstick, in syntheist ethics the ecstatic intensity in the infinite now replaces all old maxims for the existential experience and the memory of the infinite now becomes the underpinning identity-generating reference throughout life; see also relationalism and social relationalism.

INTERACTIVITY Bidirectional communication, which entails the fourth communication-technological revolution, which establishes a completely new system for reward and punishment of talents and skills, which in turn entails that a new elite – the netocrats – replace the old bourgeoisie; please compare with interpassivity.

INTERNARCISSISM A subdivision within the narcissist pathology where two or more narcissists consciously or subconsciously pretend to be obsessed with each other to conceal the extreme self-reflection occurring beneath the surface; see also hypernarcissism and interpassivity.

INTERNET The new divinity that arises when the population of the world and the world's many machines are interconnected with each other.

INTERNET AGE The era introduced when all of humanity is directly interconnected with itself in real time all around the world.

INTERPASSIVITY A concept invented by the Austrian philosopher Robert Pfaller; it describes all the meaningless quasi-actions that people carry out with the purpose of placating the other in the high-tech environment, used as an opposite of authentic interactivity, that is: a constantly ongoing false interactivity that never receives any genuine response from any co-actors.

INTERTRIBALISM Affection and care directed towards people outside one's own tribe, which during the greater part of history is something extremely rare; compare with intratribalism.

INTRACOLLABORATIVITY The joy of collaboration within one's own tribe, an attitude that distinguishes itself from individualism's idea of humanity's existence as everyone's war on everyone; within a secure collective, collaboration is closer at hand than rivalry.

INTRATRIBALISM Affection and care directed towards the tribe's own members, a propelling force behind both the outer circuit's defense of the tribe's territory and the inner circuit's sacrifices to ensure the tribe's survival; compare with intertribalism.

IRONIC POLYTHEISM Polytheism is a systematized faith in more gods than one; syntheism is not a polytheism in a classical sense, but rather an ironic polytheism since it maintains that gods can and should be created in requisite amounts.

IRREDUCIBLE MULTIPLICITY The conviction that all phenomena in existence are fundamental multiplicities that are not reducible to separate, delimited objects, such as when Friedrich Nietzsche claims that nothing in the world is reducible to less than the number two. Within a syntheist ontology the irreducible multiplicity is unavoidable since the ontology always must start with a drastic information depreciation in conjunction with the transition from mobilism to eternalism.

LIBIDO Life energy, the will to power, the will to intensity, the will to expand – libido is often connected with sexual energy but according to both Sigmund Freud and Carl Gustav Jung is a considerably broader concept that comprises all aspects of instinct, drive, desire and transcendence.

MAMILLA The matrichal breast as a symbol of eternal, boundless and unconditional love and support, as well as of a possible reunion with the mother's body and matrix, but also infantilization and complete dependence on the maternal body/society/the church/the state.

MATRIARCHY The power hierarchy between the women of the tribe, where the elder ones have authority over the younger ones; thus also the power structure in the inner circuit.

MATRIX The womb from which we all are born and, according to psychoanalysis, to which we all return at death, the symbol of the union with the Cosmos but also the dissolution of consciousness.

MEMEPLEX A cluster of memes that preferably is disseminated in the form of a synchronized unity; a memeplex can therefore be regarded as emergent in regard to the individual memes; memeplex is also used synonymously with ideology.

MEMETICS The study of how ideas – or memes – are formed, disseminated, stored and changed; memes in these studies are regarded as replicators, as a kind of mental equivalent to biological genes, and the parallels between memetics and genetics are therefore substantial.

METAHISTORY History viewed as the history of historiography, also called the historicization of history. Every new paradigm generates a new power elite that requires a new metaphysics in order to legitimize its position; this in turn requires a new historiography and about this process one can also write history, which by necessity becomes a metahistory.

METAPHYSICS Originally the philosophical occupation with that which lies beyond physical reality, comprised by the disciplines ontology, cosmology and epistemology within philosophy; Bard & Söderqvist also use the concept metaphysics as the uppermost emergence in the hierarchy of fictives, fictions, ideologies – and, as the ultimate form of storytelling, metaphysics.

MOBILIZATION Putting the completed eternalizations within the dialectics of eternalism and mobilism in motion anew – thus existence once again becomes a mobilist chaos, but this time at the metalevel, whereupon new eternalizations on the metalevel are produced by perception, and so on.

MOBILISM In part the process-philosophical reality in the dialectics of eternalism and mobilism, a chaos in constant motion; in part a synonym of process philosophy as such, including both relativism and relationalism.

MONOTHEISM The conviction that one particular god – one's own, of course – is genuine and that all others are false, in other words a sort of atheism with one tiny exception.

MORALATOR The external judge whose more or less capricious opinions underpin the demanding laws of moralism.

MORALISM From the Latin word morales, customs; a system where values and valuations are subordinated to a moralator, an external judge who demands obedience and prohibits questioning; both the Abrahamic religions and the capitalist nation states are underpinned by a moralist value system.

MORTIDO In Sigmund Freud mortido is at once the opposite of libido and its complement, a yearning for death, extinction and a return to the inorganic state that precedes birth.

NARCISSISM Compensatory self-reflection and excessive self-admiration, based on a subconscious self-contempt; the modern consumer society is largely built on an escalated hypernarcissism.

NEGATIVE DIALECTICS German philosopher G W F Hegel's revolutionizing variant of dialectics where the negation precedes the thesis that thereby becomes a negation of the negation, which ultimately results in a concretion. In this way, the Hegelian subject becomes an expression of what he calls the night of the world, which is a radical departure from Enlightenment optimism. The Hegelian revolution foreshadows important ideas in Marx, Nietzsche, Freud and Heidegger.

THE NET The metaphysical idea that the Internet is one single cohesive structure that encompasses the entire planet Earth and, as for every metatechnology, that organizes the world in accordance with its own agenda.

NETOCRACY The informationalist upper class that assumes power by virtue of its social talent, its superior information management and its ability to detect patterns and perceive nodes in a chaotic surrounding world.

THE NETOCRATS The first of three books in The Futurica Trilogy by Bard & Söderqvist focusing on the Internet Age's information-technological historiography and the new class society that emerges, conditioned by the new prerequisites that the technological revolution creates.

NETWORK DYNAMICS The aspect of system theory and complexity theory that studies how networks arise and change over time, as well as the effects within all societal areas to which this leads, a recurring metaphysical explanatory model for the Internet Age in Bard & Söderqvist's philosophy, used synonymously with relationalism.

NETWORK PYRAMID Network society's triangular power structure, developed and examined in the book The Netocrats, where it is explained that as networks become successful they are forced to break off and dispose of dead weight in order to protect the key members' limited time and valuable attention, a process constantly repeated because of outside pressure.

NETWORK SOCIETY One of three classic concepts that describe the Internet Age, to be compared to information society and communication society; according to information-technological historiography all paradigms throughout history should be categorized as network societies: networks do not just arise with the advent of the Internet but are age-old phenomena.

NIHILISM An idea according to which existence lacks objective value since it does not possess an external, objective evaluating agency or moralator; nihilism goes through three phases – the naive (unconscious), the cynical (the nihilist pretends, though he knows better, that there are objective values), and finally the affirmative (the nihilist interprets the absence of objective values as a liberating possibility that allows him to create his own, subjective values).

ONTOLOGY The metaphysical study of being, becoming, existence and reality; syntheism is built on a process-philosophical ontology, see process philosophy.

OUTER CIRCUIT The outer, mobile, sparsely populated and male-dominated half of the plastic nomad tribe, controlled by elder patriarchs in a patriarchy; compare with the inner circuit that is controlled by a matriarchy and the shamanic caste that is controlled by a priesthood.

PANTHEOS from the Greek word pan-theos, everything is God and God is everything; the second of the four divinities in the syntheological pyramid; pantheism regards everything that exists as one single cohesive phenomenon, The One, which thereby is tantamount to God himself.

PARADIGM The general worldview that harmonizes with the prevailing power structure's image of itself, replaced by a new one only when an information-technological revolution has produced a new set of conditions for all societal areas, which in turn propels extensive social changes. The theory of paradigms and paradigm shifts is originally presented by the philosopher of science Thomas Kuhn, who studies the development within the natural scientific disciplines.

PARADOXISM The concept that language arises as a treatment of paradoxical aspects of existentially formative traumas; the deepest truths about existence can therefore only be expressed as consciously constructed paradoxes, or not at all; a representative of ancient paradoxism is Heraclitus.

PARTICIPATORY CULTURE Events with varying duration where the participants build the event together; thus there are no performances and no audience in the ordinary sense. Participatory culture develops and grows in step with the Internet, for instance in the form of festivals such as Burning Man in the United States, Going Nowhere in Spain and Afrika Burn in South Africa; see also flexhibitionism.

PATRIARCHY The power hierarchy of the men of the tribe, where elder men are superior to younger men; thus also the power structure in the outer circuit, which is dominated by men.

PETER PAN SYNDROME A condition where the child refuses to grow up and remains a child while it realizes and feels the attraction of phallic adulthood. One of the prerequisites for a large-scale infantilization of society.

THE PHALLIC GAZE The big other's constantly coveted gaze that provides the only meaningful and credible existential confirmation and that distinguishes the brilliant from the mediocre.

PHALLIC INTRUSION The moment that occurs at approximately one year of age, when the child for the first time is seduced away from the security of mamilla and discovers phallus as the object that the mother is attracted to but that the child cannot give the mother, an event that generates envy in the child, which in turn initiates the child's voyage towards and yearning for adulthood while bringing about an imitation and eroticization of phallus.

PHALLUS The male sex organ and everything it symbolizes in the world of psychoanalysis.

PHENOMENOLOGY The philosophical study of experiences and consciousness; an example of a syntheist phenomenology is the dialectics of eternalism and mobilism.

PHENOMENON From the Greek word phainomenon – to show, shine, arise, manifest itself. In syntheist ontophenomenology the phenomenon replaces the classic object as a material point of reference in relation to the Universe as a whole; this phenomenon distinguishes itself from the object in that it is primarily a field made up of relations that all are equally primary and completely lack the object's phallic substance and essence.

PLASTICITY Social elasticity, the ability of the tribe members to avail themselves of separate dividuals' various talents for the benefit of the collective and give each dividual a social identity and the possibility to contribute to the common good.

PLURARCHY From the Latin word pluralis for diversity and the Greek word archos for rule; the chaotic state in the political sphere that accompanies the collapse of democracy during the paradigm shift as it moves from the mass-medial unidirectional communication and its efficient control of opinions, to the interactive multidirectional communication with its perplexing and unruly information flows.

PORNOFLATION A social-pornographic and gradually ever more extreme exposure of the most intimate in order to create awareness; is not seldom exploited to produce cheap mass entertainment.

POWER TRIAD A long-term stable power structure always has three rather than two poles, for example the American Constitution's President, Congress and Supreme Court, or Bard & Söderqvist's model that encompasses real power, imaginary power and symbolic power within every information-technological paradigm.

PRAGMATISM A philosophical school founded by Charles Sanders Peirce and William James in the United States in the 19th century that has a European equivalent in the inheritance from Friedrich Nietzsche's existentialist philosophy; the foundation is that theories and belief systems are evaluated in terms of their functionality.

PRIMITIVISM The first information-technological paradigm, arising when Man learns to use his speech organs and communicate with words around 200,000 years ago, when the human species appears on the world stage as the first species with a history.

PRINCIPLE OF EXPLANATORY CLOSURE The insight that the enormous expansion of the Universe makes ontic rationalism impossible and that the aggregate information's similarly enormous expansion in society makes ontological rationalism impossible for the very same reason; what the human brain does not have time to process it can never encompass either, which is the kiss of death for Kantian rationalism.

PROCESS PHILOSOPHY Also called the ontology of becoming, a conviction that equates metaphysical reality with difference and change; it receives its present, radical form with Alfred North Whitehead and constitutes a basic prerequisite for the syntheist ontology.

PROCESS RELIGION A religious conviction based on a process-philosophical metaphysics where syntheism is the process religion par excellence; not to be confused with the admittedly Whitehead-inspired albeit post-Christian school called process theology, which is represented, among others, by Charles Hartshorne.

PSEUDOTRIBES Tribelike constellations that however lack the plastic nomadic tribe's comprehensive array of complementing archetypes and that therefore sooner or later collapse from the discontentment that stems from members' crushed expectations of tribal satisfaction.

QUANTUM ORGANICS A better concept than quantum mechanics since the phenomenon in question has more organic than mechanic character traits.

RATIONALISM The conviction that Man is born with the capacity to mentally and intellectually understand and encompass the world logically in its entirety; however rationalism offers no logic for its own basic assumption.

REDUCTIONISM The conception that even the most complex phenomena in a meaningful way are divisible into their smallest components; according to reductionism all forms of emergence are illusory.

RELATIONALISM A radicalization of the relativist worldview, where even seemingly stable objects are dissolved and set in motion in relation to themselves, and where there are no longer any fixed points at all vis-à-vis anything other than The One, that is: the Universe as a whole; first developed by Alfred North Whitehead and later refined by the quantum physicist Niels Bohr and the mathematician David Bohm.

RELATIVISM A worldview where all objects are in constant motion in relation to each other; the objects are thus fixed within and to themselves, but completely background-independent in relation to their surrounding world.

RESSENTIMENT A hatred or contempt directed towards human existence and its prerequisites, an embittered self-contempt that is projected onto the world.

THE REVOLT AGAINST PHALLUS A psychoanalytical concept for teenage rebellion, a test of the parent generation's purported excellence and omniscience that results in the adult authorities being toppled from their pedestals, at which time the teenage subject must conquer its own phallicness, adulthood and autonomy with all that entails in terms of assumption of responsibility and search for meaning. When this revolt has been successfully carried out and has resulted in an acceptable identity, it is confirmed by the tribe through the initiation ritual.

SADOMASOCHISM A primarily erotically charged relationship between a ruler and a slave, when a sexual subculture it is limited by social codes, but as a social phenomenon it is boundless in its dialectic movement regarding the ruler's total distancing from and isolation from the slave.

SCHIZOANALYSIS An anarchic response to Lacanian psychoanalysis, primarily developed by Felix Guattari and Gilles Deleuze in France during the 1970s, whose purpose is increased dividual heterogeneity rather than the individual homogeneity that can be argued was the objective of classical psychoanalysis.

SELF-LOVE An ethical-logical decision – not an emotion – to accept oneself and one's own body with its physiological and mental prerequisites and expressions; it is not a question of narcissism, and is in fact the opposite of narcissism; see also amor fati.

SENSOCRACY A social and/or political system built around a technology of sensors that collect data from all information flows and that therefore can predict with great accuracy what every citizen at every moment requests and longs for, something that previously has been impossible because of the great amount of dishonesty that takes place at every level. In a sensocracy, means of coercion in practice become superfluous: a devastating majority of society's citizens are content to have all their needs of consumption and entertainment efficiently satisfied. The rest lack any influence and are consequently relegated to an existence outside the system.

SHADOW The part of the subject that the subject does not acknowledge and/or as a result of efficient repression does not even perceive within itself. The concept was originally introduced by Carl Gustav Jung; compare with Bard & Söderqvist's concept the asubject and G W F Hegel's concept the night of the world.

SHAMANIC CASTE the divergent minority within the plastic nomadic tribe that belongs neither to the inner circuit and its matriarchy nor to the outer circuit and its patriarchy, but instead in part acts as intermediary between the inner and outer circuits, that is: in part acting as boundary transgressors in the tribe's outer reaches as shamans and prophets toward the tribe itself, in part as diplomats and as shared priesthood toward neighboring tribes.

SINGULARITY An extraordinary historical event that in an instant fundamentally changes world history; from an anthropocentric perspective the geneses of the Universe, the living organism, and consciousness qualify as singularities, see also emergence.

SOCIAL MASOCHISM A masochistic attitude to the ruling powers on the social arena, a stubborn search for social and mortidinal submission, see further sadomasochism.

SOCIAL RELATIONALISM The concept that the principles presented by Neils Bohr in relationalist physics are equally applicable to the social sciences; see further network dynamics, relationalism and irreducible multiplicity.

SOCIAL TECHNOLOGY Techniques to control people and manipulate them in a direction desirable to the power structure; social technologies can include anything from ideology production and radio broadcasts to censorship legislation and declarations of war.

SOCIOANALYSIS Truth maximization on the social arena, or the psychoanalysis of an entire society, which should be compared with classical psychoanalysis' use of and for the dividual person.

SOCIOGRAPHY Mapping of social relations between dividuals and networks, for instance through sociograms that show who knows and communicates with whom; see also network pyramid.

SOCIOMETRY Compilation and illustration of social status and attentional power in the network society.

THE SUBCONSCIOUS Bard & Söderqvist's equivalent to classical psychoanalysis' the unconscious; the subconscious is in fact not unconscious, but chaotic and unstructured vis-à-vis the conscious and interacts both actively and reactively both with and against the conscious at all times; subconsciousness is driven by mortido or the death drive in contrast to consciousness which is driven by libido or the will to life.

THE SUBLIME The sphere where ambivalence and extimacy meet and generate maximal obsession in the subject, for example the near-death experience with its simultaneous character of infinite sadness and infinite beauty; see also ambivalence and cathexal object.

SYNTHEISM From the Greek word syntheos, meaning created god or god that arises where people create; God as a generic name for all the dreams and visions of Man, which entails a dissolution of the contradiction between theism and atheism.

THE SYNTHEOLOGICAL PYRAMID Trilateral geometric construction with Atheos, Pantheos and Entheos as the three corners in the base with lines drawn both between each other and up to the eponymous apex Syntheos; profusely present within syntheist symbolism.

SYNTHEOLOGY A syntheist theology, built around virtual divinities.

SYNTHEOS From Greek, the created god or god that arises where people create, the fourth, concluding and summarizing concept in the syntheological pyramid.

THEOLOGICAL ANARCHISM The concept that the network society offers a unique historical possibility for realizing the anarchist utopia and thus liberating the forces of the collective libido; synonymous with the British philosopher Simon Critchley's ideal mystical anarchism.

TOTALISM The conviction that it is possible to understand existence both as an entirety and in detail, just as history can be summed up and concluded, all with the aid of the philosophical genius' rationality. The idea exists going back to Plato and has never really disappeared, even when Bard & Söderqvist firmly maintain that the principle of explanatory closure means that all forms of totalism are both ontically and ontologically impossible; see also indeterminism and transrationalism.

TRANSCENDENCE To move beyond the present existence, in Bard & Söderqvist's psychoanalytical theory also the name of the fourth human drive, the sacral aspect of libido beyond the animal (instinct), the mechanical (drive) and the human (desire).

TRANSFERENCE Transference of agency, the social masochistic surrendering of one's own agency to the benefit of another agent that is considered to own both the phallic gaze and perfect knowledge.

TRANSGRESSION Overstepping of the prevailing laws, rules and norms, followed by an enjoyment of this excess, fundamental for both sexual and social perversion.

TRANSHUMANISM A broad digital lifestyle and subculture of a powerfully netocratic character; the influential ideas revolve around how the technological development develops into a post-human state colored by cryonics, artificial intelligence, chemical liberation and anarcho-libertarian utopianism, et cetera.

TRANSRATIONALISM The insight that Man's consciousness has been developed to optimize the chances of survival and procreation, not to unveil the truth about the world, which is why rationality must be conscious of its own limitations; see further rationalism and the principle of explanatory closure.

TREND An irrevocable active change of the social rules of the game, connected to a technological change of material conditions; compare with countertrend.

TRIBAL MAPPING A sociogram that comprises the entire tribe in all its multibranched diversity.

TRUTH AS AN ACT An ontological and ethical concept devised by the French philosopher Alain Badiou with inspiration from the father of existentialism, the Danish philosopher Søren Kierkegaard, which states there is never any time to test truth through the drawn-out intersubjective processes that Karl Popper and Jürgen Habermas advocate; truth, rather, appears as a decision based on intuition.

UNIMATRICHALISM A temporary, chaotic state in which the inner, matriarchal circuit has taken over the entire tribe or society.

UNIPATRICHALISM A temporary state of something that can be likened to a totalitarian dictatorship where the outer, patriarchal circuit has taken over the entire tribe or society.

UNIVERSOCENTRISM A worldview that starts from the Universe in its entirety as the center of existence; syntheism is built on universocentric metaphysics, in contrast to for instance capitalist humanism which is an anthropocentric religion.

THE WORLD STATE Socioeconomic joining of all the states in the world so that mutual dependence becomes so strong that it balances the dividing forces and supplies a necessary platform for supranational decision-making; Bard & Söderqvist use the concept repeatedly as a synonym for The Global Empire.

VOYEURISM Indirect pleasure through observing direct, vicarious pleasure in the form of some sort of sexual or social display; please compare with exhibitionism and the phallic gaze.

Digital Libido – Sex, Power and Violence in the Network Society

Translated by John Wright

Futurica Media
Stora Nygatan 7
111 27 Stockholm
Sweden

Cover design by Per Gustafsson
Body text by Fredrik Öster

Printed by Ingram Spark
ISBN 978-91-88869-23-4

ALEXANDER BARD is a philosopher, futurologist, spiritual and political activist. He has a background of almost three decades as a highly successful artist, producer and songwriter in the music industry. Bard is a globally renown lecturer and ideologue, both on the live stage and on a multitude of media platforms.

JAN SÖDERQVIST is a philosopher, futurologist and lecturer. Söderqvist is a pioneer of online television, but has been professionally active in almost all conceivable media disciplines, such as the daily press, magazines, film, radio and television. He currently writes for the Swedish major daily *Svenska Dagbladet* and works as editor for *Axess Magasin*.

Previous books by Alexander Bard & Jan Söderqvist

The Netocrats 2000
The Global Empire 2002
The Body Machines 2009
Syntheism – Creating God in the Internet Age 2014

www.ingramcontent.com/pod-product-compliance
Ingram Content Group UK Ltd.
Pitfield, Milton Keynes, MK11 3LW, UK
UKHW062309290726
14090UKWH00018B/960